PEOPLE AND ENVIRONMENT

A World Perspective

NORMAN GRAVES · JOHN LIDSTONE · MICHAEL NAISH

Heinemann Educational Books Ltd
22 Bedford Square, London WC1B 3HH

LONDON EDINBURGH MELBOURNE AUCKLAND
SINGAPORE KUALA LUMPUR NEW DELHI
IBADAN NAIROBI JOHANNESBURG
PORTSMOUTH (NH) KINGSTON

First published 1987

British Library Cataloguing in Publication Data

Graves, Norman J.
People and environment: a world perspective.
1. Anthropo-geography
I. Title II. Lidstone, John III. Naish, Michael
304.2 GF43

ISBN 0 435 34369 6

Designed, illustrated and typeset by The Pen and Ink Book Co. Ltd, London

Printed and bound in Spain by Mateu Cromo

Acknowledgements

The authors would like to acknowledge with thanks, the reviewers who made positive suggestions for the improvement of the typescript; the *Observer*, the *Guardian*, and *Geographical Magazine*, all of which proved a source of ideas and sometimes data; the *Geographical Digest* for data bases; John Fien, Eleanor Rawling and Frances Slater for providing case study material; and Christine Chitty and June Moss for typing the manuscript.

The publishers would like to thank the following for permission to reproduce photographs:

Associated Press, Figures 2.3, 2.4; Brodero, Figure 6.49; Dr Angela Brown, Figure 6.23; J. Allan Cash, Figures 1.7, 2.14, 2.15, 2.16, 2.19, 2.20, 2.23, 5.5, 5.17, 6.9, 7.15, 7.21, (top left and right), 7.22 (left), 7.47; Central Electricity Generating Board, Figure 6.42; City of Wakefield Metropolitan District Council, Figure 7.21 (bottom left); Delta Phot, Figure 7.28; J.P. Dutilleux, Figures 4.24, 4.25; Mary Evans Picture Library, Figures 1.4, 4.16; FAO photo by T. Loftas, Figure 5.21; Ferranti Electronics, Figure 6.10; Fiat, Figure 6.25; Ford Motor Company Ltd, Figures 6.19, 6.20; L. Harrington/Energy Authority of New South Wales, Figure 6.47; Intermediate Technology, Figure 4.20; Ashley Kent, Figure 8.5 (top); Lucht foto/Bart Hofmeester, Figure 6.17; Gavin Marshall, Figure 5.11; Massey Ferguson, Figure 5.5; The Milk Marketing Board of England and Wales, Figure 5.7; Municipality of Zoetermeer, Figure 7.25; Adrian Neville, Figure 1.7; The North of Scotland College of Agriculture, Figure 3.32; Nottinghamshire County Library Service, Figure 7.22 (left); *Observer*, Figures 3.31, 8.5 (centre and bottom); Port Autonome de Marseille/G. Paoli/ J.P. Jauffret, Figures 8.15, 8.17; Eleanor Rawling, Figures 7.39–44; Tennessee Valley Authority, Figures 2.28, 2.29; UN, Figure 4.19; UN/John Isaac, Figure 1.1; University of Cambridge, Figure 7.21 (bottom right); University of Dundee, Figure 3.15.

The publishers would also like to thank the following for permission to reproduce copyright material.

Action Aid, Figure 5.1; *Ashburton Guardian*, Figure 5.12; Bangladesh Population Control and Family Planning Division, Figure 4.7; John Barnes, Figure 2.5; *Geographical Magazine*/Alan Mountjoy, Figure 2.34; GOAD, Figure 6.49; *Guardian*/Shiela Latham, Figure 5.1; *Guardian*/Simon Hoggart, Figure 7.48; Perdita Huston, Figure 1.10; Madras Metropolitan Development Authority, Figure 7.36; Michelin, Figure 8.4; *New Scientist*, Figure 5.28; The North of Scotland College of Agriculture, Figure 3.32; *Observer*/Geoffrey Lean, Figure 1.14; *Observer*/Thomas O'Toole, Figure 9.31; Save the Children, Figure 5.1; *The Sunday Times*/Brian Silcock, Figure 5.27; *The Times*, Figure 1.5; Traidcraft, Figure 4.12.

Contents

Preface

This book is designed to provide a stimulating resource for GCSE. It investigates the major physical and human systems in world geography and the way in which such systems interact. It considers the impacts of human action in interfering with natural systems and the constraints and potential of natural systems for human activity. The book therefore provides coverage of issues and problems of human and environmental concern and fits well with the National Criteria for Geography. Yet it is not entirely a problem-based approach, since the potential of the interacting systems is also considered.

There is no attempt to 'cover' the world in terms of areas for study, topics or examples. The book is necessarily selective, but it does try to present a global perspective. Both case studies and models are presented in order to provide a focus for study.

The book is designed to provide information and resources for learning. Three elements go to make this possible: the text, which is intended to encourage careful reading; the graphics (photographs, maps, diagrams, tables) which demand analysis; and the questions, intended to extend and deepen the student's understanding of the main concepts investigated.

Students are very much to be encouraged to use atlases and other reference books in their study and to extend their understanding through selective reading and viewing of news media. The world's environments and human interaction with them are constantly in the news.

Exercises at the end of each section are designed to encourage further study. In all this work, attention is paid to key elements of GCSE Geography: the development of pupils' knowledge, understanding, skills and values. Activities are coded as follows to show coverage of these elements:

▲ knowledge and understanding
■ skills
● values

1

People on Earth

This book aims to help you understand some of the ways in which people **interact** with their environment. 'Interact' means how people use the Earth to stay alive and produce their children and how this affects the Earth.

You may wonder why this book starts with a chapter on people. The reason is that human beings have been so successful in staying alive and producing children that there are more people living on Earth now than there have ever been before. This is a big problem.

We do not know how many people the Earth can support. If all the land on Earth was shared out equally, there would be 3.5 hectares for every person living today. But if all the cultivated land in the world was shared out, there would only be 0.4 hectares for each person. Four-tenths of a hectare of good soil is probably enough to keep one person alive. In addition, there is another 0.8 hectares of land for each person which *could* be farmed.

There are often television programmes and newspaper stories about the 'population problem' and the 'world's starving millions' (Figure 1.1). Why does this happen if there is enough space on Earth for everyone to have sufficient food? What will happen if the population grows until all the possible farming land is being farmed? To try and find out we need to ask three more questions:

1 Why is the world's population growing so rapidly?
2 Is the population growing in all parts of the world?
3 How is the Earth's surface shared out among people in the world today?

The growing population

According to geologists and astronomers, the Earth is about 5000 million years old. Human beings may have appeared as long ago as 25 million years, although the oldest fossil remains of human beings found so far are only about 2 million years old. These fossils were found in the Omo Valley in Ethiopia. More fossil remains of early human beings have been found in East and North Africa than anywhere else in the world so archaeologists, and now biologists, think that human beings first appeared in Africa

Figure 1.1 'Starving millions': these live in Ethiopia

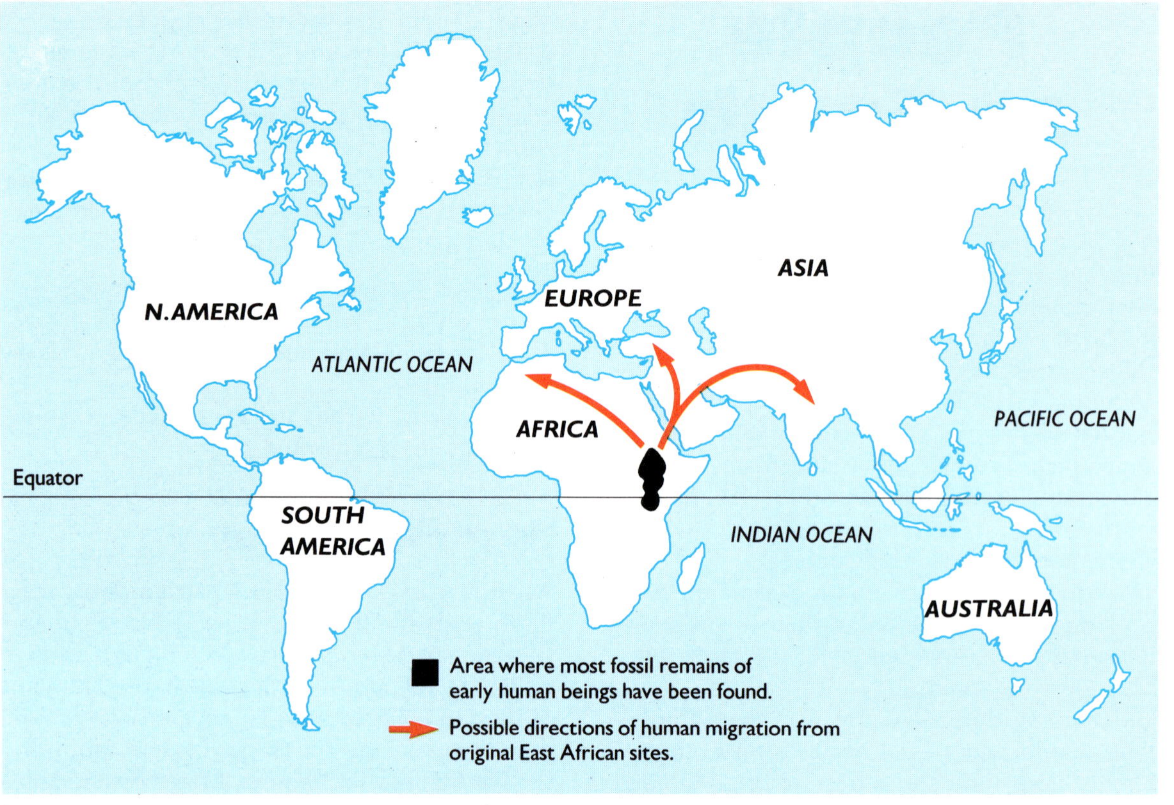

Figure 1.2 Areas where oldest fossil remains are found, and human migration routes

and then spread northwards into the Middle East. From here people spread westwards into Europe and eastwards into Asia. The areas where fossils have been found are shown in Figure 1.2.

Historians and archaeologists have estimated that it took until the time of Jesus Christ (the start of our calendar) for the human race to reach 250 million people. By AD 1000 the number had only reached 275 million. Figure 1.3 shows how the world's population has grown since then. The earlier figures are based on estimates, but as more and more countries carried out population counts or **censuses**, the figures became more accurate.

You can see from Figure 1.3 that the population grew steadily from 1500 onwards. To know how fast it grew, or to compare the changes in population of different countries, it is useful to work out the **rate of increase** (or **decrease**) as a percentage of the population each year. For example, in 1980 the population of the world was about 4432 million. In 1981 it increased by 72 million people. So the population growth for that year was 1.6%. If this rate of growth had existed every year since AD 1, today there would be 900 people for every square metre of the earth and we would all live and work in skyscrapers several kilometres high! Fortunately this has not happened – yet! A high rate of population growth is often referred to as a **population explosion**.

Year	Population in millions	Year	Population in millions
1000	275	1600	486
1100	306	1700	635
1200	348	1800	919
1300	384	1900	1571
1400	373	1980	4432
1500	429	2000	*6116

* UN projection based on available figures

Figure 1.3 The expansion of the world's population

Activity

■ **1 a** Use Figure 1.3 to draw a line graph. Call it 'The growth of the world's population from AD 1000 to AD 1980'. You could use a scale of 40 mm to 1000 million people up the side and 15 mm to 100 years along the base line. Remember that 1980 will be 4/5 of the distance between 1900 and 2000.

b On your graph label:

i) the time of slow population growth

ii) the time of rapid population growth

iii) the 'population explosion'.

What makes population change?

Imagine a class of 30 pupils. If 2 pupils move to another school, the number in the class falls to 28. If 2 new pupils then join the class the number becomes 30 again. Although some of the people in the class have changed, the total number of pupils has stayed the same. This is also true for the population of the Earth. So if the same number of people die as are born, the total population doesn't change. The population *grows* when more people are born than die. The population *falls* when more people die than are born.

Since countries are different sizes, it is easier to compare them if the figures for births and deaths are given as a proportion of their populations. For example, in France in 1984 there were 14 live births for every 1000 people (a birth rate of 14/1000). In the same year, there were 10 deaths for every 1000 people (a death rate of 10/1000). This means that for every 1000 people in France, there were 4 more births than deaths during the year. This is called the **natural rate of increase**. It is usually given as a percentage. In France in 1984, the natural rate of increase was 0.4%.

In medieval times, the birth rates were only slightly above the death rates in all the European countries. Birth rates may have been as high as 35/1000 in a single year, but as death rates were almost as high, the population did not increase much.

Changes in the death rate

Before the 18th century, the high death rate controlled the population of the world. This was caused mainly by epidemics and famines (Figure 1.4).

Bubonic Plague disappeared from western Europe by about 1720. Since then, medicine and hygiene have improved in many parts of the world. This means that people live longer and that more people live long enough to have children. There has not been a major worldwide epidemic since 1919 when influenza killed about 25 million people.

Unfortunately, this does not mean that disease is no longer important. In many countries large numbers of people suffer from diseases which make them too ill to work. In **developed countries** many people die of illnesses such as cancer and heart diseases which are not so common elsewhere in the world. In **developing countries** people are more likely to die of infectious diseases.

Figure 1.4 Plague was common in the 17th century

Infectious diseases can be controlled in two main ways. Diseases can be prevented from spreading by strict control of water supplies, sewage systems, housing and food. This is called **public hygiene**. The importance of public hygiene has only been realized fairly recently in developed countries. Figure 1.5 shows what conditions were like in London in 1849.

Vaccinations and inoculations can also prevent diseases spreading from one person to another. If people do fall ill they can often be cured if doctors and hospitals are available.

Famines were a common cause of death in Europe before about 1750. During the 18th and 19th centuries, farming methods in Europe improved. New crops such as potatoes, maize and turnips were planted to give more food for people and animals. Cattle and sheep were bred scientifically to give more meat. New machines were invented for farming. People studied the use of chemical and natural fertilizers. There were still bad harvests, but regular famines that killed many people did not happen again. The one exception to this was the Irish famine of 1846–7.

In the 19th century, canals, roads and railways were built. This meant that if one part of a country had a bad harvest, food could be moved to it from another part of the country.

A Sanitary Remonstrance

Teusday Juley 3, 1849

We print the folowing remonstrance just as it has reached us, and trust its publication will assist the unfortunate remonstrates:–

THE EDITOR OF THE TIMES PAPER

Sur, – May we beg and beseach your proteckshion and power. We are Sur, as it may be, livin in a Wilderniss, so far as the rest of London knows anything of us, or as the rich and great people care about. We live in muck and filthe. We aint got no privis, no dust bins, no drains, no water-splies, and no drain or suer in the hole place. The Suer Company, in Greek St., Soho Square, all great, rich and powerfool men, take no notice watsomedever of our cumplaints. The Stenche of a Gully-hole is disgustin. We All of us suggur, and numbers are ill, and if the Colera comes Lord help us.

Some gentlemans comed yesterday, and we thought they was comishoners from the Suer Company, but they was complaining of the noosance and stenche our lanes and corts was to them in New Oxforde Street. They was much surprized to see the seller in No. 12, Carrier St., in our lane where a child was dyin from fever, and would not beleave that Sixty persons sleep in it every night. This here seller you couldent swing a cat in, and the rent is five shilling a week; but theare are greate many sich deare sellers. Sur, we hope you will let us have our complaints put into your hinfluenshall paper, and make these landlords of our houses and these comishoners (the freinds we spose of the landlords), make our houses decent for Christions to live in.

Preaye Sir com and see us, for we are livin like piggs, and it aint fair we shoulde be so ill treted.

We are your respeckfull servants in Church Lane, Carrier St., and the other corts.

John Scott
Emen Scott
Joseph Crosbie
Hanna Crosbie
Edward Copeman
Richard Harmer
John Barnes
William Austin
Ezra Fitzgerlad
William Whut
Anne Saunderson
Mark Manning
John Turner
William Dwyre
Mary Aiers
Donald Connell
Timothy Driscoll
Timothe Murphy
John O'Grady
Maria O'Grady
John Dencey
John Crowley
Margret Steward
Bridget Towley
John Towley
Timothy Crowley
John Brown

Catherine Brown
Catherine Collins
Honora Flinn
John Crowe
James Crowe
Thomas Crowe
Patrick Fouhey
William Joyce
Michal Joyce
John Joyce
Thomas Joyce
John Sullivan
Timothy Sullivan
Cathrin Trice
James Ragen
Timothy Brian
James Bryan
Phillip Lacey
Edward brown
Mrs. brocke
Nance hays
Jeryh fouhey
Jeryh fouhey
Marey fouhey
Jerey Aies
Timthy Joyce
John Padler

Figure 1.5 Letter to *The Times*, 1849

Food supplies for European countries were also helped by imports from their colonies.

All these developments meant that people in more developed countries became healthier and lived longer than ever before. In other countries, the introduction of these 'death controls' has been slower in arriving. You will find more about this on page 77.

Activity

▲2 Look at Figure 1.5.

■ a Make a list of the problems facing the
● writers of this letter.

b Find out which organizations maintain public health in the UK today. How are the problems in Figure 1.5 dealt with by these organizations?

c Why are some people in the UK, the USA and other developed countries still living in poor conditions? Give reasons.

Changes in the birth rate

In countries where children can work to earn money or produce food, parents often have large families. If children are not allowed to work, they have to be kept by their parents' work so families will probably be smaller. In England, for example, once school became compulsory in 1870, family size began to fall rapidly (see Figure 1.6).

Date	Estimated average number of children in family
1870	5.8
1900	5.0
1930	1.6
1960	2.9
1985	1.5

Figure 1.6 Average family size in England, 1870 – 1985

Schooling has other effects too. Surveys in Brazil, Chile and Argentina, where not all children go to school, show that women who have been to school have, on average, two fewer children than those who have not been to school. School also delays the age of marriage for girls and this reduces the total number of years in which they can have children. Education makes it easier for girls and women to find jobs. Women who earn wages usually have smaller families. If they have the choice many people would probably rather have a higher standard of living than more children.

Parents who have had some schooling are also more likely to understand hygiene. This may make them more confident that their own children will survive, and less likely to want to have more children just in case some of them die. If the number of babies who die before they are 5 goes down, the actual birth rate usually drops as well.

Governments can also affect birth rates. Hospitals, health schemes, pensions and unemployment benefits mean that parents do not need to have children to look after them when they are ill, or too old to work. Many governments encourage birth control schemes and supply contraceptives. Some governments go further. China, which has over one fifth of the world's total population, discourages couples from marrying under the age of 30 and from having more than 1 child (Figure 1.7). The Indian Government once tried to encourage men to have vasectomies. Unfortunately, this frightened people away from family planning clinics.

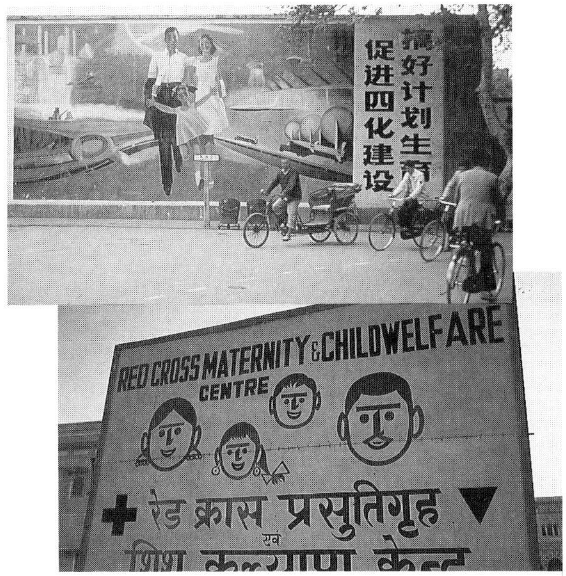

Figure 1.7 Birth control publicity from China and India

Country	Birth rate births/ 1000 persons	Death rate deaths/ 1000 persons	Mean annual change in population % natural rate of increase
Algeria	41	8	3.4
Argentina	24	9	1.3
Australia	16	7	1.3
Bolivia	47	18	3.2
China	21	7	1.4
Egypt	34	8	3.6
Germany, East	14	14	0
Iceland	19	6	1.0
India	33	13	3.0
Israel	24	7	2.3
Italy	11	10	0.4
Mexico	38	5	2.9
Nigeria	50	18	3.3
UK	13	12	0.1
USA	16	9	1.0
USSR	19	10	0.8

The rate of increase changes from year to year between censuses; the mean annual rate of increase in population is the average of those increases. Most censuses are taken every 10 years. Most between census figures are estimates.

Figure 1.8 Birth rates, death rates and annual percentage increases

Not all countries want to reduce their populations. For example, Bolivia wants an increase. To encourage growth, the Bolivian Government has closed family planning clinics and has made abortion illegal.

Figure 1.8 shows birth rates, death rates and natural rates of increase for some countries of the world.

Death rate	Birth rate
Clean water supplies	Compulsory school for all children Education for girls

Figure 1.9 Reasons for reduction in birth and death rates

Activities

▲■ **3 a** Draw a table like the one in Figure 1.9. Use a whole page. Head one column 'Death rate' and the other column 'Birth rate'. Read through this section again and list the changes which have reduced each rate. Some have been done for you.

b Look at Figure 1.8. Choose two countries where the natural rate of population increase is more than 2% each year, and two countries where the natural rate of population increase is less than 1% each year. Use your table to help you explain the natural growth rates of each of these countries.

▲■● **4** Look at Figure 1.10.

a Men and women in these countries seem to have very different attitudes to family size and contraception. Why do you think this is so?

b In developed countries, both men and women seem to agree that smaller families are better. Explain why they think this.

c How could the government of a country similar to the countries in Figure 1.10 encourage people to have smaller families?

■ **5 a** Look at Figure 1.11. Draw bar graphs to show the changes in birth and death rates and natural increase in population for each of the countries.

b All these countries have official family planning programmes.

i) In which country has the family planning programme been most successful?

ii) Which country seems to have the most effective public hygiene and medical arrangements?

▲● **6** The Bolivian Government wants to increase the population of Bolivia. It has tried to do this by closing birth control clinics and making abortion illegal. Look back to Figure 1.8.

a Suggest more efficient ways of increasing the growth of the population.

b Describe what other effects you think could happen as a result of the actions of the Bolivian Government.

Tunisia

'In my day women were enclosed within their homes. Now my daughters can go here and there. We didn't get to meet our husbands until we were married. Now we have changed our old habits. Women are free and are just as capable as men. But not the likes of me. I lived like a beast. It is obvious that I'm always left behind, overtaken by the menfolk because of my ignorance. But I'm happy to see other women are not like me now.

I had eight children. But it's much better to have a smaller number because you can feed them better, nurse them better, clothe them well and see they are clean. All the younger women have family planning. I would have done if it had been available in my time.

If the men don't like the change, it is just too bad. President Bourgiba told us we are free and that we should plan our families. All women are seeking to learn, to go about, to have a life of their own.'

Sri Lanka

Ariya lives in a small fishing hamlet north of

Figure 1.10 *Message from the Village*, Perdita Huston, 1978

Country	Year	Annual average birth rate per 1000	Annual average death rate per 1000	Natural increase %
Mauritius	1960–4	38.9	8.8	3.0
	1965–9	31.8	8.6	2.3
	1985	23	7.0	1.6
Tunisia	1960–4	46.2	11.8	3.4
	1965–9	40.6	9.5	3.1
	1985	35.0	11.0	2.5
Costa Rica	1960–4	46.1	8.5	3.8
	1965–9	39.6	7.1	3.3
	1985	31.0	4.0	2.4
Singapore	1960–4	35.6	5.6	3.0
	1965–9	26.9	5.6	2.1
	1985	17.0	5.0	1.3
Sri Lanka	1960–4	35.1	8.2	2.7
	1965–9	32.1	7.5	3.5
	1985	28.0	6.0	1.8

Figure 1.11 Population details: Mauritius, Tunisia, Costa Rica, Singapore, Sri Lanka

How a country's population is made up

So far we have looked at some of the reasons why the number of babies born and the number of people dying have changed. We have not yet mentioned the effects of the ages of the people. In general, more babies are born in countries with a lot of young people. More people die in countries where there are more old people.

Information about the ages of people in a country's population is usually shown in

Colombo. She is twenty years old and has a primary school education.

'My life is so different from my mother's. She was tied to the house and was dominated by her father and mother – like a lot of people here still are. The parents of younger girls must be instructed that if they are given the freedom to come out and work together, they will be better off. It's just like trees growing in the shade. We cannot be held in the shadows.

I'm very much afraid of marriage. My married friends, after a certain time, complain and say they are not happy. The couple doesn't get along together, because they don't really talk to each other as they should. Most women, once they have a certain number of children, think they should stop. The woman says, "Enough!" but the man doesn't care. It is not his problem. The man wants sex and the children continue to come. After a while the woman refuses relations out of fear of having more children. Then the men go and have sex outside.

Men must understand what women's lives are like. They must be taught.'

Mexico

Maria Louisa has lived her entire life in a small Zatopec Indian village. She is 40 years old, has seven children and doesn't want any more.

'But don't you need children to help with the field work?'

'No, we would need more land if we had more mouths to feed. If I could go back and choose the number of my children, I would have one or two. Look at me, I look so old; that is because we work so hard with all these children. And there isn't enough food for all of us.'

'Do you think the husbands in this village would permit their wives to control the number of pregnancies?'

'Heavens, no! They say terrible things about women who want it. Some say, "The only reason you want birth control is so you can go with other men."'

'Once the radio said, "Fathers of families, if you want to give your children a good up-bringing, take care of them well and remember that small families are better." Well, my own brother just laughed. You see, some people are very ignorant.'

population pyramids. They also show how the population is divided between male and female. Figure 1.12 shows the population pyramids for India and the UK.

The pyramid for India shows that much of the population is between 15 and 45 years old. These are the people who are most likely to have children. The wide base of the pyramid shows that a high proportion of the population are children under 15 years old. The sharp top of the pyramid shows that there are few people over 60 years old. The birth rate in India in 1985 was 38/1000 and the death rate was 15/1000. In a few years time, the children shown in this pyramid will be having children of their own. If they each have the same number of children as the present generation of parents, the total number of children born to them will be even greater than now. For this reason, India is described as having a **young population**. Even if today's children each have fewer children than today's parents, the population will continue to grow. It will be many years before India can have an **old population**.

Look at the pyramid for the UK. It shows that the number of children under 15 years old is about the same as the number of people of 15–30 years old. If these children all grow up to have the same number of children as their parents, the number of babies born will be roughly the same as now. In 1985 the rate of natural increase of the UK was 0.4%. The top of the pyramid shows us that the UK has many people over 60 years old.

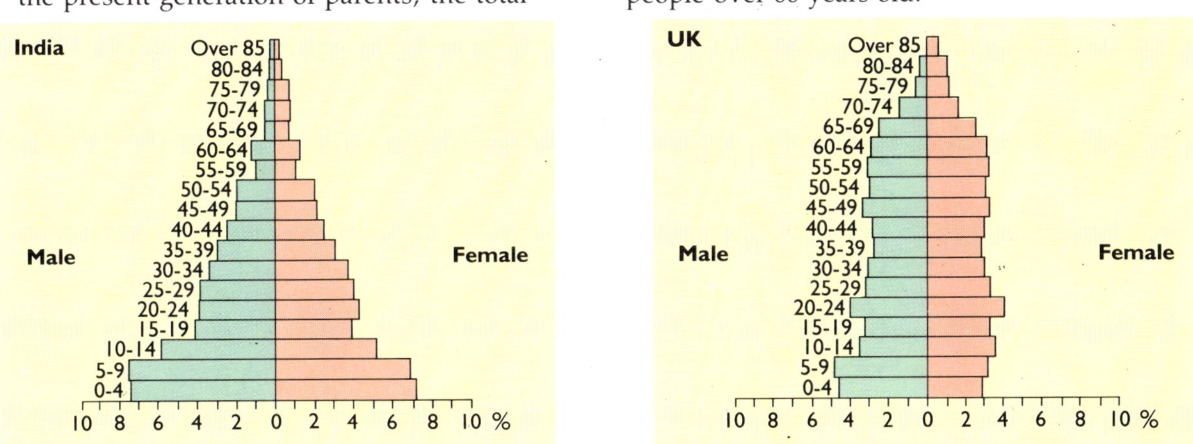

Figure 1.12 Population pyramids for India... ...and the UK

The population of the world can only change by some people being born and by others dying. The population of a single country may also change due to births and deaths, but it can also change because of people coming into the country (**immigration**) or leaving it (**emigration**). To avoid confusion, the word 'natural' is used for changes due only to births and deaths.

Although there have been slightly more births than deaths in the UK for many years, more people have left the UK to live elsewhere than have come to live in the UK. This means that the UK's total population has fallen slightly.

The governments of some countries such as Korea, Algeria and Turkey encourage emigration to help solve their population problems. Other countries such as Saudi Arabia, Bolivia, Israel and South Africa encourage immigration to provide workers.

Age range	Male %	Female %	Age range	Male %	Female %
Over 85 / 80 – 84	0.2	0.2	35 – 39	1.6	1.6
			30 – 34	2.0	2.0
75 – 79	0.2	0.2	25 – 29	2.5	2.4
70 – 74	0.3	0.3	20 – 24	3.1	3.0
65 – 69	0.4	0.4	15 – 19	3.8	3.7
60 – 64	0.5	0.5	10 – 14	4.5	4.3
55 – 59	0.7	0.7	5 – 9	5.3	5.1
50 – 54	0.9	0.9	1 – 4 / 0 – 1	6.5	6.3
45 – 49	1.1	1.1			
40 – 44	1.4	1.4			

Figure 1.13 Mexico's population, 1983

Activities

▲ **7** ■ **a** Use the information in Figure 1.13 to draw a population pyramid for Mexico.

b i) Calculate the percentage of the total population under 15 years old.

ii) Calculate the percentage of the total population between 15 and 50 years old.

iii) Calculate the percentage of the total population over 50 years old.

c Write two or three sentences to explain:

i) What is likely to happen to the total population of Mexico in the next 20 to 30 years if the rate of natural increase stays the same? (Look at your population pyramid carefully.)

ii) What is likely to happen if there are improvements in public health and the numbers of doctors and hospitals?

iii) What is likely to happen if the average family size falls to 2 children, and there are improvements in public health?

▲ **8** ● The newspaper cutting shown in Figure 1.14 suggests that the world faces problems because of the growth in the number of old people.

a List the problems explained in the article.

b Name some countries likely to have these problems in the near future. (Look back to Figure 1.8.)

c What do you think needs to be done about the problem? Give as many reasons as you can.

Figure 1.14 World faces old age boom (*Observer*)

World faces old age boom by GEOFFREY LEAN

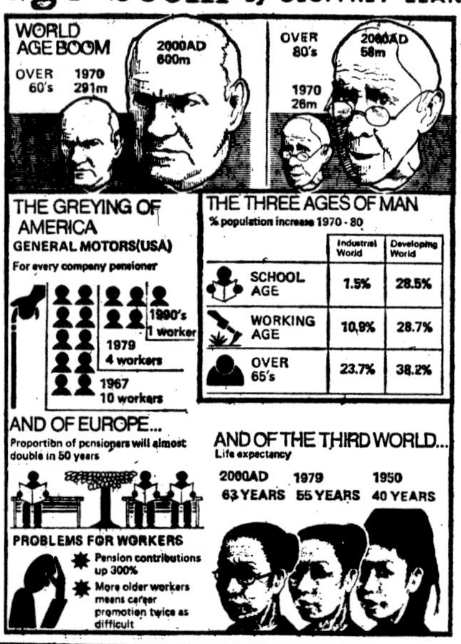

BY the end of the century there will be twice as many people over 60 alive as there were in 1970.

The number of over-80s will also double in this period.

The reasons are that people are living longer, and birth rates are falling as the pace of population growth slows down.

In rich countries, 11 of which have reached (or are close to) zero population growth, the rapid increase in the elderly will cause 'manifold social and economic consequences,' reports Mr Rafael Salas, the UN joint executive director.

A dwindling proportion of wage-earners will have to look after increasing numbers of the aged. In the United States there are now six wage-earners for every retired person; in 50 years time there will only be three.

In 1967 there were 10 workers at General Motors (USA) for every company pensioner; now there are only four, and in the 1990s there is only expected to be one.

The proportion of pensioners in Europe will almost double. This change could mean that four times as much will have to be taken from each pay packet to provide for old age.

Governments will need to shift resources from child welfare to caring for the elderly, as the old replace children as their societies' most numerous dependents. They are also likely to change their policies to encourage immigration to swell the workforce.

In the Third World, where life expectancy has been steadily growing and birth-rates are now falling substantially the growing number of the aged 'is likely to place intolerably heavy burdens on the working population.'

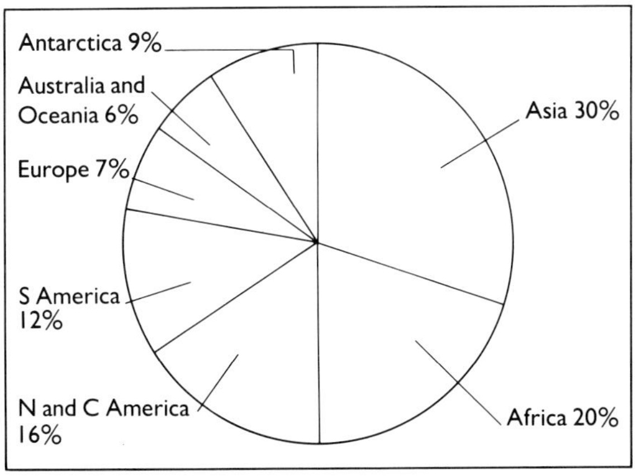

Figure 1.15 The sizes of the continents as percentages of the world surface area

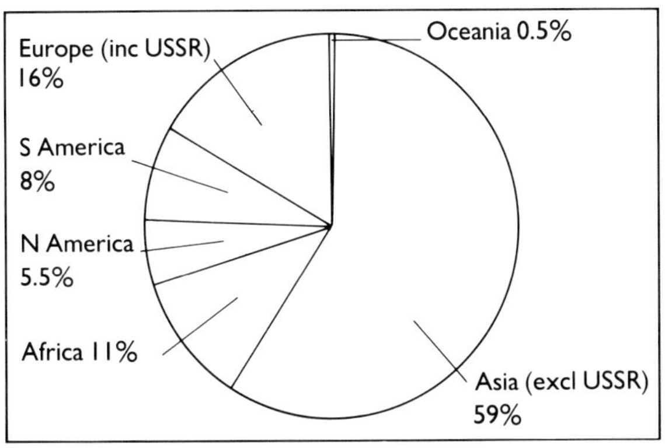

Figure 1.16 The proportions of the world's population

Where the people of the world live

Figure 1.15 shows the size of the continents and Figure 1.16 shows the proportion of the world's population living in each continent. If you look carefully at the two diagrams you will see that people are very unevenly spread over the surface of the Earth. For example, Asia has nearly two thirds of the world's population on only about one third of the land. Africa, on the other hand, has about one tenth of the world's population on one fifth of the land.

Figure 1.17 shows that people are spread very unevenly over the land of each continent. There are large areas where very few people live. There are also areas where a great many people live. Geographers try to give reasons for patterns like these on the Earth's surface.

Figure 1.18 shows that 66% of the land on earth is not suitable for cultivation. Another 23% could be cultivated. (Chapter 5 explains why it may not be wise to cultivate this land.) Only 11% is being cultivated at the moment.

It is easier to explain why some areas of the world are almost empty than to explain why other areas have a larger population. It is not always easy to tell from atlas maps why some areas have a high density of population. In

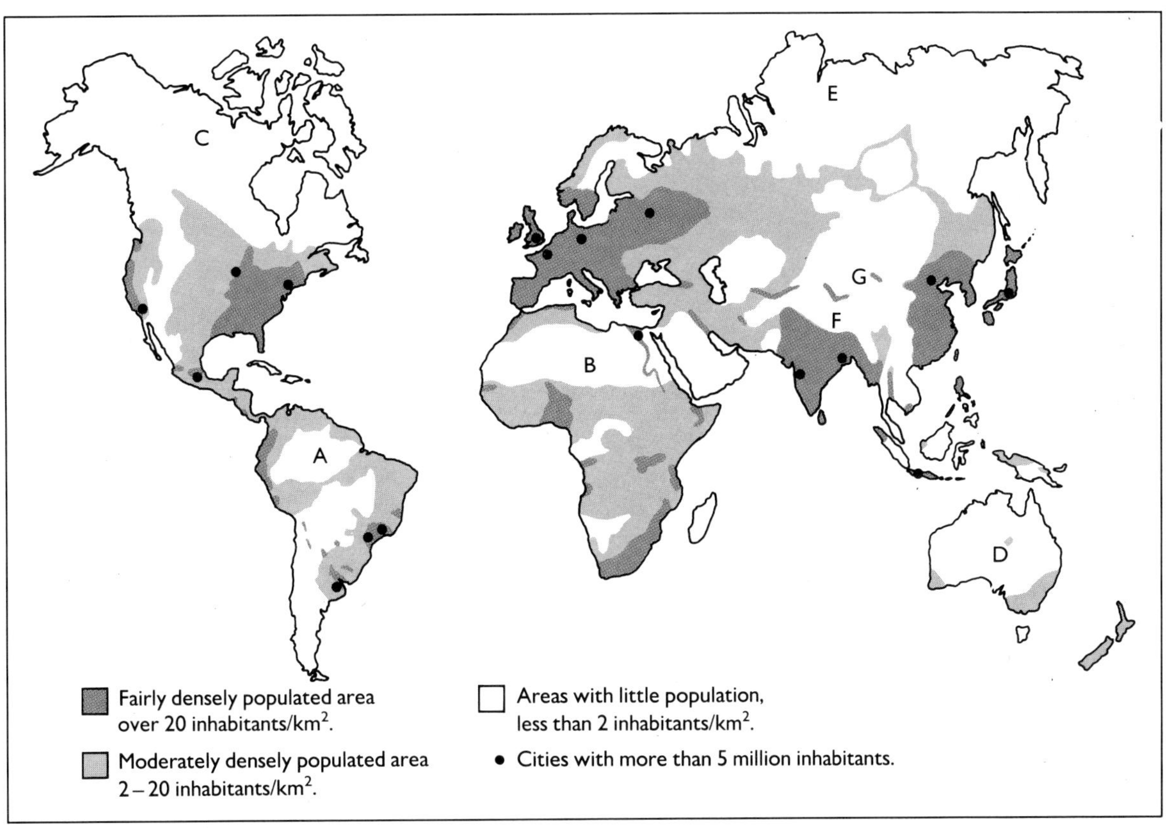

Figure 1.17 Population distribution over the world

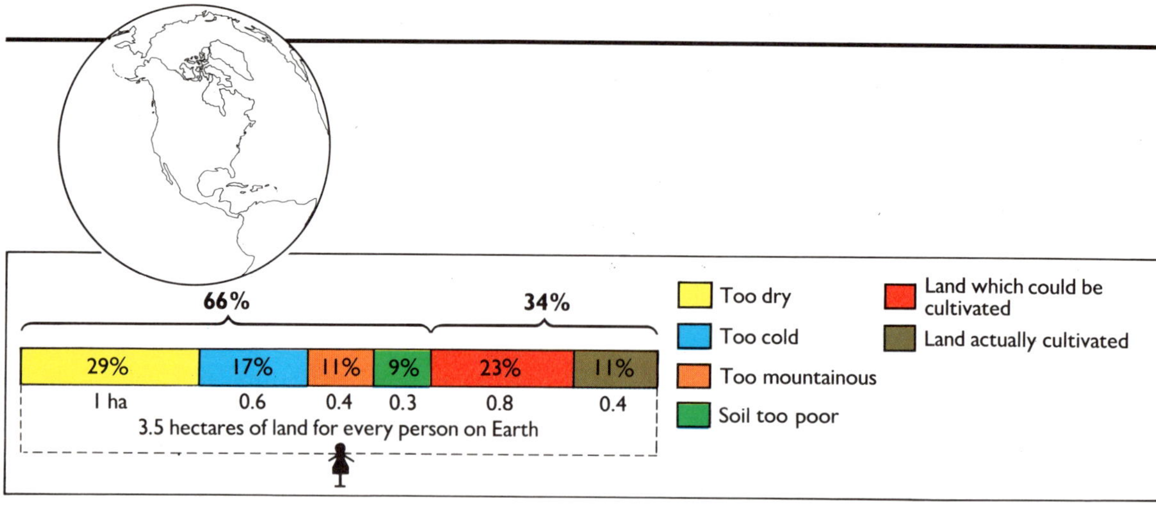

Figure 1.18 Land and cultivation in the world

general, people live wherever it is easiest for them to live. Easy areas to live in include:

where it is not too high
where it is not too dry
where it is not too hot
where it is not too cold.

Some people do live in difficult areas. Some have always lived in these areas, but some have moved into difficult areas to find iron ore, oil, uranium or other minerals. Some areas have many people because they seem to be good farming areas. Other areas with many people are based on large cities. (The reasons for people gathering in good farming areas is described in Chapter 5. The growth of cities is described in Chapter 7.)

Activities

■ **9 a** Draw a table like Figure 1.19.

b Look back to Figure 1.17. Take each continent in turn and name the areas which have less than 2 people per square kilometre. (These are labelled A – G on Figure 1.17.) Use a world map or maps of each continent from your atlas to do this.

c Look up each area on the maps in your atlas which show:

rainfall — relief
temperature — vegetation.

In your table put a tick beneath each reason which could explain why each area is nearly empty. (You may find several reasons for some areas.)

■ **10** Use your atlas to help you list the areas in each continent where there are the highest densities of population (Figure 1.17). Some are the areas around major cities. Others are larger areas. Use a world map or separate maps of each continent.

How population density is shown on maps of different scales

Although small scale maps like Figure 1.17 give us a general idea about where people live, they can hide important differences. For example in Figure 1.17 it looks as if all of Japan has a high population density. Now look at the much larger scale map of Japan (Figure 1.20). This shows that most of the larger towns are around the coasts of the islands. The areas of lowest population density are the highest parts of the mountains. Because Japan is such a long and narrow country these almost empty areas do not show up on the small scale map at all.

Even the larger scale map (Figure 1.20) hides important differences between areas. For example, Yokosuka is a small town on the peninsula south of Tokyo. On Figure 1.20 the whole peninsula has a population density of over 1000 people per square kilometre. Now look at the detailed map of just part of this peninsula (Figure 1.21). This map shows that people are not evenly spread across the peninsula. The town of Yokosuka has a high density of population, but if you travelled a little way west, you would find the houses are not close together but scattered. Still further west, you would cross Mt Okusu where there are no houses shown at all. You would have to go right down to the road on the west coast before you found scattered houses again.

This example shows that what we can find

Continent & area	Too dry	Too cold	Too mountainous	Soil too poor	Land could be cultivated
N. America					
N. Canada		✓		✓	

Figure 1.19 Copy this chart for activity 9

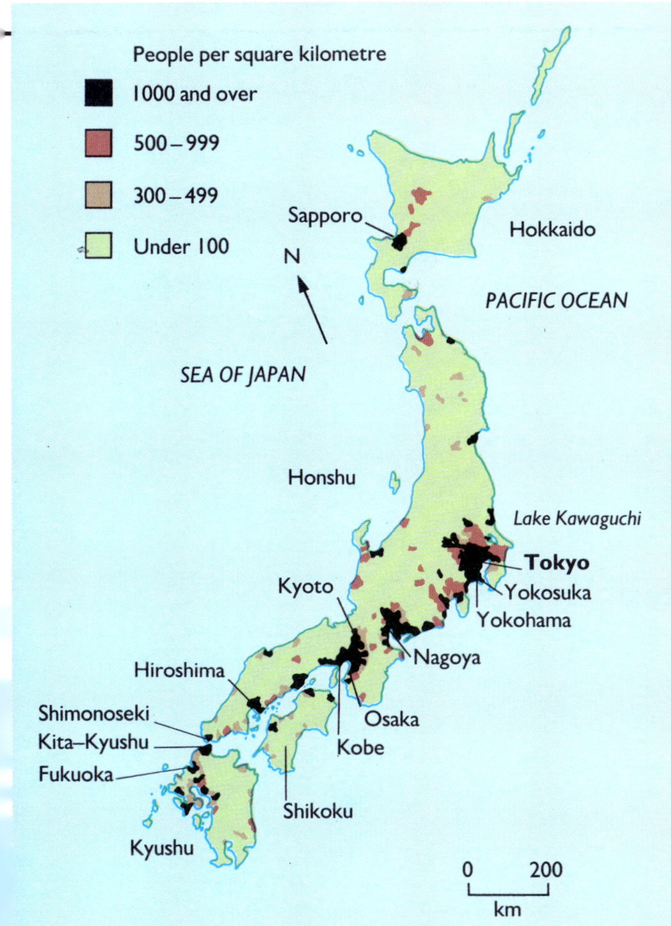

Figure 1.20 Japan, showing the population density

out about the distribution of the population of the world depends on the scale of the map we are looking at. Japan is reckoned to be one of the most densely populated countries of the world, but Mt Okusu is empty. The population density of South America is only half the world average, but there are still crowded shanty towns in many of the cities.

Depending on why we want to study the population, we must use a map drawn to a suitable scale. If we want an overall view of countries which need help to control their populations, we can use world maps of population density, wealth and area of land. If we want to plan a new National Park for Japan we will probably need a map of the whole country like Figure 1.20. If we want to find a site for a new housing estate for Yokosuka, we will need a larger scale map like Figure 1.21.

Conclusion

The growth in a country's population depends mainly on whether the number of births is greater than the number of deaths. In many countries, control of the death rate has been much more effective than control of the birth rate.

Figure 1.21 Large-scale map of an area south of Tokyo

Population densities vary enormously from one part of the world to another. Almost empty areas are usually found where it is too dry, too cold or too mountainous for most people to want to live and work there. Sometimes there are special reasons for people living and working in harsh areas.

Showing population densities on maps can give very different results if different scales are used.

Year	Birth rate (0/1000)	Death rate (0/1000)	Natural rate of population increase (%)	Population (millions)
1870	36.3	31.3	0.5	36
1880	33.9	28.3		38
1890	34.3	27.3		40
1900	35.2	24.2		44
1910	35.6	22.1		49
1920	35.0	23.0		55
1930	31.8	18.1		64
1940	30.8	16.3		71
1950	23.7	9.4		83
1960	17.2	7.3		93
1970	18.8	6.9		103
1980	14.0	6.0		117

Figure 1.22 Population growth in Japan

Activities

■ ● **11 a** Why has the world's population grown rapidly in the last 100 years? Give reasons.

b Describe the problems likely to be faced by a country whose rate of natural increase continues to be high.

c What problems will a country whose rate of natural increase is negative probably have?

▲ ● **12** Which areas of the world do you think could slowly increase their population density without causing great problems?
Carefully explain your answer using evidence from your atlas to help you.

▲ ■ **13** Look at Figure 1.22.

a Draw a graph to show the changes in birth rates and death rates in Japan from 1870–1980.

b On a copy of Figure 1.22 calculate and insert the national rate of population increase. The first one has been done for you.

c On the same graph, above your lines for birth and death rates, draw a graph to show the changes in the total population.

d Explain why the population grew from 1870 to 1920 even though the birth rate stayed fairly constant.

e Explain why the population grew from 1930 to 1980 even though the birth rate was falling.

f Describe the results of the changes in birth and death rates on the natural rate of population increase in Japan.

g If the present rate of decline continues, could Japan's death rate be reduced to zero? Give reasons.

2
The unstable Earth

Figure 2.1 shows how the whole of the Earth's surface is made up. You will see that most of the Earth is covered by oceans. Much of the land area is not very useful to human beings. The part of the Earth's surface which is either *being* used for farming, or which *could be used* for farming is very small.

We can look at the Earth in another way. Think of the Earth as a basketball or a netball. The crust of cool rock on which we live would be the thickness of a postage stamp stuck on the ball. The big difference between the **Earth's crust** and the stamp is that the crust of the Earth is constantly changing and moving.

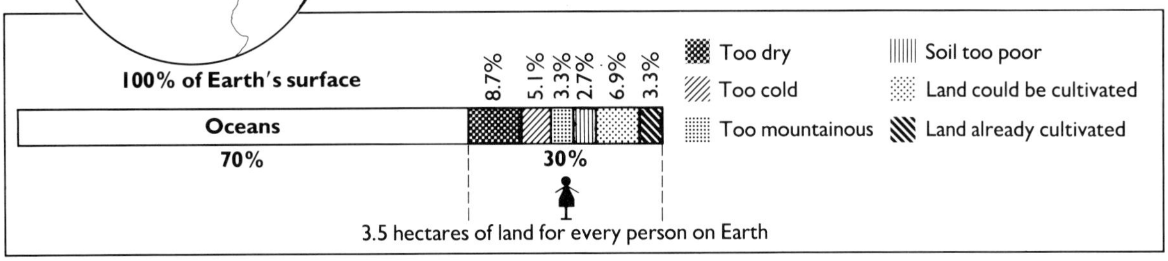

Figure 2.1 Make-up of the Earth

Both the oceans and the land are part of this crust. Since human beings live and grow their food on such a small part of the crust, it is important that we know how the crust is made and how it changes. If we can understand how the crust changes, we may be able to avoid people getting hurt. We may also prevent ourselves from damaging the land on which we live.

Earthquakes and volcanoes

At 6 o'clock in the morning on 9 February 1971 an earthquake struck the San Fernando Valley near Los Angeles. The earthquake lasted only one minute, but it killed 64 people. The local hospital had been built to stand up to earthquakes, but it still collapsed. There was other damage too. A motorway overpass collapsed. A reservoir had to be drained because of a crack in the dam. An electricity transformer station was badly damaged.

This earthquake was described as only 6.6 on the **Richter scale**. (The Richter scale is a measure of the size of earthquakes. It goes from 0 for a *very* gentle movement to 9 for a very severe shock. See Chapter 9 for more about this.) The 9 February 1971 earthquake was only one of many earthquakes which have struck California. Figure 2.2 shows where earthquakes have struck since 1850.

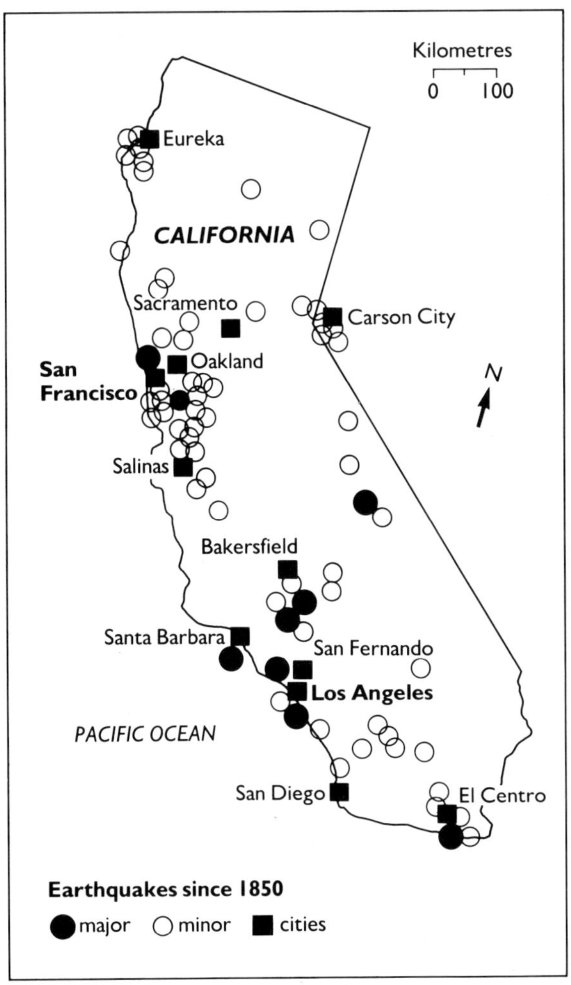

Figure 2.2 Californian earthquakes since 1850

A severe earthquake which makes buildings collapse can kill many people. Imagine being

Figure 2.3 Earthquake destruction

asleep at the top of the building shown in Figure 2.3 when this earthquake struck.

In a developed country, if you survived the earthquake itself, you would probably be rescued and cared for fairly quickly. In less developed countries, surviving the earthquake may just be the start of your problems. It might be a long time before you are rescued. There might be no doctors to look after you and not even any clean water to wash your injuries.

Activity

▲ 1 Look at Figure 2.3.
■ a Describe the ways in which people can be hurt *during* an earthquake.
● b Describe the ways in which an earthquake can be a danger to people's health *after* the initial shock.
c Explain why more people may be hurt *during* an earthquake in a developed country, but more people are likely to suffer *after* an earthquake in a less developed country.

Figure 2.4 Mount St. Helens erupting, 1980

Mount St. Helens eruption, 1980

In 1980 Mount St. Helens in Washington State in the west of the USA erupted (Figure 2.4). It had been dormant since its last eruption in 1857.

In 1975 a team of scientists from the US Geological Survey had forecast that Mount St. Helens would erupt again. They did not know exactly when, but only that it would happen 'perhaps before the end of the century'.

Seven weeks before the eruption the experts realized that the eruption was coming soon. The area around the volcano was evacuated. Only people with special permits were allowed to go into a wider zone around the mountain. One of the people with a permit to stay in the central zone was a geologist called David Johnston. A month before the eruption, Johnston said 'my feeling is that when it goes its just going to go like that . . . (he snapped his fingers) . . . bang!' He was correct. Afterwards, searchers found only a pile of black ash where his trailer caravan had stood. Figure 2.5 is a newspaper account written about the 1980 eruption.

Many other people died because they refused to stay out of the area. Two tourists from California were found dead in their car which had been covered by boiling mud. A young father was found dead with his arms wrapped round the bodies of his two small sons.

Activity

■ 2 Read the newspaper account of the Mount St.
● Helens eruption (Figure 2.5).

a Describe what happened to the mountain when the eruption took place.

b List six results of the eruption which were disastrous for people who lived in the area affected by the volcano.

In other eruptions, the lava seeps out of the volcano fairly quietly. This does not mean that it always flows slowly!

▼ **Figure 2.5** The eruption of Mount St. Helens

● **For once it was a disaster that was expected. Even so, when Mount St Helens actually did explode in Washington State last week, it did so with a suddenness and intensity that stunned the experts – and left some 100 people dead. JOHN BARNES reports from Vancouver, Washington State.**

GEOLOGIST David Johnston was manning the Goldwater Two observation post five miles north of the summit of Mount St. Helens. For seven weeks the 9,677 feet snow clad volcano had been emitting signs of imminent eruption and Johnston was at one of a string of monitoring points reporting back to the government Geological Survey base some 40 miles south of the summit at Vancouver, Washington State.

At 8.32 am last Sunday Johnston's voice was heard shouting over a crackling radio link-:"Vancouver, Vancouver. This is it. The mountain's going." They were the 30-year-old geologist's last words. He died instantly as the volcano exploded with a force 500 times greater than the atomic bomb dropped on Hiroshima.

The noise was heard 200 miles away as a deep rumble. But to Bert Delfinso, a logger only 25 miles away, it looked "like the end of the world. Heavy, thick clouds boiled up, white and blue, lightning flashes crackled through the mountains. It rained mud balls – little balls a quarter-inch in diameter. And after that the ash came down. It was so powerful and quick the way the clouds built up. It just got black and I mean pitch black."

Within seconds the volcano had put on a display of spectacular devastation. The crater's north wall collapsed as a four-cubic-mile mass of volcanic gas, ash and rock was blasted up with such force that some fine debris soared 16 miles high into the stratosphere. Snow was instantly melted and avalanches of mud and rock hurtled down the volcano's slopes at 100 mph flattening homes, cabins, sawmills, bridges and 125 square miles of fir trees.

One great flow of debris blocked off the outlet of Lake Spirit north of the summit. A 200ft natural dam began to form, holding back a rapidly expanding mass of water fed by the melted snows.

Then the ash, sometimes as hot as 100 degrees Centigrade, began to fall. Near the crater itself – now some 2½ miles wide and 5,000 feet deep – it was eight feet thick. On the Green River, just north of the volcano, it fell on the state fishing hatchery and incinerated 10 million salmon. Over 100 miles away it rained down on the wheat fields and the orchards which provide America with a third of its apples. Meanwhile the fine ash that had reached the stratosphere was turning into a great grey plume.

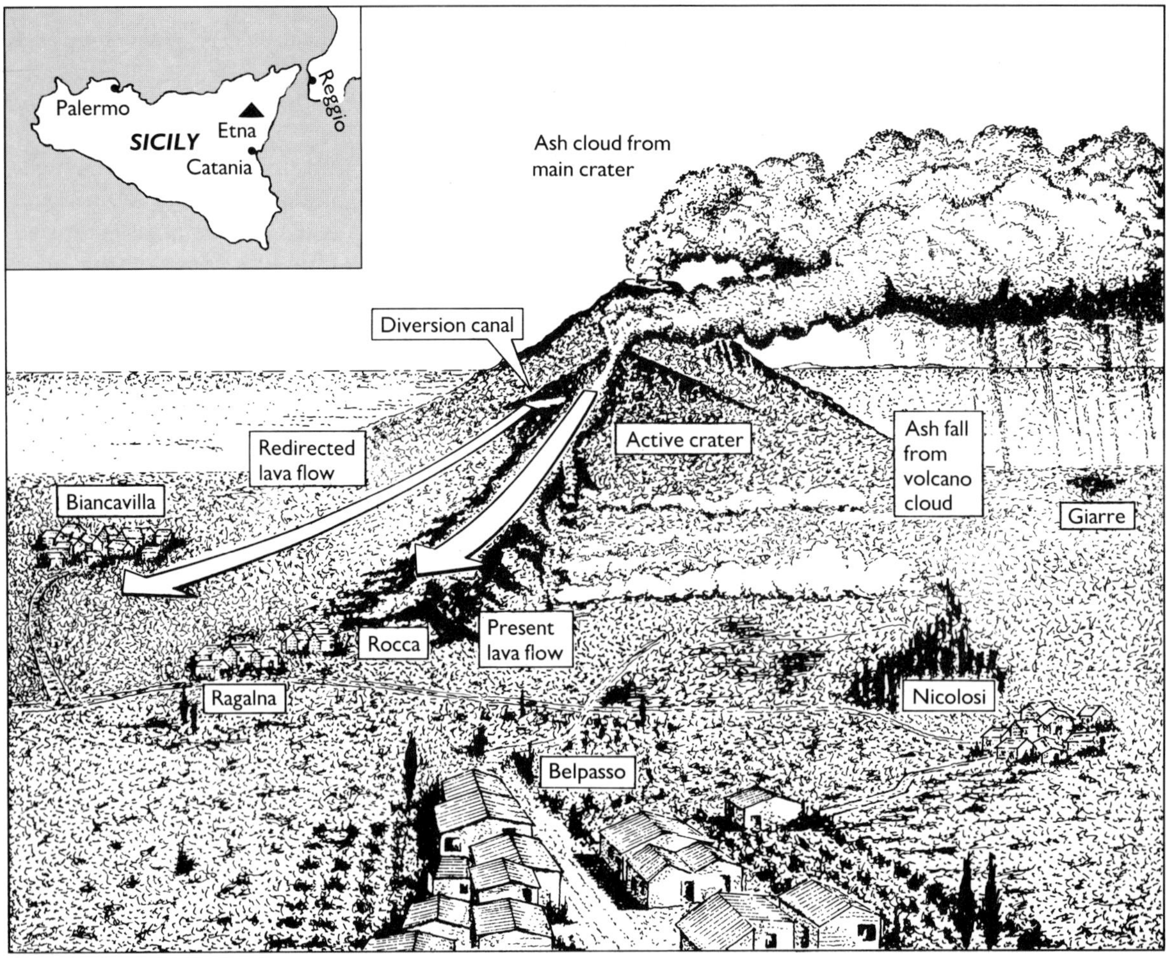

Figure 2.6 Mount Etna lava diversion plan

Mount Etna's eruption, 1983

Mount Etna is on the island of Sicily in the Mediterranean Sea. It is Europe's largest volcano. At the end of March 1983 a small crater 2400 metres up the side of the mountain began to erupt. Millions of tonnes of lava flowed out and covered the side of the mountain with huge tongues of molten rock. Some of these tongues were 6 kilometres long. The molten rock was so hot it glowed. The lava carved out a channel for itself about 6 metres wide and 15 metres deep. The lava at the side of the flow cooled enough to become solid walls of rock. The lava in the middle raced along at about 16 kph – about twice the speed of a fast walker! After about 1 kilometre it began to slow down.

The lava flow burned up 1 hotel, 3 restaurants, 25 houses and many orange groves. A month later the main crater at Etna's summit, 3500 metres above sea level, began to erupt.

Lava flows from Mount Etna have affected the lives of the people who live nearby for centuries. The farmers used to try to change the direction of the lava flow away from their houses and farms. Since none of the farmers wanted the lava to destroy the land, there were often disagreements about which direction the lava should be sent. In the 19th century it was made illegal to try to change lava flows. This law was changed in 1983 so that an attempt could be made to alter the flow of the lava using explosives. Figure 2.6 shows what was done.

A wide canal was dug down the mountain-side leading away from the villages at the foot of the mountain. Then a hole was blown in the 'wall' of the lava flow so that the lava could overflow down the canal. This idea was only partly successful because the mountain produced more lava than before. The lava overflowing into the canal only ran for 350 metres before it cooled and hardened. The rest of the lava carried on down its original course.

Activity

▲3 ■ ● Write an account of the arguments for and against the plan to change the flow of lava from Mount Etna with explosives, from the point of view of

a someone who lives in Rocca

b someone who lives in Biancavilla.

Use the text and Figure 2.6 to help you.

Earthquakes in the UK

There have not been any volcanic eruptions in the UK for many millions of years, but this does not mean that the Earth's crust under the UK never moves rapidly. There are several earthquakes recorded every year. Usually they are so slight that they are only noticed by scientists using sensitive instruments.

In 1983 the UK suffered its biggest earthquake for 50 years. The earthquake happened at 4.00 a.m. and lasted for 30 seconds. It reached force 5 on the Richter scale.

The place on the Earth's surface above the actual movement of the earthquake is called its **epicentre**. The epicentre of this earthquake was between Gretna Green and Longtown. This is just on the English side of the border between England and Scotland. Figure 2.7 shows the area most affected by the earthquake.

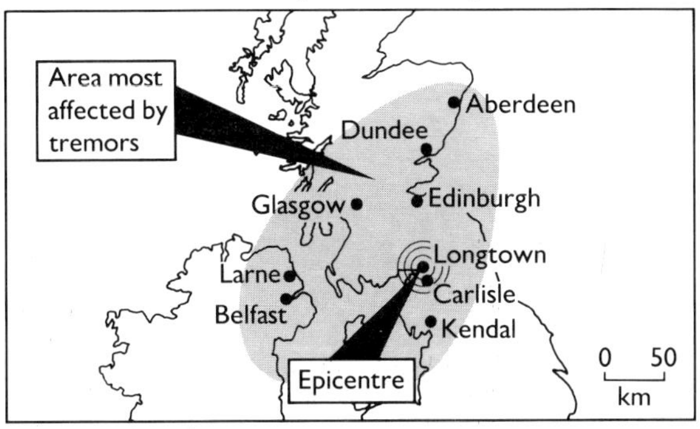

Figure 2.7 The biggest earthquake to hit the UK for 50 years

Water mains and drains cracked. Bricks and tiles fell off buildings and dozens of chimney pots crashed. Inside the houses, beds slid across floors, furniture fell over and crockery crashed off shelves. One person who was near the epicentre said that the earth shook and roared 'like a thousand express trains'. Another person said 'it was as if a giant hand was shaking the house'.

Activity

■ **4** Look at Figure 2.7.
Calculate the size of the area affected by the earthquake:
a from south-west to north-east
b from south-east to north-west.

Earthquake and volcano patterns

Some areas have many earthquakes and volcanic eruptions. One area in California had 100 earth tremors in one week in 1980. Often earthquakes and volcanoes happen where many people live. If scientists could find out if there are patterns in where and when earthquakes and volcanoes occur, they could warn people in advance. This would reduce the number of people hurt every year by these catastrophes.

Figure 2.8 shows the areas in the world where there have been most earthquakes and volcanic

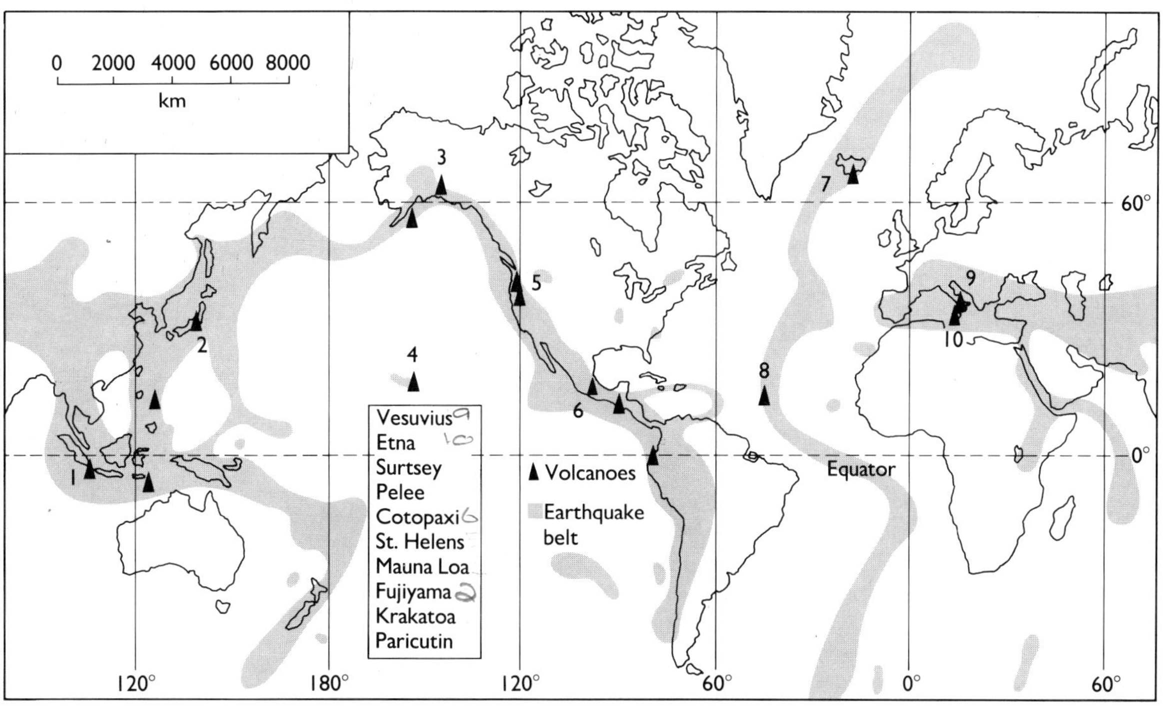

Figure 2.8 World map showing volcanoes and earthquakes

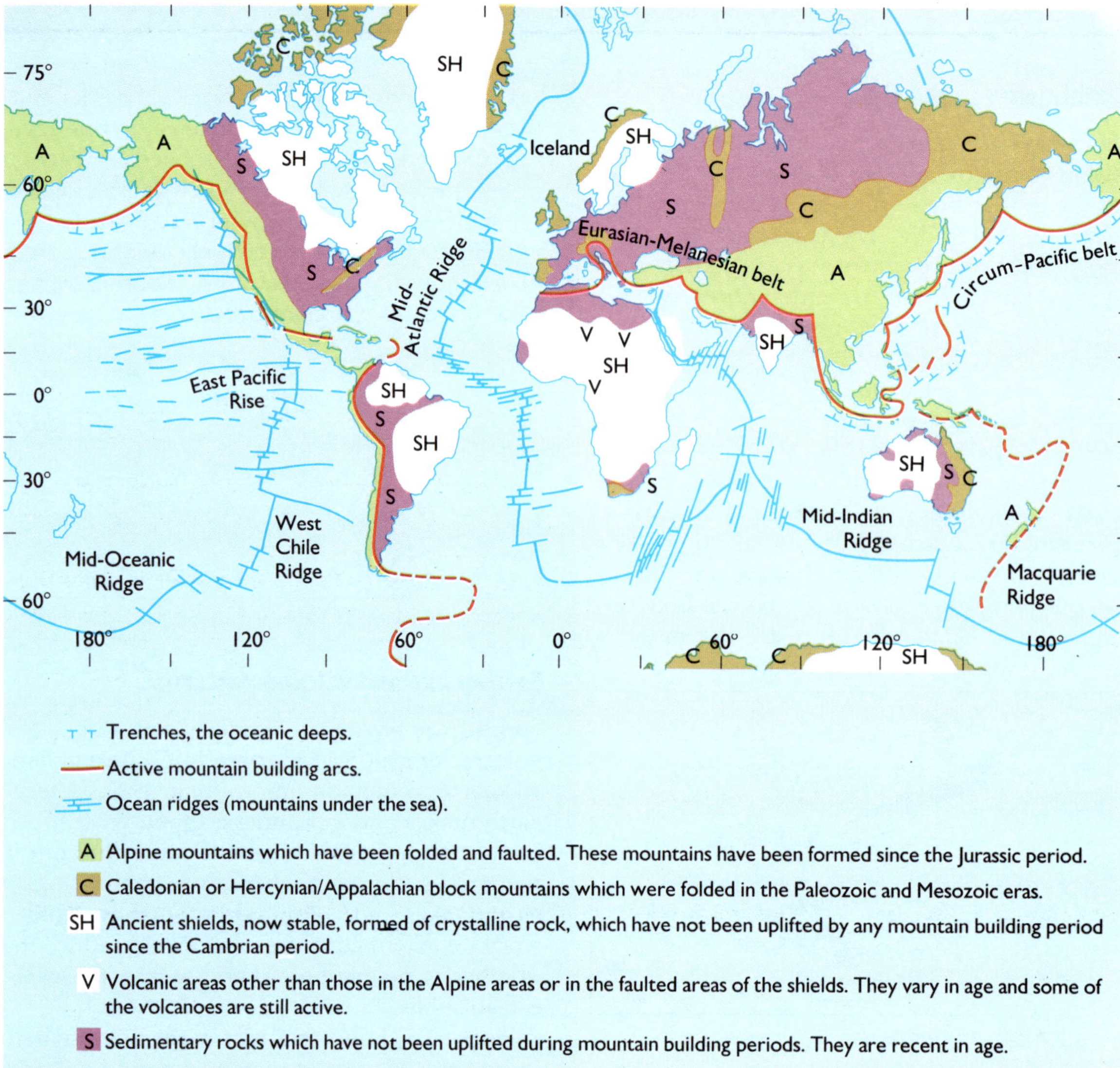

Figure 2.9 The structure of the Earth's surface

eruptions. You can see that there are three **belts** of activity. One runs around the rim of the Pacific Ocean. The second belt runs across Europe and Asia from Spain through the Alps and Himalayas. The third belt runs from north to south through the middle of the Atlantic Ocean. One way to try and explain this pattern is to compare it with the patterns of other features.

Look at an atlas map of the world which shows the mountains. You will see that the pattern of mountains and the pattern of earthquakes and volcano belts seem to be similar.

Figure 2.9 shows the main rock ages and mountains of the Earth's crust. (If you don't know the names of the geological periods Figure 2.10 will help you.) If you compare this map with an atlas map of the world's mountains and the map of earthquakes and volcanoes (Figure 2.8) you will see that, once again, the patterns are similar.

Geological period	Number of years ago (millions)	Periods of mountain building (orogenies)
Quaternary	3	
Tertiary	65	Alpine
Cretaceous	135	
Jurassic	180	
Triassic	225	Hercynian Appalachian
Permian	280	
Carboniferous	345	
Devonian	395	Caledonian
Silurian	430	
Ordovician	500	
Cambrian	570	
Precambrian	3500	Precambrian
Earth formed	4500	
Palaeozoic		
Mesozoic		

Figure 2.10 Geological time scale

Activities

- **5** Copy Figure 2.8. Name the volcanoes numbered 1–10. Mount St. Helens may not be named in your atlas. Why not?

- **6** Make a copy of Figure 2.9.
  - **a** Colour the mountains which were formed in the Alpine Orogeny in yellow. Name each mountain range.
  - **b** Colour the mountains which were originally formed in Hercynian Appalachian and Caledonian times in red. Name the largest mountain areas in each continent.
  - **c** Name the oceans of the world.
  - **d** **i)** From your atlas, find out whether the Alpine or the Hercynian Appalachian and Caledonian mountains are usually higher.
    ii) Write down as many reasons as you can think of why the mountain type you have chosen is higher.

Plate tectonics

Many people have noticed how the continents appear to match each other like the pieces of a jigsaw puzzle. This pattern made scientists wonder whether the continents may have once been together but have since drifted apart. Moving continents may not seem very important to us since they obviously move very slowly. However, the patterns of earthquakes, volcanoes and mountains are similar, so it is not difficult to see that there may be some link between them and the moving continents. The study of the links between these things led to the theory of **plate tectonics**.

In the early 1900s it was suggested that the continents as we know them today were once one huge land mass. This land mass was called **Pangaea**. It was divided into a northern part called **Laurasia** and a southern part called **Gondwana**. In Triassic times, this huge land mass began to split up. Pieces of the crust drifted apart to form new continents and oceans. You can see this in Figure 2.11.

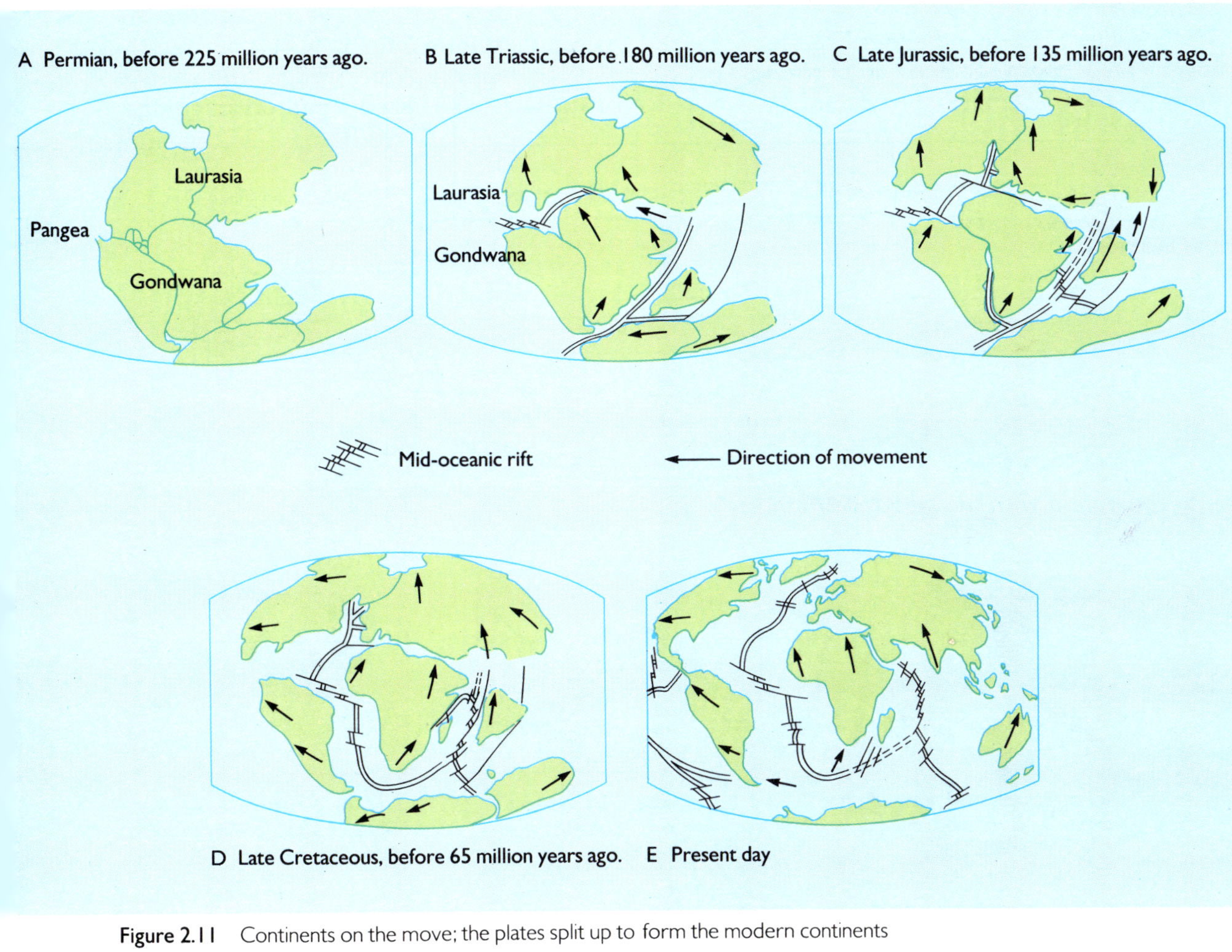

Figure 2.11 Continents on the move; the plates split up to form the modern continents

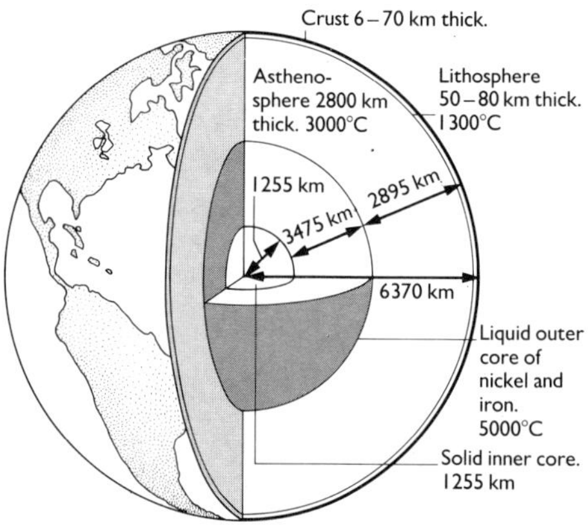

Figure 2.12 Inside the Earth

Inside the Earth

Figure 2.12 shows how the centre of the earth is made up. It shows that the **lithosphere** (solid rock) which includes the crust has an average temperature of about 600° C at depths of 80 km. The **mantle** is also solid rock. It has an average temperature of 3000° C. In between the lithosphere and the mantle is the **asthenosphere** which is partly melted. The difference in the temperatures of the two layers of solid rock sets up **convection** movements in the asthenosphere. (These are rather like the movements you can see in a pan of soup on a cooker.) Near the surface, the upward movements in the asthenosphere spread out horizontally. These horizontal movements make the crust split. This makes the huge continental plates move slowly. In some places they are pulled apart. In other places they are pushed together. Sometimes they slide sideways along one another.

Moving plates

Figure 2.13(a) shows how a convection current in the asthenosphere rises, separates and forms a **mid-ocean rift**. The convection current sinks again where the oceanic plate meets the continental plate. As it sinks it carries some of the solid rocks of the crust downwards. These rocks melt back into the asthenosphere. The place where they are carried down is called the **subduction zone**.

Figure 2.13(b) shows what happens when plates separate. As the rift widens, an ocean basin forms and melted rocks from the asthenosphere spread out and harden and become the ocean floor. This is called **sea floor spreading**. The place where the melted rock comes out is called the **zone of construction**. As the ocean floor forms, the new volcanic rock from below builds up into a ridge. The zone of construction is now called a **mid-oceanic ridge**.

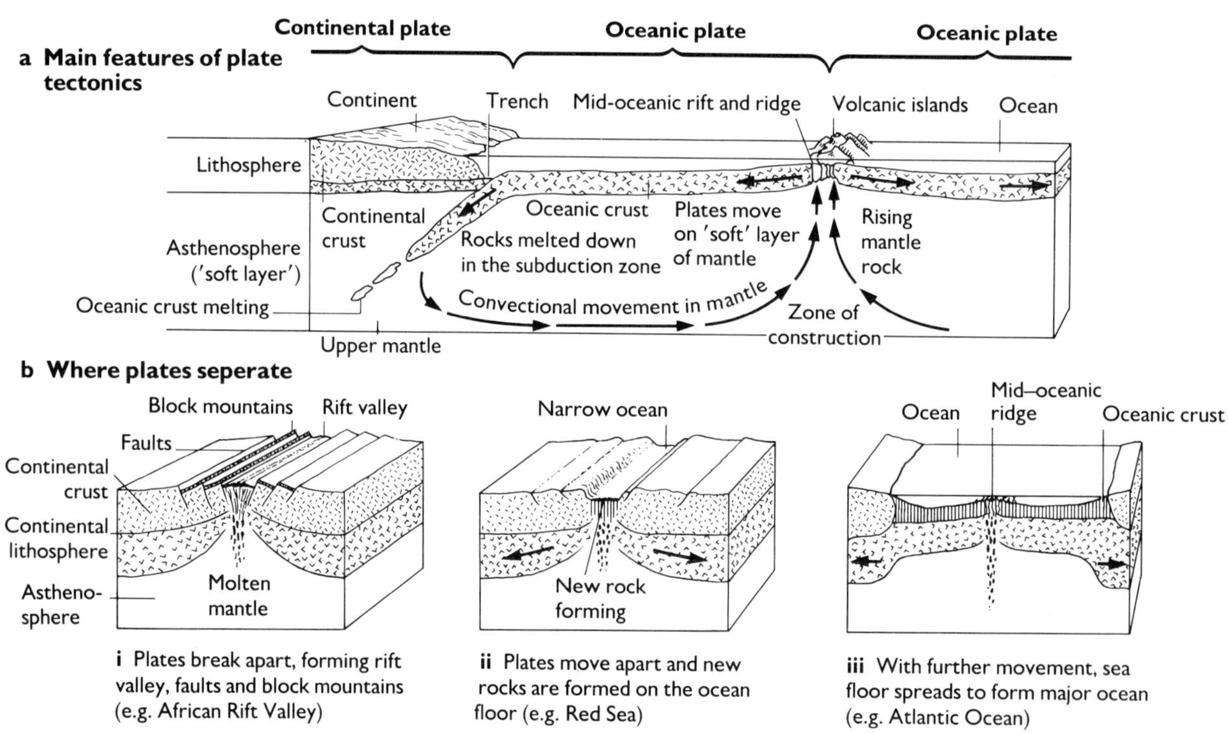

Figure 2.13 Plate tectonics

When volcanic rocks reach the surface they make volcanic islands.

Figure 2.13(c) shows what happens where oceanic plates meet. Rock from one plate is carried downwards into the hot molten asthenosphere and melts in the subduction zone. Where the rock is dragged down, a deep ocean trench forms. This movement weakens the crust and molten rock can escape to the surface and form islands of volcanic mountains.

Figure 2.13(d) shows how the movement of the plates helps explain mountain building. Over many years, layers of sediment are deposited on the ocean floor and the continental shelf. The sediments may be compressed together to form **sedimentary rocks**.

If the sediments are sand or clay brought down to the sea by rivers, they will form **sandstone** or **shale**. Other sediments are the remains of dead animals or sea creatures. These sediments form **chalk** and other **limestones**. When two continental plates meet, they press against these layers of sediment and very slowly force them to wrinkle or fold. The pressure can force the rocks into very complicated folds. This can lift them to great heights. This is the way young sedimentary rocks are lifted up to form new mountains like the Alps (Figure 2.14).

In Figure 2.11 you saw how India broke away

Figure 2.14 The Alps

from Gondwana in late Triassic times and travelled north-eastwards towards the Asian block of Laurasia during the late Cretaceous period. As the Indian plate met the Asian plate, it pushed and folded the sediments up to make the Himalayan Mountains – the greatest mountain range in the world (Figure 2.15).

A period of time when plates push together and mountains are forced up is called an **orogeny**. If you look back to Figure 2.10 you will see that there have been four main orogenies. During an orogeny, older, folded mountains which appear to have been worn down by erosion are sometimes lifted up again. Old mountains which are uplifted like this are called **block mountains**. In Hercynian times

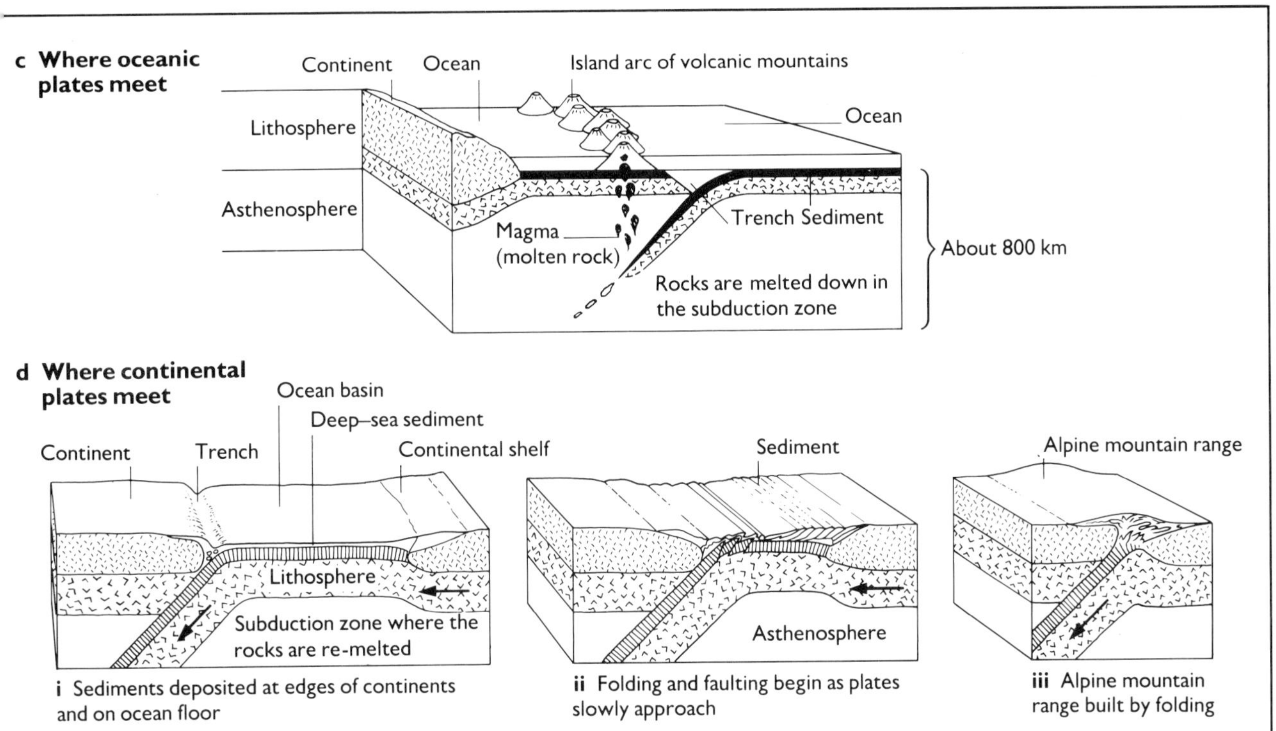

sediments were folded to form mountains in the centre of what is now Europe. By Alpine times these mountains had been worn down again. When the movements which pushed up the Alps took place, these old Hercynian mountains were lifted up again. The uplifted blocks are what we know today as, for example, the Black Forest and the Rhine Uplands in Germany, and the Vosges and the Massif Central in France (Figure 2.16).

Because the old rocks were so hard and brittle, they often shattered as they were lifted. This caused fault lines of broken rock. For example, the Rhine Rift Valley was formed between two series of faults along the edges of the Vosges and the Black Forest.

The ripples of these huge movements spread outwards as far as the UK and the rocks of south-east England were gently folded. These folds have been eroded and today form the North and South Downs.

Plates, volcanoes and earthquakes

You should now be able to see why scientists think that the earthquakes and volcanoes we described at the beginning of this chapter fit into the world-wide pattern of plate movements. At the edges of the plates, the crust is weak and molten rocks can force their way to the surface. Movements of the plate edges are felt as earthquakes.

Although it is interesting to work out how the mountains and valleys of the world are formed, there are far more important reasons for doing so. If scientists can find out more about plate movements, then they may be able to predict major earthquakes and volcanic eruptions. This would save many lives. On Mount St. Helens, scientists were able to measure the Earth's surface bulging upwards. In California, lasers are beamed from one mountain top to another. This has helped scientists to find out that the plates are moving about 5 cm per year.

So far, however, not enough is known to be certain of when an eruption or earthquake will take place to within a few years. It was fairly easy to put Mount St. Helens out of bounds. Scientists would have to be very certain that an earthquake was about to happen before they suggested evacuating the whole of Los Angeles and San Francisco!

At the moment, all that the scientists will say is that there is a 50:50 chance that an earthquake of the same strength as the San Francisco 1906 earthquake will occur again before 1990. If 'the

Figure 2.15 The Himalayas

Figure 2.16 Massif Central

big one' strikes during the afternoon rush hour, it has been predicted that 30000 people would be killed, 15000 people would be injured and 300000 people would be made homeless.

Activities

▲■ **7** Look at the maps in Figure 2.11 which show the break up of Pangaea.

- **a** Which is the older ocean – the Atlantic or the Pacific?
- **b** Draw two more maps to show how the world may look in 50 million years time and 100 million years time.

▲■ **8** Use your atlas and the maps in this chapter to find out:

- **a** the names of the main mid-oceanic ridges and their heights
- **b** the names of the main oceanic trenches and their depths
- **c** three examples of volcanic islands
- **d** two examples of island arcs (islands formed from fold mountains).

▲■● **9** Find the island of Iceland in your atlas. Then read this description: 'Iceland is a large island. There are major faults running north-south across its centre. There are younger volcanic rocks in a belt running north-south across the centre of the island. There are older volcanic rocks in the east and west. There is a lot of volcanic action in the centre of the island. A volcanic island called Surtsey rose out of the sea 100 kilometres south of Iceland in 1963.'

Now look carefully at the position of Iceland in Figure 2.9.

- **a** Why are there different types of rock forming belts across Iceland? Give reasons.
- **b** Explain why there is volcanic activity in Iceland.
- **c** Why do you think Surtsey erupted?
- **d** Suggest what is likely to happen to Iceland in the (distant) future.

Changes in the rocks

The theory of plate tectonics helps us to understand earthquakes and volcanoes but these are not the only ways in which the surface of the Earth moves.

The surface of the Earth is continuously changing its form and even the rocks which make up the surface change. There are basically three classes of rock. They are named according to how they were formed.

Igneous rocks

Igneous rocks are formed when the molten rock from the asthenosphere, deep under the surface, cools. If the molten rock cools very slowly underneath other rocks, large crystals have time to grow. This results in rocks like **granite**. If the molten rock flows out on to the Earth's surface and cools quickly, the crystals are too small to be seen without a microscope. This results in rocks like **basalt**.

One of the constituents of granite, called **felspar**, breaks down to form **kaolin** (china clay). This is used in medicines and 'china' cups and saucers, as well as for putting a smooth surface on paper.

Granite is usually **impermeable**. This means that water does not pass through it. Soils which are formed on granite are usually thin, acid and not very fertile.

Sedimentary rocks

Sedimentary rocks are formed from small particles of rock which accumulate and become compressed. The particles are sometimes carried by the wind and deposited in front of some mountain barriers. This has happened in northern China and parts of northern Europe. The rocks formed from wind-blown sediments are called **loess** (in Germany) or **limon** (in France). Soils formed on loess are usually fertile. (You'll find more about them in Chapter 7 in the section on farming settlements in Germany.)

Most sedimentary rocks, however, have accumulated in lakes and seas. They are usually laid down in layers and fossils of plants and animals are sometimes found in the layers.

Some sedimentary rocks, like **sandstone**, come from other rocks which are broken down by weathering and erosion. For example, granite is made of crystals of quartz, felspar and mica. When the felspar changes to china clay, the quartz and mica crystals are left as grains of **sand**.

Other sedimentary rocks come from the remains of dead animals and plants. **Chalk** and other **limestones** are made of the shells and bodies of sea creatures. **Coal** is made from the remains of trees.

Some sedimentary rocks such as **gypsum**, **anhydrite** and **rock salt** are caused by chemicals being deposited when shallow lakes evaporate rapidly. These rocks are mined for use in the chemical industry.

Sedimentary rocks are more easily weathered and eroded than igneous rocks. They usually form much deeper and more fertile soils than granite.

Metamorphic rocks

Metamorphic rocks are formed when igneous or sedimentary rocks are changed by great heat and pressure from volcanic eruptions or mountain building. Chalk and limestones are changed into **marble**. Shale (or mudstone) is changed into **slate**. Coal is changed into **graphite**. Metamorphic rocks are more resistant to erosion than sedimentary rocks. This means that they are like igneous rocks and don't usually make very fertile soils.

Activity

■ **10 a** Figure 2.17 shows you how to begin a table of igneous rocks. Copy the table. Find out about as many other igneous rocks as you can and complete the details of the table for each one.

b Draw out two similar tables and complete them for

i) sedimentary rocks

ii) metamorphic rocks.

Name of rock	Description	Can water soak through	Resistance to erosion	Soils	Uses
Granite	Crystals of quartz, felspar and mica	No	Very hard	Thin and acid	Building, road stones

Figure 2.17 Use this diagram for question 10

Weathering and erosion

The rocks which form the Earth's surface are broken down as well as being built up. They are broken down by the weather (**weathering**) and by the movement of ice, wind, water and animals (**erosion**). The whole process of breaking down rocks is called **denudation**.

When rock is affected by weathering its surface is broken down, but the pieces remain on the spot. Obviously if weathering takes place on a cliff face, gravity will make sure the pieces reach the bottom of the cliff!

When rock or soil is eroded, the ice, water, wind or animals move over the surface and may carry away pieces broken off the rock. These pieces will then be deposited somewhere else.

Figure 2.18 summarizes the main types of weathering. Once rock surfaces are broken down by weathering, the various agents of erosion can carry out their work more easily.

Types of weathering

1 Physical weathering

a Water fills cracks in the rock. When water freezes it expands by 10% of its volume. This forces cracks apart. When ice thaws, cracks fill up with water again. Water freezes and again expands by 10%. The cracks are made larger.

b Seeds fall into cracks in the rock. The seed germinates and grows. As it grows it exerts pressure on the crack and makes the crack larger. This can also happen when roots of a tree or plant creep into a crack in rock.

c During very dry periods the water in a rock evaporates. This makes the rock contract. During wet periods the rock absorbs water and expands. The expansion and contraction leads to cracking.

d If soil is eroded from the ground surface the weight is removed from the rock underneath. The rock expands slightly and may crack.

e During the day, when the sun shines, dark coloured crystals absorb more heat than light coloured crystals. The dark crystals expand more quickly than the light crystals and this makes the rock surface break up.

f In very hot dry areas the outer layers of rock become hot and expand. The inner part of the rock stays cool. This may make the outer layer break away from the inner parts like the layers of an onion.

2 Chemical weathering

a Rainwater falling through the air dissolves carbon dioxide from the atmosphere. The rain becomes weak carbonic acid.

When this acid falls on granite, the felspar is changed into china clay (kaolin). The granite is then left as particles of mica and quartz embedded in soft clay.

When this acid falls on chalk and other limestones, the calcium carbonate breaks down into calcium bicarbonate which is soluble.

b Rainwater may fall through air polluted with sulphur dioxide which comes from the burning of oil and petrol. The sulphurous acid dissolves rocks and building materials. It also kills vegetation and may leave slopes open to erosion.

c When plants and small soil animals die they rot down to form humus in the soil. Rainwater soaks through the soil and dissolves the humus. The water becomes humic acid. The acid dissolves the rock underneath the soil.

Figure 2.18 Types of weathering

They can erode the rocks, transport the eroded material and deposit it elsewhere.

There are three main agents of erosion. These are ice, wind and water. In some cases human beings and other animals have become important agents of erosion.

Erosion

During The Great Ice Age in Quaternary times, ice sheets and valley glaciers covered large areas of Europe, Asia and North America. They are still found in some areas of Scandinavia, the Alps, the Pyrenees, the Himalayas and the Rocky Mountains today. The glaciers cut deep, steep-sided troughs in old river valleys. Figure 2.19 is a photograph of a glaciated area. The materials cut from these valleys were carried down from the mountains and deposited over large areas of lowland. The deposited material is called **glacial drift** or **boulder clay**.

In deserts, the wind is an important agent of erosion. Small particles of sand are carried by the wind. Millions of sharp sand particles carried quickly by the wind can wear away very hard rocks. Many strange shaped rocks found in deserts have been caused in this way. Figure 2.20 shows a desert area which has suffered wind erosion.

Figure 2.19 Glaciated area in Norway

Figure 2.20 Desert showing signs of wind erosion

The wind is also important as an agent of erosion because it can remove soil from land left unprotected. One of the largest areas in the world which has suffered from soil erosion by the wind is the Great Dust Bowl of America.

Case Study

The Great Dust Bowl, USA

At the end of the 19th century, millions of people emigrated from Europe to the United States. A large number of immigrants moved westwards to search for new farmland. These farmers were used to farming in the east of America and in Europe where there was frequent rainfall and the natural vegetation was forest. When they crossed the river Mississippi they found that the land was not forest but natural grassland. These grasslands were the Great Plains.

The farmers were encouraged to settle in the Great Plains by the offer of cheap land from the US Government and the railway companies.

The climate of the Great Plains becomes drier as you go further west. The climate also becomes hotter in summer and colder in winter. When rain does fall, it falls in very heavy showers. Strong winds often blow. The soils are very porous and the rivers have cut deep valleys. This means the soil is very dry.

The farmers tried to grow crops such as wheat and cotton. They used the methods they had used back east and in Europe. They grew a crop on the land every year.

Year	Rainfall (mm)	Year	Rainfall (mm)	Year	Rainfall (mm)
1919	380	1931	405	1943	380
1920	380	1932	360	1944	520
1921	410	1933	320	1945	380
1922	380	1934	350	1946	660
1923	610	1935	290	1947	580
1924	300	1936	215	1948	610
1925	405	1937	290	1949	560
1926	410	1938	375	1950	680
1927	405	1939	325	1951	410
1928	610	1940	410	1952	230
1929	460	1941	650	1953	310
1930	455	1942	670	1954	240

Figure 2.21 Rainfall in Goodwell, West Oklahoma, USA

For a number of years they were successful, but slowly the soil was exhausted. There were several years of drought. Figure 2.21 shows the rainfall figures for Goodwell in West Oklahoma from 1919–54. The wind blew the top soil away from a million acres of land. This land became known as the Dust Bowl of Kansas, Nebraska and Oklahoma.

Farmers were ruined. Thousands of families were forced to leave the Plains. Even today, much of the land is left unused and useless.

Although ice and wind are both important agents of erosion, water is the main agent of erosion at work in the world. The sea constantly wears away parts of the coastline. The material which is worn away is usually deposited somewhere else along the coast.

On land, water flowing over the surface can move huge amounts of material. Sometimes water on a hillside saturates a thin layer of soil and makes it move downhill. This is called **solifluction**. Sometimes a river in flood moves huge boulders.

The actions of human beings and other animals often encourage the work of other types of erosion. If too many animals are allowed to graze on the land, the soil may break up and be blown away, as happened in the Dust Bowl, or it may be washed away. Ploughing the land down a slope instead of across it allows water to flow down the furrows and wash the soil away. Cutting trees down on a slope also leaves the soil open to erosion.

Soil erosion is a problem in all types of National Parks. Figure 2.22 shows a footpath in the Peak District National Park which has been closed. So many people have walked along the path that all the grass has been killed. The footpath has been worn into a groove and the rain has made it into a gulley.

In the National Parks of Tanzania, the protected animals have increased their numbers so much that they are over-grazing the vegetation. This is leading to soil erosion by wind and water. Many animals have been shot to keep their numbers down.

Figure 2.22 Closed footpath in the Peak District

Figure 2.23 Peculiarly shaped sandworn rock features in a desert

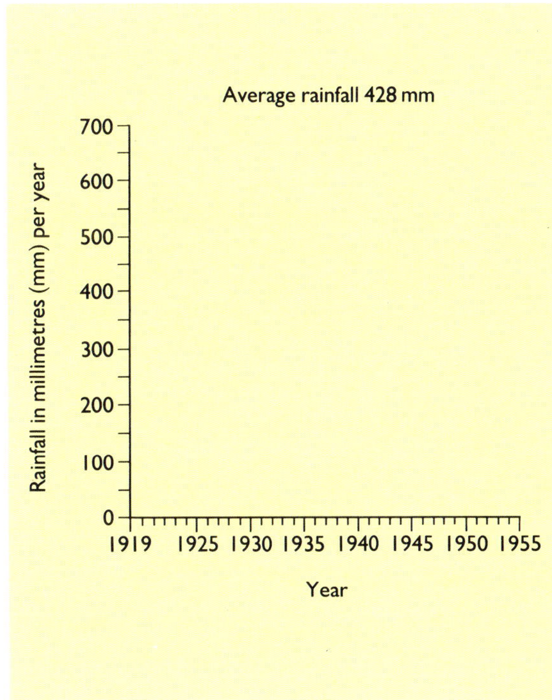

Figure 2.24 Outline for a block graph of the annual rainfall at Goodwell (W. Oklahoma)

Activities

▲ **11** Look back at Figure 2.18 which summarizes the different types of weathering. For each of the following areas, suggest which types of weathering are probably most active. Explain the reasons behind your answer.

- **a** A granite cliff face in Scotland from October to March
- **b** A bare granite rock in the Sahara Desert
- **c** An area of bare limestone rock in the Peak District
- **d** A concrete roof in Tokyo
- **e** Sandstone lying under the soil of the Amazon rain forest
- **f** Clay in south-east England

▲ ■ **12** Study Figure 2.23 which shows rocks eroded by the wind in a desert.

- **a** Draw a diagram and label it to show where the erosion has been greatest.
- **b** Suggest reasons why the rock should be eroded like this rather than evenly all over. (*Remember* – there may be several reasons.)

▲ ■ ● **13** Study the rainfall figures for Goodwell, West Oklahoma, between 1919–54 (Figure 2.21).

- **a** Copy Figure 2.24. Complete the graph to show the rainfall totals for each year.
- **b** Now answer these questions:
  i) What was the highest rainfall recorded in any one year between 1919 and 1954?
  ii) Which year had the lowest rainfall?
  iii) What was the **range** of annual rainfall totals during this period? (The range is the difference between the highest and the lowest.)
  iv) Describe how the range of rainfall compares with the average rainfall during this period.
  v) Which figure would have been most useful for early settlers to have known – the average rainfall *or* the range of rainfall totals? (Remember that actually they did not know either!) Explain your reasons.
- **c** **i)** Explain why farmers who moved into the area around Goodwell before 1931 would have had an unpleasant surprise during their first 10 years of farming.
  ii) Explain why farmers who moved into the Goodwell area between 1940 and 1950 would have had different ideas about what they could grow.
- **d** Write an account to explain why there was so much soil erosion in the Great Plains in the 1930s.

How water shapes the land

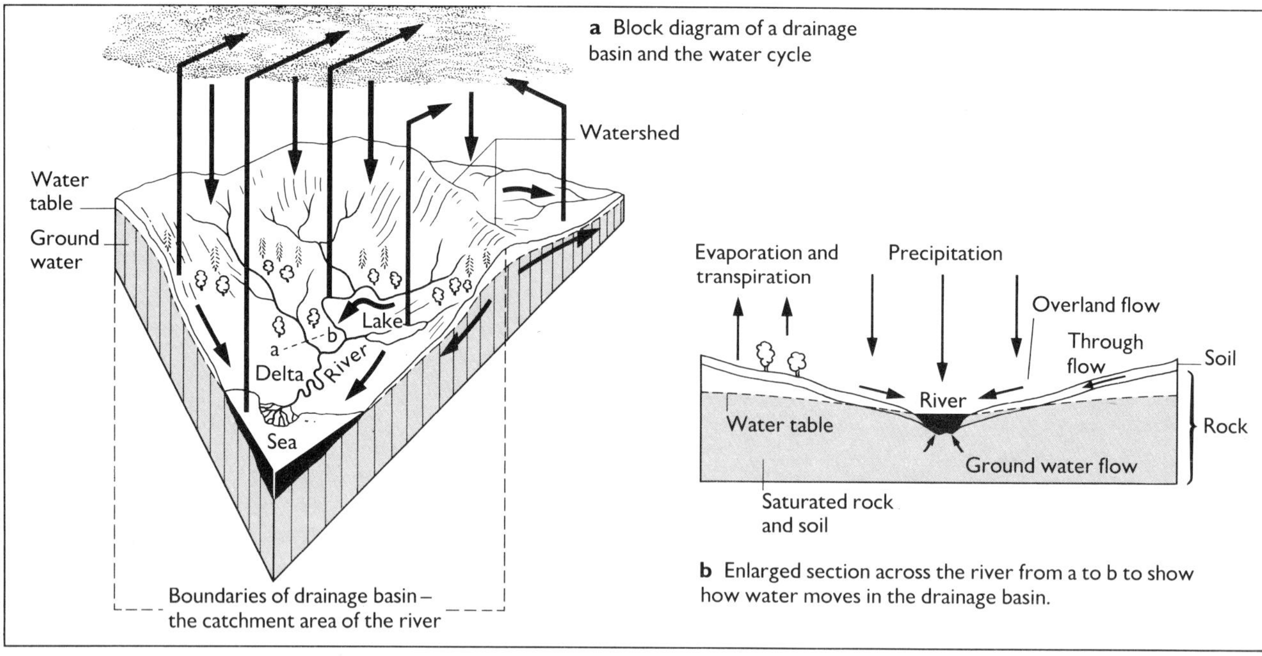

Figure 2.25 The hydrological cycle

Water plays an important part in weathering and erosion. About 97.5% of all the water on Earth is in the oceans. The other 2.5% is fresh water. It is found in four main places.

1 in the ice sheets of the Arctic, Antarctic and the high mountain areas
2 in the ground and soil
3 in the rivers and lakes
4 as water vapour in the atmosphere.

Water is constantly moving between these storage places. The movement of water between the four main water storage places is called the **water cycle** or the **hydrological cycle**. Figure 2.25 shows the water cycle in an imaginary river basin.

Water causes erosion in two main ways:

1 By **hydraulic action** – the water moves the rock particles. Some particles are dissolved in the water flowing over the surface. Some particles are light enough to be carried in suspension in very little water. Larger particles up to the size of boulders are rolled or bounced along a river bed.
2 By **abrasion** – the rock particles bang together as they move downstream and break one another up. It usually happens in a river and is called **attrition**. The boulders and stones bouncing along break up the river bed and make it deeper. They also wear away the river bank.

Figure 2.26 shows how a river makes its valley. Rainwater which flows over the surface carries small particles of soil downhill towards the river. There is a constant movement of water and soil particles down the slopes of the drainage basin into the river and then eventually to the sea (Figure 2.26(a)).

The power of the river to erode and transport material depends on the amount of water flowing down it. This is called its **discharge**. The discharge is affected by the amount of precipitation (rain, hail, snow etc.) and the size of the drainage basin (which forms the catchment area). The discharge of a river gets larger downstream because more water flows into it from its tributaries and from ground water (Figure 2.26(b)).

The increase in the discharge of the river causes changes in the river channel and in the landforms produced by the river. The width and depth of the channel **increases** downstream. The **gradient** (or slope) of the channel tends to **decrease**. A river also becomes more winding downstream. The large bends in the river are called **meanders** (Figure 2.26(c), (d) and (e)).

This is how it works. Water falls to the surface of the earth mainly as rain, hail or snow. The water is drained from the surface of the land either by soaking into the land or by running off over the ground. Most of the water reaches the

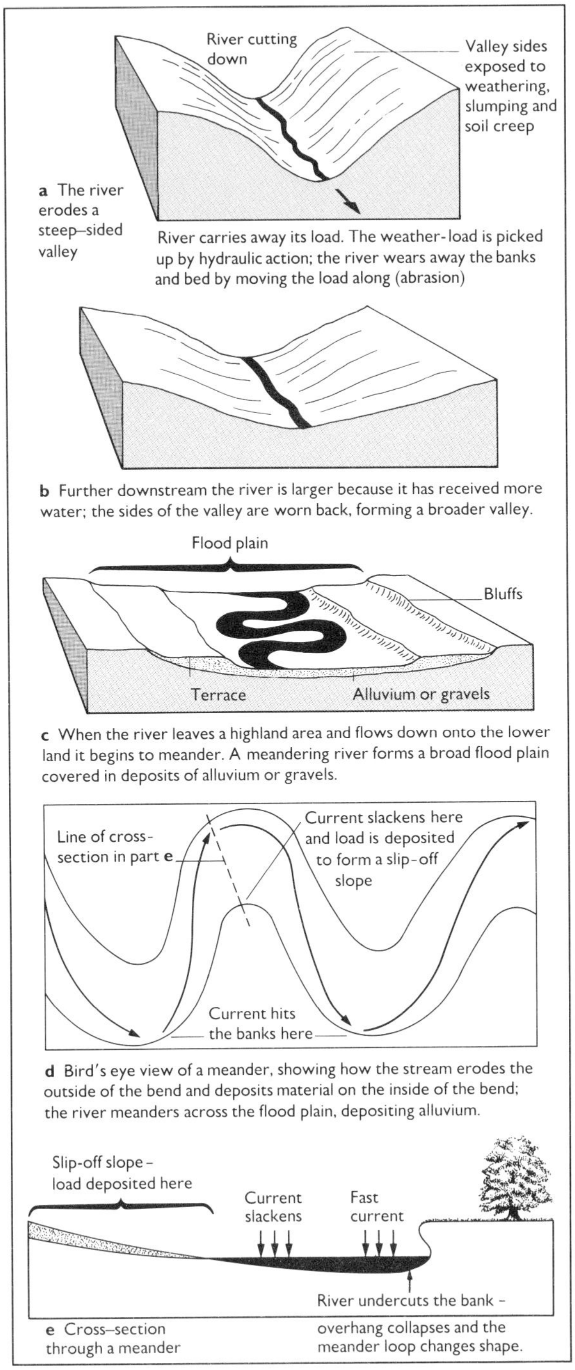

Figure 2.26 River at work

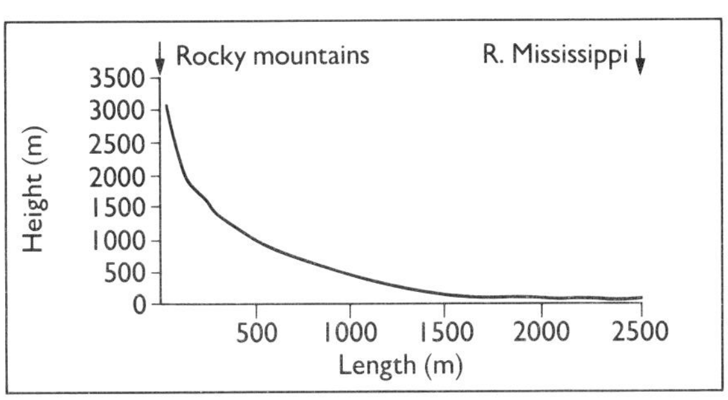

Figure 2.27 Profile of the Arkansas River, a major tributary of the Mississippi

rivers by these two routes. The rivers pour their water into the seas and oceans. This is shown in Figure 2.25(b).

Some of the water in the ground is absorbed through the roots of plants and trees. Then the water is transpired through their leaves back into the atmosphere. Some water evaporates from the surface of the ground. But most water returns to the atmosphere by evaporation from the sea. Since 70% of the surface of the Earth is sea, this is not surprising. Once the water has returned to the atmosphere, it is available to fall once again somewhere else.

These movements of water can be very quick. On a warm day, rain which falls can evaporate in a very short time. The movements can also be very slow. Snow which falls on a mountain top may take many years travelling downhill as part of a glacier before it melts and evaporates again. Some water soaks into porous rocks under the ground. It has been estimated that the water which is being pumped out of the Great Artesian Basin in Australia today, originally fell as rain 20 000 years ago!

Drainage basins and erosion by water

Most water eventually flows into rivers. Some water goes over the surface, some soaks through the ground. The whole area which collects water for a river is called its **drainage basin**. The line which separates one drainage basin from the next is called the **watershed**. Figure 2.25 shows you a river flowing to the sea and the way the hydrological cycle works over a single drainage basin. The movement of water in a drainage basin also makes rock particles move.

Because smaller rock particles and soil move downhill, river basins are important for farming. The flood plain areas and deltas where the river reaches the sea are particularly important farming areas in many parts of the world.

A river wears its channel unevenly. So a river flowing from a highland area to the sea may have a profile from source to mouth rather like the Arkansas River (Figure 2.27).

If people alter anything in a drainage basin, the effects may be felt many miles away or many years later. The Tennessee Valley of North America is an example of human interference in a drainage basin which caused major problems.

Case Study

The Tennessee Valley, USA

The early British settlers in North America settled on the plain between the Appalachian Mountains and the Atlantic Ocean. No settlers moved further west for many years. One of the reasons why the settlers did not move was because of the barrier formed by the Appalachians. The Appalachian Mountains are not very high but they are very rugged. The main ridges run from north to south, parallel to the coast.

The first people to find routes through the mountains were frontiersmen like Daniel Boone. In 1775, Daniel Boone discovered a route which became known as the Wilderness Road through the Cumberland Gap. Other routes were found later. The routes through the mountains climbed up the valley of an eastward flowing river and then went down again along the valley of a westward flowing river. Farmers followed the frontiersmen to the west. In this way settlers from the coastal plain reached the Tennessee Valley in the late 1700s. Between then and 1920 the soil on the hillsides began to wear away and from time to time there were disastrous floods. The main reason for this was that the farmers used ways of farming which worked well on the coastal plain but which were not really suited to the Tennessee Valley.

The first thing the farmers in the Tennessee Valley did was to cut down the forest to make farmland. Trees were cut down on the steep slopes and on the flatter land. Sometimes the bare soil was attacked by the wind and the rain before crops could grow to protect the land. A great deal of soil was washed downhill or blown away.

A second problem was caused by the crops grown. The farmers found that maize and cotton grew well in the Tennessee Valley. They grew these two crops every year until the humus in the soil was used up. Without humus the soil was just like dust. The crops did not grow well in this poor, dusty soil and so the rain could wash even more soil downhill.

Finally, when the farmers ploughed their land, they found it was easiest if they ploughed up and down the slopes. This meant that the rainwater could flow down the furrows made by the ploughs. The water could flow faster down the furrows, so it could carry a lot of soil. So much soil was washed down the slopes into the river Tennessee that the river became almost blocked with silt and often flooded. Figure 2.28 shows how a typical hillside looked after the soil had been washed away.

By 1933 about 2 million people lived in the

Figure 2.28 Eroded hillside with gulleys

Tennessee Valley. Because of the damage to the soil, most of these people were very poor. In 1933 many people were unemployed in America. President Roosevelt decided to make work for people by setting up schemes to improve the country. One of these schemes was to try to repair the damage done to the Tennessee Valley. A committee was set up to organize the work. The committee was called the **Tennessee Valley Authority** (often called the **TVA**).

The TVA organized various schemes to improve the valley. Firstly, they slowed down the rate of soil erosion on steep slopes. They did this by planting the hillsides with coniferous trees. Planting the trees in areas which were once forests is called **re-afforestation**.

Next, soil erosion on farmland was reduced by training farmers to farm the land more carefully. The farmers were trained to plant different crops each year and to fertilize the soil. They were taught to plough across the slopes and not up and down. This is called **contour ploughing**. It prevents rainwater from rushing downhill and carrying soil with it.

Thirdly, dams were built to slow down the flow of the river. This prevents the floods which used to wash away the river banks. More than 30 dams were built and many of them are used to generate electricity from hydroelectric power stations. Figure 2.29 shows part of the Tennessee Valley after it had been reclaimed.

Figure 2.29 Tennessee Valley after reclamation

Activities

▲14 ● Read the description of the Tennessee Valley again.

a List the ways in which the early farmers made soil erosion more likely.

b List the ways in which the TVA tried to improve the area.

■15 Look at Figures 2.28 and 2.29. Draw a sketch of each photo and label it to show the features which are

a the causes and results of soil erosion

b designed to limit or prevent soil erosion.

The Tennessee Valley shows that what happens in one part of a drainage basin can have effects on other parts. Poor farming methods led to faster soil erosion. The soil erosion led to the river flooding and breaking its banks.

The Tennessee Valley was changed in order to repair the damage caused by poor farming. The St. Lawrence Seaway is an example of the way in which one river system has been changed so that it can be used for transport.

Case Study

The St. Lawrence Seaway, North America

The St. Lawrence river forms part of the boundary between the United States and Canada. The drainage basin of the St. Lawrence includes the whole area around the Great Lakes. The water from the drainage basin flows into the Great Lakes and then down the St. Lawrence to the sea.

Many rivers begin with steeply sloping channels in their upland stages. As they reach lower land, the profile of the river becomes more gentle (look back at Figure 2.27). The profile of the Great Lakes–St. Lawrence channel is not smooth at all. The course of the drainage system is broken in many places. The lakes lie at different heights. The Niagara Falls lie between Lake Erie and Lake Ontario. There are rapids on the St. Lawrence between Lake Ontario and Montreal. These breaks in the flow of the water are shown in Figure 2.30.

The early settlers in this area realized how useful the Great Lakes were for travelling right to the centre of the continent. However, boats could not travel from the sea up through the Great Lakes because of the breaks in the channel. The first attempt to bypass the Niagara Falls was made in 1824. The first successful bypass, however, was the Welland Canal which opened in 1833. This canal has been rebuilt several times. Today the canal has eight twin locks which lift ships nearly 100 metres between Lake Ontario and Lake Erie.

There have been other schemes to improve the route for ships through the Great Lakes. In 1954 it was decided to convert the St. Lawrence from Montreal to Lake Ontario into a seaway – the St. Lawrence Seaway. This was finished in 1959. The whole seaway is at least 8¼ metres deep, so that ocean-going ships up to 9000 tonnes can travel through it to the Great Lakes. This saves the time and cost of unloading cargoes on to smaller ships or barges.

The dams and locks which were built as part of this scheme have provided the water power for many hydroelectric power stations. The cheap power and easy transport has meant that many industries have been set up in the St. Lawrence Valley and around the Great Lakes. Figure 2.31 shows the complete Great Lakes–St. Lawrence waterway and the area around the Lakes which it serves.

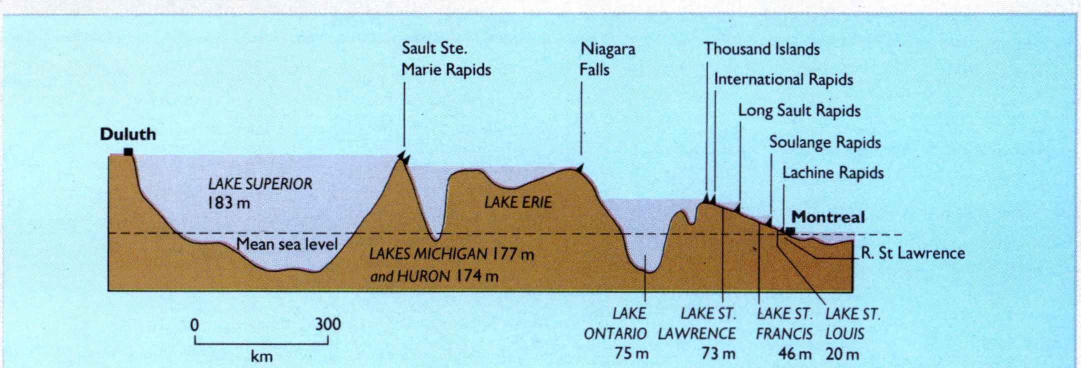

Figure 2.30 Profile of St. Lawrence river

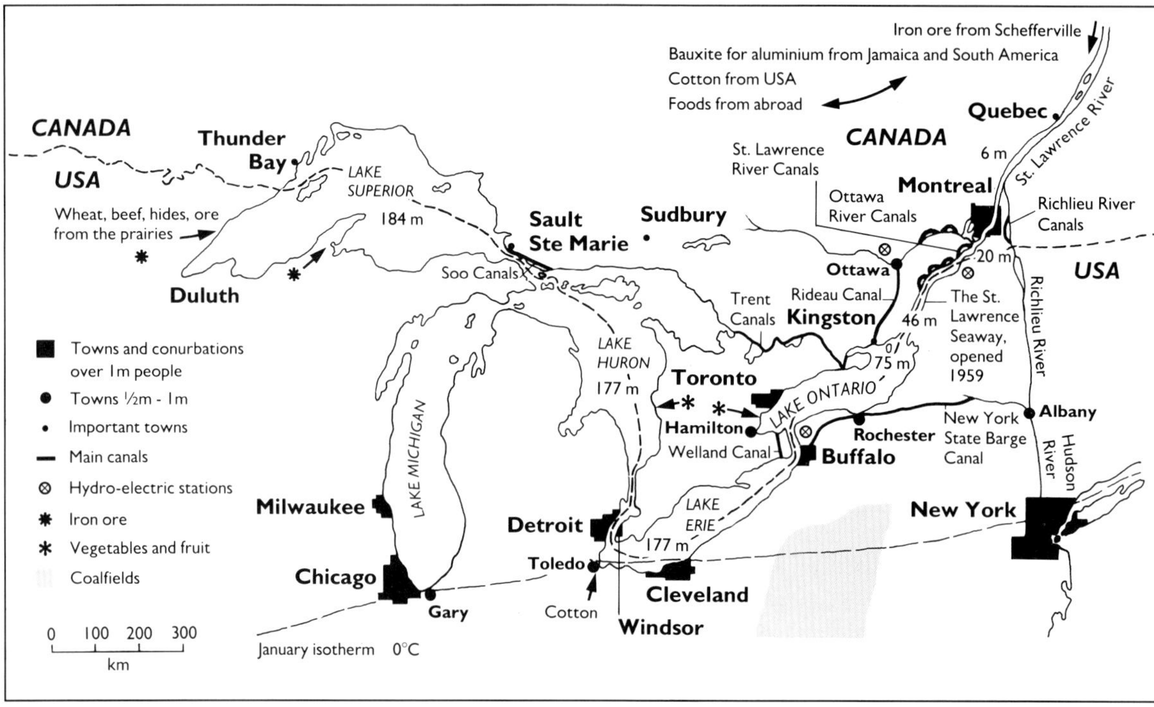

Figure 2.31 Great Lakes and St. Lawrence water transport system

Activity

▲16 ■ Imagine that you have been asked to write a booklet on the Great Lakes–St. Lawrence waterway system to help cargo boat skippers. Use your atlas and Figures 2.30 and 2.31 to help you. The questions below are hints.

a *The importance of the area*

i) Which large cities are served by the Great Lakes–St. Lawrence waterway?

ii) Which raw materials are produced in the area and which must be imported?

b *The water transport system*

i) How far is it from Quebec to the grain port of Thunder Bay?

ii) What is the difference in sea level between Quebec and Thunder Bay?

iii) Use the spot heights in Figure 2.31 to draw a profile of the Quebec–Thunder Bay route. Label the problem areas.

iv) Describe the problem areas a boat has to pass through on its way up the water system. Describe how each problem has been overcome.

c *The weather*

i) What particular problem is caused by the weather? (An **isotherm** is an imaginary line joining all places with the same average temperature. The 0°C January isotherm suggests the answer.)

ii) North of the 0°C January isotherm, the average January temperature is below freezing. What effect will this have on the lakes and what can be done about it?

Rivers are not just important for transport and power supplies. They are also an important source of water for life. Australia is a continent which has great shortages of water. We will now look at a scheme which changed the watershed of a drainage basin to provide water supplies for people and for growing their food.

Snowy Mountains Authority set up 1949

Work on last power station completed 1974

Cost $800 000 000

145 km of tunnels, 80 km of aqueducts, 16 large dams

Provides 2344 million m^3 of additional water for irrigation

Irrigated area of Victoria and New South Wales increased by 2600 km^2

Capacity of 3740 MW of peak power to be integrated with thermal power in New South Wales, Victoria and the Australian Capital Territory

Two major parts to the scheme: the Snowy-Tumut Development in the north, and the Snowy–Murray Development in the south

Other results:
new road communications e.g. the Alpine Way
new settlements e.g. Thredbo Alpine Village in the mountains, and Coleambally in the Murrumbidgee lowlands
expanding townships
recreation in the mountains, including skiing, fishing, sailing, camping
Kosciusko National Park 6500 km^2 1967

Figure 2.32 Snowy Mountains fact sheet

Case Study

The Snowy Mountains Scheme, Australia

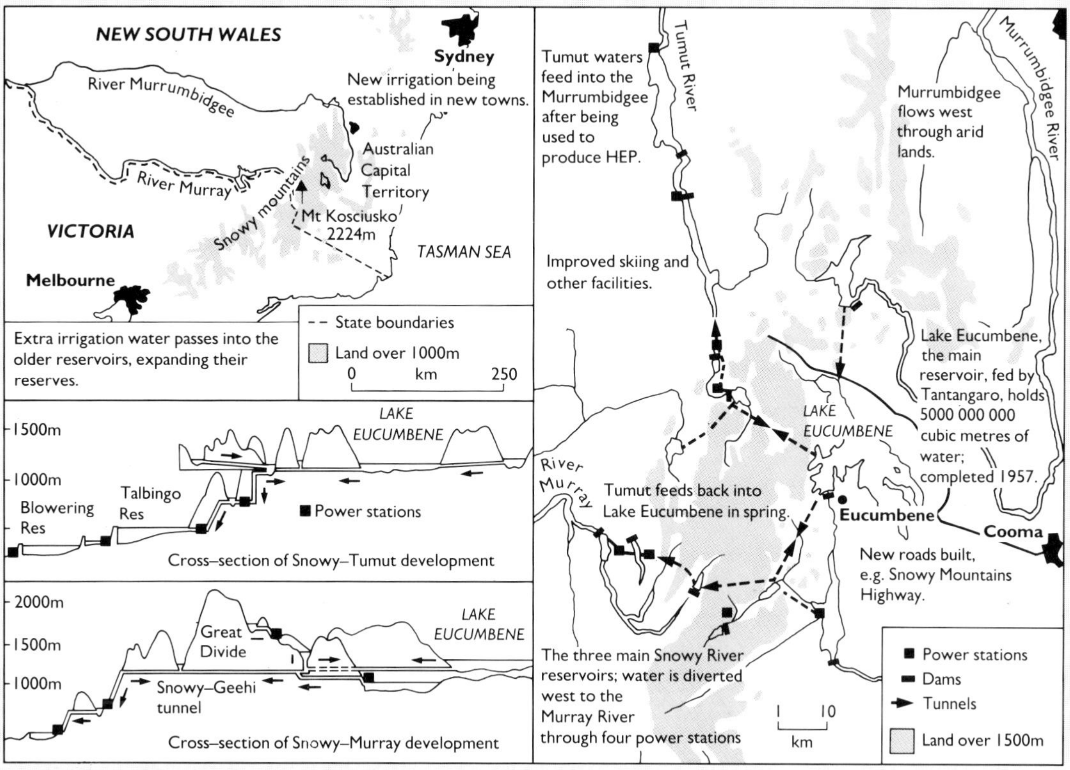

Figure 2.33 Snowy Mountains Scheme

The Snowy Mountains (Figure 2.33) are part of the Great Dividing Range of Australia. The Dividing Range is well named. It divides the plain along the east coast, which is well populated and has plenty of rain, from the lowlands to the west, which have a low density of population and much less rainfall.

The lowlands around the river Murray have been irrigated for a long time. Small reservoirs were built in the foothills of the mountains in the 1880s. This water allowed farmers to grow grass for dairy cattle as well as wheat, barley, sugar beet and fruit. However, the rainfall in the basin is fairly low and the same amount doesn't fall every year. Another problem is that the high temperatures make the rain which does fall evaporate very quickly. Most of the water used for irrigation has to come from the snow melting in the Snowy Mountains.

Since Mount Kosciusko and the Snowy Mountains (Figure 2.33) are the watershed for the Murray drainage basin, much of the rain which falls on the mountains used to flow quickly down to the sea through the Snowy river. A hundred years ago it was suggested that some of the water which ran down the Snowy could be diverted back through the watershed to feed more water into the Murrumbidgee river. The Murrumbidgee could then feed the Murray.

The Snowy Mountains Authority was eventually set up in 1949, and the whole scheme was completed in 1974. The maps and diagrams in Figure 2.33 show the main features of the Snowy Mountains Scheme. Figure 2.32 is a fact sheet about the scheme.

The Snowy Mountains range, as its name suggests, is not an easy place to build such a huge scheme. You can read Alan Mountjoy's description of the construction problems in Figure 2.34.

The whole Scheme – in many respects resembling the Tennessee Valley Authority project – had to be planned and carried out almost like a military operation. The enemy was the terrain and the weather. Hostels, barracks and transportable camps for the work force had to be built, new roads constructed and air strips cleared. Stocks of food and fuel had to be laid in during the summer, and snow-clearing plant established at strategic points, for much of the area is covered in deep snow for half the year. In winter construction traffic was organized in convoys and road clearance was continual; the Authority is proud that no road was closed by snow for more than twenty hours. Thus, a rugged, remote and inhospitable mountainous part of the Southern Alps has been opened up; an area almost as large as Norfolk, Suffolk and Essex combined.

Figure 2.34 Construction problems (extract from *Geographical Magazine*)

Activities

▲ ■ ● 17 Look at Figures 2.33 and 2.34. Write one or two paragraphs to explain the problems which faced the planners and builders of the Snowy Mountains Scheme.

▲ ■ ● 18 Briefly explain the effects that the Snowy Mountains Scheme has had on each of the following:

a the size of the drainage basin of the Murray–Darling

b the position of the watershed between the Murray–Darling drainage basin and the Snowy drainage basin

c the amount of electricity available in New South Wales and Victoria

d the area of land which can now be irrigated

e the land use of the land around Mt. Kosciusko

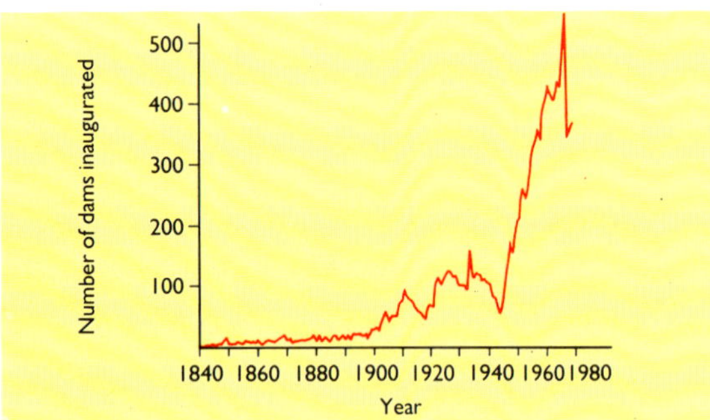

Figure 2.35 Construction of dams in the world

The effects of dam building on drainage basins

The case studies of the Tennessee Valley and the Snowy Mountains Scheme show how people can change their environment. Sometimes, however, the changes have effects which were not intended. Both the Tennessee Valley Scheme and the Snowy Mountains Scheme involved building dams. We will now look at some of the effects of building dams on the balance of drainage basins.

Figure 2.35 shows the number of dams built in the world since the mid 1800s. Some of the dams are quite small, but some are very large and make very large lakes.

In Africa and North America about 20% of all the rainwater which runs from the land into rivers is now controlled by dams.

Dams may be successful in controlling the discharge of water by rivers, but their lakes can cause great changes in the drainage basin. (Figure 2.36).

The main effect of a dam in a river basin is that the river can no longer carry its load from source to mouth. So silt which was carried downstream is deposited in the lake behind the dam. The streams which are allowed to flow out of the lake carry very little silt. This can have many effects downstream. The Aswan High Dam in Egypt is an example of this.

Figure 2.36 Changes in drainage basins caused by dams

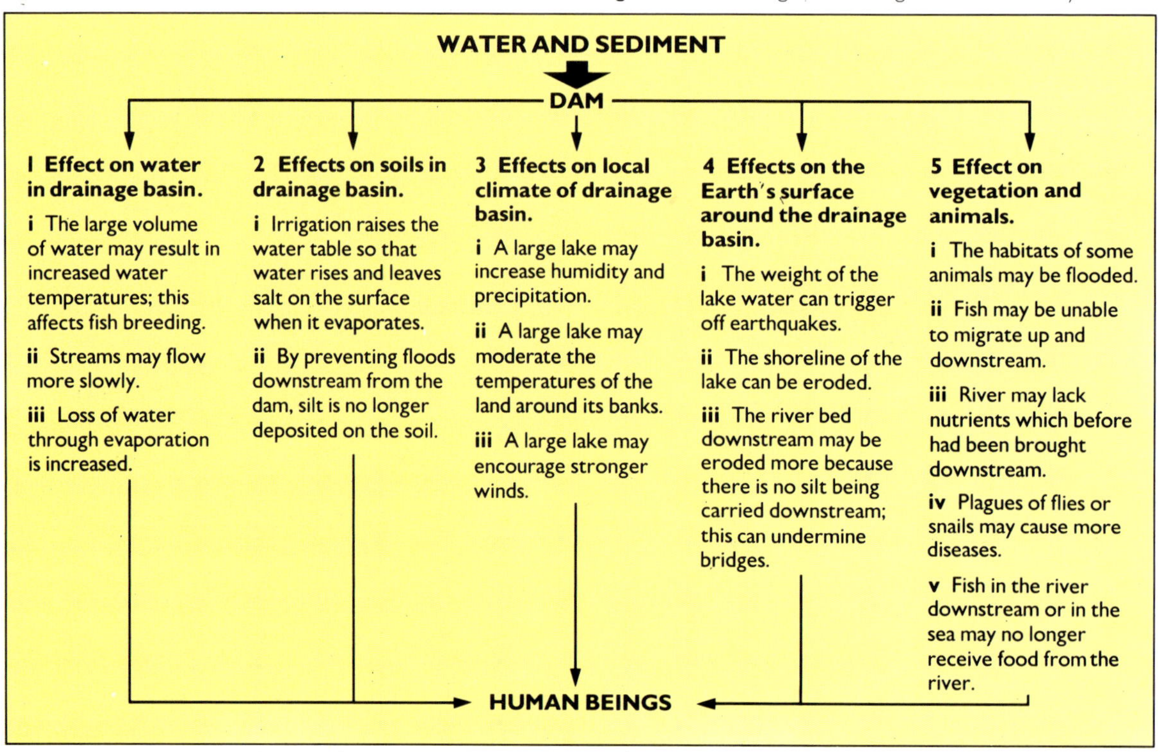

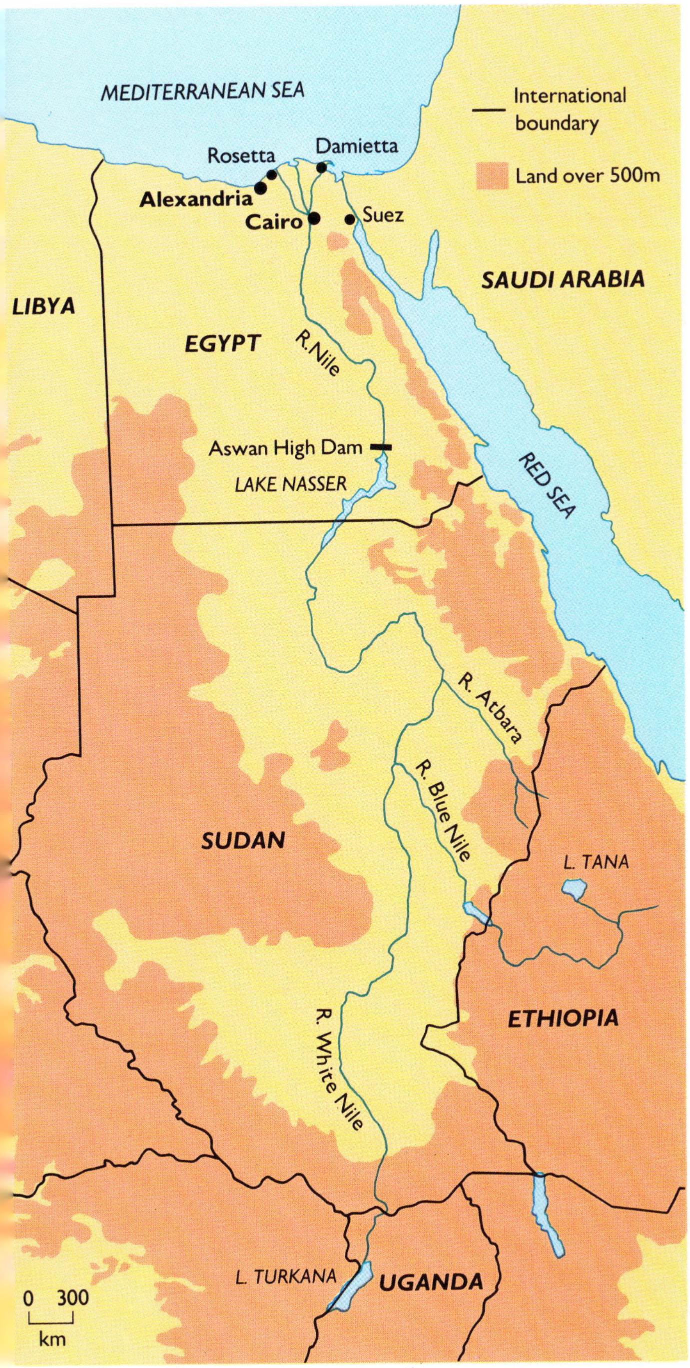

Figure 2.37 The position of the Aswan High Dam

The figures show the silt concentration in the river in parts per million downstream from the dam.

BEFORE: averages before the dam was built

J	F	M	A	M	J	J	A	S	O	N	D
60	50	45	42	43	85	674	2702	2422	925	124	77

AFTER: averages after the dam was completed

J	F	M	A	M	J	J	A	S	O	N	D
44	47	45	50	51	49	48	45	41	43	48	47

Figure 2.38 Sediment of the Nile before and after the building of the Aswan High Dam

Case Study

The Aswan High Dam, Egypt

Figure 2.37 shows the location of the Aswan High Dam. This dam was completed in 1970. The dam created Lake Nasser. Lake Nasser is 560 km long.

Before the dam was built, much of the water which flowed down the Nile flowed straight into the sea through the Nile Delta. Although the climate of Egypt is a desert climate, the rainy season in the Ethiopian Highlands used to make the Nile flood. The floods watered the land along the river and also deposited a layer of fertile silt in which crops were grown. In the dry season, only a small area of land could be irrigated directly from the river. The silt which reached the sea built up the delta. The river also carried nutrients to the Mediterranean Sea which led to large shoals of sardines.

Each year at flood time, many bilharzia snails were washed into the sea where they were eaten. This no longer happens and so there are more snails in the river and reservoir. Bilharzia snails carry a disease which affects human beings.

Since the dam was built, the flood waters of the Nile have been stored and used for irrigation all the year round. This increased the area of crops by 700 000 hectares between 1952 and 1977.

The water flowing from Lake Nasser is also used to generate hydroelectric power. About half of all Egypt's electric power is generated from the Aswan High Dam.

Even though building the dam has had advantages, there have also been problems. As Lake Nasser lies in a very hot area where the sun shines almost every day, there is much evaporation. It is estimated that over a quarter of all the water is lost through evaporation.

A second problem is caused by the silt. Most of the silt is deposited in the lake. Figure 2.38 shows how the amount of silt carried in the Nile changed after the dam was built. The farmers downstream from the dam no longer have their fields fertilized by the silt which was dropped by the flooding Nile. There are more bilharzia snails in the rivers so there is more disease. Finally, there is less silt for building up the river bed and delta. This has caused erosion in both the river and the delta. For example, the Rosetta headland was being eroded at the rate of 20–30 metres a year although this rate is now slowing down.

These case studies show how human beings can affect the natural changes in the Earth's surface. Sometimes this happens accidentally. Sometimes people set out to change the Earth's surface and find that the changes they make are not quite what they expected. Perhaps you can now see why we must study the natural systems of the Earth's surface. Our Earth is a small planet with a fragile surface. We must handle it with care!

Activities

■ **19** Study Figure 2.38 which shows the amounts of silt in the Nile before and after the building of the Aswan High Dam.

a Draw graphs to show the changes in the amounts of silt each month before and after the dam was built.

b Describe the differences you notice in the amounts of silt carried before and after the dam was built. During which months is the largest amount of silt carried today?

▲ ■ ● **20 a** Draw up a table with two columns. In one column list the advantages of the Aswan High Dam. In the other list the disadvantages.

b Many of the disadvantages were not known before the dam was built. From what is known now, do you think that the dam should have been built? Give reasons.

c Explain how you think difficult decisions like building a dam should be made. What things should be most important in the minds of people who have to make decisions on schemes like the Aswan Dam Scheme?

3

The living planet

People from other parts of the world often say that the British are always talking about the weather. If this is true, it may be because we have a lot of weather to talk about! There is football in winter — unless the weather prevents it. There is tennis in summer – unless the weather prevents it. Planes fly in and out of Heathrow, Prestwick and the other airports – unless the weather prevents them from doing so. The reason we talk so much about the weather is that often we do not know until the day of the football or tennis match, or the day we are due to fly, whether or not the weather will prevent these events happening. The weather can change from day to day.

In summer, many people head south to the sunnier climates of the Mediterranean. But it is not always true that it is hotter in the south of France than in southern England. It *is* true, however, that the chances of finding hotter weather are greater in the Mediterranean than in England.

These examples show the difference between **weather** and **climate**. The weather in London may be hotter than the weather in Rome on one or two days in the year. The average temperature in Rome, however, over say 30 or 40 years, is much higher than in London. Some hot desert areas have been known to have more rainfall in a single storm than London gets in a month. However the monthly or yearly averages of rainfall are very low in a desert. It is the average weather conditions over a long period of time that give us the figures to describe the climates of different areas. So, in general, Rome has a hotter climate than London and London has a wetter climate than desert areas.

What causes weather?

The energy which causes all the weather in the world comes from the sun. The sun is Earth's nearest star. Its surface burns at 6000 °C. The heat from the sun is **transmitted** (given out) as radiant energy towards the Earth. However, only 1/2 000 000 000 of the energy which leaves the sun reaches the outer edge of the Earth's atmosphere. Even after that, only about half of the energy which reaches the Earth's atmosphere actually gets through to the Earth's surface. Figure 3.1 shows how the shortwave radiant energy from the sun is absorbed and scattered on its way through the atmosphere.

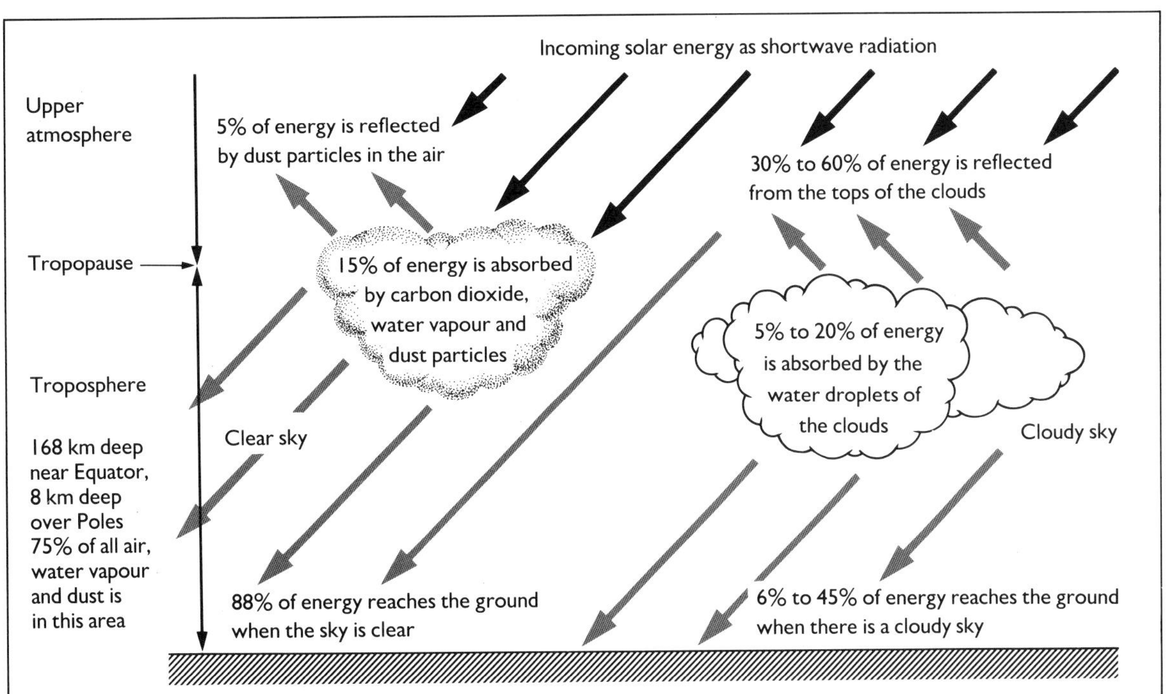

Figure 3.1 How energy from the sun is lost before it reaches the Earth's surface

The radiation from the sun travels through space at the speed of light until it hits something. The 'something' can be molecules of gas, such as the gases of the atmosphere. It can be liquid, such as the water droplets which make up the clouds, or the waters of the oceans, seas, lakes and rivers. Or it can be solid, such as the particles of dust which float in the atmosphere or the solid material of the Earth itself. When the radiation hits these particles of gas, liquid or solid, it is either **reflected** or **absorbed**. If the radiation is reflected, it just bounces off in another direction. If the radiation is absorbed, the particle itself gets warmer. The particles which are warmed then radiate heat energy themselves. However, because they are not as hot as the sun, they radiate longer wave radiation. Longwave radiation can't escape easily from the atmosphere so it is absorbed by other particles. This means that the whole atmosphere slowly warms up. In this way, the atmosphere acts like a large blanket and limits the amount of heat energy lost by the Earth. As you can see from Figure 3.1, the water droplets in the clouds reflect or absorb much of the shortwave radiation coming from the sun. They can also reflect and absorb much of the longer wave radiation coming from the Earth. This is why a cloudy night in winter is nearly always warmer than a clear night.

The closer you are to the Equator the hotter the climate. The main reason for this is shown in Figure 3.2. The sun is large and far away, so the energy radiating from it probably reaches the Earth in parallel lines of radiation. Figure 3.2 shows how 'bundles' of rays hitting the Earth in different places have different effects.

The rays which reach the Earth at the Equator are at right angles to the ground. The energy of these rays is concentrated on the area marked **a**.

The rays which reach the Earth nearer the North or South Poles hit the ground at a much lower angle. The energy of their rays is spread over a much larger area like the one marked **b**.

The amount of energy from the sun which reaches the Earth's surface is called **insolation**. Figure 3.2 shows that the further you are from the Equator, the less energy you receive from insolation.

Other things also affect the amount of energy received by different parts of the Earth. The clouds and ice at the Poles reflect the sun's radiation back into space more than the rich and dense vegetation of the areas around the Equator.

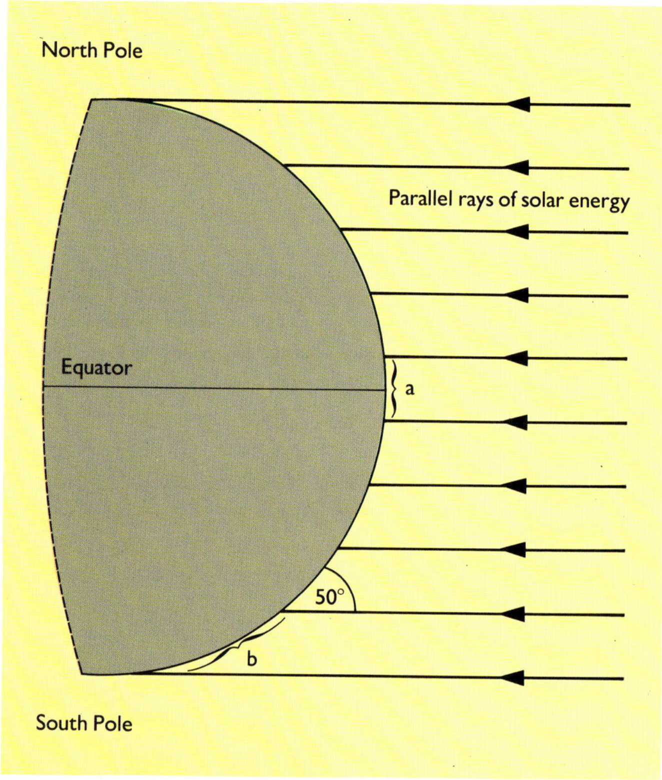

Figure 3.2 Insolation

More heat is received by the Earth near the Equator than near the Poles so since the atmosphere acts like a blanket to stop the heat energy escaping, this ought to mean that the atmosphere over the Equator gets steadily hotter and hotter. This obviously does not happen. Heat energy is moved from the areas near the Equator to the areas near the Poles by the movements of air and water vapour in the atmosphere and by the movements of water in the ocean currents.

It is the movements of air and water vapour caused by the sun heating the Earth that cause the different climates and weather of the world.

Activity

- **1** Use Figures 3.1 and 3.2 to make a list of the ways heat from the sun is lost before it reaches the Earth.

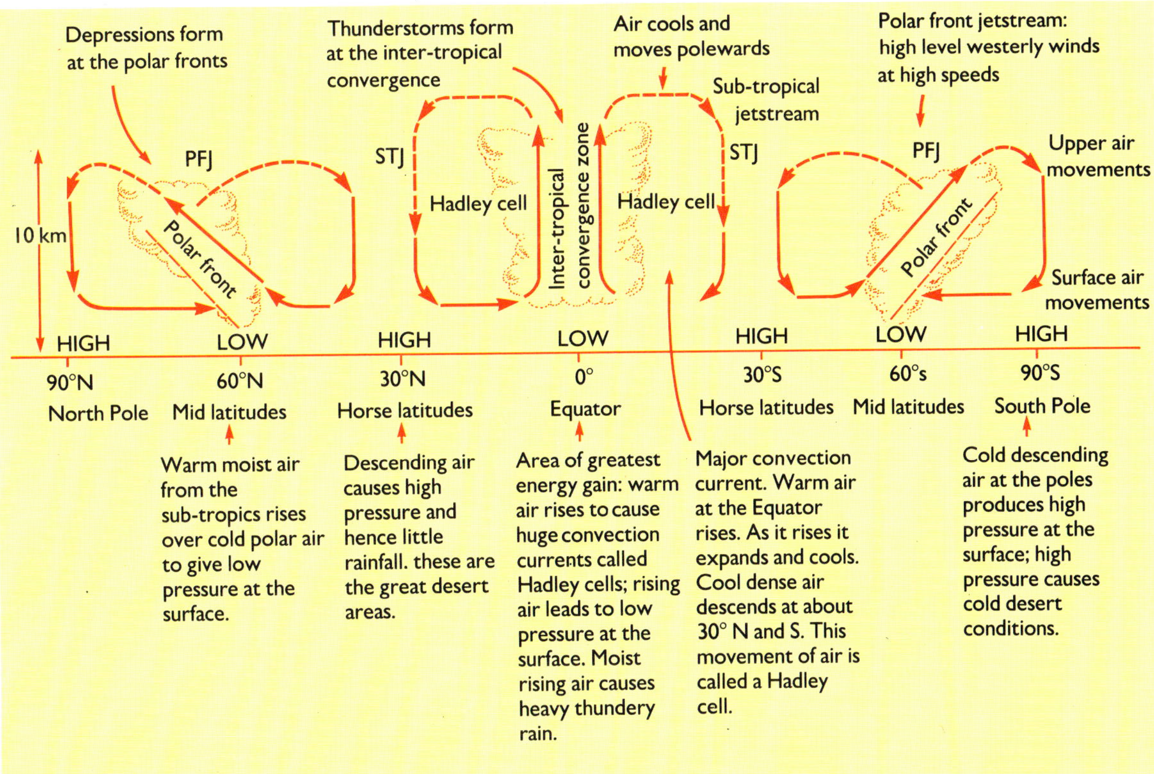

Figure 3.3 Simplified cross-section of the Earth's surface and atmosphere to show the circulation of the atmosphere

Movements of the atmosphere

The pressure belts

Figure 3.3 shows the overall pattern of air movements for the whole Earth. This pattern is called the **general circulation**. The main driving force of the atmosphere is the rising air around the Equator. Air gets less **dense** (heavy) as it is warmed by the longwave radiation given off by the Earth. Because the air is less dense, it rises. As the air rises, it cools and spreads out towards the Poles. When it cools, it becomes more dense and sinks again towards the Earth. This sinking happens at about 30° north and 30° south of the Equator. The sinking air forms the high pressure area at the **horse latitudes**. The sinking air stops air rising from the hot land underneath. This means that there is very little rain. The sinking air is the main reason for the hot deserts of the world.

The air which sinks in the horse latitudes either moves back towards the Equator near ground level or moves towards the Poles. The air which moves towards the Equator forms the **Trade Winds**.

Over the Poles, the air is cold and dense. It sinks to form the polar high pressure areas. From the polar high pressure areas, winds blow towards the Equator.

At about 60° north and 60° south, the winds blowing from the polar high pressure areas meet the warmer, moist air moving north and south from the high pressure of the horse latitudes. The zone where different types of air meet is called a **front**. The zone where cold polar air meets warmer air from the horse latitudes is called the **polar front**. Along the polar front, warm air tends to rise over colder air. This creates localized low pressure areas, known as **depressions**. In these depressions the colder polar air swirls around the low pressure area. Where the warm moist air rises over the cold air this often leads to rain. The depressions usually move along the polar front. It is not known why they move as they do, but they seem to be affected by a narrow belt of very high speed westerly winds in the upper atmosphere called the **polar jet stream**.

In the low pressure areas between the Tropics of Cancer and Capricorn the rising of the warm moist air gives heavy thundery rain.

Rainfall and cloud occur in areas of low pressure because the air rises and cools to condensation level. Clouds are then formed and rain may follow.

In the areas of high pressure, the air is sinking. As the air sinks it gets warmer and so rain is unlikely. The high pressure belts cause

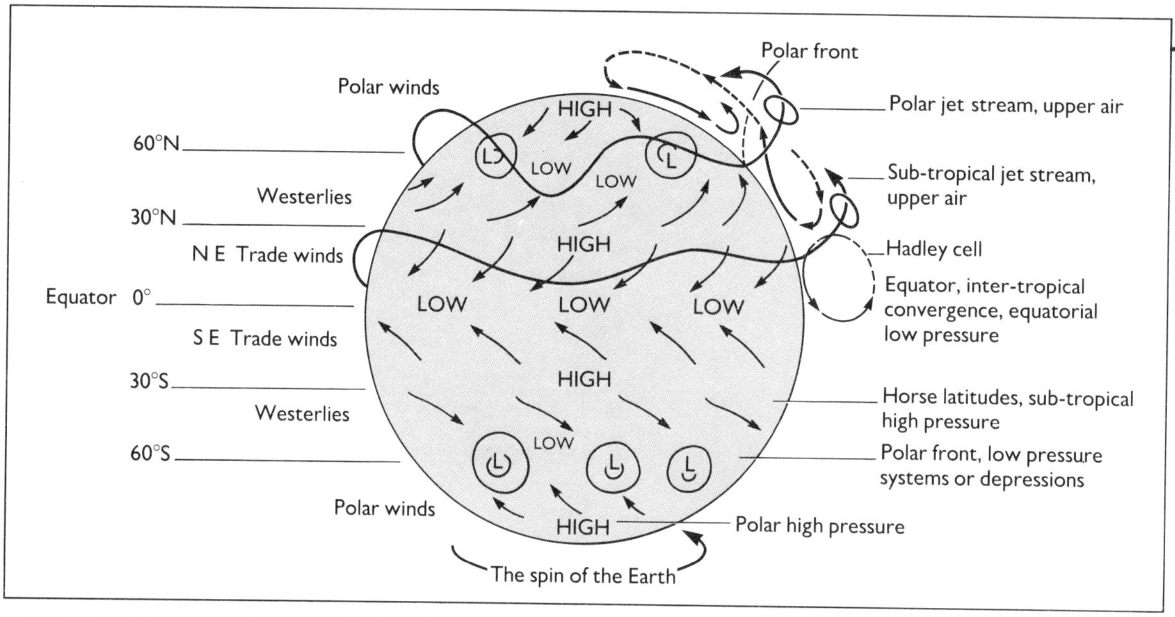

Figure 3.4 Main pressure belts and winds on the spinning Earth with a uniform surface

the great desert areas of the world. The high pressure over the Poles causes cold deserts. The high pressure in subtropical areas causes hot deserts.

The winds

Winds are caused by air moving from areas of high pressure to areas of low pressure. This is shown in Figure 3.3.

The winds can't blow straight from high pressure to low pressure because of the spinning of the Earth. The effect of this spinning is shown in Figure 3.4. The winds which blow from the high pressure area 30° north and 30° south towards the low pressure area over the Equator blow from the north-east and south-east. In the days when most trading was by sailing ship, these winds were given the names **North-East Trades** and **South-East Trades**. They were called Trade Winds because the skippers of the ships could rely on them.

The pattern of winds shown in Figure 3.4 is very simplified because it assumes that the Earth's surface is quite smooth and either all land or all sea. In fact, the continents and oceans make a great difference to the pattern. Figure 3.5 shows how the patterns of pressure and winds change between January and July.

The main reason why land and sea have an effect on pressure and winds is that land and sea heat up and cool down at different speeds. The land heats up more quickly than the sea in summer, and cools down more quickly than the sea in winter.

In winter heat stored by the land surface is quickly lost into the atmosphere. The heat stored in the oceans is given off much more slowly. This means that the land is colder than the sea in winter.

Warmer air rises and cooler air sinks. When the temperature of the land falls in winter, huge cells of high pressure build up over the continents.

In summer, the land heats up rapidly and the warmed air rises. This rising air causes low pressure over the land compared with the sea.

The difference in the speed of heating and cooling between land and sea is not the only reason why the pattern of winds changes between January and July. The second reason for the difference is the tilt of the Earth.

Figure 3.6 shows how the Earth is always tilted at the same angle as it orbits the sun.

On 22 December the sun is directly overhead at noon at the Tropic of Capricorn. On 21 June it is directly overhead at noon at the Tropic of Cancer. This means that the Tropic of Cancer receives most heat from the sun on 21 June and the Tropic of Capricorn receives most heat from the sun on 22 December. The sun is overhead at the Equator on 21 March and 23 September.

The zone around the Earth where the sun is directly overhead at noon is called the **heat equator**. This is where the air rising from the hot ground starts the circulation of the atmosphere. Look back at Figure 3.4 and imagine the heat equator moving north in June and south in December. You can see how this movement of the heat equator makes the pressure belts, winds and weather systems move north and south as well. This causes the differences between summer and winter. It also explains why there are winter conditions in the northern hemisphere when there are summer conditions in the southern hemisphere.

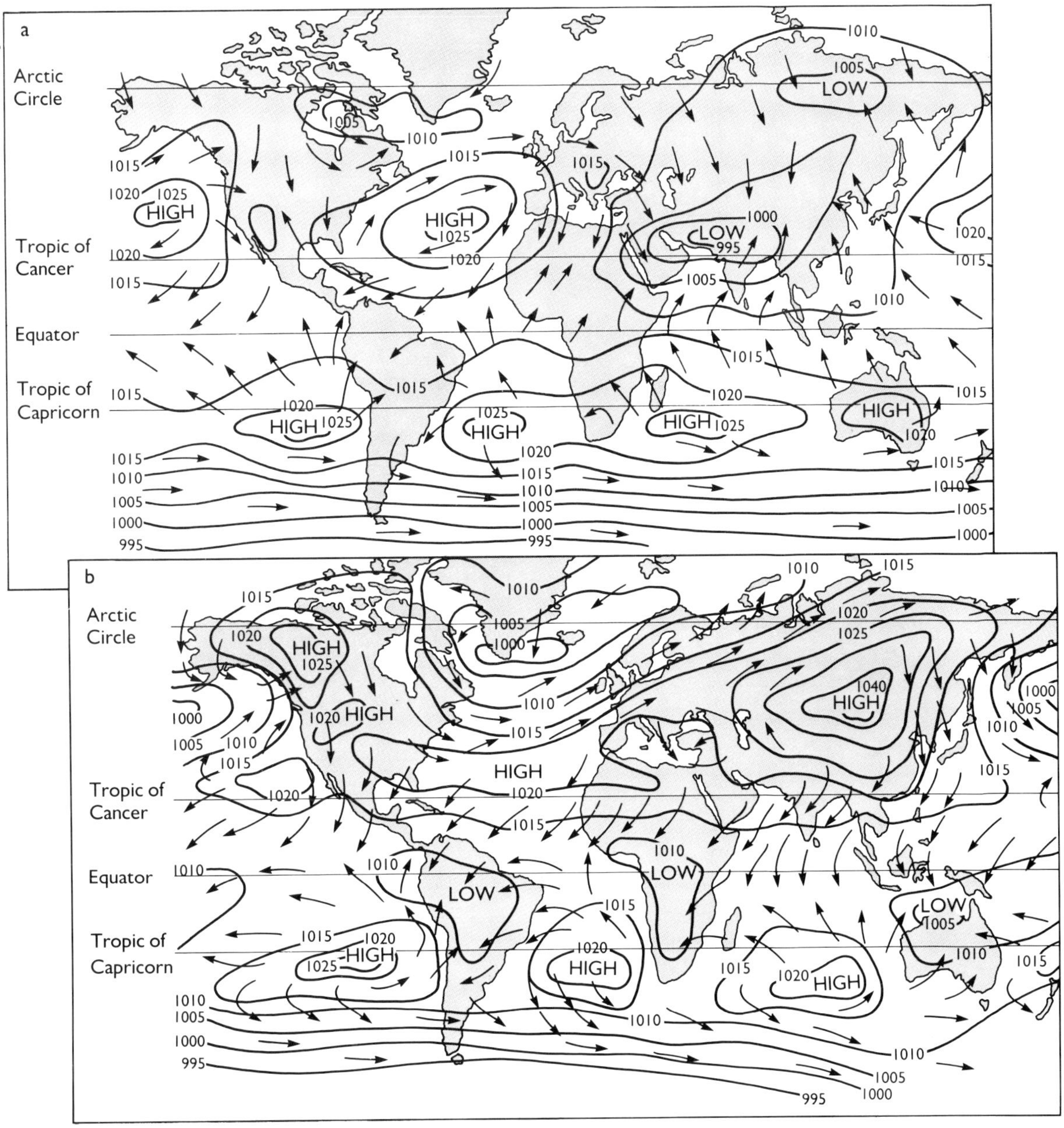

Figure 3.5 a World pressure and winds in July
b World pressure and winds in January (pressure in millibars)

▼ Figure 3.6 The seasons occur because of the constant tilt of the Earth's axis

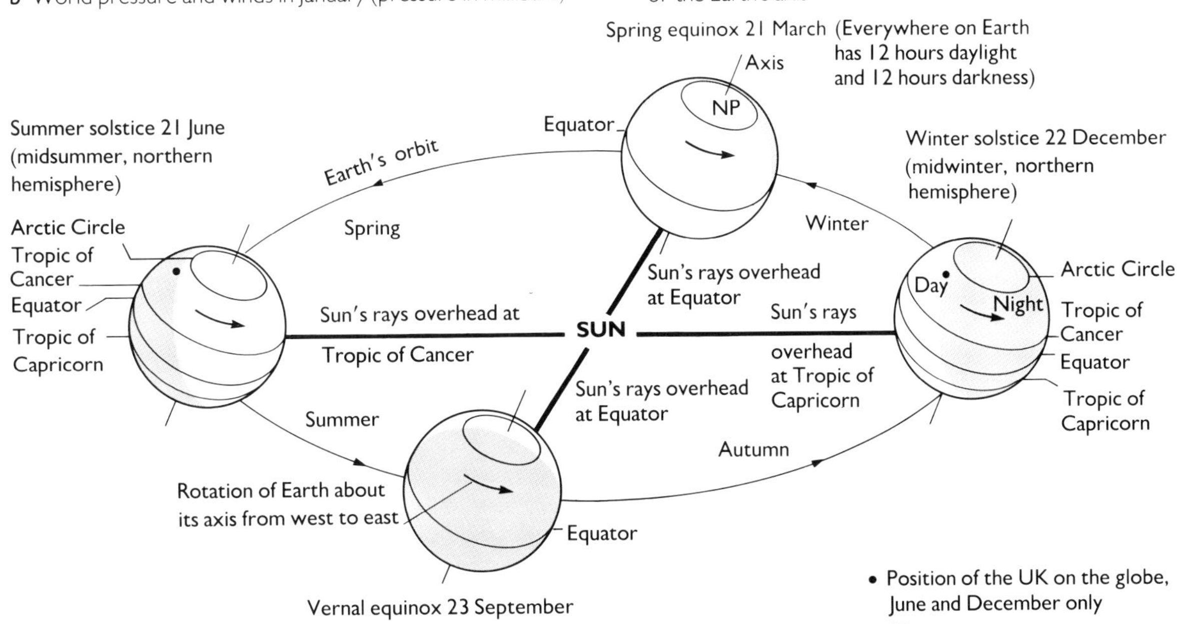

• Position of the UK on the globe, June and December only

Activities

▲2 Study Figure 3.4.

■ **a** For which two days of the year is Figure 3.4 most accurate? Explain why this is so.

b Rome is 42° north of the Equator. Most of its rain falls in the winter months. Explain why this is so.

c i) What is meant by 'heat equator'?

ii) Use Figure 3.6 to describe the northward and southward movements of the heat equator during the year. Start the year from when the sun is overhead at the Tropic of Capricorn on 22 December. Begin your writing: 'First the heat equator moves northwards towards the Equator. It reaches the Equator on ....

▲3 Study Figure 3.5.

■ **a** Explain why there are areas of high pressure over North America and Central USSR in January.

b On an outline map of the world:

i) Draw in the series of low pressure areas (below 1010 millibars) which run east to west between the Equator and the Tropic of Capricorn in January.

ii) Draw a line from east to west through the centre of these low pressure areas. Label it **'Inter Tropical Convergence Zone (ITCZ)'**.

iii) Draw in the winds which blow in towards the ITCZ. Label them 'NE Trades' and 'SE Trades'.

iv) Draw a line to show roughly where the heat equator is in mid-January. Label your line 'heat equator' (see Figures 3.3, 3.4, 3.6).

c i) Explain why the heat equator and the ITCZ are south of the Equator in January (see Figure 3.6).

ii) Explain why the South-East Trades and the North-East Trades meet roughly along the line of the ITCZ.

iii) Explain why the low pressure areas are further south over South America, Africa and Australia than over the oceans. (Hint: which heats up faster – land or sea?)

d i) Draw two sketch maps to show East Africa, India, the Arabian Sea, the Bay of Bengal and SE Asia. On the first, show the winds and the approximate position of the ITCZ in January. On the second, show the winds and approximate position of the ITCZ in July.

ii) During which month would you expect the heavy monsoon rains to fall? Why?

Air masses

In high pressure areas air is affected by the Earth's surface underneath it. A body of air which has been affected by the Earth's surface over a large area is called an **air mass**.

Air masses over the large continents and oceans of the world are affected by the temperature and humidity of these areas. The high pressure areas where air sinks towards the Earth's surface near the Tropics form *warm* air masses. The high pressure areas near the Poles form *cold* air masses.

Air masses which form over oceans usually contain more water vapour than the air masses which form over land masses. Air masses formed over oceans are usually called **maritime** air masses and those formed over large areas of land are called **continental** air masses.

The area where an air mass forms is called its **source area**. There are four main types of source area. These are **Tropical maritime**, **Tropical continental**, **Polar maritime** and **Polar continental**. They are usually abbreviated as **Tm**, **Tc**, **Pm** and **Pc**. There are also the air masses which form over the Arctic and Antarctic ice fields. These are very cold and dry. These air masses are usually abbreviated **Ac** and **Aac**. Figure 3.7 shows the source areas of the air masses in and around an imaginary continent. It also shows how the winds are affected by the different air masses. Figure 3.8 shows the

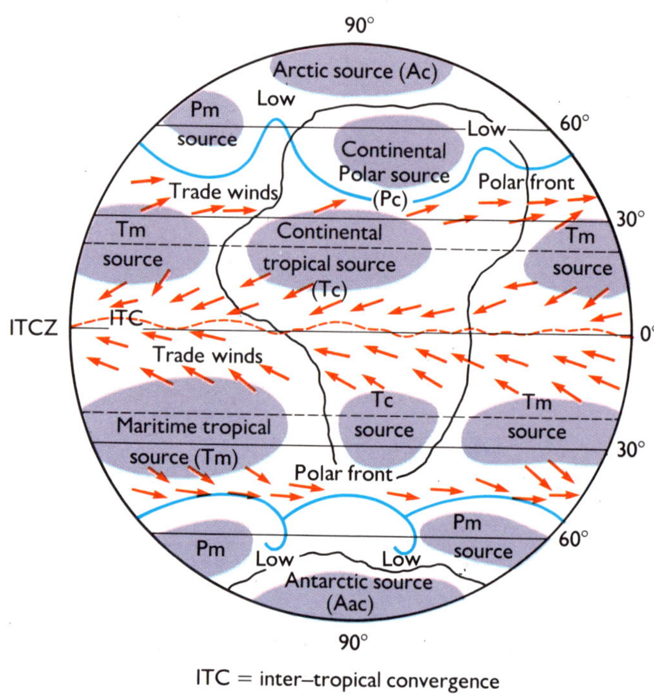

Figure 3.7 Sources of air masses on a globe with an imaginary continent

source areas of air masses in North America and the winds which come from them.

Where two air masses from different types of source region meet, the air does not mix straight away. Often the warmer or moister air is forced to rise over the colder or drier air. Where these air masses meet is called a **front**.

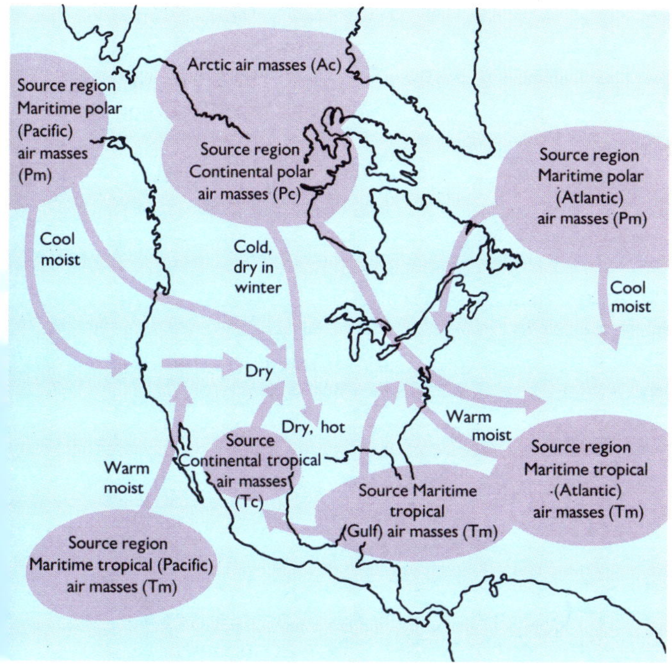

Figure 3.8 Air masses and their movement in N America

Depressions and hurricanes

When low pressure systems develop along the front between the polar and tropical air masses (called the polar front), depressions often form. When low pressure systems develop along the inter-tropical convergence zone, revolving tropical storms may occur. These are called **hurricanes** (or **cyclones** or **typhoons**).

No one really understands what causes depressions, although they may be affected by high level waves in the westerly winds. For some reason a wave is formed in the polar front and warm, tropical air is pulled into the centre of low pressure. A spiral of winds is set up which blows in an anti-clockwise direction in the northern hemisphere. Cold polar air swings round behind the warm sector of tropical air. Eventually it lifts the warmer air away from the ground. A front which has been lifted away from the ground is called an **occluded front**.

Depressions travel from west to east. A depression may take a few hours or a few days to pass over Britain, depending on how fast it is moving. Often, one depression follows another. Depressions bring very changeable weather because of the two types of air mass and the winds which are swirling in an anti-clockwise direction. The weather in a depression is shown in Figure 3.9.

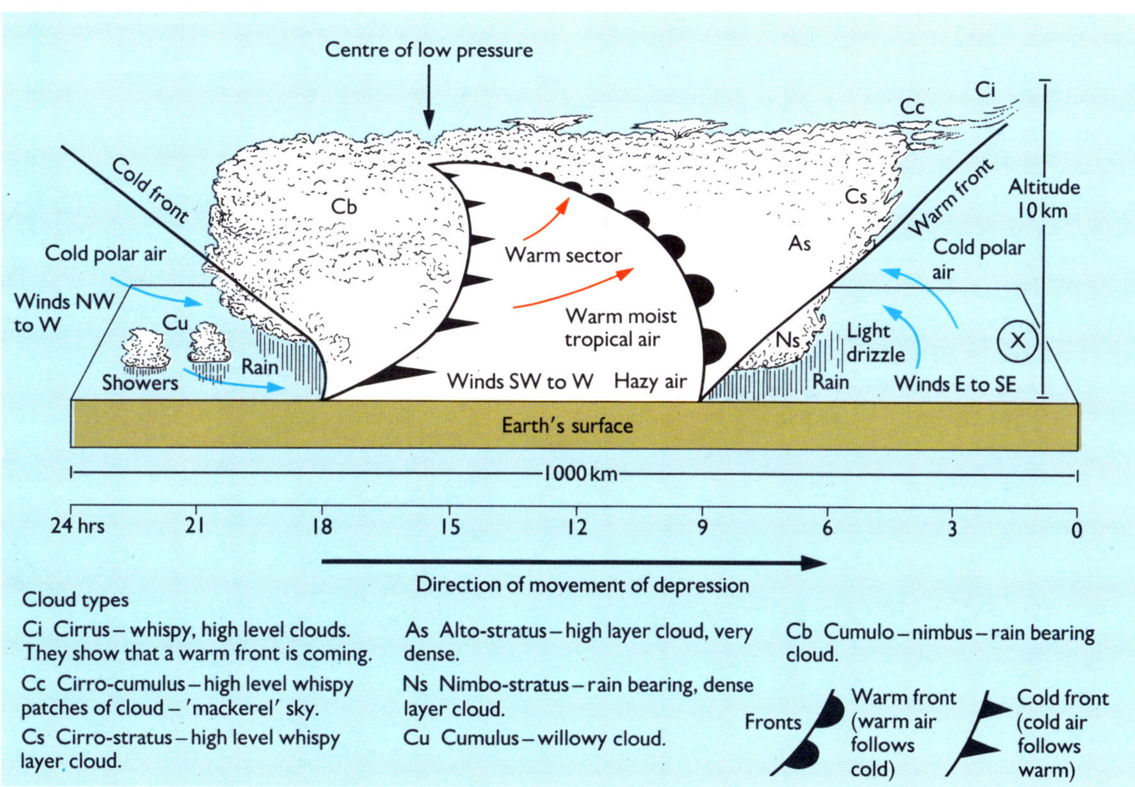

Figure 3.9 The weather in a depression

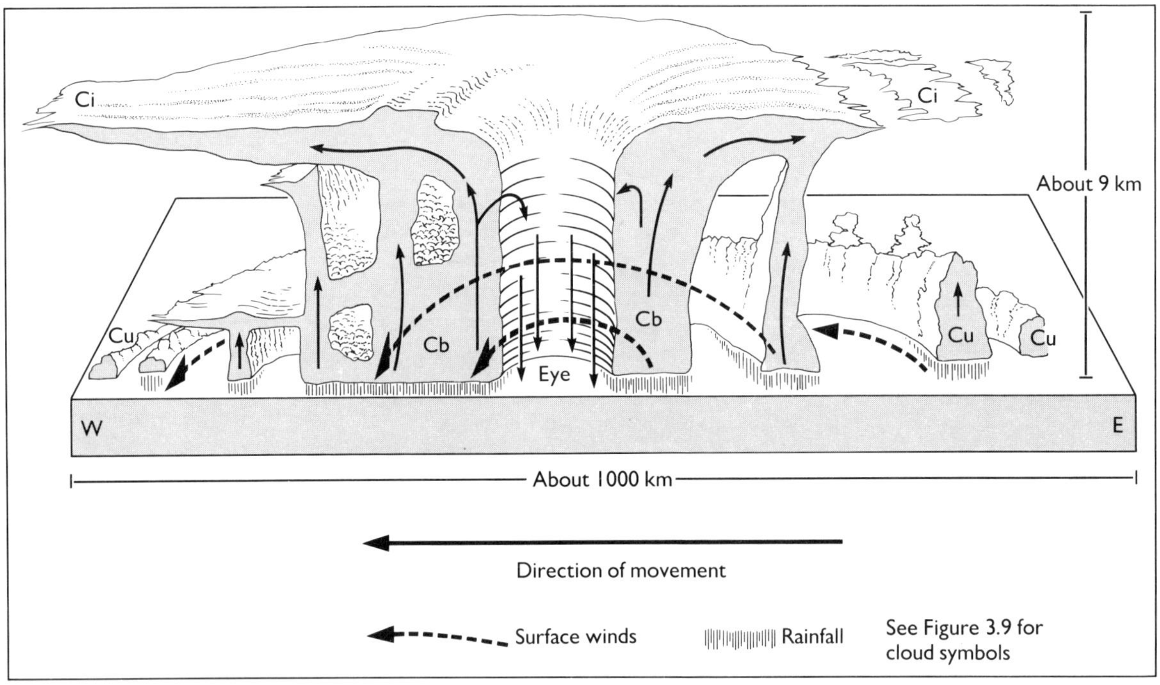

Figure 3.10 The weather in a hurricane

In tropical areas low pressure revolving tropical storms are called hurricanes, cyclones or typhoons. Because the air masses on either side of the inter-tropical convergence zone (ITCZ) are similar, there are no clear fronts and no warm sector. No one is quite sure why hurricanes happen. It is known that they occur over oceans when the sea temperature is higher than 27°C. Once a low pressure cell has formed, water vapour evaporates from the warm sea surface and the air rises very rapidly. This causes huge towering cumulo-nimbus clouds. As the air rises, the water vapour condenses and gives torrential rain. Then the dry air sinks gently in the 'eye' of the hurricane. The low pressure caused by the rapidly rising moist air makes very high winds swirl around the centre of the hurricane. The torrential rain and high winds of a hurricane often cause great damage and many people may be killed. Figure 3.10 shows the weather in a hurricane.

Weather	Now	In 6 hr	In 9 hr	In 15 hr	In 18 hr	In 24 hr
Cloud type **Wind direction** **Temperature** **Rainfall**						

Figure 3.11 The weather in 24 hours (for question 6)

Activities

▲■ **4** Use Figure 3.8 and your atlas to answer the following questions:

a What type of air mass can cause very cold, dry weather in New York in winter?

b What type of air mass is likely to cause drought conditions in Colorado and Kansas?

c What type of air mass is likely to bring heavy snowfall to
i) Vancouver and
ii) Montreal?

d What type of air mass is likely to form the warm sectors of depressions in North America?

▲■ **5** Weather in western Europe is affected by air masses very like the air masses which affect the western parts of the USA.
Draw a map to show the UK and the west coast of the continent of Europe. On your map draw arrows to show the four main air masses which affect the UK. Beside each arrow describe the kind of weather which each air mass is likely to bring.

▲■ **6** Imagine you are standing at point X in Figure 3.9.
Copy and complete Figure 3.11 to show the weather you would expect over the next 24 hours. The depression is 1000 km across and is moving from west to east at about 40 kph.

Weather maps and forecasting

Every evening after the BBC news on television there is the weather forecast. Many of us watch it with only half an eye unless we have something important planned for the next day or so. For some people, such as sailors, farmers, mountaineers, aircraft pilots or people working on high rise buildings, the weather forecast is much more important. The weather affects their work and safety.

The weather forecasts for the UK are prepared by the Meteorological Office at Bracknell. Each forecast is based on more than a million separate observations of temperature, pressure, wind, humidity etc. This information comes from 110 weather stations in the British Isles, from aircraft in flight, from weather ships anchored at sea, from instruments carried up by balloons and rockets, from satellites, from radar stations which can 'see' rain and from other weather forecasting stations all over the world. All this information is fed into the Meteorological Office's powerful computer twice a day. It has been estimated that the sums done by the computer in 1 minute would take 64 000 mathematicians a whole year to do with pencils and paper!

The results of each forecast are very accurate for the weather above 15 km. This is very important for the RAF and for the airlines. The problem comes when the Meteorological Office tries to forecast what will happen at ground level. The Earth's surface has a great effect on the lower layers of the atmosphere. This can cause changes in the weather over very short distances. (Have you ever spent a day in the rain and then been told that somewhere, only a few km away, people have enjoyed brilliant sunshine?) Because of this, human forecasters use their experience of how particular weather patterns are affected by the hills, valleys and plains of different parts of Britain. Then they can produce a forecast of weather on the ground. The TV weather forecast is prepared in the London Weather Centre by meteorologists who receive information from Bracknell. Figure 3.12 shows the symbols used on TV weather forecasts.

People who need more information can ask the Met. Office for a really detailed weather forecast for their own particular area. For example, a building firm which wants to lay concrete will pay the Met. Office for information about the likelihood of frost on their building site. If frosts are forecast, they will mix anti-freeze with the concrete. Anti-freeze is expensive, but not so expensive as re-laying concrete which will not set after a frost. On the other hand, it is cheaper to pay for a detailed weather forecast than to waste anti-freeze when frost is unlikely.

Oil companies also pay for weather forecasts to save themselves the expense of sending supply ships out to oil rigs when the winds are too strong and the seas too rough for them to unload.

To help in forecasting, weather forecasting centres draw daily charts which summarize the weather. These are called **synoptic charts**.

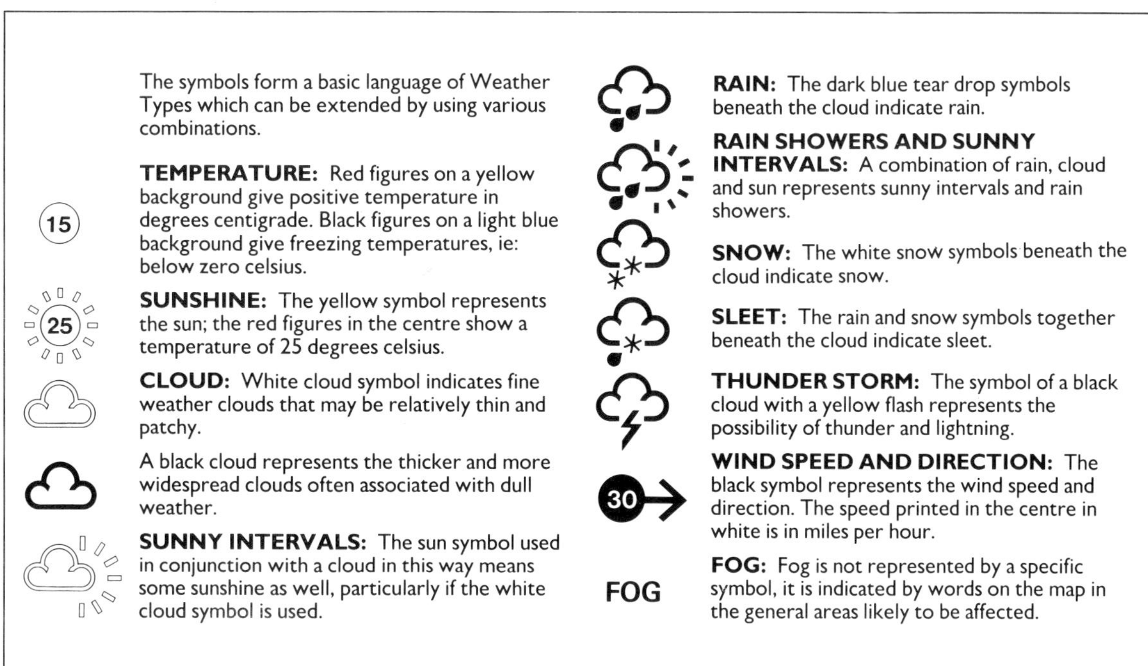

Figure 3.12 Weather symbols used in TV forecasts

A depression crossing the north Atlantic, January 1984

In the first few days of January 1984, a series of depressions formed over the Atlantic and moved eastwards over the British Isles. Figure 3.13 is the key to the weather charts and maps. Figure 3.14 shows the north Atlantic weather charts for 12 noon on Sunday 1 January, Monday 2 January, Tuesday 3 January, Wednesday 4 January and Thursday 5 January. Figure 3.15 shows satellite photographs taken on Monday 2 January and Thursday 5 January.

Let's look at the patterns of the weather on each of these days (Figure 3.14). On 1 January at 12 noon the chart shows a series of low pressure areas in the north-west of the map area. They are labelled LA, LB, and LD. There are high pressure areas to the south labelled H and HM. The meteorologists at the Weather Centre give each low and high pressure area a letter to help us follow them across the charts from day to day. There is a front between the two air masses which is running across the centre of England from west to east. To the south-west of the British Isles, around 47°N, 37°W a depression is forming.

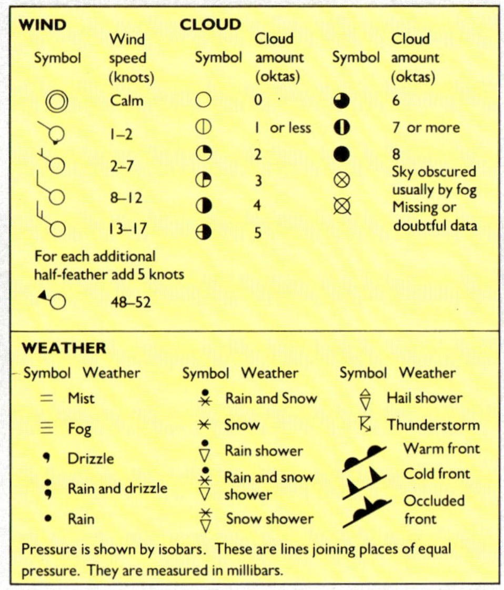

Figure 3.13 Symbols used on synoptic weather charts

The chart for 2 January at 12 noon shows that this depression is now well formed. It has moved to the east and its warm front now lies across Ireland and south-west England. The

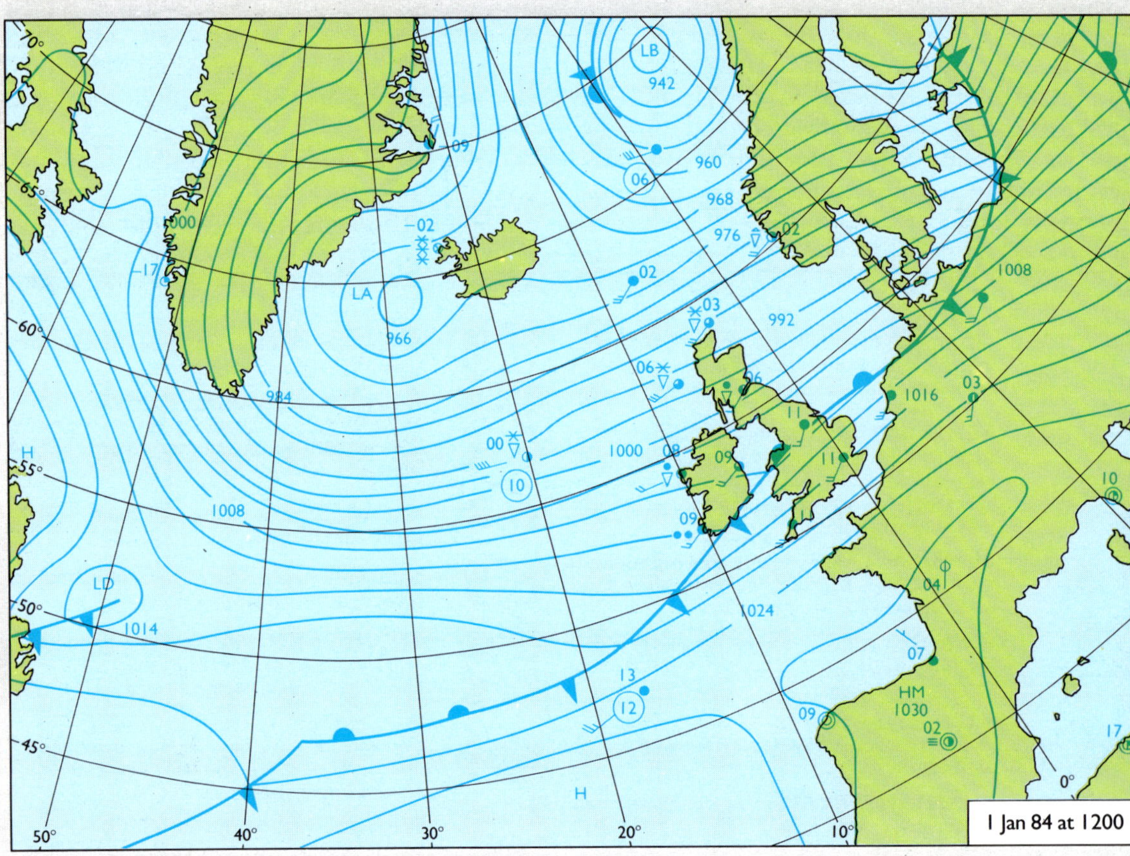

Figure 3.14 Weather maps of the North Atlantic

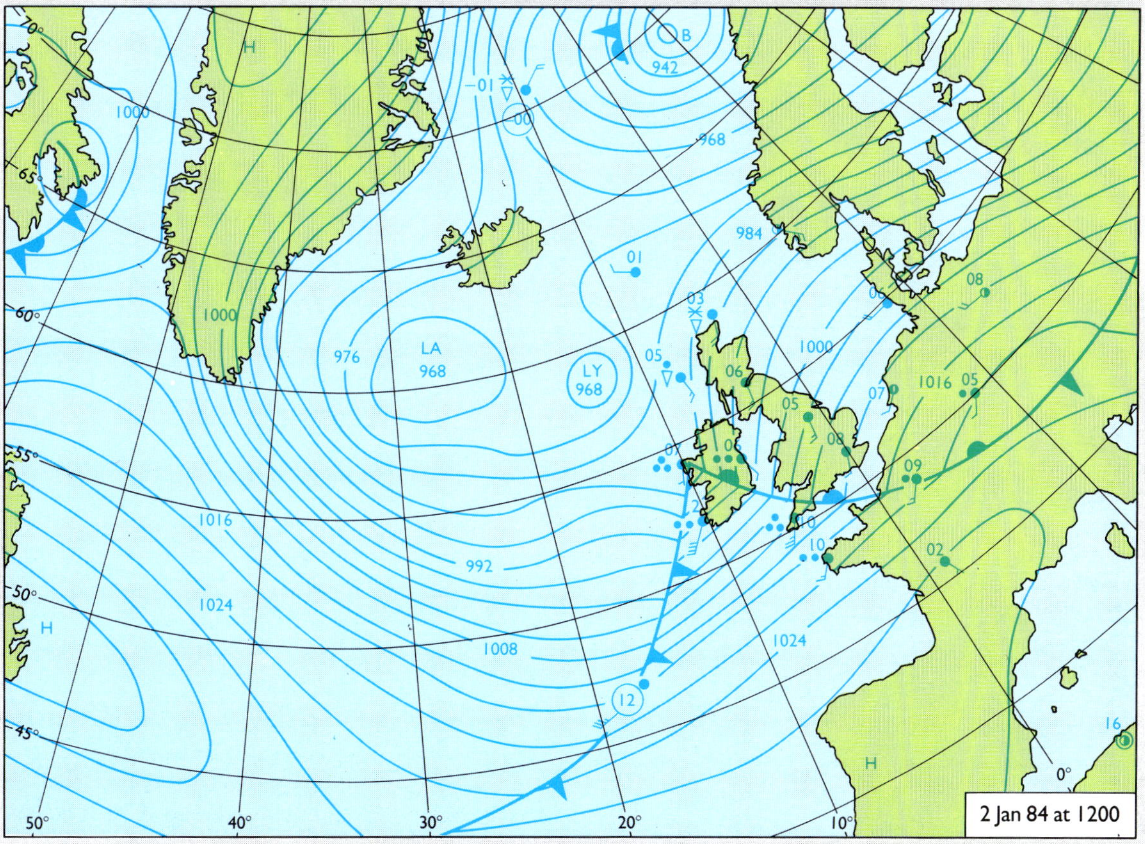

2 Jan 84 at 1200

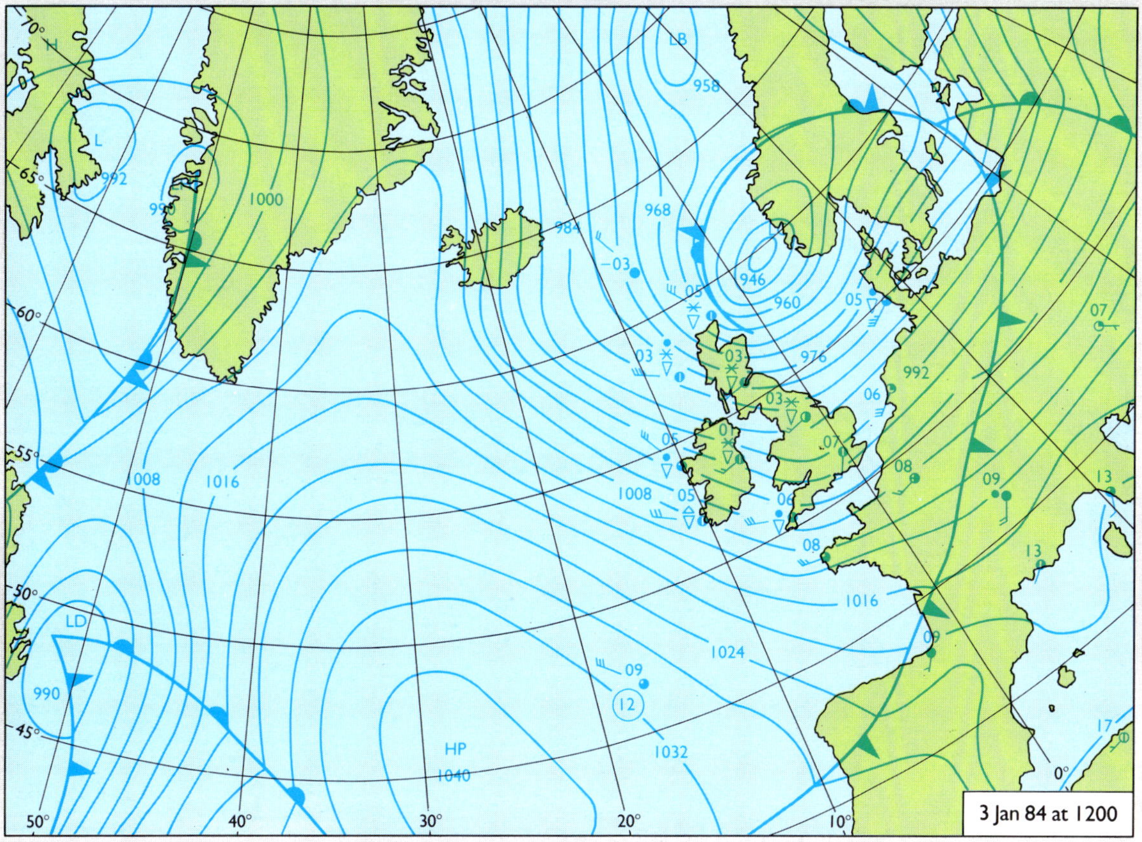

3 Jan 84 at 1200

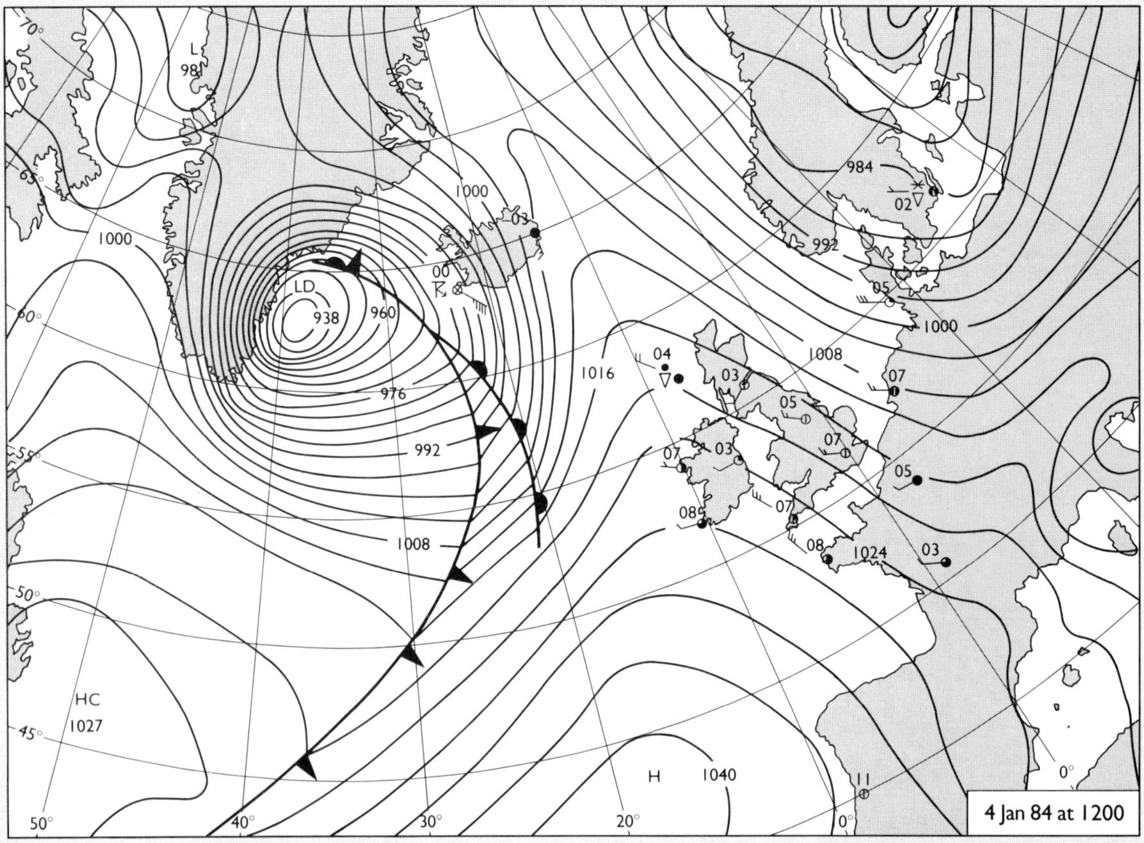

4 Jan 84 at 1200

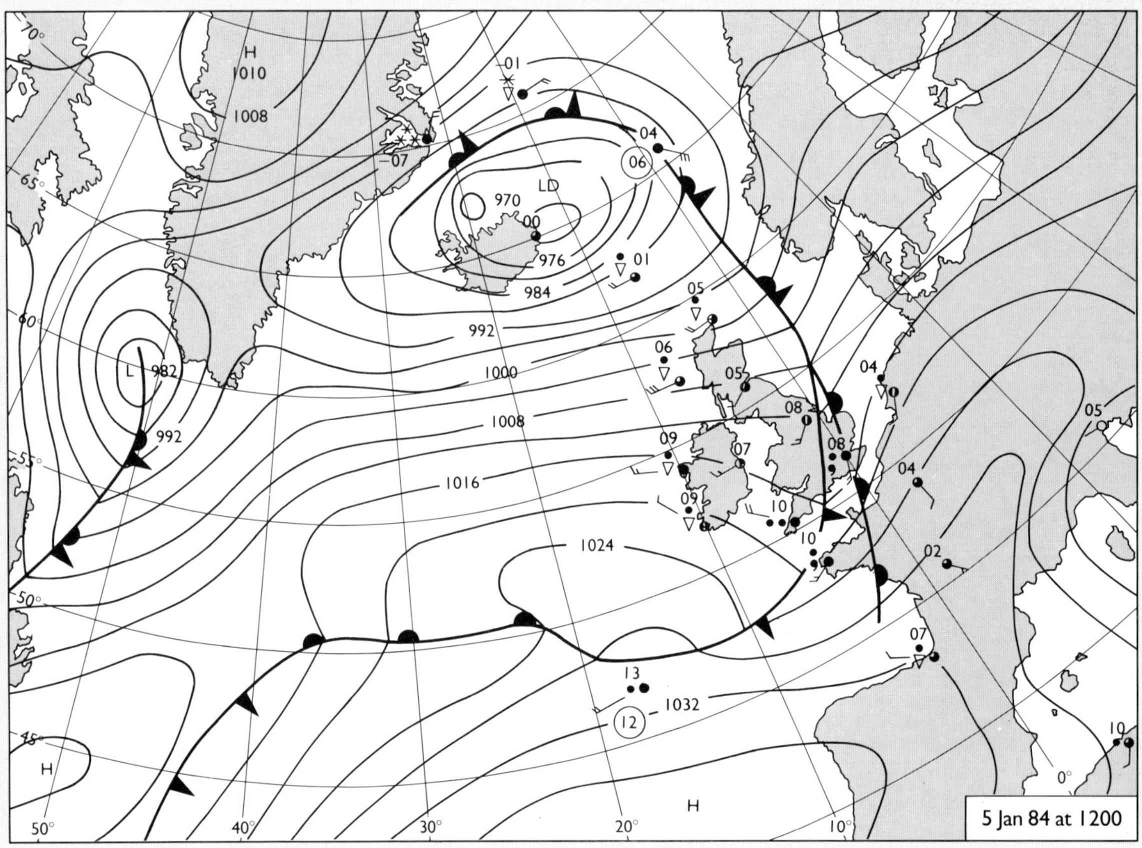

5 Jan 84 at 1200

a
b
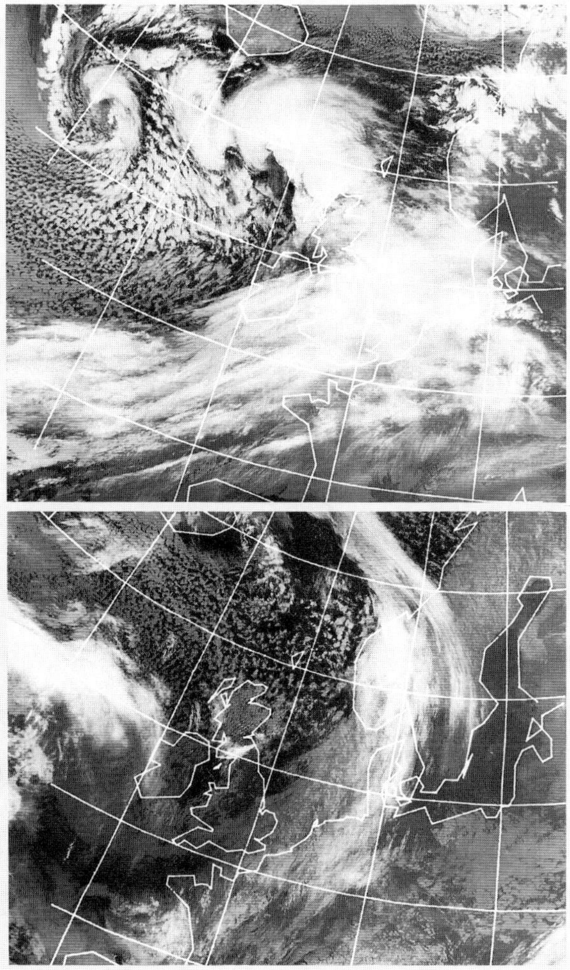

Figure 3.15 Two satellite pictures of weather

satellite picture (Figure 3.15(a)) shows the situation 3 hrs 4 mins later than the chart at 15.04. The picture shows the clouds of the warm front over most of the British Isles. It also shows the swirling of the clouds as the winds blow around the low over the Atlantic to the west of Scotland.

By noon on 3 January, this depression had passed on over Europe. Out in the Atlantic another depression had already formed. The low pressure at the centre of this new depression is labelled LD.

By noon on 4 January, LD had moved northwards. The isobars are very close together. This shows that the pressure is falling very rapidly as you get closer to the centre of the low. The 'feathers' of the arrows show that the wind speeds are up to 45 knots (over 70 km per hour). The cold front has started to catch up with the warm front. This means that the warm air is being lifted away from the ground to form an occluded front.

By noon on 5 January, the chart shows that the depression has been nearly filled in. The map of observations (Figure 3.16) shows that there is drizzle over the country. The satellite photograph (Figure 3.15(b)) shows that by 14.27 on that Thursday, the clouds had moved away to the east and the skies over Great Britain were fairly clear. The whole country was by then under polar maritime air again. Away to the west, the next depression can be seen on the chart. The clouds along the front can be seen in the satellite photograph (Figure 3.15(b)) taken at 14.27 hrs.

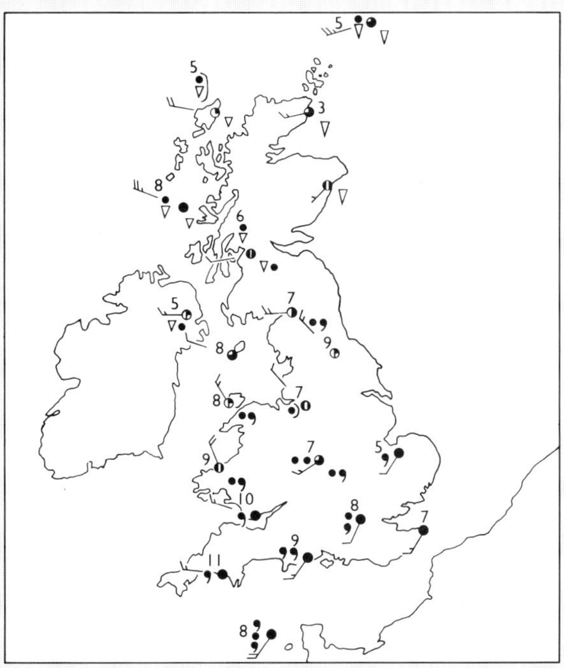

Figure 3.16 Observation map

Activities

■ **7** Examine your own home area on the charts for each of the five days. Describe the weather your area received during these days.

▲ ■ **8** Study Figure 3.16 and the chart for 5 January (Figure 3.14).

a **i)** Describe the weather in the north and west of the UK.

ii) Describe the weather in the south and east of the UK.

You should mention the temperature, wind direction, wind strength, cloud cover and precipitation (rainfall).

b Explain why the north and south of the country had these differences in their weather on that day.

Case Study

A cyclone crossing the coast of eastern India, May 1979

Figure 3.17 shows the movements of a cyclone north-westwards across the Bay of Bengal towards Madras in May 1979.

The Bay of Bengal is an area well known for cyclones. Large cyclones affected the area in 1971, 1974 and 1977. On Wednesday 9 May, the storm was spotted on the weather charts in the south of the Bay of Bengal. On Thursday 10 May it had moved north. It was under special watch by the Cyclone Warning Radar Station at Madras.

The temperatures along the coast were much higher than normal. On Friday 11 May, the cyclone centre was off the coast to the east of Madras. The winds got stronger. On Saturday, the storm crossed the coast north of Madras near the village of Pallepalem. At times the wind reached 75 knots (120 km per hour).

On Sunday the storm passed to the north of Pallepalem and the temperatures dropped 12°–14°C below normal. There was very heavy rain, but the winds died down during the day. By Monday 14 May, the storm had more or less died away, but the heavy rain and some thunderstorms continued.

This storm caused great damage to the villages along the coast. The people knew that it was dangerous to go out in the high winds. They stayed still, lying down. However, floods followed the high winds and many people were drowned. After the storm, 10 000 people were either dead or missing. 500 000 homes were wrecked and 120 000 hectares of crops were ruined. 1500 fishing boats were lost and 12 000 fishing nets were lost or destroyed.

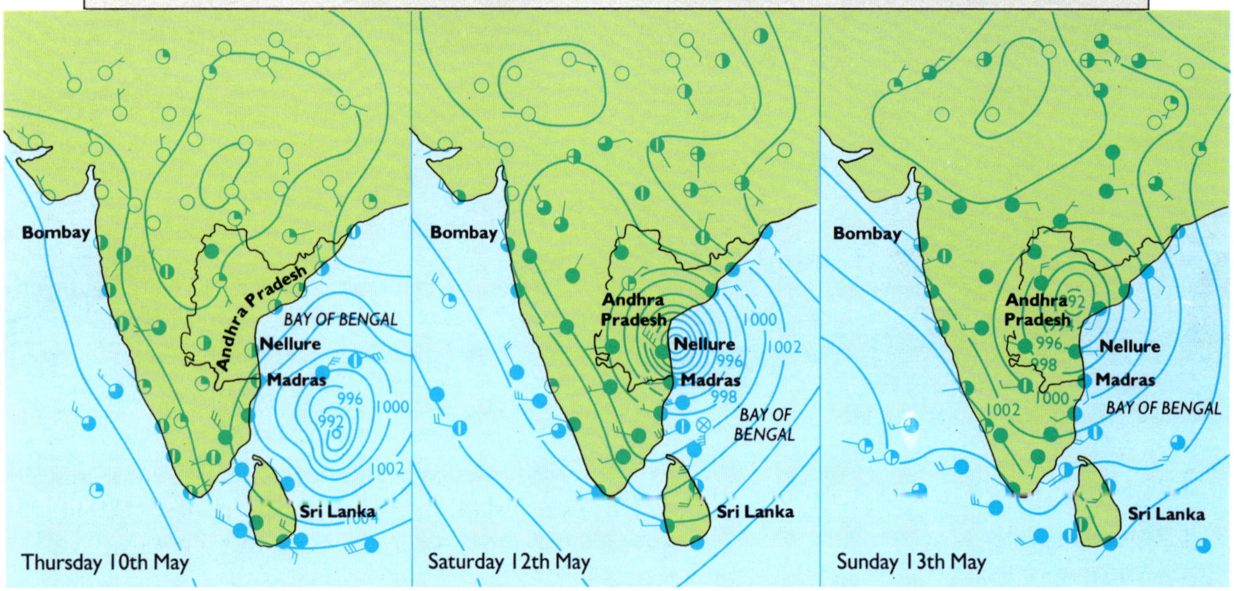

Figure 3.17 Synoptic weather charts showing cyclone movement

Activities

■ **9** Draw an outline map of the Bay of Bengal.

- **a** Add Madras and Nellare to your map.
- **b** On the map draw a line to show the track followed by the eye of the cyclone.
- **c** Mark the points reached by the eye of the cyclone each day. Write notes about the weather information given for each day on your map.

▲ ■ **10** Imagine you are a weather observer in Madras. Beginning on Thursday 10 May, write a description of the weather (wind speed, wind direction, rainfall, pressure, temperature) for each day until Monday 14 May (6 days).

▲ ■ ● **11** Imagine you are at the cyclone radar tracking centre in Madras. It is Wednesday 9 May. You can see the cyclone on your screen and you can work out the speed at which it is moving. Write a warning to be broadcast on the radio warning people about the cyclone. Tell them what to expect in the next few days. You suspect that the eye of the cyclone will pass over the town of Nellare. Give special advice to the people of Nellare about what they should expect.

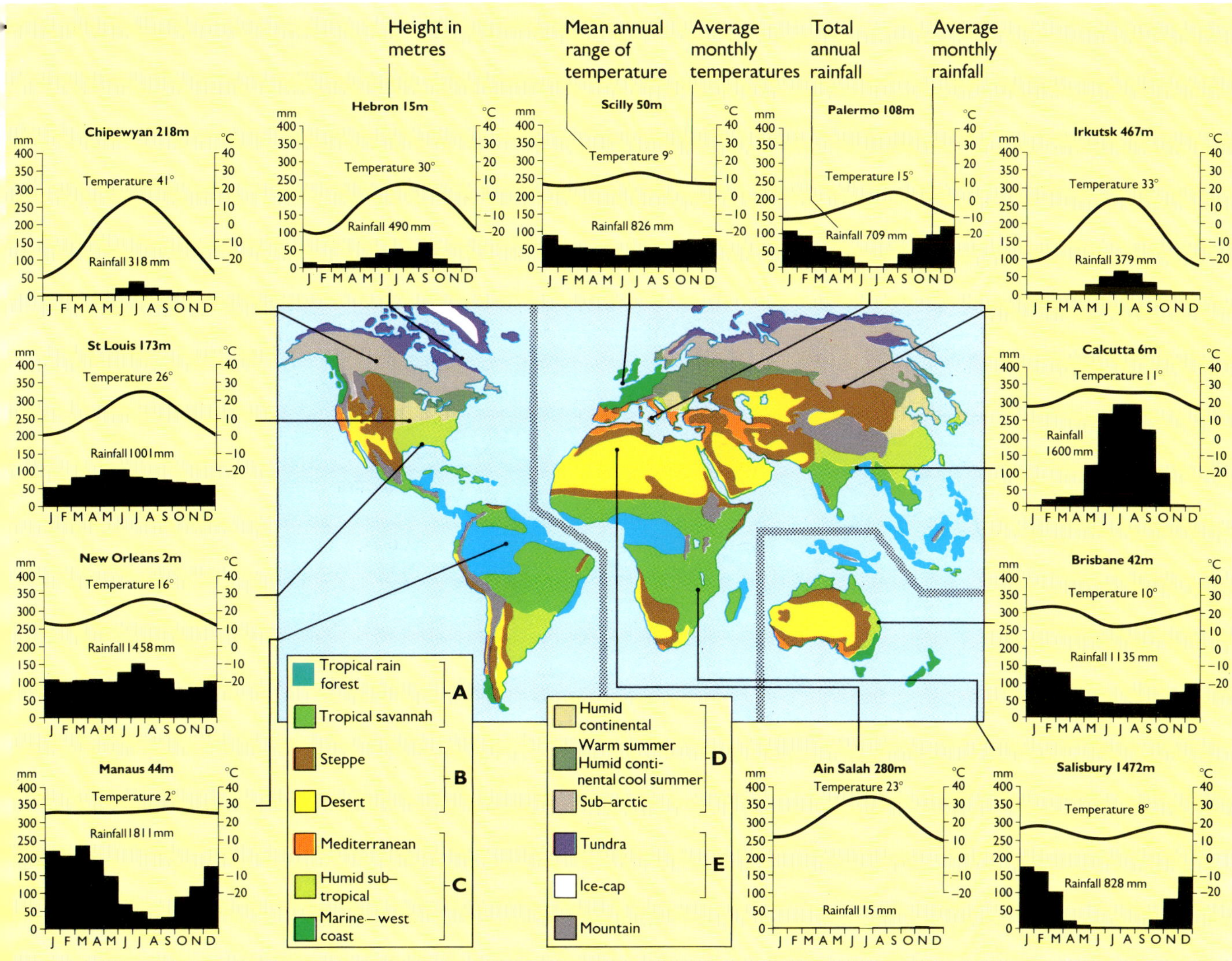

Figure 3.18 Examples of climatic types in the Köppen classification of climates

The pattern of world climates

The general patterns of weather over 30 years or more give us the climate of a place. As more information about places all over the world became available, maps were drawn of the world climates. (Your atlas probably has maps of the world which show January temperatures, July temperatures, ocean currents, winds, total annual rainfall and when most of the rain falls.)

From these maps, some **climatologists** (people who study climate) have tried to produce maps to show the areas which have similar climates. Figure 3.18 is a simplified version of Köppen's classification which was first produced in 1918. It also shows rainfall and temperature graphs for a town or city which is typical of the main climate types.

The climate types can be simplified even further into five groups.

Group A
Tropical rainy climates. Every month has an average temperature above 18°C. There is no winter season. There is a high annual rainfall. Much more rain falls than can evaporate.

Group B
Dry climates. There is low rainfall. More water could evaporate than actually falls as rain.

Group C
Warm temperate climates. Temperatures are usually quite mild and rain falls all through the year. The coldest month has an average temperature between 3°C and 18°C. At least one month has an average temperature above 20°C.

Group D
Snowy forest climates. The coldest month has an average temperature of just below freezing. The average temperature of the warmest month is above 10°C.

Group E
Polar climates. The average temperature of the warmest month is below 10°C. There is no true summer.

Activities

▲ ■ **12 a** Use Figure 3.18 to draw a sketch map of South America. Mark and label the climatic types.

b Add other labels around the margin of your map to explain why South America has these climate types. Figures 3.2 to 3.8 and pages 43–48 and 57 will help you with this.

▲ ■ **13 a** Use Figure 3.18 to draw the five main groups of climate types on an outline map of the world.

b For each of the five groups, describe where they are found in the world.

c Explain why the groups of climate form this pattern. You should mention pressure, wind direction and distance north or south of the Equator.

▲ ■ **14 a** Study an atlas map of annual world precipitation. On an outline map of the world:

i) Draw in the areas with a high rainfall (2000 mm or more per year).

ii) Draw in the areas with a low rainfall (less than 500 mm per year).

iii) Draw in the areas with a medium rainfall.

b Use the other climate maps in your atlas and the information in this chapter to find areas of the world which show that the following statements are true:

i) Onshore winds tend to bring rain.

ii) Offshore winds and winds blowing across land masses tend to bring little or no rain.

iii) Winds which blow down from a mountain range tend to bring little rain.

iv) Land masses outside the tropics cool rapidly in winter and cause high pressure conditions. This causes low rainfall.

v) Air which moves over warm water tends to hold more moisture than air which moves over cold water.

vi) The polar front and the ITCZ are areas of rising air where there is heavy rainfall.

Natural vegetation

The kinds of plants which we can grow depend on the climate and the soil. If we want to grow tropical plants in the UK we have to keep them indoors or in a greenhouse. This allows us to control the temperature, the amount of water available and the amount of light they receive. When we do this, we are trying to copy the climatic conditions of the plants' natural home.

In their natural surroundings, plants get light energy, carbon dioxide and water from, or through, the atmosphere. The chemical nutrients come from the breakdown of plant and animal material in the soil.

The study of which conditions will allow most plant growth is important if human beings are going to be able to feed themselves in the years to come. Some geographers have tried to put together all the different pieces of information on climate to show which areas are most suited to plant growth. The information they have used is:

1 The average temperature of the warmest month.
2 The annual range of temperature – the difference between the warmest and the coldest months.
3 The growing season in months – the number of months when the temperature is high enough for plants to grow.
4 The amount of solar radiation received.
5 The total precipitation.

Figure 3.19 shows the world divided into six zones. Zone F is the least productive part of the Earth's land surface for plant growth. Zone A is the most productive part of the Earth's land surface.

Figure 3.20 shows the plant productivity zones on a cross-section from north to south across an imaginary continent. Figure 3.20 also shows the types of natural vegetation found in each zone. Figure 3.21 shows the zones of natural vegetation on a map of the world.

If we studied the distribution of different types of animals, birds and insects as well as the types of plants, we would find that the vegetation zones each have their own particular kinds of animal life. When the natural vegetation zones and their animal life are described together, we call the different areas **biomes**. The main biomes are forest, savanna, grassland, desert and tundra.

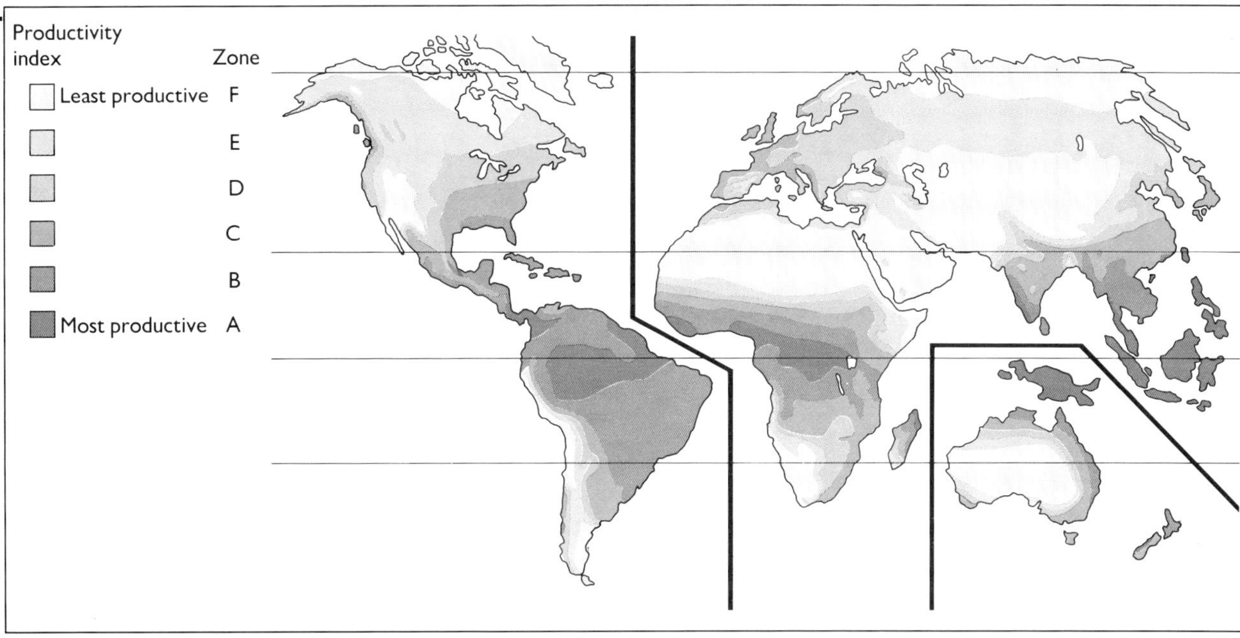

Figure 3.19 World productivity for plant growth

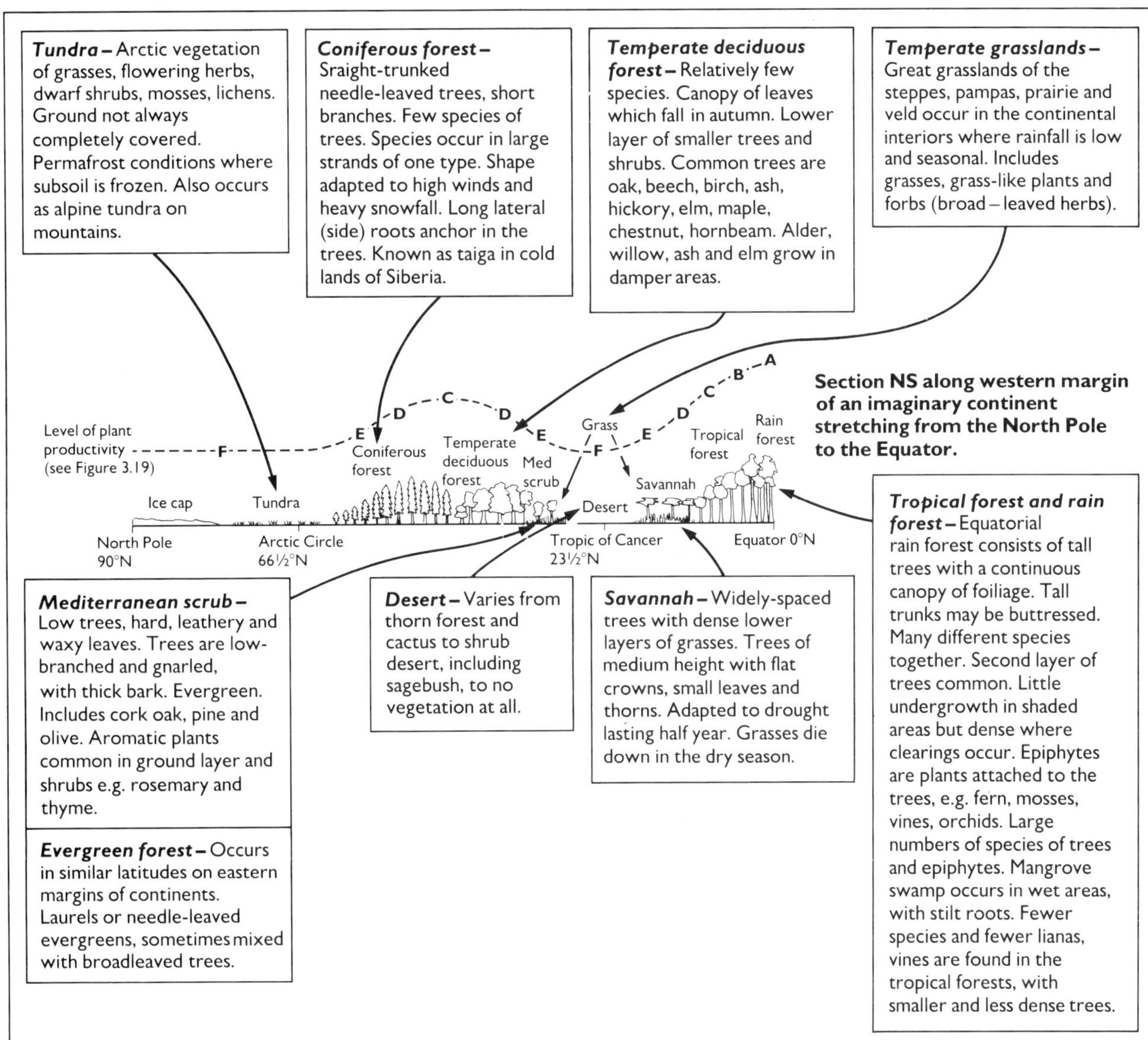

Figure 3.20 Cross-section showing plant productivity and the major types of natural vegetation

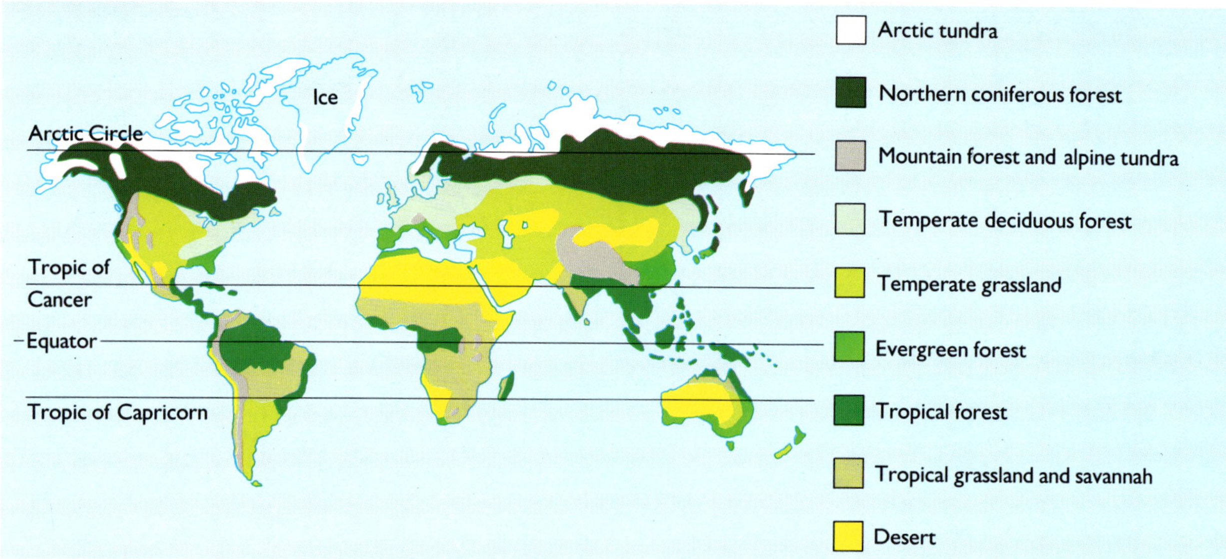

Figure 3.21 The world's natural vegetation zones

Activities

▲15 ■ Look at the maps of temperature and rainfall in your atlas and at Figure 3.19 which shows plant growth productivity in the world.

a Draw 3 sketch maps of South America side by side.

i) On the first show the annual rainfall.

ii) On the second show the average temperatures in January.

iii) On the third show the natural vegetation.

b Describe the differences and similarities between:

i) your maps of temperature and natural vegetation

ii) your maps of rainfall and natural vegetation.

c Use the information you have discovered to explain whether rainfall or temperature seems to be the most important factor which influences natural vegetation.

▲16 ■ Look at Figure 3.21.

a Draw up a table to show which types of vegetation are found in areas of each productivity level as shown in Figure 3.19.

b Write a paragraph to explain which types of vegetation are most productive and which are least productive.

▲17 ■ In many parts of the world there is no natural vegetation left because of farming, industry or settlement by human beings.
Which types of natural vegetation are *least* altered by human beings? Why do you think this is so? Give reasons. (Hint: look back to Chapter 1 for a map of population distribution in the world – Figure 1.17.)

Soils

Without soils, there would be no vegetation. Soil supports plants by holding their roots. Soil also provides nutrients and moisture for plant growth. However, we could also argue that without vegetation, there would be no soil. Vegetation is a very important factor in making soils.

Soil begins as bare rock. Gradually the bare rock is weathered into small particles. These particles are the first stage in making soil. There is more to soil, however, than just rock particles. Soil is a mixture of rock particles, soil water, humus, mineral salts, lime and air.

Soil water is the thin film of water which clings on to the rock particles. The plant roots take the water they need from this film of water. When rain falls on the ground, it sinks down through the soil and wets the soil particles. Eventually the water reaches the **water table**, where the rocks are saturated with water. As the roots of the plants absorb water, or water evaporates from the soil surface, more water is drawn up from the water table. The water moves through the soil by **capillary action**, that is, it is 'pulled up' through the minute spaces in the soil.

The water can only move through the soil by capillary action if the soil particles are the right size. If the particles are too large, water sinks straight through and can't be pulled up. Also, water sinking through the soil washes the useful nutrients downwards. This is called **leaching**. Leaching sometimes causes very poor soil. On the other hand, if soil particles are too small and tightly packed, water can't get through at all. Then the water stands on the top or flows off the surface. If there is heavy rain

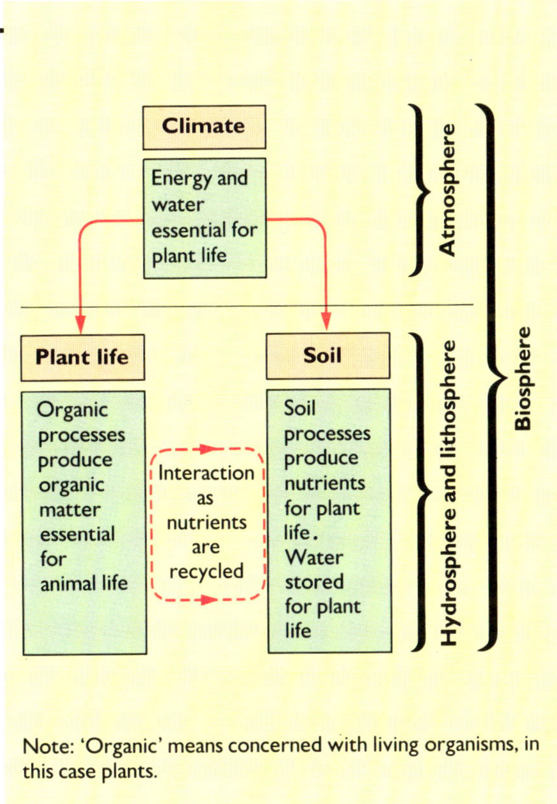

Figure 3.22 Climate controls the biosphere

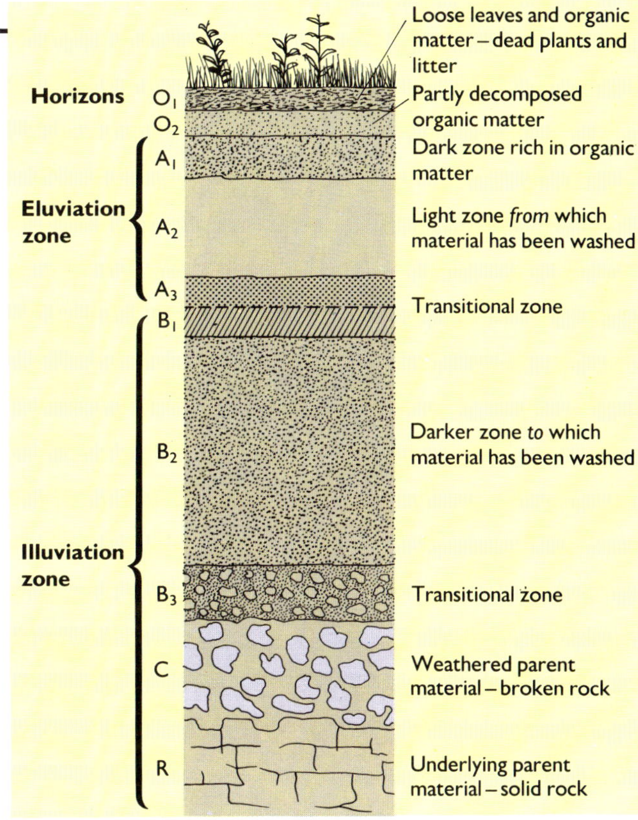

Figure 3.23 Horizons in soil

and the water can't soak down or flow away, the soil becomes **water-logged**. Water-logged soils are short of oxygen. This means that the vegetation and animal materials can't break down properly.

Humus is a sticky substance made when animals and plants die in the soil. Their bodies and animal wastes decay with the help of insects, bacteria and other creatures living in the soil. Humus is black, so soil with a lot of humus is usually a dark colour. Humus makes the soil rich in the nutrients needed for plant growth. It forms a sticky coating round the soil particles and helps them to clump together into soil **crumbs**. A soil with good crumbs is said to have a good structure. The humus stores water and prevents the nutrients being washed out of the soil when it rains. If the soil crumbs are broken up by over-use in farming the soil can't hold soil water and the nutrients can be washed out by the rain. This means that the soil loses both its structure and its fertility.

The soil water contains various mineral salts. These provide the nitrogen, phosphorus, potassium and other elements that plants need for growth. Some of the mineral salts come from the rock which formed the original soil. Other minerals are formed when humus breaks down.

To be fertile, soils need some calcium carbonate. This is the chemical name for a white substance found in chalk and limestones. Calcium carbonate is important for three main reasons. Firstly, calcium is needed for plant growth. Secondly, calcium carbonate and other carbonates help soil particles to stick together to make soil crumbs. Thirdly, calcium carbonate and other carbonates are alkaline. They prevent the soil from becoming too acid.

Good soil always has plenty of spaces between the soil particles and the crumbs. These spaces are filled with air. The oxygen in this air is needed by the plant roots and creatures which live in the soil. Oxygen is also needed by the bacteria which help humus to decay. Creatures such as earthworms, mice, moles, foxes, rabbits and badgers all help to let air into the soil.

The links between climate, plant life and the soil are shown in Figure 3.22.

If you have ever looked into a hole dug in the ground, you will probably have noticed that soils have layers of different colours. These layers are called **horizons**. Horizons are caused by water moving up and down in the soil. They take a long time to form. Usually water collects **organic material** (material from living things) from the upper horizons and deposits it in the lower horizons. The removal of material is called **eluviation**. The depositing of material is called **illuviation**. The effects of this movement are shown in Figure 3.23.

If the balance between eluviation and illuviation breaks down, the soil may become useless. For example, if tropical forests are cut down so that the heavy rainfall just soaks through the soils, all the organic material may be washed into the lower layers of the soil. This leaves the top soil with poor structure and few nutrients.

Sometimes the opposite can happen. If the soil is left bare so that water can evaporate easily, mineral salt can be carried up to the surface. This causes salt caking on the surface.

Geographers have tried to classify soils so that they can be mapped. The United States Soil Conservation Service completed a soil classification in 1970. The classification describes ten **orders** of soils. These are then broken down into 47 suborders, 185 great groups, 1000 subgroups, 5000 families and 10000 series. These figures for the subgroups, families and series are for the United States alone. Imagine how detailed the classification would be for the whole world!

The orders of soils are described in Figure 3.24. Figure 3.25 shows how soil orders are distributed in the world.

Order	Characteristics of the soil	Associated vegetation	Fertility and value to people
Entisols	No horizons.	Varies – could be any type.	May be very infertile, e.g. in tropical or polar deserts. Can also be very fertile, e.g. on tropical or subtropical flood plains, such as the Ganges and Brahmaputra.
Inceptisols	Young soils with one or more horizons. There is soil water for more than half the year.	Tundra or mountain tundra. Can also be found in e.g. the Tropics.	Can be productive when carefully farmed and where climate is favourable.
Histosols	Contains much organic material near the surface. Organic horizon may be the only one.	Heath and moor on peat bogs. Woodland or grass on old lake floors in mid latitudes.	Can be very fertile and productive when properly managed, e.g. vegetables on drained and fertilized lake floors. Peats used in gardening and farming and as a fuel.
Oxisols	Minerals weather to sesquioxides and iron in soils of loamy texture. Minerals deposited at depths of 2 m. Heavy rainfall may cause washing out of minerals (leaching).	Forests in equatorial and tropical areas.	Traditionally areas of shifting cultivation. Not naturally fertile, but can be productive with addition of lime and fertilizers and good management. Can become infertile quickly.
Utisols	Soils with a B horizon of deposition, usually yellow-brown in colour from iron. Deeply weathered bedrock.	Tropical and subtropical forests.	Not naturally fertile, but can be productive with careful management.
Vertisols	Clay soils which crack and move with a heaving movement as they dry. Horizons not strongly marked. Soil 'turns' as surface material is washed into cracks and cracks close in the wet season.	Grassland and savanna.	Fertile, but difficult to cultivate because it is heavy and sticky when wet, and develops deep cracks when dry, e.g. black cotton soils of USA. Much left as savanna grassland.

Alfisols	Non-acid soils with grey, brown or red top soil, and a marked B horizon. Soil water available more than half the year. Some leaching in the A horizon.	Woodland and Mediterranean types of vegetation.	Fairly fertile and productive for farming. High in soil water and carbonate content. Farming has been continuous for centuries in parts of western Europe and China.
Spodosols	Soils with a clear horizon of deposition, dark in colour and sometimes cemented as **hard pan**. Above is a leached, ash-grey coloured horizon. Acid and low in plant nutrients.	Coniferous forest.	Infertile and may be badly drained where hard pan occurs, leading to standing water. Can be productive when fertilized and properly managed, e.g. deep ploughed to break up hard pan, lime and fertilizers added.
Mollisols	Deep, dark brown to black surface horizon. Loose structure when dry. Strong in calcium and clay.	Grasslands of mid-latitudes.	Naturally fertile, with good crumb structure and a high level of calcium and other carbonates. The great grain producing areas of the world. Once open grazing for cattle.
Aridisols	Soils with no soil water for long periods. No significant darkening of upper horizons by humus.	Scattered desert plants, short-lived grasses, forbs, cacti and shrubs.	Traditional use by nomads and their grazing animals. Can be productive where water is available.

Figure 3.24 Characteristics of the ten soil orders

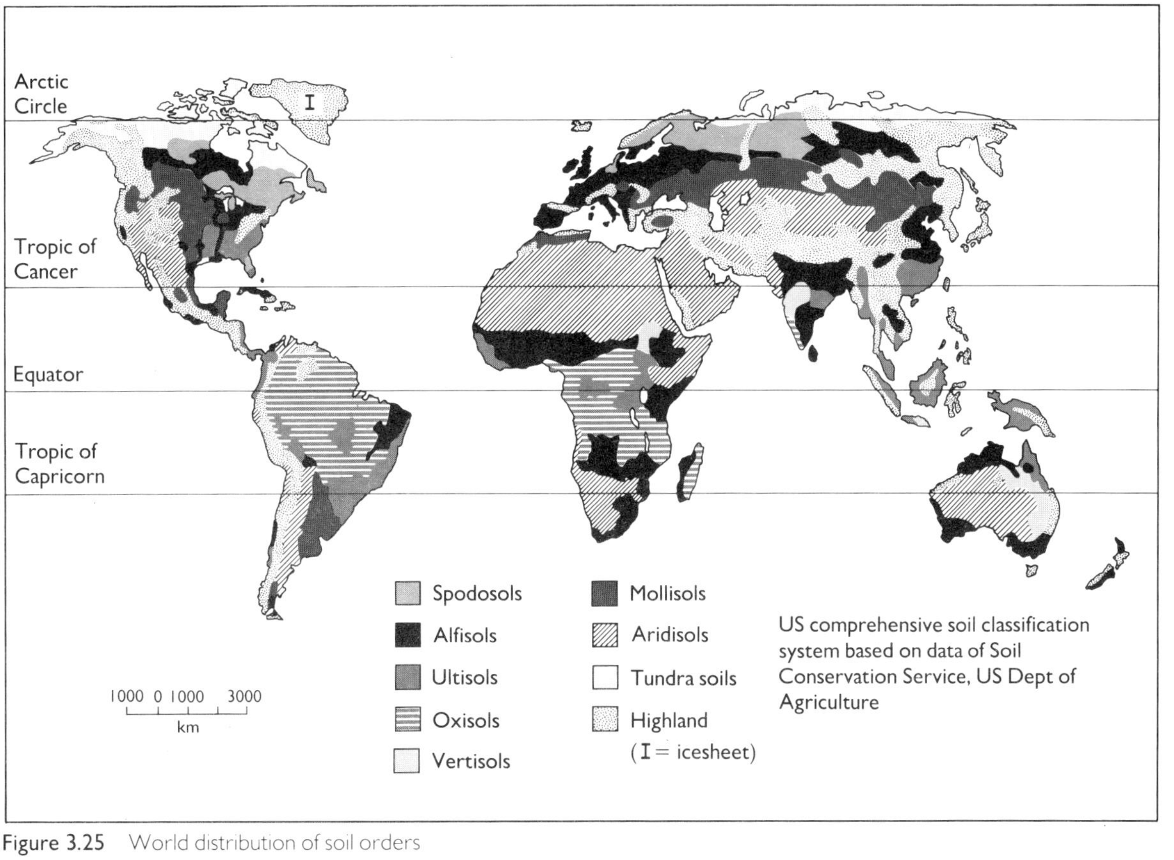

Figure 3.25 World distribution of soil orders

▲ **18** ■ Study Figure 3.23 and answer the following questions as fully as you can:

a What happens in the eluviation zone?
b What happens in the illuviation zone?
c What is a 'transitional zone'? What do you think affects what happens in the transitional zone?
d Why is the rock called the 'parent material'?
e What causes the organic matter to decompose?
f What causes the decomposed organic matter to be washed down in horizon A1?
g Why does material collect in horizons B1 and B2?
h Describe what would happen if the vegetation cover was removed and the soil was ploughed and planted with the same crop for a number of years.

▲ **19** ■ Get some garden top soil and a glass jar.

a **i)** Quarter fill the jar with soil.
ii) Add water until the jar is about three-quarters full (can you see any air bubbles given off?).
iii) Cover the jar and shake it well.
iv) Let the soil settle for a day or so.

b **i)** Draw the jar and the layers of soil in it.
ii) Describe the different layers in the jar. (Measure the thickness of the layers. Describe the size of the particles in each layer. Describe the colour of each layer. What is left floating on the top of the water?)
iii) Explain why air bubbles were given off when you added the water.

c **i)** Repeat this work with different kinds of soil and compare your results.
ii) Try to explain why there are differences between the soils.

▲ **20** ■ Take some garden soil.

a **i)** Rub some soil between your fingers. Describe what you notice.
ii) Wet a little soil and rub it in your palm. Does it leave a stain? Does it roll together into a lump?
iii) Put a single soil crumb on a sheet of paper. Squash it with your finger. Are the particles well stuck together? What do you notice about the paper afterwards?
iv) Look at the roots of a weed you have pulled out of the soil. Describe the amount of soil which is sticking to the roots. Examine the way in which the roots are connected to the soil crumbs.

b **i)** Explain why some parts of the soil are gritty and other particles of the soil feel smooth. Which type of particle makes the soil roll into a lump?
ii) Explain how the particles of the soil crumb are stuck together.
iii) Draw a diagram of a single soil crumb with a root attached to it. Label the diagram to show how the crumb is held together and how the root is attached to it.

▲ **21** ■ **a** **i)** Choose two areas in your school field or a nearby park. One area should be where many people walk on the ground or the grass, the other areas should be where few people walk.
ii) Take two empty food cans of the same size and cut the bottom out of each.
iii) Push and screw the cans into the ground to a depth of about 3 cm.
iv) Pour 250 ml of water into each can and measure the time it takes for the water to sink into the ground.

b You may find there are differences in the length of time taken for the water to soak in. Explain why this is so. It could be because the soil types in your two areas are different. You can test this in the ways described in Activity 19. If the soil is the same in the two sites, explain why the number of people walking on the soil may be important.

c Why may the results of experiments like this be important for people who design farm tractors? Give reasons.

▲ **22** **a** Draw two sketch maps of Africa.
i) On the first map show the climate types according to Köppen's classification (Figure 3.18).
ii) On the second map, show the soil types according to Figure 3.25.

b For each soil type shown on your map:
i) Describe the soil.
ii) State which climatic zone it is found in.
iii) Explain the effects the climate has had on the formation of the soil.
iv) Look at your two maps. How closely do the patterns of climate and soil types match? For each soil type which does not seem to be affected by the climate, explain how the soil type was formed.

Ecosystems

All living things depend on each other and on their environments. Plants, animals and the physical world exchange energy and matter between themselves. The various groups of plants, animals and environments found over the Earth's surface are called **ecosystems**. An ecosystem is like a games field and its players. The players and the grass are the living organisms. They interact with each other and with their coaches and groundsmen. The changing rooms and the weather are their non-living environment. The living organisms are sometimes called the **biotic organisms**. The non-living parts are often called the **abiotic environment**.

Figure 3.26 is a model of an ecosystem. In a natural ecosystem, matter includes compounds or elements such as water, oxygen, hydrogen, carbon, nitrogen, sulphur and phosphorus. These are all important for plant growth. Energy is light and heat energy from the sun. The energy from the sun is changed into chemical energy in plants. The chemical energy can then be transferred from one organism to another through the **food chain**.

The food chain works like this. Plants are stores of chemical energy. The plants are eaten by **herbivores** (animals which eat plants). Some of the energy is used up by the plant eaters, but some is stored in their bodies. The herbivores are then eaten by **carnivores** (flesh eaters) and **omnivores** (animals which eat plants and flesh).

Dead plants and the wastes and dead bodies of animals are broken down so that the nutrients can be returned to the soil. The plants and animals are broken down by **macroconsumers** such as insects, worms and snails and **microconsumers** such as bacteria and fungi.

Ecosystems can be many different sizes. The biomes mentioned earlier in this chapter are examples of ecosystems at a large scale. Smaller examples include a stream, a watershed, a forest, a salt marsh, a freshwater estuary, a freshwater pond, a marsh, a swamp, a sand beach, a rocky shore and so on. All these examples are affected by one another. In Chapter 2 you saw how a stream can be affected by changes anywhere in its drainage basin. You also learnt how the marine ecosystem of the eastern Mediterranean has been changed by the changes in the flow of the river Nile.

Figure 3.27 (overleaf) is an example of a prairie ecosystem. It shows the flows of energy and matter through the ecosystem.

Energy from the sun enters the ecosystem as sunlight. Most of the light energy is reflected or radiated back into space as heat. The prairie grasses use about 1% of the light energy. Most of the energy is used by the grasses for transpiration. Only a small part of the 1% is used to make more grass. Of all the grass which grows, only a little is actually eaten by the prairie dogs (the **consumers**).

▲ ■ **23** Look at Figures 3.18, 3.24 and 3.25.

a Draw up a table to show which soil orders are strongly linked to climate zones and which orders do not seem to be linked to climate zones.

b i) Which soil order is naturally fertile?

ii) Describe the area of the world in which this fertile soil order is mainly found.

iii) In which climate zone is this soil order most commonly found?

c Briefly explain what makes some soils less fertile than others.

▲ ■ **24** On a certain mountain top, the soil is only a few centimetres thick.

In a forest at the foot of the mountain, the soil is many metres thick.

Using the information from this chapter and Chapter 2 give as many reasons as you can why there is this difference in soil depth.

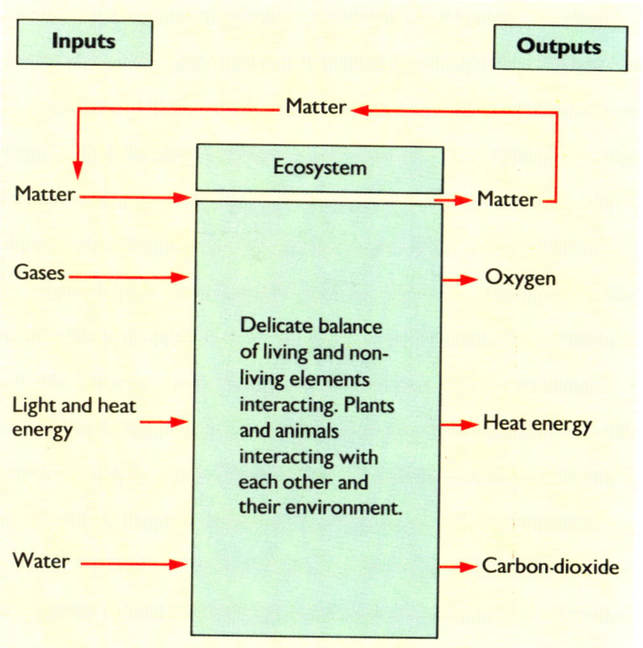

Figure 3.26 A simple model of an ecosystem

Most of the food energy consumed by the prairie dog is used to keep the animal warm and to give it energy to move. Much energy is lost to space as heat. A small amount of food energy is used by the prairie dog for growth. The small amount of grass that is converted into prairie dog tissue is available to the next stage in the food chain – the black-footed ferret and the prairie falcon. These animals use most of this food energy for warmth and movement. They only store a small part in their new tissues. If there are no other animals which prey on the black-footed ferrets and prairie falcons, then their dead bodies, the dead bodies of uneaten prairie dogs, the unused parts of the prairie dogs which were eaten and the grass which was not eaten are decomposed. The warmth caused by the rotting transfers the rest of the heat which came into the ecosystem as sunlight, back into space.

Figure 3.28 shows a salt marsh ecosystem. This is rather more complicated than the prairie ecosystem.

Some ecosystems are very complicated. The more complicated an ecosystem is, the easier it is for the balance of the ecosystem to be disturbed. In the case of the prairie ecosystem prairie dogs were the only energy source for the black-footed ferret. As the prairie dog towns, or burrows, have been broken up by ploughing, the black-footed ferret has become nearly extinct.

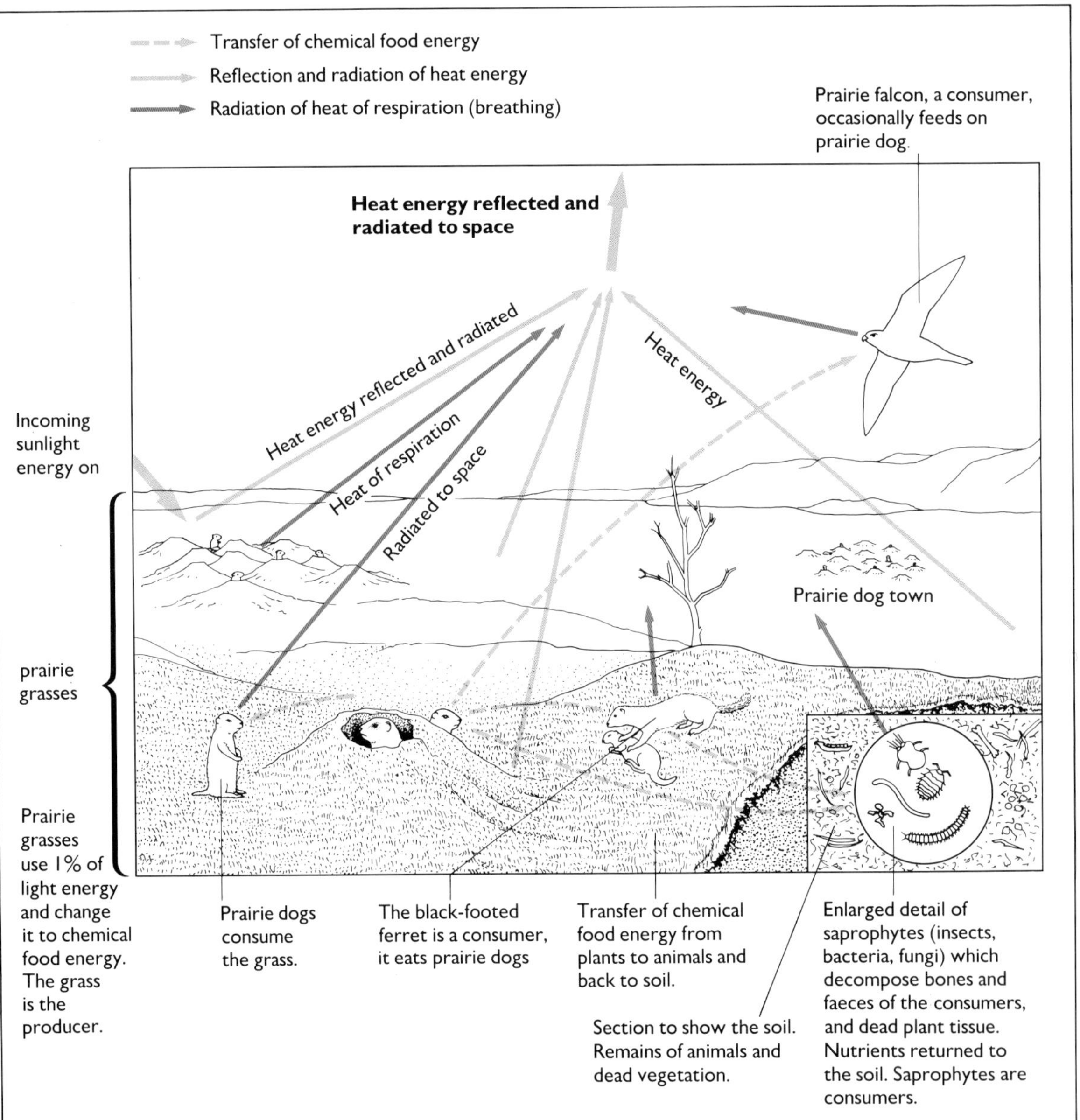

Figure 3.27 Energy flow through a simple prairie ecosystem

Activities

■ **25** Study Figures 3.27 and 3.28 which show two types of ecosystems. Draw a flow diagram like Figure 3.28 to show the different levels in the food chain of the prairie ecosystem from prairie dogs to black-footed ferrets.

▲ ■ **26** Study Figure 3.28 which shows the salt marsh ecosystem.

a Write a description of the ways in which energy is transferred from sunlight through the salt marsh ecosystem and eventually is lost back into space.

b Describe what would happen if:

i) The number of marsh hawks and owls increased.

ii) The number of marsh hawks and owls was reduced by egg collecting.

iii) The salt marsh becomes polluted by chemicals – e.g. by a large oil spillage.

How energy moves through an ecosystem

Life on Earth would not be possible if plants did not convert carbon dioxide and water into carbohydrates, oxygen and fats. This is called **photosynthesis**. **Chlorophyll** (which makes plants green) can change carbon dioxide and water into carbohydrate and oxygen so long as there is light energy available.

Photosynthesis makes plants into producers of energy. The energy stored in the plants is then transferred to the consumers which eat plants. There is usually a large number of first order consumers, fewer second order consumers and still fewer third order consumers. The levels of consumers are called **trophic levels**. This comes from the Greek word 'trophe' which means food. The levels are called this because each level of consumer in the food chain stores less energy than the lower levels. Energy is finally lost when it is radiated back into space as heat.

Figure 3.29 (overleaf) shows a food chain with a sparrow hawk as the top consumer. In an oak woodland there are millions of tiny creatures such as greenfly, worms, ants and caterpillars which live on living or dead vegetation. These tiny creatures provide the food for large numbers of small birds such as sparrows, robins

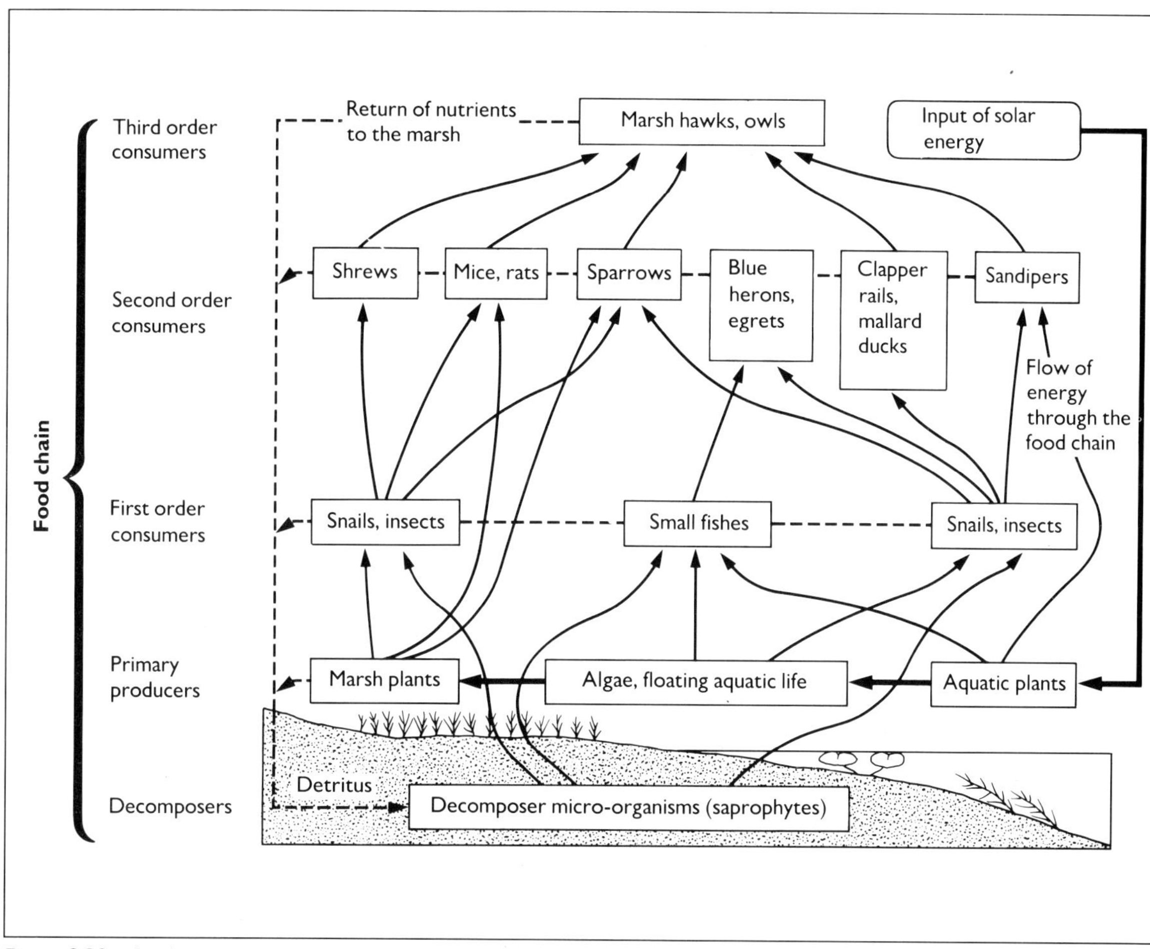

Figure 3.28 A salt marsh ecosystem

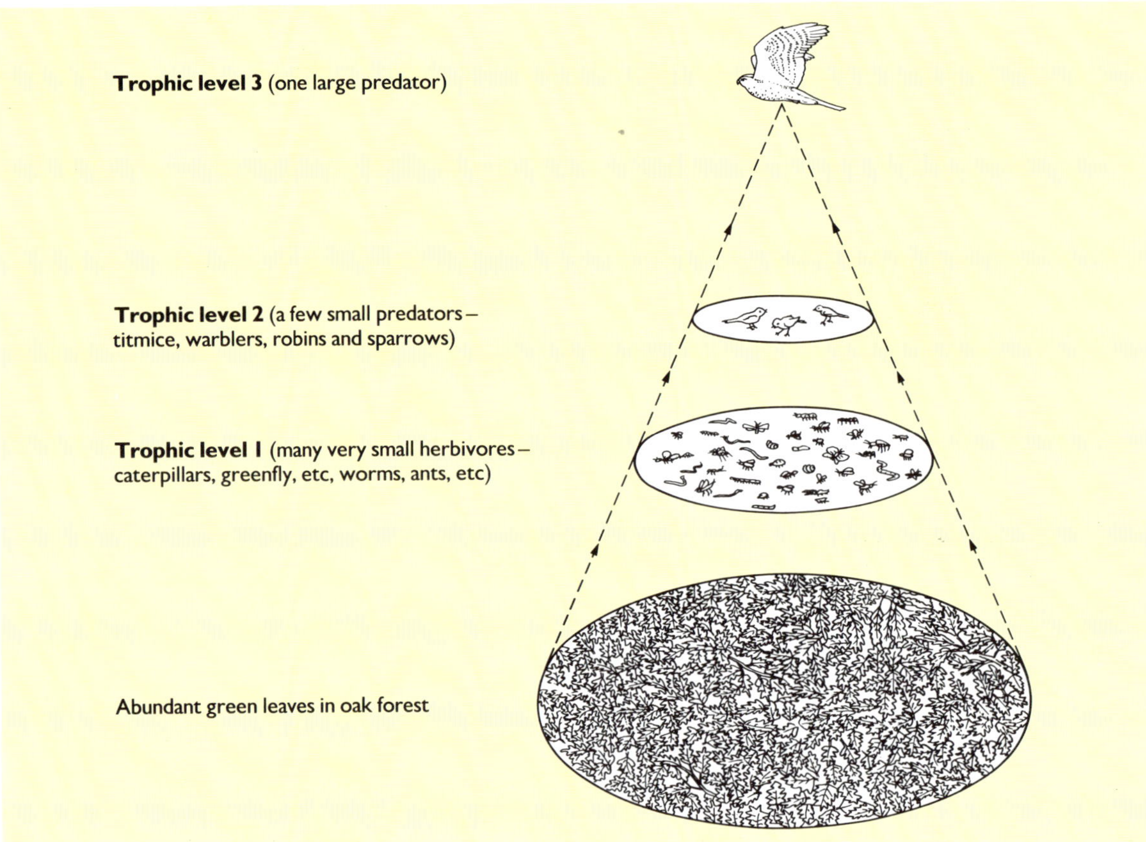

Figure 3.29 A simple food chain

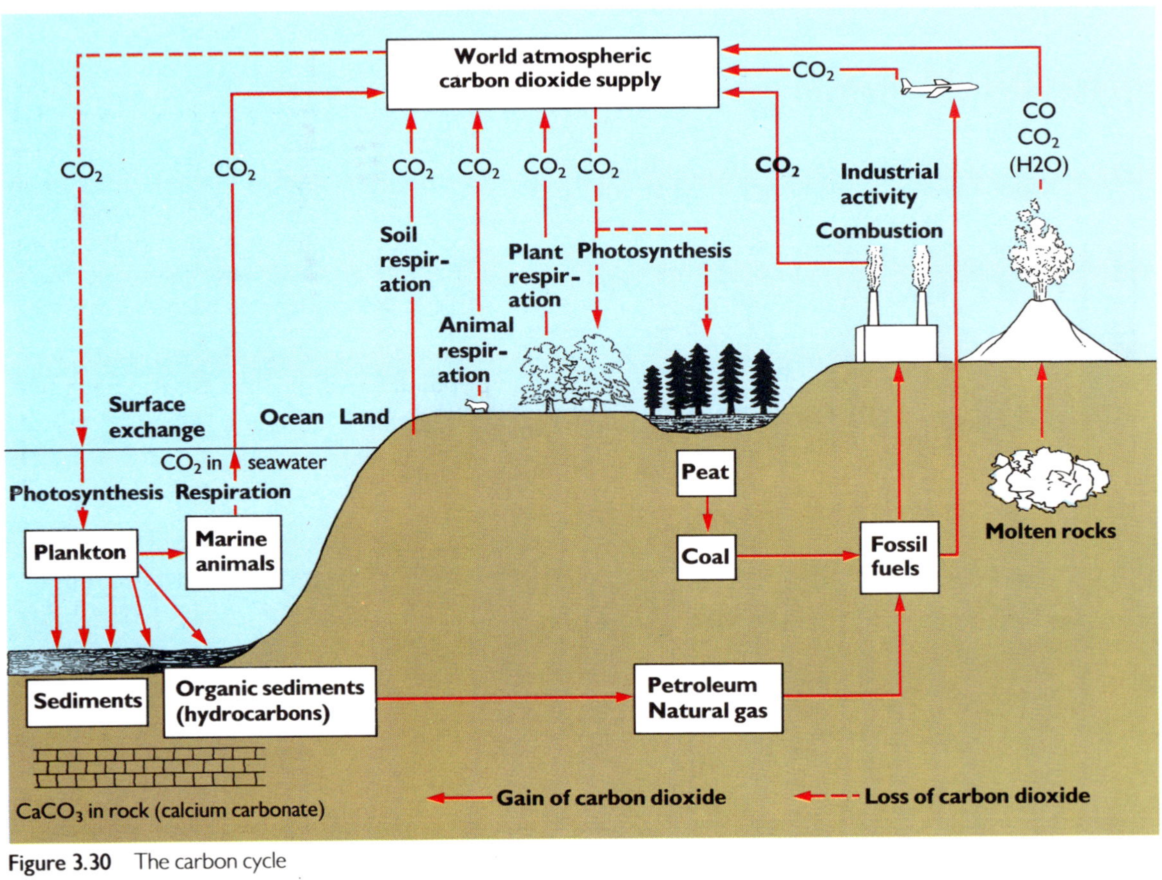

Figure 3.30 The carbon cycle

and titmice. In any one area of woodland, there is probably only one large predator – the sparrow hawk – which lives on these smaller birds as well as other small animals. In this way, the energy from the sun which is stored in the leaves of the oak woodland moves up the food chain to the sparrow hawk.

Matter also moves through an ecosystem. Matter is not lost to the system like energy, but it is **recycled**. Carbon is one of the main parts of carbohydrate. Figure 3.30 shows the **carbon cycle**. You will notice that carbon itself does not appear in the diagram. This is because it is mainly stored as carbon dioxide in the atmosphere, or as dissolved carbon dioxide in the oceans.

Respiration (breathing) is very important in the carbon cycle. Animals take in oxygen and release carbon dioxide into the atmosphere. Plants take in carbon dioxide and by the process of photosynthesis release oxygen into the atmosphere. Volcanoes also release carbon dioxide. People can increase the amount of carbon dioxide in the atmosphere by burning peat, oil, coal and other fossil fuels. People can also increase the amount of carbon dioxide in the atmosphere by cutting down trees and other types of vegetation. When trees or plants are cut down it reduces the amount of carbon dioxide being changed into oxygen by photosynthesis.

Activities

▲ 27 Look at Figure 3.29.
■ ● A small amount of a pesticide spray falls on the leaves of an oak woodland. It is not enough to kill the worms and insects living there. Eventually the sparrow hawk dies from the poison. Explain how this could happen.
What are your views on pesticides?

▲ 28 Study Figure 3.30.
■ **a** Draw a table with two columns.
i) Head the first column 'Gains of carbon dioxide'.
ii) Head the second column 'Losses of carbon dioxide'.
iii) List the ways in which the atmosphere gains and loses carbon dioxide.
b i) What kinds of rocks contain large amounts of calcium carbonate?
ii) There is one other major form of combustion not shown on the diagram. What is it?

People and ecosystems

Natural ecosystems are very delicately balanced. It is very easy for human beings to upset this balance with their modern technology. Sometimes people have changed ecosystems deliberately.

For example, huge areas of the prairies were changed from a grassland ecosystem to farmland growing wheat. Some species of animals have expanded in numbers, while many others have become extinct. People also alter the inorganic environment. Dry areas are irrigated. Damp areas are drained. Large areas are covered in concrete.

Human beings have also changed ecosystems accidentally. The accidental changes can be divided into five groups:

1. Where people have changed the vegetation in drainage basins and speeded up erosion and deposition.
2. Where people have farmed the soil or grazed animals and caused changes in the structure and fertility of the soil.
3. Where people have changed the ground water and surface water by pollution of various sorts. This may include fertilizers and pesticides as well as more 'accidental' problems such as acid rain.
4. Where people have changed the climate. This may be at a very small scale where wind breaks of trees are planted or a reservoir is built (remember that water heats up and cools down more slowly than land). At a larger scale, a power station pouring hot water into a river or lake can cause warming of the environment many miles away.
5. Where people alter plant and animal populations. This may cause some species to become extinct. Grey squirrels were brought to Britain in 1876 as pets to be kept in parks. Since they are bigger than the red squirrels which were already here, the red squirrels have nearly been wiped out. Another example is Giant Hogweed. This was brought to Britain as an ornamental plant but has spread so much that it is destroying traditional river bank ecosystems. (This problem is described in more detail in Figure 3.32.)

There are many ways in which human beings have changed ecosystems. Here are three examples in a little more detail.

Example 1: Forest clearance

Figure 3.31 Deforested hillside in Amazonia forest

Human beings have changed the land by removing forests for many centuries. This is called **deforestation**. Timber is used as a resource in many ways. In the UK it is used for building, furniture and paper. In many parts of the world it is still an important fuel. Woodland has also been cut down to make space for farming. In the Middle Ages, most of western Europe was woodland.

Today, most deforestation is taking place in the tropics. About 11 million hectares of forest is cut down every year. This is equal to about half the total area of the UK.

The cutting down of these forests has very serious effects on other parts of the tropical forest ecosystem and may also affect the whole world ecosystem.

First, iron and aluminium oxides may accumulate in the soil due to more rapid weathering. Eluviation may become faster and the nutrients will be leached out of the upper horizon of the soil. The wetting and drying of the soil may cause the surface to become hard and cracked. Soil like this is called **laterite**. Laterite soil is very difficult to farm.

Second, soil erosion may become much faster. The trees normally protect the soil. When the trees are removed the soil is open to weathering and heavy rain splash. This can lead to such severe soil erosion that mud flows and landslides can happen.

Third, the removal of forests can cause an increase in the amount of carbon dioxide in the atmosphere. This could cause the heat balance of the atmosphere to change. Carbon dioxide absorbs heat energy from the sun as it passes through the atmosphere. By AD 2050, this could mean a rise of between 1.5°C and 3.0°C. This would lengthen the growing season for cereals. However, it could also make the deserts grow even larger. It could make the ice caps and glaciers melt. The level of the sea would then rise and many coastal areas could be flooded.

Figure 3.31 shows a deforested hillside in the Amazonia Forest of Brazil. Some landowners in Amazonia are in such a hurry to clear the land that they just burn the timber.

Activities

▲29 ■ Make a list of as many reasons as you can think of to explain why natural vegetation protects the soil from erosion and keeps it in good condition.

▲30 ■ Explain how deforestation in a river basin can increase the rate of soil erosion.

Example 2: Pollution and acid rain

Pollution is the name given to material put into the natural world in such large quantities that ecosystems are upset. Pollution can affect the air, the soil or the water, but is usually part of a cycle. This means that once one part of the ecosystem is affected, the pollution eventually affects all the other parts. This may mean that what starts as air pollution will eventually pollute the soil and the water.

There are some natural sources of pollution. These include volcanoes, earthquakes, dust storms and salt sea spray. The chief cause of pollution, however, is people.

Human beings have major effects on the biosphere. They gather things up, extract minerals from rocks, take nutrients from soils, and move and dump materials. They cover large areas of the ground with concrete. They put large quantities of natural and artificial substances into the biosphere, which can pollute rainfall (this is known as **acid rain**). These include phosphorus from sewage, nitrogen monoxide from vehicles, sulphur dioxide from furnaces and boilers, hydrocarbon from oil spillage, poisons of all kinds from pesticides, and radioactive fallout from nuclear weapons and power stations. There is also the waste heat from our homes, factories and cities.

Example 3: Giant Hogweed

Many of us have seen Giant Hogweed which grows along the banks of many streams and is also found along country roadsides (Figure 3.32). If you have touched the leaves or the stems you may have suffered afterwards!

The sap of the plant makes human skin very sensitive to light, so that the sun can cause rashes and blisters. Severe cases need hospital treatment. Children are particularly attracted to these spectacular plants, which are true giants with leaves 1 metre or more wide and flowering stems 3 or 4 metres tall. Children often use these reddish, bristly stems as 'telescopes' or blowpipes and then suffer from blistering of their mouths and eyelids.

Giant Hogweed was brought into the UK as an ornamental garden shrub in the late 19th century. Now it threatens other plants and animals by dominating river banks and leaving easily eroded soil when it dies back in winter.

Giant Hogweeds produce about 5000 seeds each. Many of these are shed into rivers and streams and are carried downstream where they then grow in silt on the flood plains and river banks.

Giant Hogweed has become such a problem that special leaflets have been produced to help farmers and local authorities control it. Part of a leaflet about the plant is given in Figure 3.32.

Activity

▲31 a i) Write a list to summarize the reasons
■ why Giant Hogweed is a problem.
● ii) Explain how Giant Hogweed seeds are spread.
iii) Study the map of the pattern of Giant Hogweed before 1974 and since 1974 in Figure 3.32. Describe the pattern of the new areas of Giant Hogweed since 1974.
iv) Explain why whole river catchment areas should be chosen for control programmes.

b i) Describe how Giant Hogweed can change a river bank ecosystem.
ii) Describe the effects on a river bank ecosystem of each of the possible ways of controlling Giant Hogweed.

Methods of control

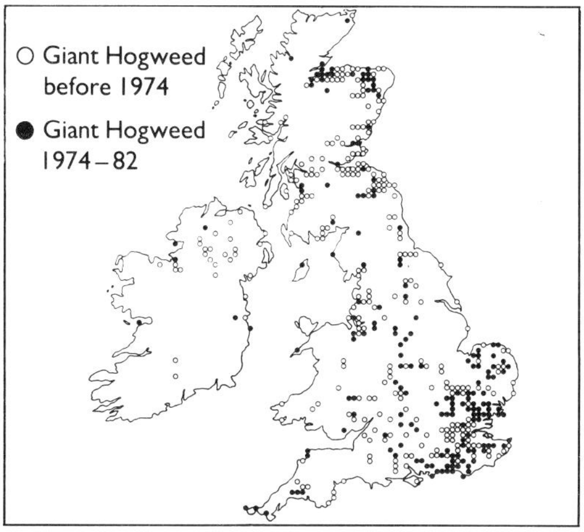

Cutting – Individual plants may be killed by cutting them below ground level with a spade. Cutting at or above ground level allows abundant growth from the base and is seldom worthwhile. The method is laborious and may miss younger plants. Adequate protective clothing, including rubber gloves and boots, should be worn and contact of the plant with the face should be avoided.

Ploughing – Seedlings and young plants spreading into agricultural land are normally completely killed by ploughing. Ploughing is not, however, practicable in most situations where giant hogweed becomes a problem.

Grazing – Where practicable, giant hogweed may be controlled by grazing with cattle or pigs, which relish the plant and suffer no ill effects.

Herbicide Application – The best herbicide so far tested for control of mature giant hogweed is *glyphosate* (Roundup). This is non-selective, therefore care must be taken to minimise deposition of the chemical on other plants. For example, it is not suitable for spraying from machines that produce very fine droplets which are subject to drift.

Figure 3.32 Giant Hogweed

4
Earning a living

Systems made by people

Chapters 2 and 3 describe the world systems which work well without human beings interfering. Mountains are built and rocks are broken down into soils without any human help. In fact, when people do interfere, they often stop the system working properly.

Now let's look at the kinds of world systems which have been developed by human beings. Let's begin by describing a very simple example of an **economic system**.

Imagine how a factory worker spends her wages. She probably spends her money partly on food, partly on clothes and partly on rent or mortgage repayments. She may also manage to save a little of her earnings in a bank savings account. Although she spends money in shops, we know that the shops get their stocks of goods from the producers. You can see this in Figure 4.1 which shows the flow of money from a factory worker's wages through the economic system.

Some goods, such as foods like eggs, come straight from a farm. As the farmer does not get the eggs from anyone else, he is called the **primary producer**. Farming or agriculture is part of the **primary sector** of the country's economy.

Shops buy other goods, such as clothes, from a wholesaler. The wholesaler buys them from the factory. The clothing factory buys its cloth from a textile factory or textile mill. If the cloth is made of cotton or wool, the raw materials will have come from cotton plantations or sheep farms. The making of goods such as cloth or clothes belongs to the manufacturing sector or **secondary sector** of the economy.

The shops which sell food and clothes do not usually produce the raw materials. Neither do they make their own goods. They just sell the goods which other people have made. The whole business of getting things from the producers to the people who want to buy them is called **commerce**. Commerce includes the bank which lends the money, the driver who delivers the goods, the insurance companies who insure the goods, the warehouses which store them until they are needed and the shops which offer them to the public for sale. All these people and organizations are part of the commercial or **tertiary sector** of the economy.

Some economists say there is a fourth level in the economy. They call this the **quaternary sector**. This sector includes all the people who plan how the economy should run. It includes financiers who encourage investments in

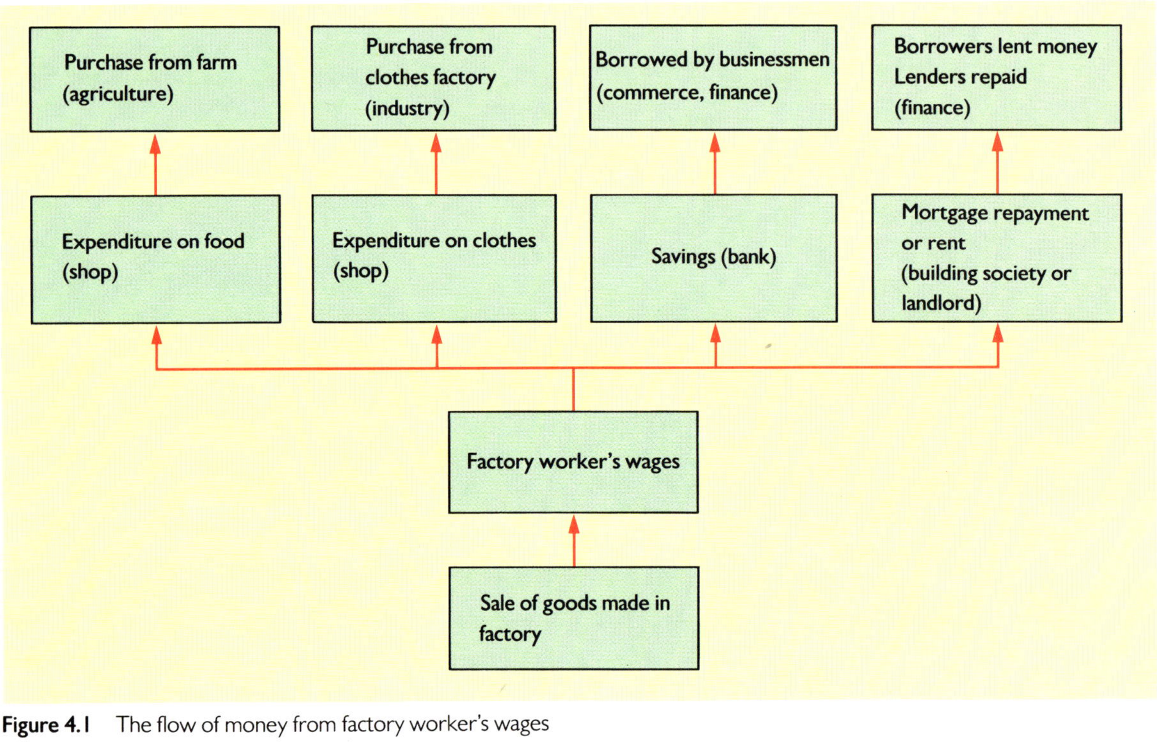

Figure 4.1 The flow of money from factory worker's wages

particular industries, the scientists who research and develop new products, consultants who advise large firms like ICI and the top managers of the economy.

The four sectors of the economy of a country are shown in Figure 4.2. You will notice that there are arrows pointing in both directions between each sector. The upward arrow shows that the goods which are sold in the tertiary sector started off as raw materials in the primary sector. The downward arrow shows that decisions made in the quaternary sector can have effects in all the other sectors. For example, the decision to build a new Ford car plant in Spain has an effect in all the other sectors. (You can find out more about this in Chapter 6.)

A country's economy is a giant system for producing goods (e.g. cars) and services (e.g. television programmes). It is also a giant system for providing people with jobs and a way of earning their living.

Whichever way you look at it, every part of an economy is linked to every other part. Look back at Figure 4.1. The factory worker receives wages from her employers. Her employers get the money by selling the electrical goods produced in the factory where she works. If the factory worker decides to buy clothes, she becomes part of a chain which links her to the clothes shop, back to the clothes factory, back to the cloth factory, and back to the producer of the original fibre.

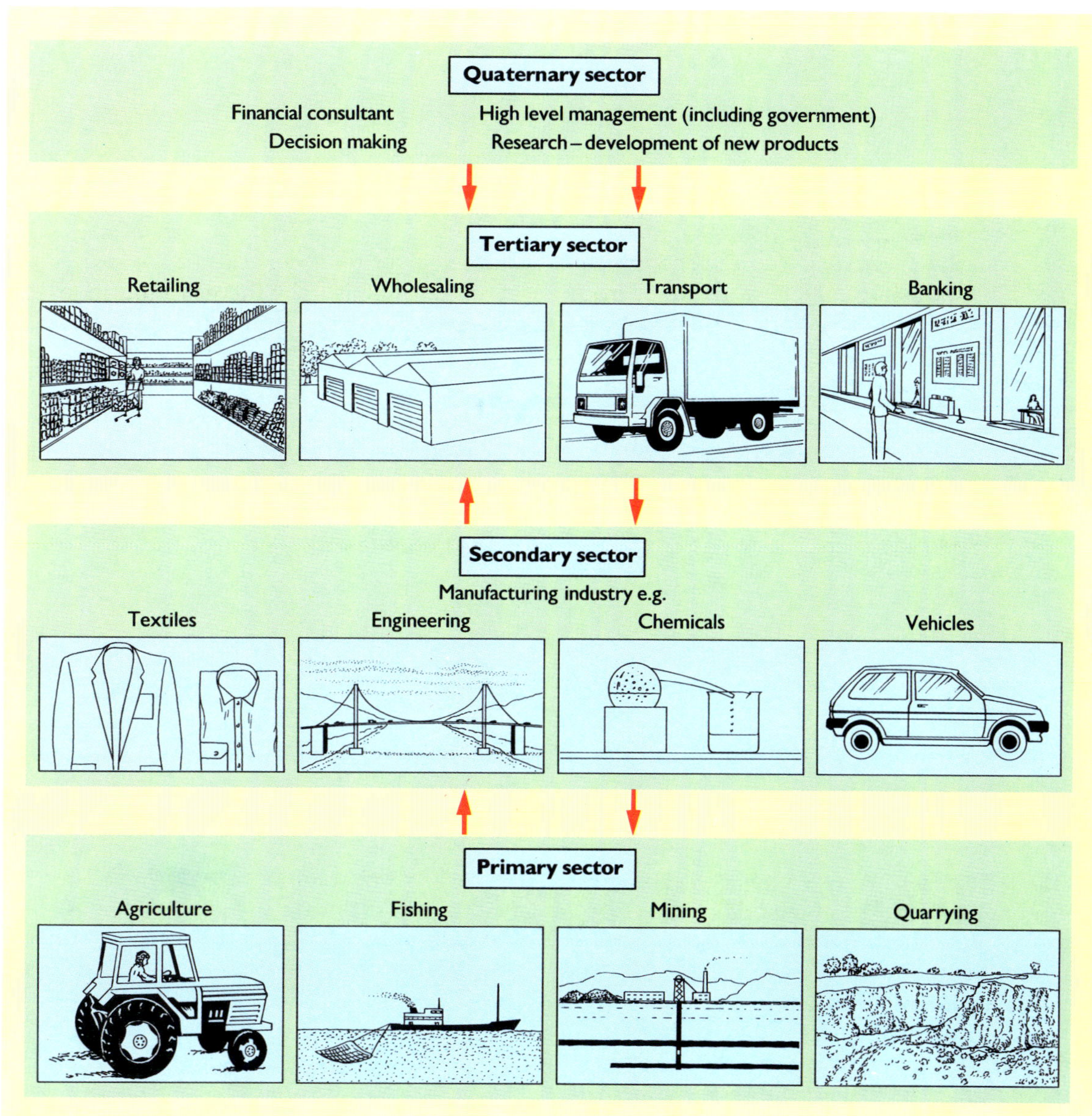

Figure 4.2 The four sectors of the economy

Activity

▲ 1 a Here is a list of economic activities. Make a
■ table like Figure 4.3.
Write down each activity in the correct column.

coalmining
banking
quarrying
car making
nursing
picture painting
financial decision making
management consulting
road hauling
teaching
calculator manufacturing
systems analysing
oil prospecting
broiler house operating
airline piloting
farming
stockbroking
computer programming
landscape gardening
oil refining

b Some activities could be put into two columns. Explain why each of these activities is difficult to place.

Primary sector	Secondary sector	Tertiary sector	Quaternary sector

Figure 4.3 The classification of economic activity

Types of economy

In the last section we saw how a worker spent her money on food, clothing and shelter (her house or flat). These are the three basic needs of human beings all over the world. The importance of each of the needs may be different in different parts of the world. For example, in a hot climate, clothes are not so important for keeping warm.

Although everybody has the same basic needs, people do not all try to satisfy their needs in the same way. In the UK and many other countries in the world, there is a **money economy**. The factory worker in our example sells her time and skill in the electrical goods factory. She uses the money she earns as wages to buy the food, clothing and shelter she needs.

There are areas in the world where a money economy is not very important. For example in New Guinea there are people living in villages who build their own houses, grow their own food and make their own clothes. They sell some plants or animals to outsiders for money. Then they use the money to buy things they cannot make themselves, like steel knives. The kind of economy where people satisfy most of their own needs is called a **subsistence economy**. There are not many people left in the world with a completely subsistence economy, but there are still many groups of people who live entirely on the food they can grow or catch themselves (see Chapter 5).

The countries of the world can be divided into countries with a mainly money economy and countries with a mainly subsistence economy. Countries where the economy is based on money usually use a lot of machinery and power supplies. Because each person can produce a lot, the average income of the people is high. These countries are often called **developed countries**.

Countries where the economy is still partly subsistence usually use very little machinery or power. Because output per person is low, the average income of the people is low. These countries are often called **developing countries**.

It is important to remember that the words 'developing' and 'developed' tell us something about the kind of *economy* in different countries. These words do not tell us anything about how civilized a country is, or how old its traditions and culture are. For example, India is a developing country but it had architecture, art, music, dance and literature many years before the Greeks and Romans.

It is difficult for nearby countries or areas to have different types of economies without being affected by one another. Once people start mixing, they soon start to copy one another. The case study of the Apa Tani people of north-east India shows how quickly change can come.

Case Study

The Apa Tani people

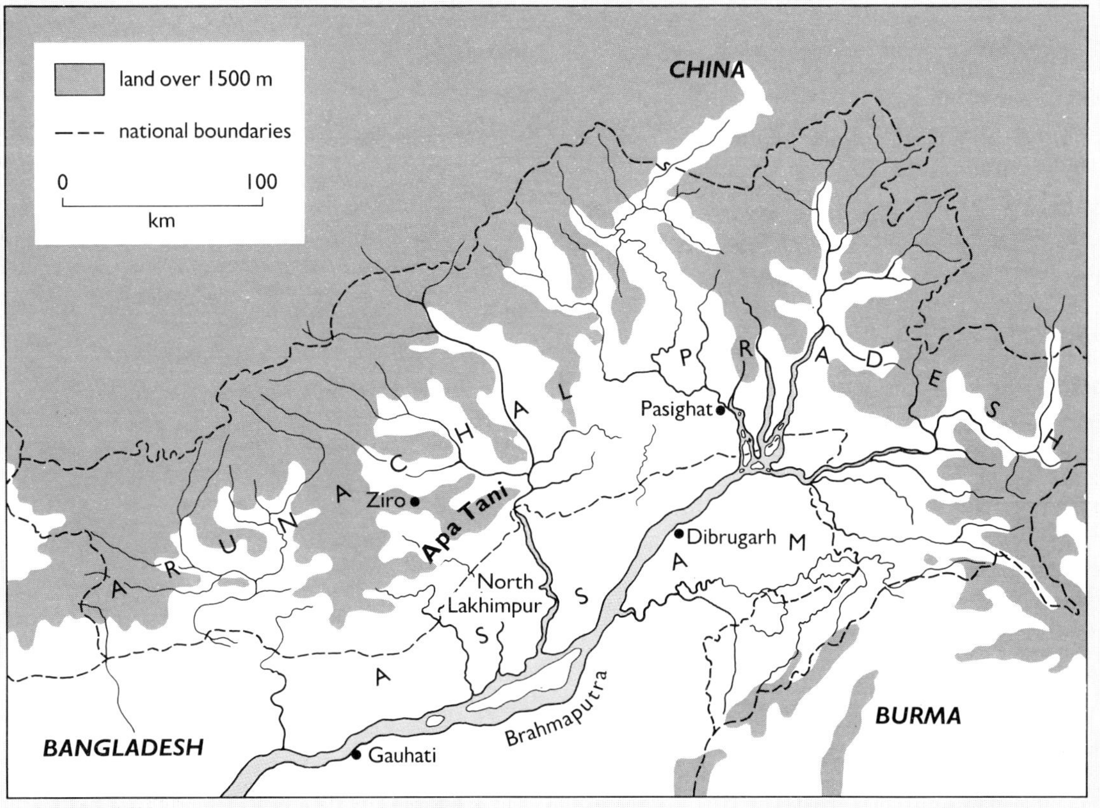

Figure 4.4 The location of the Apa Tani valley in N.E. India

The Apa Tani people live in the State of Arunachal Pradesh in north-east India. They live in a valley only 3 km wide and 10 km long. This is so small that it could not be shown on a map of the whole of India. Figure 4.4 shows a small part of India in the foothills of the Himalayas. The valley of the Apa Tani can just be seen.

An **anthropologist** (a person who studies the lives and customs of groups of people) visited the valley three times – in 1944, in 1962 and in 1978 – to study the way of life of the Apa Tani.

In 1944 there were no roads into the valley. The only way in was through the forests growing on the hills all around. It seemed that no one had ever visited the area before. The Apa Tani people grew their own food which was mainly rice. They built their own houses and made their own clothes. They governed themselves by a village council. Their only trade was to barter their spare rice for pigs and cattle with the people who lived in the Nishi Valley.

In 1962 the anthropologist went back. He found that the Indian government had taken over the whole area and had built a new town at Ziro. The Indian Government had made Ziro the administrative centre for the whole area. Schools had been built. Some of the Apa Tani people who had done well at school were employed by the Indian Government as administrators.

By 1978, on his third visit, the anthropologist found that a road had been built from Ziro to the River Brahmaputra in Assam. This had caused a growth in trade between the Apa Tani people and the 'outside world'. Ziro had become an important town with 59 shops! Instead of a subsistence economy and some bartering, the Apa Tani people had started to use money. Some of the Apa Tani people had gone on to higher education in universities and colleges. Some of these people had become government officials. Two of the Apa Tani people had become doctors and one had become an air force pilot. There were other changes too. Cars, jeeps, lorries and motor scooters were now in the streets of Ziro. However, traditional crafts such as weaving, pottery and clothes making were beginning to die out because the people could buy pots, pans and clothes which had been made in factories.

The Apa Tani way of life changed. Both men and women used to be involved in growing food. Now, the men worked at other jobs and the farming was left to the women.

Finally, there were more 'mixed marriages' because the Apa Tani people were meeting the Nishi Valley people as well as people from other parts of India.

Although there have been changes, many of the old customs and traditions have been saved because the Indian Government has prevented too many people from outside going into this area and this has protected the Apa Tani way of life from too much competition.

There have been many changes in the Apa Tani way of life. The economy has changed from a subsistence economy to a money economy and the economy has become a little more developed than it was before. This sort of development nearly always happens when a remote area is linked to more developed areas by road, rail or air.

The development of an economy is not all good. Almost always it means that traditional crafts are lost and the farming pattern changes. It also means that people may leave the area if they think they can earn more or do better somewhere else.

Activities

▲ **2 a** Describe
- i) a subsistence economy
- ii) a barter economy
- iii) a money economy.

b For each of these types of economy, explain
i) the advantages ii) the disadvantages.

c All sorts of things have been used as 'money' at some time. They include beads, cattle, shells, cigarettes, pieces of metal or paper and plastic cards (Figure 4.5). There are six things which are important for something to be 'money'. Money should be:

1) portable	4) acceptable
2) durable	5) scarce
3) uniform	6) divisible

i) Write a sentence to explain why each of these six things is important for money.
ii) Explain why each of the examples in Figure 4.5 makes good or bad 'money'.

▲ ■ ● **3 a** Why is it difficult for subsistence or barter economies to continue in the modern world? Give reasons.

b Write a paragraph to explain the advantages and disadvantages of modern money economies.

Figure 4.5 Different kinds of money that have been used

World differences in development

We can use the amount of money which moves through the economy of a country as a way of measuring how developed that country is. If the value of all the work done in each sector of the economy is added together, the result is the **Gross Domestic Product** of the country. This is often called the GDP.

Since the goods and services which are included in the GDP are produced by people, you may expect that countries with large populations produce more than countries with small populations. This would be true if every worker produced the same amount every year in every country. However, workers in different countries do not produce the same amount.

For example, the USSR has a GDP of $1.28 million and Japan has a GDP of $1.23 million. These figures seem very similar. But the USSR has a population of 272 million people and Japan has only 120 million. This means that Japanese workers are more than twice as productive, on average, as workers in the USSR.

For this reason, it is more useful to study maps and tables of average **GDP per head** of population for each country rather than use maps which just show the total GDPs.

There are problems in measuring GDPs. The most obvious problem comes from collecting the figures. If a villager in India sells some rice in the market for money and then spends the money on buying a calf, it is very unlikely that the exchange will ever be reported to the government. In the UK, on the other hand, most wages and purchases are reported in one way or another.

A second problem is that GDP is not always a measure of people's standard of living. This is because only things which are exchanged for money are included in GDP. In the UK, some goods, such as blood for transfusions, and some services, such as youth work, are given freely. If these were paid for, the GDP of Britain would go up, but the welfare of the country would not be increased.

Thirdly, some expenditure, for example an increase is spending on defence, appears as an increase in GDP although the average person does not enjoy any increase in his or her standard of living.

Fourthly, GDP can be increased by using more non-renewable resources such as coal or oil. When the resources run out, GDP will fall again. This is a particularly important consideration for the UK.

Country	Gross domestic product per head (US $)	Country	Gross domestic product per head (US $)
Afghanistan	160	Libya	8560
Algeria	2129	Malawi	200
Argentina	2560	New Zealand	7580
Australia	11190	Portugal	2534
Bangladesh	144	Sweden	14500
Brazil	2214	Switzerland	17150
Colombia	1334	Tanzania	299
France	12130	UK	8950
W. Germany	13520	USA	12530
Greece	4540	USSR	4701
India	253	Yugoslavia	2789
Ireland	5350	Zimbabwe	815
Japan	10330		

Figure 4.6 Gross Domestic Product per head of population for selected countries

Finally, a high GDP per head does not mean that everyone in the country is equally well off. Neither does a low GDP mean that everyone is very poor. Wealth is very rarely divided equally among the people of a country.

Despite these problems, the GDP per head does give some indication of the state of development of a country. Figure 4.6 shows the GDP per head for a number of countries. The figures are given in United States dollars (US$) so that the countries can be compared.

The poorest country in the table is Bangladesh. It has a GDP of $144 per head. Switzerland is the richest country. It has a GDP of $17150 per head. This means that the average Swiss man or woman can have almost 120 times more goods and services than the average Bangladeshi.

An average Swiss family will have a good house, good furniture, a washing machine, central heating, a refrigerator, dishwasher and video recorder. They will have many clothes. Their children will go to school. They will be looked after by doctors at home or in hospitals if they are ill. They will have holidays once or twice a year.

The average Bangladeshi family will have a poor house, with very little furniture. They will have few clothes. Their children are unlikely to go to school, and if they do, it will only be for a few years. They will suffer from a shortage of doctors and hospitals if they are ill. They will have no labour-saving machines in their house. Much time will be spent in collecting firewood and fetching water from a river or a well.

Figure 4.7 Advertisement for the Bangladesh Population Control and Family Planning division

The Swiss family will spend only a small part of their money on food. The Bangladeshi family will spend most of their money on food and there will still be times when they are hungry.

Figure 4.7 is an advertisement by the Bangladesh Population Control and Family Planning Division. It shows what living in a developing country is like in both pictures and figures. Figure 4.8 shows the country of Bangladesh and its roads and railways.

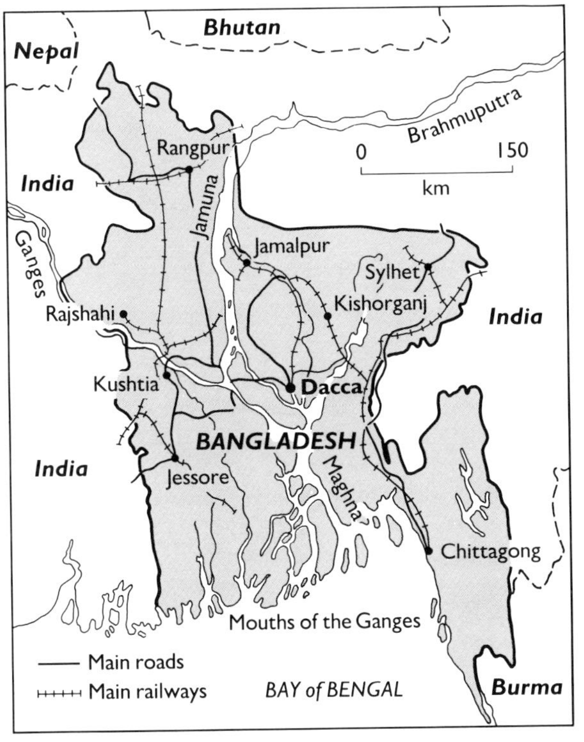

Figure 4.8 Bangladesh

In the example above we took the two extreme cases from the table of figures. A look at the whole table shows there are great differences in the wealth of many countries. Even a large country like Brazil with many natural resources has a GDP per head which is only about one quarter that of the UK and one fifth that of the USA. The question is, how do these differences happen?

Why are some countries richer than others?

To answer this question, the first thing to look at is where the wealth – or GDP – of different countries comes from. Figure 4.9 shows the percentages of the GDP created by the different sectors of the economy.

Figures 4.6 and 4.9 together show that the countries where GDP is low are usually the countries where most of the GDP comes from the primary sector – that is, mining and farming. On the other hand, the countries with a high GDP are those countries where only a small percentage of GDP comes from the primary sector.

Country	GDP per head (US $)	Percentage of GDP originating in			
		Agriculture	Mining and Manufacturing	Trade Tourism Transport	Others
Afghanistan	160	63	20	11	6
Algeria	2129	7	40	18	35
Argentina	2560	9	27	23	41
Bangladesh	144	48	8	21	23
Brazil	2214	10	27	16	47
Colombia	1334	23	23	5	49
France	12130	4	27	18	51
W. Germany	13520	2	40	15	43
Greece	4540	16	19	19	46
India	253	32	17	19	32
Ireland	5350	11	35	18	36
Libya	8560	2	55	11	32
Malawi	200	38	13	17	32
New Zealand	7580	11	24	30	35
Portugal	2534	9	30	8	53
Sweden	14500	3	22	16	59
Switzerland	17150	6	40	26	28
Tanzania	299	43	7	12	38
UK	8950	2	26	15	57
USA	12530	3	26	23	48
Yugoslavia	2789	13	41	30	16
Zimbabwe	815	16	5	20	59

Figure 4.9 Origins of Gross Domestic Product in selected countries

Countries where most of the GDP comes from the primary sector do not have many industries (the secondary sector) or transport companies, banks and insurance companies (the tertiary sector).

This is why the terms 'developing economy' or 'less developed economy' are often used for economies where the primary sector is most important. 'Developed economies' are the ones where secondary and tertiary sectors are most important.

There are many reasons why some countries do not have well developed secondary and tertiary sectors. We can see some of these reasons by studying coffee.

Case Study

Coffee production

Coffee is the second most important primary product in world trade after oil. Most people in the developed countries drink coffee.

Figure 4.10 is a list of the main coffee producers in the world. It also shows their GDP per head. All these countries have fairly low GDPs and most of their GDPs come from the primary sector of their economies. Figure 4.10 shows how important coffee is to some of these countries. Figure 4.11 describes how coffee is grown and processed into instant coffee.

Country	GDP per head	% population employed in Primary	Manufacturing	Services
Brazil	2214	44	18	38
Columbia	1334	30	18	52
Costa Rica	1476	36	19	45
Dominican Republic	1338	65	10	18
Ecuador	1171	56	13	12
El Salvador	636	60	13	27
Guatemala	1159	65	15	17
Haiti	297	90	6	4
Honduras	591	67	10	23
Mexico	2250	45	20	25
India	253	74	13	13
Indonesia	519	64	9	27
Nicaragua	874	68	20	12
Papua New Guinea	815	60	15	25
Peru	1122	42	19	32
Venezuela	4170	16	27	57
Angola	790	60	16	24
Cameroon	793	81	10	9
Central African Republic	328	92	5	3
Ethiopia	142	80	15	5
Ghana	402	58	13	29
Ivory Coast	1174	86	6	8
Liberia	536	74	0	26
Kenya	432	32	18	50
Malagasy Republic	332	80	8	12
Rwanda	250	91	3	6
Burundi	235	85	7	8
Tanzania	299	90	5	5
Togo	391	76	12	12
Uganda	356	23	28	49
Zaire	225	75	13	12

Figure 4.10 The main coffee producing countries of the world (1984)

How Coffee is Grown and Processed

Coffee requires a warm climate and flourishes in the tropics. After the trees are several years old fragrant white flowers bloom, and these soon give way to green berries. Six months later they ripen into red 'cherries' containing two coffee beans. The cherries are picked and spread on the ground to dry in the sun for several weeks. Lower grade coffees are prepared by the dry method; the sun-dried cherries are crushed in a hulling machine to remove the skin and pulp, leaving the green beans. The wet method involves soaking the cherries for three days before hulling, and is used for the better grades of coffee. Finally the green beans are graded and packed in 60-kilogram sacks for export.

When coffee is landed in the consuming countries, it normally passes through the hands of a dealer who sells the beans to a processor. The green beans are roasted in heated metal cylinders, bringing out their flavour, and different varieties of coffee are usually blended together to improve the taste. Finally the roasted beans have to be ground before they reach your coffee pot. Roasting and grinding adds considerably to the value of the green beans. But it takes place where the coffee is drunk, not where it is grown, so much of the profit from the crop goes to the consuming countries.

Increasingly the beans are processed into instant coffee. Instant, or soluble coffee is manufactured by brewing freshly roasted and ground coffee in huge percolators. Using the spray-dried method the brew is dispersed into small droplets. These are sprayed into a stream of hot air and the water is evaporated, leaving a powder of pure coffee.

Figure 4.11 How coffee is grown and processed

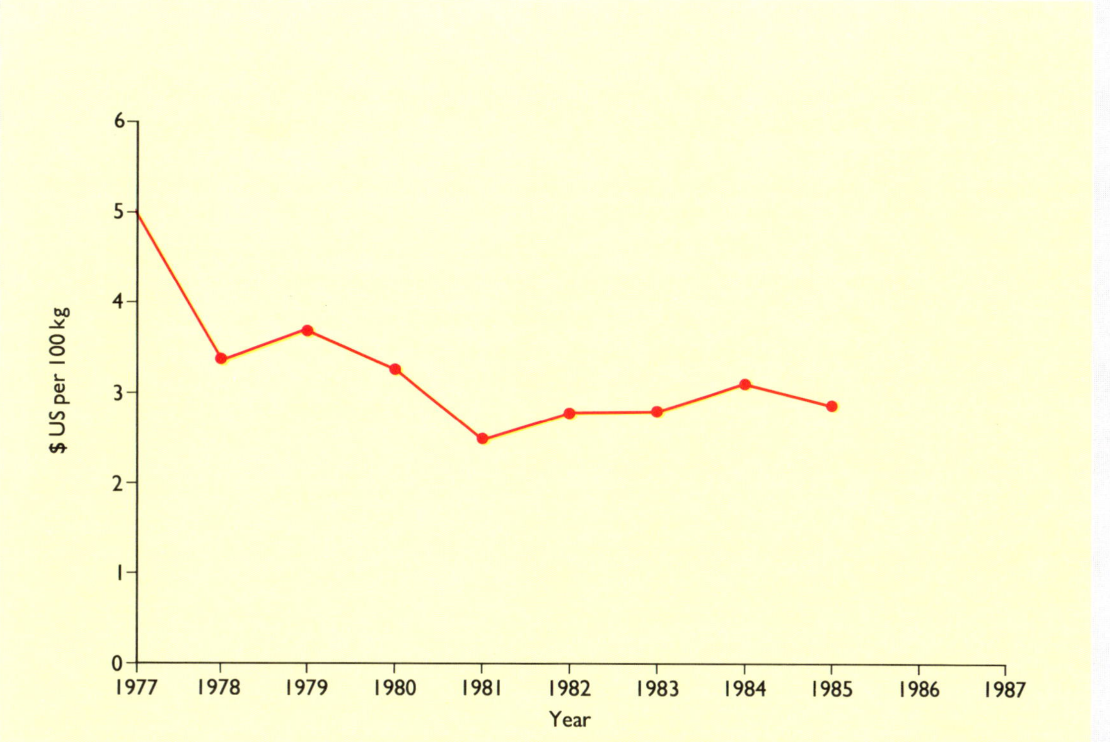

Figure 4.12 Variations in the price of coffee

Figure 4.12 shows how the prices the buying countries pay for the coffee change from year to year. There are many countries selling coffee in the world, but only a few countries buy it. This means that the buyers can buy coffee from whichever country will sell at the lowest price. If there is a good harvest, the exporting countries have a lot of coffee to sell, so they often have to take a lower price. If there is a bad harvest, then the price may rise. However, when the price of coffee goes up, many people change to drinking tea for a time, so less coffee is bought. The countries which grow coffee do not know how much coffee they will be able to sell, nor what price they will get. This makes it very difficult for them to plan their economy for the years ahead.

There is a second problem which faces countries which earn most of their money from selling primary products like coffee. They have to buy their manufactured goods from more developed countries which have a developed secondary sector. The prices of these manufactured goods have been rising steadily for many years. This is called **inflation**.

Figure 4.13 shows how the number of bags of coffee needed to buy one 16 tonne truck rose from 1975 to 1985. Look back at Figure 4.12. The price of coffee did rise in 1977, but it soon fell again. Over the whole ten years the price of coffee did not rise by nearly as much as the cost of manufactured goods from developed countries.

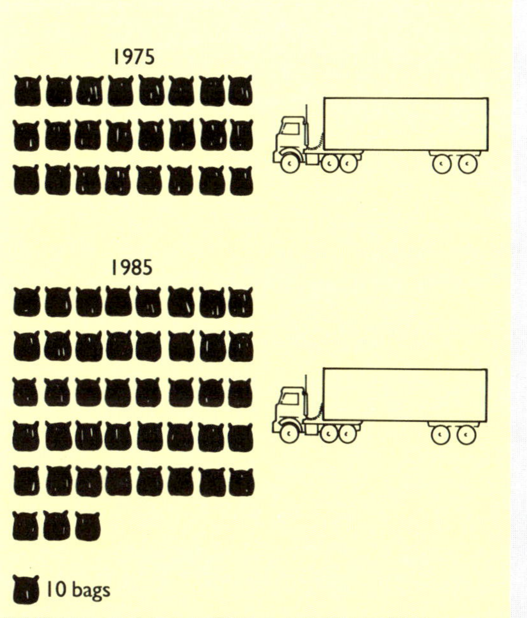

Figure 4.13 The changing terms of trade between coffee and trucks

The amount of exports from one country needed to buy things from another country is called the **terms of trade**. If the prices of primary products like coffee do not go up as fast as the prices of manufactured goods, the primary producers have to sell more and more each year to buy the same amount of manufactured goods. This is described as 'the terms of trade moving against the primary producing countries'.

Finally, in Figure 4.11 we saw that the roasting and blending of the coffee beans and the making of instant coffee is done in the country which imports the beans. Figure 4.14 shows how the cost of a jar of instant coffee can be split up. You can see that most of the money stays in the developed countries. This means that when you buy a jar of coffee you are adding much more to the GDP of your own country than you are adding to the GDP of the country which grew the coffee beans.

This jar of coffee costs £1.10 in the shops: where do the pennies go? (figures for 1984)

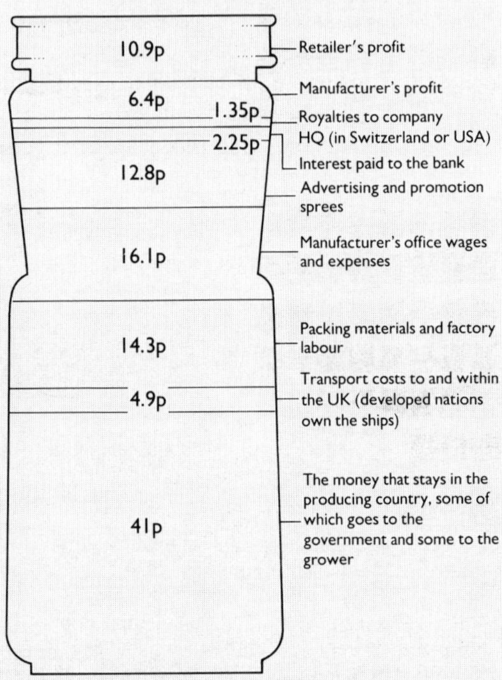

Figure 4.14 Distribution of money derived from the sale of a jar of coffee

Activities

- **4** Read the description of how coffee is grown and processed (Figure 4.11).
  - **a** Draw a flow diagram like the one begun in Figure 4.15 to show all the stages from planting the trees to drinking the instant coffee.
  - **b** Shade in the boxes which describe what happens in the growing country in one colour and the boxes which describe what happens in the importing country in another.

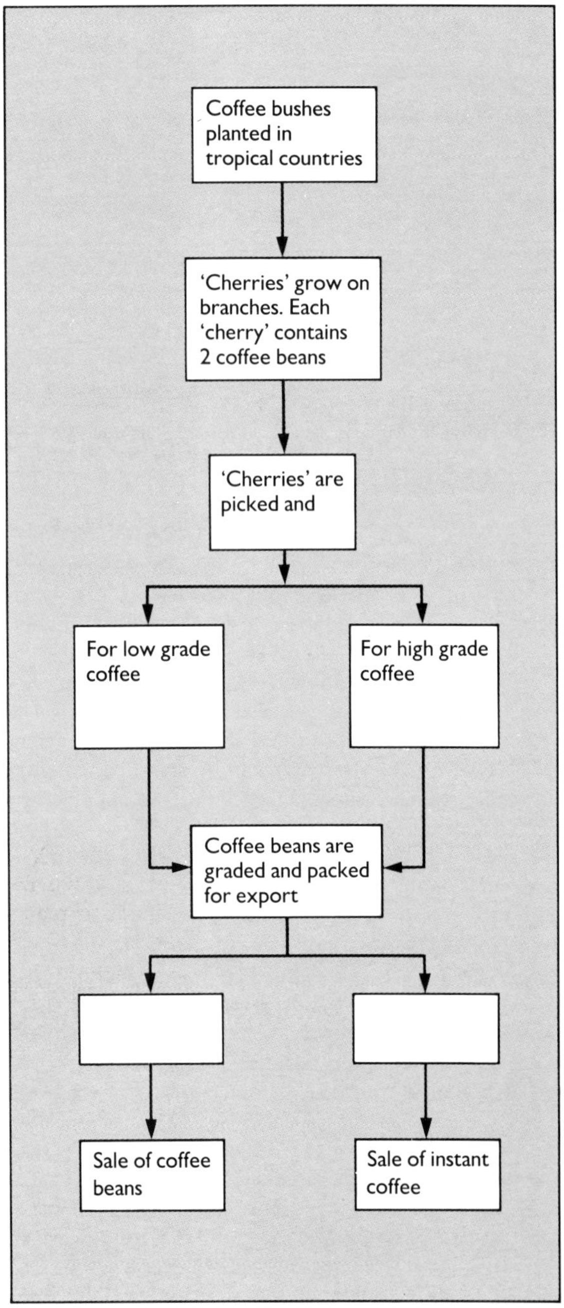

Figure 4.15 Stages in the growth and processing of coffee

▲ 5 Look at Figures 4.12 and 4.13.

■ a Describe how the price of coffee beans has
● varied since 1945.

b In April 1986 in the UK a 100 g jar of instant coffee cost £1.10 in a supermarket. Prestel reported that the London price for coffee beans was £1945 per tonne.

i) Find out how much a 100 g jar of coffee costs now.

ii) Find out the present price for coffee from Prestel or a newspaper.

iii) Which has gone up more in price – the cost of beans or the cost of instant coffee?

c Imagine you are a government planning officer in Burundi. Explain why you would find it difficult to plan to build new schools or new hospitals for next year.

d Imagine you are a coffee grower. You have worked out that if you work hard, you can save up to buy your own truck in 5 years time. Describe all the problems you might face while you try to save for your truck.

▲ 6 a Make a copy of the jar in Figure 4.14. Shade
■ in a dark colour the part of the drawing
● which represents extra GDP to the coffee growing country. Shade in a light colour the part which represents extra GDP to the importing country. Comment on this.

b Describe how the jar of coffee makes work in the secondary sector, tertiary sector and quaternary sector of the UK.

Underdevelopment is a problem for all of us

The case study of coffee shows that there are two main problems facing the countries which grow coffee. The first is that the price of coffee varies from year to year. The second is that much of the value of the processed coffee stays in the developed countries of the world. So why haven't the producing countries set up their own factories and selling organizations? One answer is that there are often very high tariff barriers to protect industries in the developed countries from competition.

There are three other possible answers to the question. Firstly, there must be knowledge of the technology to build and operate factories and a transport system. The country needs people with the skills to manage the factories and organize the transport. Some countries make discoveries earlier than others. Workers in the UK were the first to invent powered machines to spin and weave cotton cloth (Figure 4.16). The UK could then import raw cotton, process it into cotton cloth and then export it again. This made great profits and increased the GDP. The extra wealth meant that time and money could be spent on inventing and developing new equipment.

Secondly, some workers must spend their time and energy building factories, roads and railways. This is called **capital development**. While they are doing this, perhaps for many years, they must be fed, clothed and housed. This could mean that the people who stay as farmers have to produce more food. It could

Figure 4.16 Spinning cotton in Lancashire

also mean that everyone must eat a little less food so that there is enough to go round. In both cases, the people who are developing the industries have to be kept by the people who are producing food. New methods of farming might be the answer to this problem. This is how the UK managed capital development 200 years ago.

Capital development can be helped by developed countries. For example, the Tanganyika Instant Coffee Company owns one factory near Mount Kilimanjaro in Tanzania. 10% of the company is owned by a co-operative of local coffee farmers. The other 90% is owned by the Tanzanian Government. Tanzania needed the help of multi-national corporations to set up the one factory. To sell their coffee, the factory needs the help of an English company called Traidcraft. Traidcraft specializes in selling things made in developing countries.

In this case developed nations have helped to develop a manufacturing industry by supplying technology and making it possible for Tanzanians to sell its product. There are many other cases though where technology is kept from developing countries or where selling is made difficult. In earlier times many European countries took over countries in South America, Africa and Asia as colonies. These colonies were used to supply the 'home' country with raw materials. Later on, the colonies became independent nations. They were still kept as raw material suppliers by developed countries because the developed countries put high taxes or import tariffs on manufactured goods but low tariffs on raw materials. This makes it easier for other countries to export their primary products and more difficult to export manufactured goods. France, Netherlands, Belgium, Spain, Portugal and the UK all had colonies in other continents.

The third answer to the question is that development may depend on the values of the people. What people value in life varies greatly from country to country. Some people may not value wealth very highly. They may prefer a more relaxed lifestyle to producing goods and services and earning more money. For example, it does not follow that the average Swiss citizen is happier than the average Zimbabwe citizen just because GDP per head in Switzerland is 21 times higher than GDP per head in Zimbabwe.

These suggestions why some countries, such as Bangladesh or Afghanistan, are less developed today can be summarized like this:

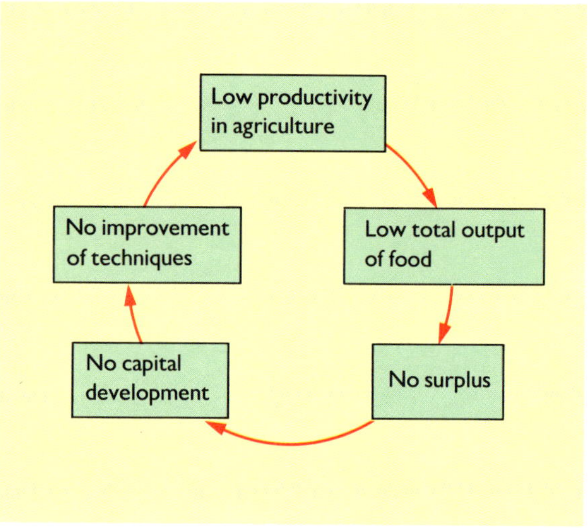

Figure 4.17 The vicious circle of underdevelopment

1 In recent years agricultural productivity has not been high. It has not increased so food cannot be put aside for capital development. i.e. all the food being produced is being used up. Population growth has made it even more difficult to grow spare food.
2 In the past the technology of industrial growth was not known in these countries.
3 In the past, these countries may not have valued money wealth very highly. Before modern communications, people in these countries would not have been able to compare themselves with people from more developed countries.
4 The countries which import raw materials have often prevented their former colonies from developing manufacturing industries by putting high import tariffs on manufactured goods.

These four reasons to explain underdevelopment have often been shown as a simple diagram. Figure 4.17 shows the vicious circle of underdevelopment. On the other hand, developed countries can be shown as an open spiral rather than a vicious circle. This is shown in Figure 4.18.

If these two diagrams showed the exact way countries develop, then less developed countries could only stay less developed. Developed countries would just go on growing. Of course this is not true. The case study of the Apa Tani people showed that when they had contact with the people of India; their economy started developing. The development of the Apa Tani economy seemed to start when a road and schools were built. We could say that it was 'capital' and 'knowledge' which triggered off development.

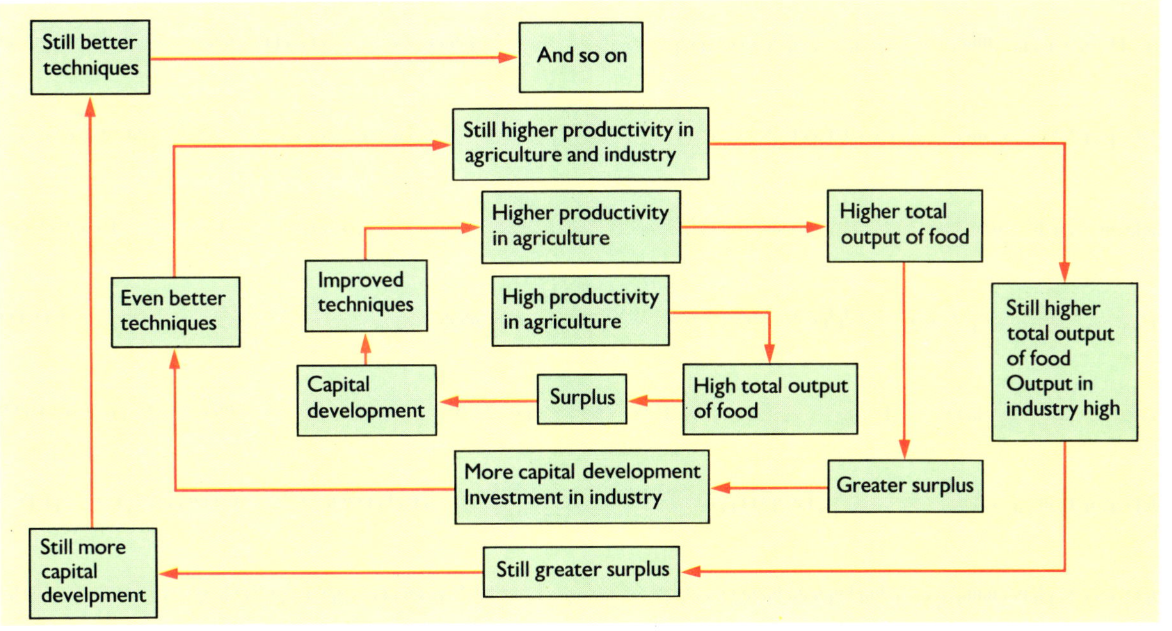

Figure 4.18 The open spiral of development

If less developed countries do not have to stay less developed, neither do more developed countries have to keep on developing. In the 1930s rich countries did not grow very fast and for most of the 1970s and 1980s there has only been slow growth. In fact, most economies in the world are developing to some extent. The main difference is the rate at which they are developing. Unfortunately, these rates are so different that the gap between the rich countries and the poor countries has been getting much wider since 1945.

Some countries like Libya were very poor in 1945. But by 1980, as Figure 4.6 showed, their GDP was high enough for them to join the list of wealthy countries. The reason for this rapid growth was that developed countries invested a lot of money in them because they needed the oil. The high GDP per head has also been helped by the relatively low populations. Remember, however, the warnings about GDP per head. In particular, remember that oil drilling is part of the primary sector. Unless these countries use some of their oil wealth to develop secondary, tertiary and quaternary sectors, they will suffer a fall in GDP when the oil runs out. The same argument is true for the UK when its petroleum supplies run out.

Other countries, like Malawi and Tanzania, have not had a great deal of capital put into them by developed nations. The countries which have not been given capital have not developed very quickly at all.

Activities

▲**7** Explain what each of these terms means.
- **a** Gross Domestic Product
- **b** Developed country
- **c** Capital development
- **d** Productivity
- **e** Colony

▲**8** ● **a** Using the information in this chapter make two lists. Call one list 'Things which make some countries rich. Call the other list 'Things which keep some countries poor'.

b For each list, put a 1 beside the reason you think is most important, a 2 beside the second most important reason, and so on . . .

Reducing the gap between rich countries and poor countries

If the reasons we have suggested for some countries remaining poor are correct, they may give us a clue about helping them to become richer. We have described the effects of the terms of trade moving against the coffee producing countries. We have explained the problems of capital development. We have also mentioned high tariffs which make it difficult for developing countries to develop their industry and export manufactured goods rather than primary goods.

Rich countries can help poorer countries by making changes in all these areas. However, it is important to realize three things.

1 Great improvements in a country's standard of living can't be achieved overnight.
2 The rich countries will have to make some sacrifices if they want to help the poorer countries.
3 If the poorer countries are helped to start manufacturing, then they may compete with the richer countries.

Let's look at this in more detail.

Firstly, it takes time for an economy to develop. Even if some factories are built, it takes time for workers to be trained to work in them.

Managers are needed to run the factories. People are needed to service the equipment, to supply packaging for the goods, to arrange insurance, to transport the products and to find buyers. In the early days, many of these jobs have to be done by people from more developed countries. It may take many years before the country develops all the sectors of its economy. At the start of this chapter we explained how all the four sectors are linked together. An economy can't really grow until it has all four sectors.

Secondly, richer countries can help poorer countries by lending the money for factory machinery, roads or other capital equipment (Figure 4.19). They can also help by supplying money for training people to develop the economy. This money can be either a gift or a loan. If it is a loan the richer countries can't expect any interest on it for many years.

For example, suppose a developing country wants to develop its textile industry. Developed countries like the UK, West Germany and France may lend it large sums of money to buy and install modern spinning and weaving machinery. Until all the machinery is bought and installed and is working properly the country will not be able to pay interest on the loan. Even when the machinery is earning money, the country will be prevented from developing even further if all its earnings have to be paid out as interest.

The third problem of giving help to developing countries is competition. Once the developing country starts making textiles, it may sell these in the UK, France and West Germany. Because the machinery was bought with a loan or a gift and wages are likely to be low, the imported textiles will be cheaper than British, French and German textiles. This can cause the textile industry of the richer countries to decline.

This problem has led some people to demand that the European industries should be

Figure 4.19 A 'self-help' project in the Congo. The Federal Republic of Germany has given funds to help purchase tools and equipment and to subsidise training.

protected by high import duties. Unfortunately, this would make it even more difficult for the developing countries to earn money. It would be more sensible for the richer countries to change to making types of products which the developing countries do not yet make.

There is a further problem about sending money to developing countries to help them build up their economies. If the UK, France or West Germany sends money to developing countries, this may slow down the rate of growth of their own GDPs. This must happen if poorer countries are to become richer. However, governments in the developed countries are often afraid that they will lose votes if they do not try to keep their own economies growing.

The developing countries in the United Nations have called for a **New International Economic Order** to help solve some of these problems. They say that there are four main areas which need to be changed.

Firstly, the developing nations want international agreement on raw materials and their prices. This would prevent the terms of trade from moving against the developing nations. There have been several attempts at making agreements between buyers and sellers of primary commodities to keep prices steady. For example, there have been four International Coffee Agreements. The first Coffee Agreement was signed in 1962 by 42 exporting countries and 17 importing countries. The exporting countries wanted to reach an agreement amongst themselves because of the disastrous years they had experienced in the 1950s. Figure 4.12 showed you that during the 1950s coffee prices fell to such low levels that the coffee crops were hardly worth harvesting. These low prices were because more coffee was being grown than the importing countries wanted to buy. The purpose of the 1962 Agreement (and the three others which have been signed since then) was to try to make sure that just enough coffee is grown to supply the needs of the world without growing so much that the prices fall. Here is the way the Coffee Agreements work. The coffee exporting countries and the coffee importing countries get together to decide how much coffee should be sold in the world and how this amount should be divided up among all the coffee growing countries. The amount each country is allowed to grow is called its **quota**. The idea is to make sure there is enough coffee for sale at fair prices for consumers, and enough buyers at fair prices for producers. This is arranged by deciding on two **trigger prices**. If coffee prices rise to the higher trigger price, all quotas are automatically increased. If coffee prices fall below the lower trigger price, all quotas are cut back to keep coffee off the market.

There are two important problems about this system which make it difficult for agreement to be reached. The first problem is deciding the quota for each country, that is, how much each producing country should be allowed to sell. All the producing countries want to have as large a share as possible. The second problem is that all the producers would like the prices to increase each year in line with inflation. The importing countries do not want this to happen.

Another problem is that the coffee growing countries are in competition with each other. The South American countries want larger quotas than the African countries. The smaller producing countries like Ecuador think that they should have relatively larger quotas than larger producing countries like Brazil. This competition makes it difficult for the coffee producers to be united in their negotiations with the smaller number of coffee importers.

There are also commodity agreements for tin, copper and cocoa, but the problem of low and variable raw material prices has still not been solved.

The second area the developing countries want changed is the international money system so that they can get long loans at low rates of interest. The **World Bank** was set up to give help in this way.

Thirdly, the developing countries want the richer countries to give them aid without telling them how to spend it.

And fourthly, the developing countries want the richer countries to control the world's largest companies. These large companies have branches in different countries. They are called **multinational corporations**. Because these companies operate across the world, it is difficult for any one government to control them or tax them. Often the multinational corporations have more power and money in a developing country than the government of that country.

Is economic growth important?

Most of the developed countries have an economy which depends on the mass production of goods in factories. These goods are then distributed over great distances by sea, air and road. This kind of economy needs complicated links between the four sectors of the economy.

Some people now think the disadvantages of this system are greater than its advantages. In Tanzania, the government has decided not to try to develop just by increasing the GDP. They want to develop the way their people think of their society and get them to work together.

For example, rather than trying to ignore traditional ways of farming and change to western ways, the Tanzanians are trying to make the traditional ways more efficient. They think that it is silly to use tractors and western ploughs which plough quickly but compress the soil with their wheels, and put people out of work. Instead they are making new steel ploughs which can be pulled by oxen. This makes the farming more efficient, it does not damage the soil and it keeps people in jobs. Another advantage is that oxen do not need expensive petrol which has to be imported. This is an example of **intermediate technology** (Figure 4.20).

Tanzania is also trying to encourage people to work together. In country areas the people are encouraged to live in self-help villages. These are called **Ujamaa villages**. In these villages people help one another and develop their own skills. A good farmer can show other people how to increase their yields of crops. The people can work together to dig wells. Someone may be good at making ploughs or storage jars and can specialize in that. The idea is that slowly the village will develop its own kind of economy and lifestyle by improving on the traditional lifestyle.

Some people think that the developed countries have become so developed that we have all stopped being individual human beings. We all wear similar clothes from similar shops, we all eat the same processed food and we all work more or less the same hours. For example, Coca Cola, Levi Jeans and Space Invaders are found everywhere in the UK, Europe, the USA and Australia. One result of our development is that all these things can be owned by nearly everyone. The other result is that ordinary people have lost the power to make their environment personal because they have to use the standard products.

Figure 4.20 Intermediate technology

Activities

▲ ● **9 a** Explain the effects of not linking the trigger prices to world inflation on
- **i)** producing countries and
- **ii)** importing countries.

b Suggest a new system of making sure that the price of coffee is fair to both the producing countries and the importing countries.

■ ● **10** Figure 4.21 shows some photos taken in various parts of the world. For each photograph:

a Describe what the photograph shows.

b Say whether you think the photograph was taken in a developed or a developing country. Give your reasons.

c Try to suggest in which part of the world each photograph was taken. Give your reasons.

▲ ■ ● **11** The photographs in Figure 4.22 show water being raised from a well and put into an irrigation channel.

a Describe the techniques being used to raise the water.

b Explain how this job would probably be done in a developed country.

c Draw a table with two columns. Head one column 'Advantages' and the other column 'Disadvantages'. Under your two headings, list the advantages and disadvantages of the method of raising water shown in the photographs for a developing country.

d Suggest some ways in which the water raising could be improved by using intermediate technology.

So far we have described what has happened to the development of the Apa Tani people, the Tanzanians and the countries which grow coffee. The Apa Tani people came into contact with people with a more developed economy and copied many of their ways. The Tanzanians

Figure 4.21 Developed and developing countries

Figure 4.22 Raising water from a well and distributing it for irrigation

have decided not to try to copy the western type of development. They are developing their traditional type of economy in their own way. The coffee growing countries have found that the terms of trade and import tariffs in developed countries make it almost impossible for them to earn enough to develop. They are like many other countries which try to develop their economies by trading raw materials with more developed countries. We will now look at a group of people who do not want to change to a developed economy.

Case Study

The Amazonian Indians

Five hundred years ago early travellers from Europe began to explore the Amazonian forests. They thought that the Indian tribes were living in a paradise on Earth. The Indians got everything they needed from the forests. When the explorers first went to Amazonia there were about 6 million Indians living in 230 tribes. By 1900 there were only about 1 million Indians left. Many of them had died because the explorers brought diseases like measles, smallpox, influenza, malaria and tuberculosis. The Indians had no natural immunity to any of these diseases.

Between 1900 and 1983, 87 tribes were wiped out of existence. The latest estimates are that only between 50 000 and 100 000 Indians remain alive. The surviving Indians live mainly in the forested areas of the Amazon river basin. They live an entirely subsistence way of life.

Although the forest is home for the Indians, other people see the forest in different ways. The Brazilian Government sees the Amazon forest as a large area of land which could be farmed by the millions of poor people who are living in north-east Brazil. The large timber companies see the forest as a large stock of trees for hardwoods. A single tree can be worth thousands of pounds. The mining companies want to clear the forests so that they can get at the iron ore, bauxite, tin, diamonds and gold which they know are there. Cattle men want to clear the forest and let grass grow for huge ranches. If these people have their way, the Indians will just become third-class citizens without any money or qualifications.

Figure 4.23 shows the Xingu National Park which was set up in 1961 along the Xingu River. This was to be reserved for 14 Indian tribes to allow them to live their traditional lifestyle. The Brazilian Government also set up an official organization to help the Indians. This is called FUNAI (an abbreviation of its Portuguese name).

The Government and FUNAI agreed on four important principles. These were that:

1 The traditional culture of the Indians should be respected.
2 The Indians had a right to permanent possession of their traditional lands.
3 FUNAI should support any Indians who wanted to become part of the modern world, but should not force them to do so.
4 FUNAI should protect the Indian tribes from any upset caused by contact with outsiders.

Figure 4.23 Xingu National Park area

Unfortunately these four principles did not last for long. Laws were passed by the Brazilian Government which allowed Indians to be moved from their land by force in special circumstances. They could be moved if tribes fought against one another; if there were minerals, such as coal, iron ore or oil, under the land; or for 'reasons of national security'.

In 1970 a new highway was routed through the Xingu National Park. This cut off the northern part of the park and made it easy for cattle farmers to move on to Indian land to the south.

The tribes united under the chief of the Megkronotis tribe – Chief Raoni. In 1976 the Megkronotis tribe's land had been virgin forest. By 1980 about 80% of the forest had been pulled down and burned. Figure 4.24 shows the Megkronotis Indians in the ashes of their forest. In 1980 work started on more forest clearing. Raoni went and asked the farmer to stop clearing the forest while he went to **FUNAI** to decide where the settlers' land ended and the Indians' land began.

While **FUNAI** thought about the problem, the farmer carried on clearing the forest. In the end Raoni sent warriors from several tribes to frighten the workers away. He told them to hit the workers hard enough so that they would go away. The warriors hit the workers rather too hard. One of the warriors remembered that farm workers had killed his cousin. Because of this, and because the farm workers were badly injured, the warriors decided to kill them.

Raoni knows about life in the modern world. In 1976 he took part in a film about his tribe called 'Raoni'. Figure 4.25 shows Raoni in a shop in São Paulo. He is buying a rifle. Although he and his companions are wearing trousers you can see that Raoni still has a thick twig stretching his lower lip to make him look fiercer. The other Indian with Raoni in São Paulo is N'groire. The name 'N'groire' means jaguar hunter. He had never been to a town before this trip. He needed help to open doors and to turn on taps. He had never seen stairs before.

Even though Raoni has seen the modern world and uses a rifle, he does not want his people to become part of it. The Indians would rather be killed than lose their land. Raoni has said 'If we lose our land, then the whites will destroy the whole forest. Where will we go to hunt the tapir, the ant bear, the panther? What will we eat? There will be no game left . . . . We will fight and maybe we will die . . . but we are slowly dying anyway.'

Figure 4.24 Members of the Megkronotis tribe in the ashes of their forest territory

Figure 4.25 The Chief of the Megkronotis tribe in a São Paulo shop

What this story shows is that the Indians do not want to change their style of life, or at least not as quickly as the developers would like. The Amazonian Indians are part of the group of people who still live in tribes in various parts of the world. This group includes Eskimos, Pygmies, Aborigines, Bushmen and many others. They make their living through killing wild creatures and harvesting wild plants. They usually live in deserts, rain forests, polar regions and other areas which are too dry, too wet or too cold for the kind of lifestyle which people have in the developed world.

You may be asking if it matters if these tribes of people are civilized to death. There are a number of reasons why we should all be concerned. Firstly, there are about 200 million people who choose to live in tribal societies. Have we any right to stop them living their lives in their own way?

Secondly, most of these groups manage to survive in areas in which our way of life could not survive. These groups show us how to use scarce resources.

Thirdly, if these old cultures die out, vast amounts of knowledge will die with them. The Amazonian Indians, for example, use over 750 different plants for medicines. Many of these plants have not been studied by western scientists. For example, the World Health Organization believes that the tribal peoples of the Earth use more than 3000 different plants for contraceptives. These may be safer than the artificial chemicals used in the developed world. The Lua Tribe in northern Thailand grows 75 different food crops and tribes in Burma use 300 different food plants. These are just some of the ways in which we could learn from the 'backward' people of the Earth.

Fourthly, the rain forest areas like Amazonia are very complex ecosystems. Once the trees are removed, it is difficult to preserve the quality of the soil (see Chapter 3). The soil loses its fertility and is quickly washed away. So, a forest which provides food and shelter for the Indians will probably be of little use as open land. The ranches of today will be the deserts of two or three years time.

Activities

▲ ■ ● 12 Use the information in this section and what you learned about the Amazon basin's climate and ecosystem in Chapter 3 to list the advantages and disadvantages of clearing the Amazon forest from the point of view of

a The Brazilian Government which wants to increase Brazil's GDP as fast as possible.

b The chief of an Indian tribe which lives in the Amazon forests.

c A meteorologist who is concerned with the world's weather.

d A botanist who is trying to develop new types of crops which can resist diseases in south-east Asia.

▲ ■ ● 13 Cutting down the Amazon forest would increase Brazil's GDP. It would also destroy plants, animals, people and ecosystems which the whole world may need.

a List the points for and against a world tax on rich countries so that Brazil could be paid to leave the Amazon forest alone.

b What would be the problems of organizing this kind of scheme?

▲ ■ ● 14 A group of Aborigines in northern Australia is living a traditional life in a semi-desert area. The land is owned by the Aborigines. Uranium ore is known to exist there. A large multinational mining company wants to mine the uranium. The company offers the Aborigines 10% of the profits.

a List the advantages and disadvantages of this offer to the tribe.

b Decide whether you would advise the tribe to take the money or not. Explain the reasons for your decision.

The quality of life

We have just described the way in which the Indian tribes of the Amazon are fighting against the kind of changes which come from 'western' style development and rising standards of living. We must assume that they enjoy their way of life. They do not seem to want the same way of life as the factory workers, farm workers or office workers in the rest of Brazil.

Although the Indians are worse off in money and goods than the town dwellers of Brazil, it does not mean that they are less happy or ought to change their way of life.

Figure 4.26 Singapore

Figure 4.27 Singapore: older buildings

In the same way, if Tanzanians in Africa prefer to develop through Ujamaa villages and intermediate technology rather than through industrialization in towns, there is no reason why they should not do so.

However, many poor countries are trying to develop in the same way as western countries. For example, Brazil has already developed important secondary and tertiary sectors of her economy. This has led to an increase in GDP although Brazil has not caught up with the USA or West Germany yet.

Figures 4.26 and 4.27 show Singapore. Here industry and commerce have been developed and have led to a steadily rising GDP. There are disadvantages about developing economies in this way. In Singapore the growth of industry and commerce has led to the growth of the city itself. This results in traffic congestion, pollution and stress. It also means that buildings tend to be built more for speed and the use to which they will be put than for architectural style. Big commercial cities all over the world look much the same.

There is more to quality of life than just the balance of advantages and disadvantages of growth. In many countries of Europe and parts of North America people have realized that a

Figure 4.28 Nijmegen, in the Netherlands

Figure 4.29 Wroclaw, in Poland

Figure 4.30 New Orleans, USA

Feature	Poor	Average	Good
State of repair of buildings	−2 −1	0	1 2
Interesting architecture			
Amount of greenery visible (trees, gardens, window boxes etc)			
Sense of spaciousness			
Smell			
State of pavements			
State of roads			
State of street signs			
Cleanliness			
Traffic congestion			
Separation of pedestrians from traffic			
Safety level			
Is the street a pleasant place to be in?			
Column total			
Overall score	**Total poor scores**		**Total good scores**

Figure 4.31 Quality of urban landscape checklist

town is likely to be more pleasant to look at and live in if it grows bit by bit and buildings are conserved.

Figures 4.28, 4.29 and 4.30 show towns which have been changed slowly and carefully. This only happens when people begin to value the beauty of a site or a town or a landscape more than the short term economic advantages. You will find more about this in Chapter 7.

Activities

▲■● **15 a i)** List the things in your town or village which add to your quality of life.

ii) List the things in your town or village which take away from your quality of life.

b For your first list, describe the things you would lose if people in your area and your local council became poorer.

c i) For your second list, describe how your quality of life could be improved without anyone becoming poorer.

ii) Describe how your quality of life could be improved but only at someone else's expense.

▲■● **16** Choose 3 streets in your local area. One of them should be a shopping street.

a Make 3 copies of Figure 4.31. For each street, give a score for each of the features listed.

b Use your score sheets to help you describe how pleasant or unpleasant you found each street.

c Explain which features of each street made it more pleasant to be in and which features made it less pleasant to be in.

▲■● **17** Study Figures 4.26 and 4.27 which are photographs of Singapore. Describe the features of each photograph which show that Singapore has a developed economy.

▲■● **18** Study Figures 4.28, 4.29 and 4.30.

a For each photograph describe the view.

b Explain your own reaction to each photograph. You should describe the features of the photograph you particularly like and those which you do not particularly like.

c Explain why you think they were chosen as examples in the section on the quality of life. Do they make the quality of life better or worse?

5

Farming for food and materials

The three essential things people need in order to live are food, clothing and shelter. Figure 5.1 shows that this chapter is mainly concerned with one of these needs – food. Most of our food is produced by farming. However, there is more to farming than just food. Cotton and linen come from farm crops. Leather and wool come from animals. Rubber and cork come from trees. In fact, agriculture is probably the most important of all economic activities. About two thirds of the world's population work at some form of farming.

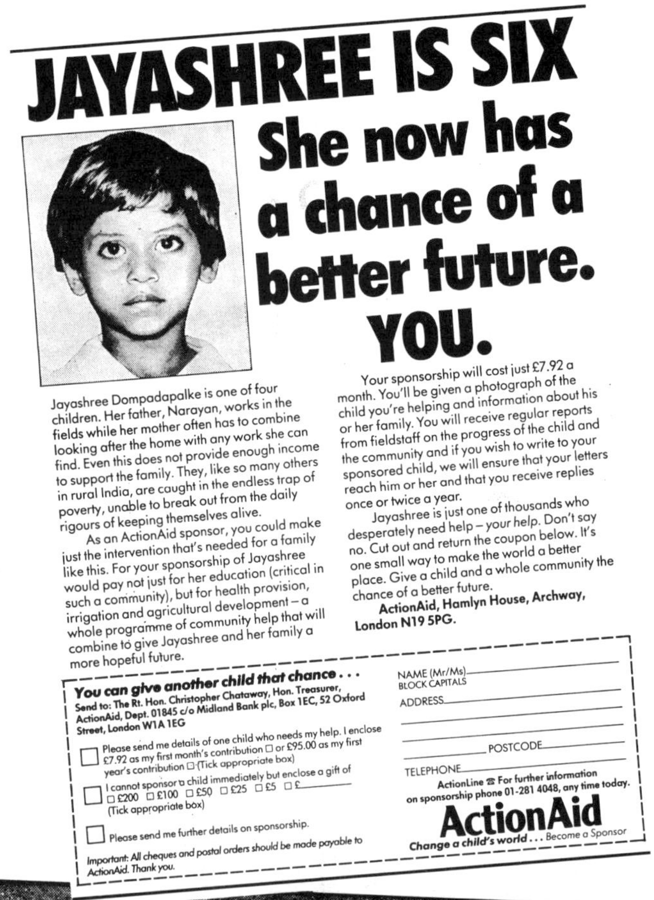

Figure 5.1

The best gift for many children this Christmas is the gift of life. A bowl of food for a starving boy in Ethiopia. A nurse's care for a sick child in Uganda. Father Christmas can't make it happen. You can. They don't need toys. They need food, medicine and shelter now. Five pounds will feed the little boy for a month. Twenty pounds will help to build a new life for that child in Uganda. This Christmas spare a thought for these and many other children. Please send a donation to The Save the Children Fund using this coupon or ansaphone 01-701 0894 for Access/Barclaycard.

To: The Save the Children Fund, Dept 323118
17 Grove Lane, London SE5 8RD.
I enclose £ ______ (sae please, if you need a receipt).
Or debit my Access/Barclaycard account No. ______
Or you can send through National Giro No. 5173000.
Signature ______
Name ______
Address ______

Save the Children 323118

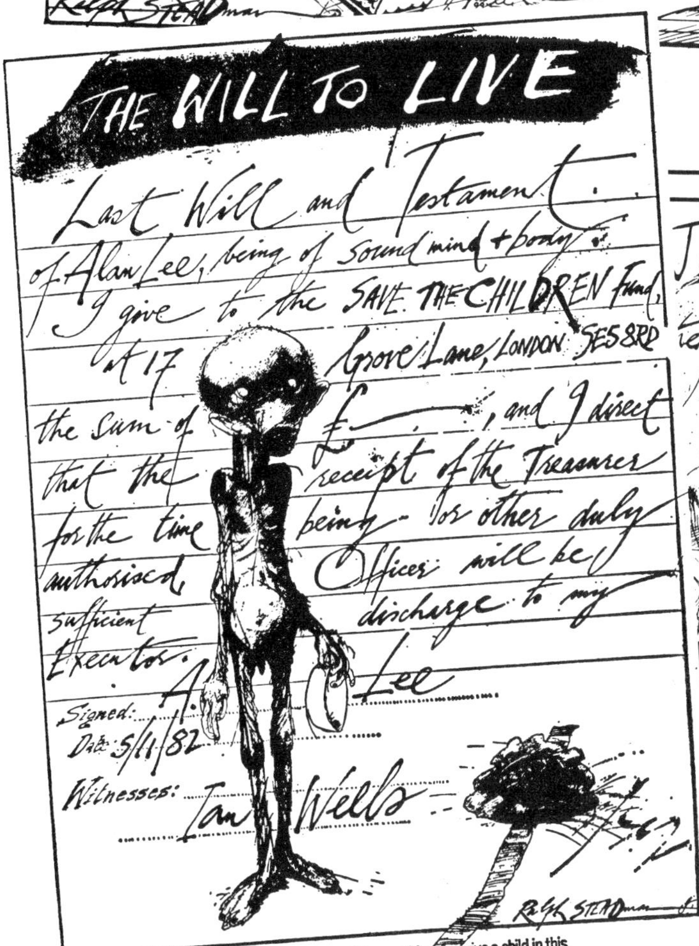

Your legacy to Save the Children could give a child in this country or the third world their only chance. If you would like to know more about our work for children at home and overseas write to Peter Lindsey at the address below.

Save the Children

The Save the Children Fund, 17 Grove Lane, London SE5 8RD.

This does not represent a legal document.

Every day of every month of every year, millions of children are in desperate need of food. And shelter. And medical help.

85p in every £1 you contribute to Save The Children gets through to where it matters – in over 50 countries – caring for children through mother and child health services, nutritional programmes, education and training schemes.

Don't ignore the children, they're crying out for your help.

Please send a donation direct using the coupon below (s.a.e. please, if you need a receipt) or through National Giro No. 5173000 or ansaphone 01-701 0894, quoting your Access/Barclaycard account details.

To: The Save the Children Fund, Dept 320
17 Grove Lane, London SE5 8RD.
Please use this donation £ ______ to help your work.
Or debit my Access/Barclaycard account
No. ______
Signature ______
Name ______
Address ______

Save the Children

The early beginning of agriculture

The word **agriculture** means the cultivation of land. Cultivation of land probably began about 12000 years ago. Before that, hunting animals, fishing and gathering fruit were the main ways of providing food. About 200 million people in remote areas of the world still live by hunting and gathering to some extent.

Farming probably began when people started to settle in more or less permanent villages. The first villages may have been where good lake or river fishing was possible. Perhaps the first cultivated plants grew from the remains of food dropped in waste heaps. Later on, wild plants were transplanted into patches of land near the village. Finally, people learned how to collect seeds from their plants and save them for the next year. In many tribes the men go hunting and the women go gathering. This means women probably developed agriculture. Animal farming may have begun when hunters brought back the young of the animals they had killed. Once they were fenced in and protected, 'tame' animals could breed.

Archaeologists think that animal farming and crop farming both began at about the same time in the Middle East, Central America, West and Central Africa and South East Asia.

There have been many changes since farming began – most of them in the last 300 years. Farmers have learned to rotate crops so that they do not remove all the nutrients from the soil. Natural and artificial fertilizers are now used. Many insect pests and weeds can be controlled. Different strains of plants and animals have been made by cross-fertilizing. This has meant larger crops, faster growth, more resistance to disease and the ability to grow in harsh areas of the world. New tools have helped farmers to produce food in difficult areas and have speeded up farming.

These changes are only true for part of the world. In many other parts of the world farming has not changed much for thousands of years.

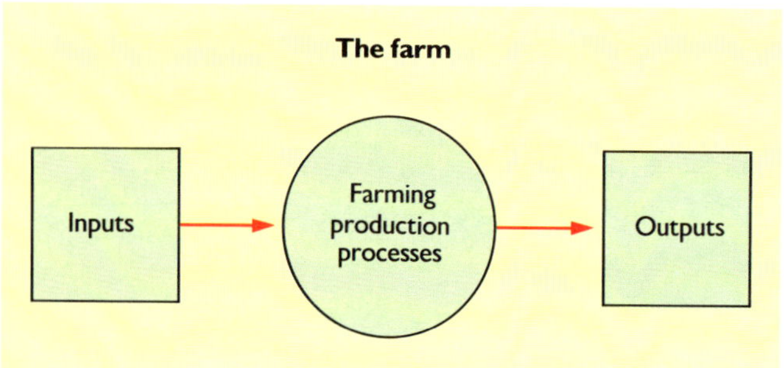

Figure 5.2 A simple farm system

Activities

▲1 ● Make lists of the advantages and disadvantages of getting food by:

a Hunting and gathering

b Subsistence farming (producing enough food only for your own family).

c Modern 'scientific farming'.

▲2 ● The development of machinery is one important way of improving agricultural production. Write down the likely effects of the invention of more efficient machinery on

a Workers in industrial areas

b Farm workers in western countries

c Undernourished people in tropical areas

d Villages in western countries where farming is the main occupation

e Poor farmers in less developed countries.

The farm system

Figure 5.2 shows a simple farm system. The **inputs** are all the things which are needed for farming. What goes on in the farm makes use of these inputs. The **outputs** are the things produced by the farm either for eating or selling.

To make the system work properly year after year, there has to be a constant supply of inputs. The inputs might include new seed, new machinery or a new barn. Inputs might also include animal manure. These could all be bought from outside the farm using money from savings. This would not be a very good way of running a farm, so it is more likely that the money would come from the profits from what is sold in the market and the manure would come from the farm animals. Using some of the outputs to provide inputs like this is called **feedback**. Figure 5.3 shows a simple farm system with feedback.

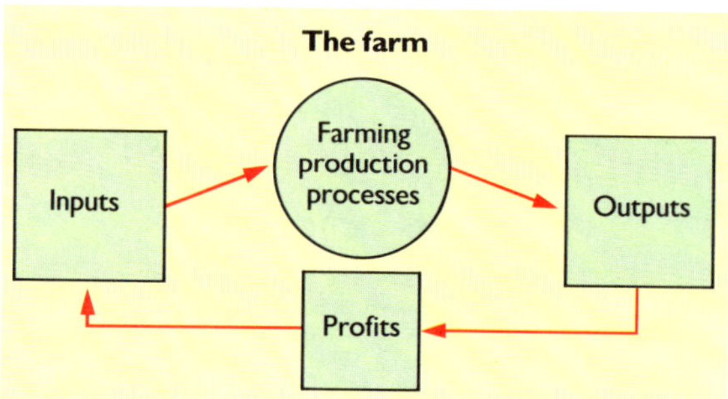

Figure 5.3 A simple farm system with feedback

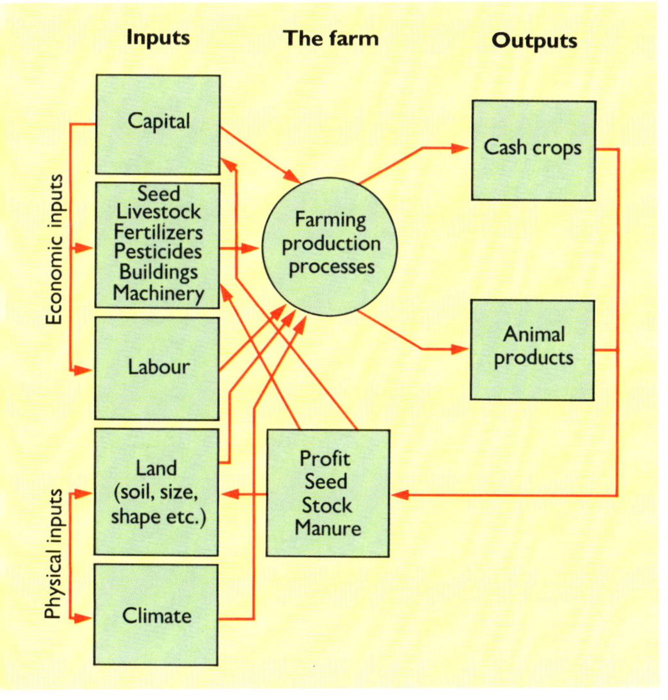

Figure 5.4 A farm system

Figure 5.5a Rice farming in Indonesia

So far we have described the farm system by just using words like 'input' and 'output'. Figure 5.4 shows a systems diagram for a farm which produces crops and animals. The diagram shows many of the inputs but does not give much detail about what happens on the farm (called the **farm production processes**) or the outputs. These will be explained in more detail later. We will now describe the inputs to the farm system. The inputs have important effects on farmers' decisions about how to manage their farms.

Physical inputs

The land

The land is obviously very important for farming. Farming is difficult in mountainous areas. It is usually easier in flatter, low-lying areas. It has been suggested that crop farming is difficult and inefficient where the slopes are more than 11°. Where the slopes are greater than 18° it may be impossible. In hilly areas animal farming is more likely than crop farming. The effects of this difference on population density are described in Chapter 1. Temperatures are important. Most grasses stop growing when the temperature falls below about 6°C. Temperature falls on average by 1°C for every 200 metres of **altitude** (height). This reduces the number of months of the year during which grass can grow on higher land. Rainfall may be heavier and winds stronger in upland areas. The photographs in Figure 5.5 (above and overleaf) shows the differences in farming which occur in three different areas.

Chapter 3 described the importance of soil. The best soils for farming are deep, fertile loams with good drainage. Crop farming is difficult on heavy clay soil, acid soil and thin soil.

Climate

In the section above we described how climate changes with altitude. In Chapter 3 we described how the climate changes across the globe. It is obvious that the climate limits the sort of farming which is possible in an area. For example, wheat will not normally grow further north than 60°N. Maize will not normally grow further north than 45°N unless it has been specially bred.

Frosts are useful if they break up the soil or kill pests. But they are a problem if they kill plants or kill the early blossom on fruit trees.

Rainfall is important. For example, cotton will only grow where there is between 550 and 1150 mm of rain in a year.

Wind can dry out the soil and make plants lose too much moisture. Wind can cause soil erosion. Crops can be flattened by a strong wind or a thunderstorm.

Figure 5.5b Sheep driving in the UK

Figure 5.5c Wheat farming in the USA

Activity

▲ 3 Draw systems diagrams like Figure 5.4 to show
■ each of the following types of farm.

a A subsistence farm in an area where no money is used at all
b A dairy or beef farm from which no crops are sold
c A wheat farm

Economic inputs

Capital

One of the main economic inputs to farming is **capital**. Capital is the money needed to buy new equipment or buildings. In some developing countries capital can be very difficult to find. Moneylenders sometimes charge very high rates of interest. This means that most of the farmer's profit goes in paying off interest. If there is only a small profit to be made, the farmer cannot expand his or her business. If the farm is at nearly subsistence level, the farmer may never be able to replace equipment.

A farmer also needs to get produce to the market. If the market is a long way away, or the journey is difficult, the farmer will try to grow crops such as wheat which are easy to transport. If the market is near or the journey is easy, then the farmer can grow lettuces or tomatoes which are more difficult to transport. This idea was first suggested by J H von Thünen in the 19th century. He owned an estate in northern Germany. Figure 5.6 shows the way von Thünen thought that farmers should use their land to make the greatest profit. He

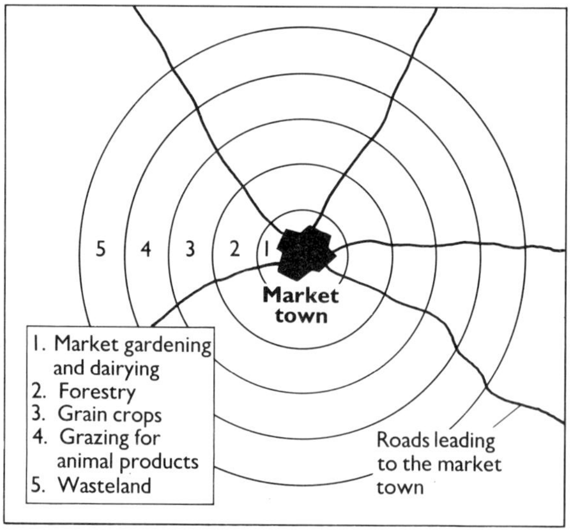

Figure 5.6 Land use rings based on von Thünen's theory of 1826

assumed that the land was all flat and that all the soil was the same quality. He also assumed that transport was equally easy from all directions.

A farmer must also consider the cost of wages. A coffee plantation needs more workers than a wheat farm on the American prairies. A farmer has to decide whether the cost of wages makes it worth while to grow one crop rather than another.

Politics and culture

In communist countries the government may control all the major decisions about farming. It may own the land, decide what should be grown, the way it should be grown and the price at which it will be sold. In other countries, governments may pay subsidies for certain kinds of farming to make it worth the farmers' while. For example, in the UK, farmers are paid a subsidy by the Government for every sheep they keep on the moorlands. This is because the Government does not want the moorlands to be wasted. In addition it wants to cut down the need for importing wool or meat.

Sometimes farmers are given **quotas** of crops. This means that they can only grow a certain area of some crops. For example in East Anglia farmers are told they may only grow a certain amount of sugar beet. If they grow more than this the British Sugar Corporation may refuse to buy the extra crop.

In the **European Economic Community (EEC)** dairy farmers are guaranteed a certain price for their milk. Far more milk is produced than customers want to buy at a fixed price. The result is the 'milk lake' and 'butter mountain' we read about in newspapers.

Social customs are also important in farming. In some countries such as France, farms used to be split up amongst the children when their father died. This meant that over the years the farms became broken into smaller and smaller pieces of land. The situation became so serious in France that the Government had to reorganize the land into farms large enough to work properly. 7 million hectares of land have been reorganized since 1941.

New developments

Farmers in the 1980s can do many things which farmers in the 1950s could not do. Many of these new possibilities are due to developments in seeds, livestock, fertilizers, pesticides, buildings and machinery, and irrigation.

Figure 5.7 Modern dairy or milk shed (roundabout system)

New types of seeds have allowed wheat to be grown much further north on the prairies. Temperate breeds of cattle which produce a lot of meat have been crossed with tropical cattle which can resist great heat. This has produced cattle which can be kept on the ranches of the Amazon basin. Chemical fertilizers have made it possible for some farmers in East Anglia to grow nothing but barley year after year.

Milking parlours have been designed so that one milker sitting down can milk a large herd of dairy cows. The cows walk on to a roundabout to get food and are milked as the roundabout goes round (Figure 5.7). This means that the cows are brought to the milker which saves the milker from moving.

Combine harvesters cut and thresh grain crops much faster than used to be possible. This reduces the number of people needed to bring in the harvest.

Artificial watering (**irrigation**) has been used in India and Egypt for thousands of years. In recent years some farmers have used irrigation on crops in areas which are not really dry and have found that their yields have increased. In other areas, huge water control schemes like the Snowy Mountains Scheme (Chapter 2) have made it possible to irrigate much more land.

The result of all these developments has been that much more food is grown by the world's farmers than ever before.

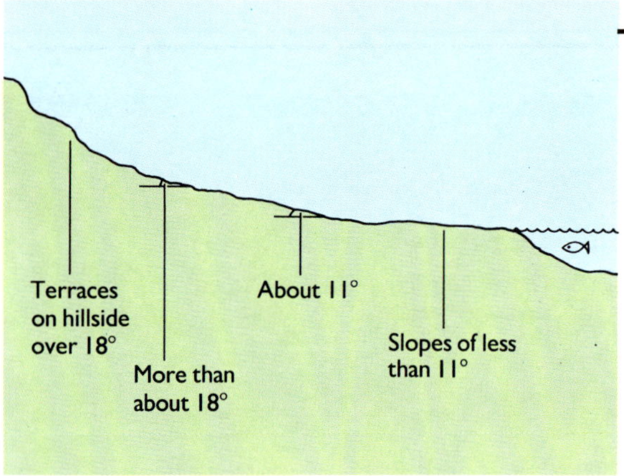

Figure 5.8 Cross-section of agricultural land

Activities

■ **4** Figure 5.8 shows a simple cross-section from a mountain range down to the sea. Copy the diagram and label it to show the advantages and disadvantages of the mountains, hills and lowlands for farming. The photographs in Figure 5.5 may help you.

▲ **5** Study Figure 5.6 which shows von Thünen's
■ ideas of rings of land-use around a town.

a **i)** Make a list of all the products which would be produced in Zone 1 – market gardening and dairying.
ii) Explain in one or two sentences why these types of farming needed to be near the town.

b **i)** Explain why von Thünen put the forestry zone so near the town.
ii) Describe the kinds of areas where forest land is found today.

c Von Thünen assumed that the town was in the middle of a plain where all the soil was the same quality and all the roads were the same quality. Draw 3 other diagrams to show how the rings would change:
i) If one of the roads were made into a dual carriageway so that transport on that road became faster and cheaper.
ii) If there were a granite hill to the south-west of the town and an area of especially fertile loam soil to the north-east of the town.
iii) If there were another smaller town some distance to the north-west of the town.

▲ **6** Study the photograph of modern dairy
■ farming (Figure 5.7).

a Explain how milking in this type of milk shed is cheaper in time and labour than in older types of milk shed.

b Explain the ways in which this type of system is more expensive than older systems.

Types of farming

Figure 5.9 shows the main types of farming in the world. If you study the key, you will see that words such as **commercial**, **subsistence** and **nomadic** are used. You may understand these words already. Check through the following section to make sure.

All the different types of farming in the world can be divided up in a number of different ways. The ways can be summarized as pairs of words. The pairs include:

arable/pastoral
sedentary/shifting or nomadic
subsistence/commercial
intensive/extensive

Arable/pastoral

Arable farming is the cultivation of soil to produce crops. Pastoral farming is animal or livestock farming. The livestock can be kept on cultivated land or on natural or semi-natural pasture.

Sedentary/shifting or nomadic

Sedentary farming is where the farmers stay in the same place. They use permanent farm buildings and farm the same land. Shifting cultivators clear an area of forest by felling the trees and burning the undergrowth. Then crops are grown for a number of years until the soil loses its fertility. The farmers then leave the old clearings and make new ones in another part of the forest. The undergrowth and trees grow back in the old clearings and the soil slowly becomes fertile again (see Chapter 3).

Nomads are people who move about with their animals to make the best use of scarce pasture and water.

Subsistence/commercial

Subsistence farmers only produce enough food for their own families (see Chapter 4). In a good year there may be a little spare to sell. In a bad year the family may go hungry. Commercial farming aims mainly at producing crops for sale, although the farmers and their families may use a small amount of what they produce. Commercial farms may be owned by large companies and be run by managers and a large staff rather than by a 'farmer' as we usually imagine. Plantations are nearly always run by companies and managers.

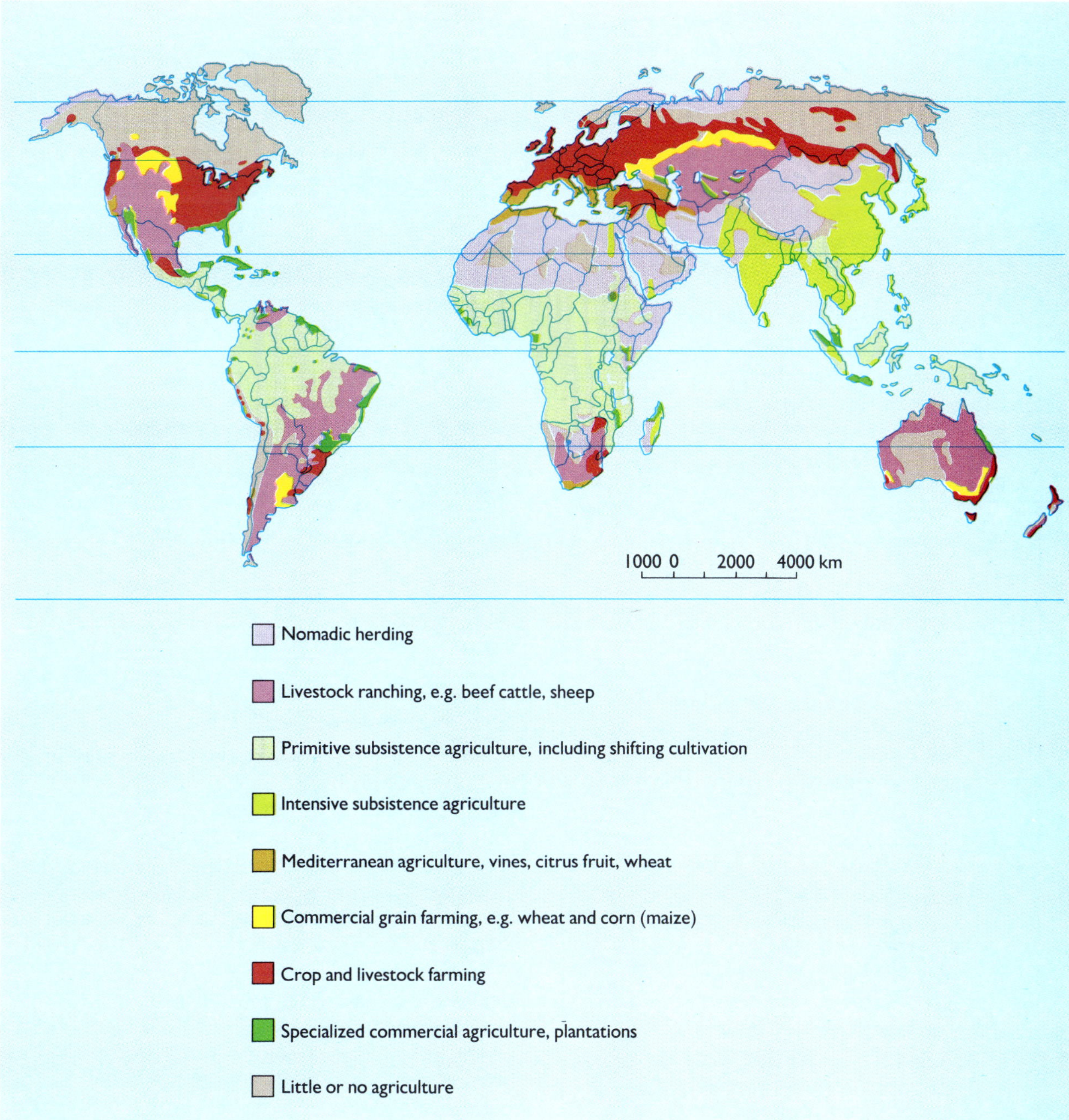

Figure 5.9 World farming

Subsistence and commercial farms can be arable or pastoral. If they are both arable and pastoral, they are called **mixed farms**.

Intensive/extensive

Intensive farming aims to get the greatest possible yield out of a certain area of land. An intensive farm can be arable or pastoral. So that it can get the greatest yield from the land, the other inputs to the farming system are increased. This can mean that many hours of labour are put into a small area. It may mean extra fertilizers, or special seeds, or irrigation or drainage. It may go so far as to cover the land with glasshouses so that even the climate can be improved.

Extensive farming tries to get the greatest yield from the lowest amount of inputs by using large areas of land. This means that yields per hectare of land are usually low. Extensive farming is usually found where there is plenty of cheap land which cannot be used in a more profitable way.

Activities

▲ 7 Read back through the last section. Use one word from each pair of words above to describe the following.

a A flower grower in Holland
b A hill sheep farmer in the Lake District of England
c The Apa Tani people before 1968
d A new cattle rancher in Amazonia, Brazil
e A wheat farmer on the prairies of North America
f A sugar cane farm in Queensland, Australia
g Lapp reindeer herders
h A dairy farmer near London
i A rice farmer on terraced land in Java
j A vine grower in southern France

▲ ■ 8 Look at the map of farming types (Figure 5.9).

a On an outline map of the world, shade in all the areas of intensive subsistence agriculture. Give your map a title.

b i) Compare your map of intensive subsistence agriculture with the map of population density (Figure 1.17).
ii) Describe the population density in the areas of subsistence agriculture.
iii) Explain why there seems to be a link between intensive subsistence farming and population density.

▲ ■ 9 a On other outline maps of the world, draw separate maps to show:
i) Livestock ranching
ii) Commercial grain farming
iii) Primitive subsistence agriculture
iv) Crop and livestock farming.

b i) Compare your maps one at a time with the maps of climate (Figure 3.18).
ii) Describe the links between each type of farming and particular types of climate.
iii) Explain why there seem to be these links.

c i) Compare your maps one at a time with the maps of soils (Figure 3.25).
ii) Describe whether each type of farming seems to be linked with a particular type of soil.
iii) Explain why there seems to be this link.

Case Study

'Strowan', an intensive crop farm in New Zealand

Strowan is a small farm on the edge of Ashburton. Ashburton is a market town 80 km south of Christchurch in the South Island of New Zealand.

To the west of Ashburton is Mt. Somers which is the beginning of the snow covered mountain ranges called the Southern Alps. To the east of Ashburton, the coastal plain slopes down to Canterbury Bight and the Pacific Ocean.

Old Mr Marshall bought Strowan in 1951 and his son Gavin, who now owns the farm, took over in 1964. Gavin Marshall runs Strowan as an intensive farm. He keeps up to date on new developments by reading various farming magazines and by going to occasional day courses at the Lincoln Agricultural College. His own son will one day take over Strowan and in 1983 was studying farming full-time at the College.

Figure 5.10 is a sketch map of Strowan and Figure 5.11 is photographs of the farmhouse and buildings. Here is a description of the farm.

The farm

The farm has a total of 90 ha of land on the very edge of the Ashburton built-up area. The farm is roughly square in shape and has roads on 3 sides. Strowan used to be divided into 20 small paddocks. These have now been joined together to make 3 large paddocks. A new track has been made across the centre of the farm.

Soil

The soil is a heavy silty loam. There is a layer of silt 30 cm deep lying on top of 90 cm of clay. Originally this land was covered in grass. There were some swampy patches. The farm has been drained using tile drains. These are porous tubes of tile laid end to end in the soil. Water soaks into the tubes and is then drained away. Although parts of the farm have to be drained, irrigation is used for all the crops except clover. A water main for irrigation is buried beside the track which runs across the centre of the farm. There are hydrants every 90 m along the water main to take the water off on to the cropped land. The water is pumped from a well. The local authority allows Mr Marshall to pump up a certain number of litres of water per second throughout the year. Artificial fertilizers are also used to make the soils more fertile and to make the yields greater. The chemical spraying is one of the important jobs to be done on the farm.

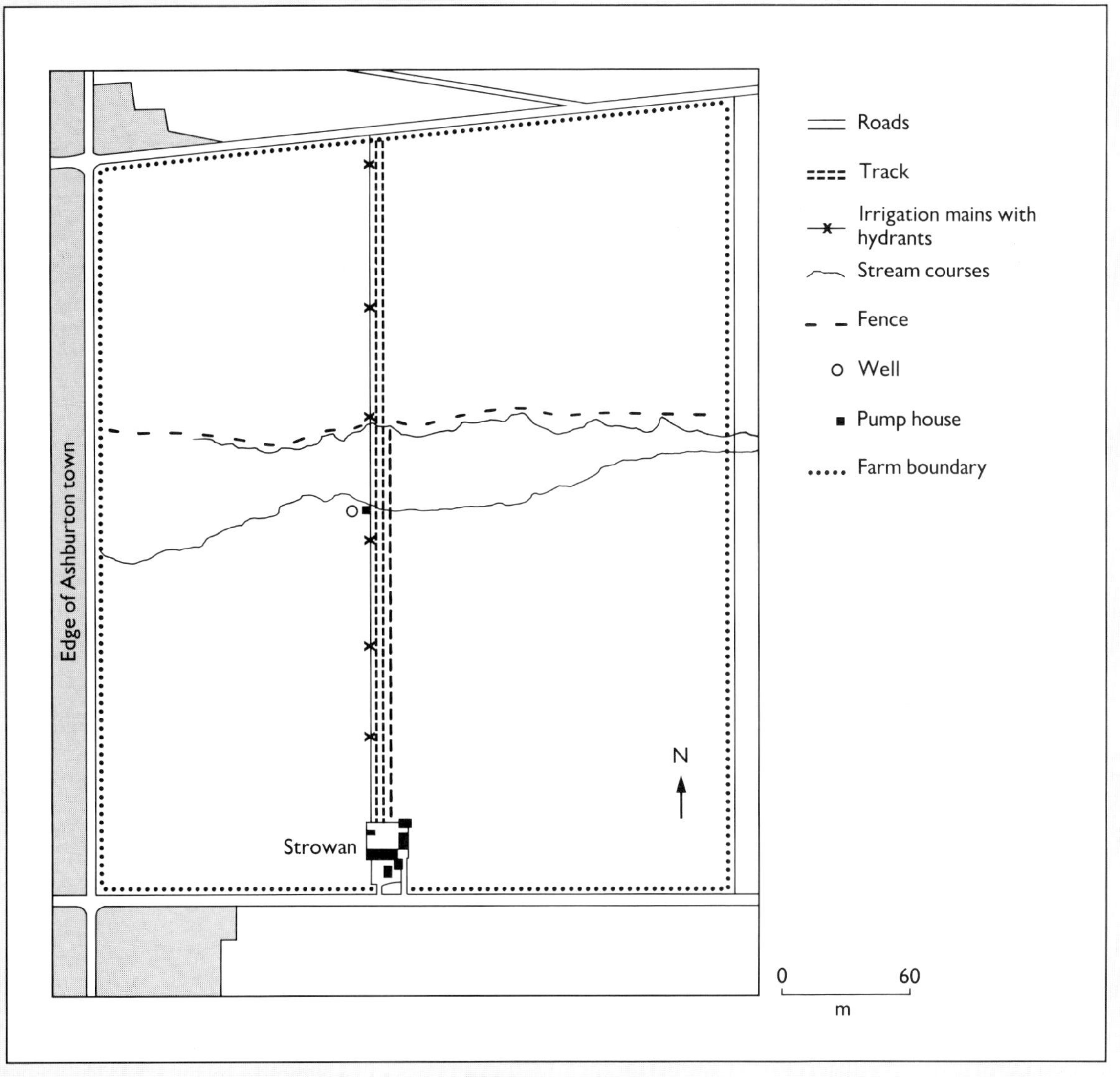

Figure 5.10 Sketch map of Strowan

Figure 5.11 Strowan farmhouse and buildings

Crops
Mr Marshall grows wheat, barley, peas and clover in rotation. In each field, white clover is grown for two years. Clover and peas are members of the plant family called **legumes**. They are leguminous. Plants in this family can 'fix' nitrogen from the air into the soil.

Peas are grown for one year. The peas also replace nitrogen in the soil. The pea crop is dried and exported to the Middle East and Asia. The grain crops – wheat and barley – take a lot of nitrogen from the soil. For this reason they are alternated with the peas and clover as part of the five year rotation. The wheat goes to make flour and the barley is used for animal feed or to make malt for beer brewing.

Ashburton has driest year since 1915

Last year was the driest recorded since 1915 according to Ashburton Domain weather figures

During 1982, 460.4 millimetres of rain fell at the domain, the second lowest annual rainfall in the 73 years records have been kept.

The lowest figure ever recorded was the 1915 annual fall of 381mm, the third lowest was 465 in 1964 and the highest was 1146 in 1938.

There were 94 wet days last year.

The heaviest fall of rain in one day last year was 36mm on Sunday, April 4 according to Ashburton man, Mr Dave Mitchell who researched the records. He has a particular interest in high intensity falls and found that a downpour of rain and hail on that day registered 27mm in nine minutes.

The rainfall for 1982 was 290mm (11 inches) lower than the average annual figure of 750mm from when records began in 1909 until the end of last year.

However, Mr Mitchell said the rainfall between September and December was above average. "I think we had the right rain at the time."

A farm advisory officer with the Ashburton Ministry of Agriculture and Fisheries, Mr Kim Stevenson said the weather was "very dry" up until last winter and this tended to distort the 1982 calendar year rainfall figures.

WET SPRING

A good rainfall about four months ago heralded the turning point and "set it up" for this growing season. "Good strategic rainfall" since then has resulted in good growth, he said.

"The crops are looking good, the feed supply is a lot better than last year, a lot of hay has been made and stock have put on condition. It's a definite improvement on last year."

"We could always do with some more rain but we are reasonably happy and I think the farming community is reasonably happy."

"It has been a morale booster. Now we need a few weeks of warm dry weather to get the harvest in and then some rain to establish the autumn crops," he said.

SUNNIEST YEAR

The Domain records also showed that last year was among the sunniest ever with 1924.5 hours of sunshine up until November. Readings for December were not available.

February 15 was the hottest day in 1982 when the temperature reached 38.5 degrees celsius, the second hottest February day since 1909.

The hottest day last month was on December 17 when the temperature reached 32.7, compared to December 1981 when the maximum was 32.3. The minimum for December that year was 4.4 compared to 1.7 on December 2, 1982.

Rain fell on nine days last month with a total of 42.66mm. Of this, 13mm fell on the wettest day, December 12, when thunder was also experienced here. There were no frosts.

Figure 5.12 Extract from the *Ashburton Guardian*

As well as spraying artificial fertilizers, Mr Marshall uses chemicals for pest control. The wheat seed is treated with fungicides before it is planted. Both the wheat and barley crops are sprayed against rust and aphids. A general weed killer is used on the soil before the peas are planted. Even the clover may need spraying against aphids and moths.

Marketing
The New Zealand Government has a guaranteed price for wheat. This makes sure that it is worth while to grow it. Mr Marshall has a contract to sell his barley to the South Island Export Barley Society. This is a co-operative which was set up in 1981. The basic barley price is usually known in advance because the Malting Companies in New Zealand set the price each September (September is spring time in New Zealand!). Since the Malting Companies do not know how good the harvest will be, they will also buy barley at an 'open pool price' once the harvest is in. Depending on whether the yields and quality of the barley are higher or lower, this open pool price may be higher or lower than the fixed price. Mr Marshall often chooses to take the risk and goes for the open pool price.

Clover is the most risky crop for marketing. The clover seed is collected for sale overseas. Sometimes the price is low and sometimes it is very high.

Labour and machinery
Mr Marshall needs extra help from one extra person for a total of about 2 months in the year. The farm owns the following machinery:

1 90 HP two-wheel drive tractor	2 cultivators
	1 roller
1 8 tonne truck	3 harrows
1 utility truck	1 weed spraying trailer
1 mower	
1 plough	1 seed drill

There are 4 grain silos for storing grain and 2 sheds as part of the farm outbuildings.

Climate
Sometimes there is a steady drying wind from the mountains. This can be a problem, particularly with ripe barley. Special wind-resistant types of barley have to be grown. Another problem is caused by heavy rain after irrigation. When this happens the soil gets too wet. Figure 5.12 is a report from the local newspaper *Ashburton Guardian*. It gives an idea of what the weather is like in Ashburton and the things the farmers worry about. Ashburton Domain is the main park in the town.

Activities

▲ ■ **10 a** Use one of each of the 4 pairs of words on page 100 to describe Strowan.

b i) What features show that Strowan is an intensive farm?

ii) Explain why Mr Marshall uses intensive farming methods on his land.

▲ ■ **11 a** Draw up a table with 2 columns. Head one column 'Natural factors' and the other column 'Economic factors'. Under these headings make lists of all the factors which influence Mr Marshall's decisions on what to grow and the ways that he grows his crops.

b Which list if the more important? Explain why the factors in this list are more important than those in the other list.

▲ ■ **12 a** Draw a systems diagram of Strowan like the one in Figure 5.4. Show the inputs, processes, outputs and feedback.

b Can you suggest any ways of improving this system? Write a paragraph to explain how the system could be improved.

▲ ■ **13** Look back at the section on water in Chapter 2 (page 34).

a i) What happens when the soil on Strowan gets too wet after there has been rain and irrigation?

ii) What might happen to the soil if Mr Marshall used his tractor on the land after irrigation and rainfall?

b What are the long term dangers of irrigation by sprinkler and draining the land by buried pipes?

c If the well is on Mr Marshall's land, explain why Mr Marshall has to get permission to pump water for irrigation.

d Explain the advantages and the disadvantages of making the 20 small paddocks into 3 large paddocks.

▲ ■ **14** Read the newspaper article (Figure 5.12).

a Sort out the information which is on rainfall, sunshine hours and temperatures.

b Describe the climate of Ashburton as far as you can from this information.

c What does the article suggest to you about the importance of the climate to the farmers?

Case Study

Rubber plantations in Malaysia

Everyone knows that in 'Fourteen hundred and ninety-two, Columbus sailed the ocean blue', but what did he do in 1496? The answer is he brought back from Haiti a ball which bounced.

The ball was made from **latex** from a wild rubber tree. At that time no one could see much use for natural rubber. It got very sticky when it was hot and very brittle when it was cold. But in 1839, Charles Goodyear discovered how to solve this problem by **vulcanizing** the rubber. He mixed the rubber with sulphur and heated it up. This made a kind of rubber which was not so badly affected by heat or cold. This meant that more uses could be found for rubber.

The wild rubber trees grew mainly in the Amazon forests of Brazil. There are so many different trees in a tropical rain forest that the wild rubber trees were very spread out. This made collecting rubber a very slow process.

In 1876, the India Office of the British Government asked Sir Henry Wickham to collect some seeds of the wild rubber trees from Brazil. He collected 70000 seeds and delivered them to Kew Gardens. The seeds were germinated and the seedlings were taken to Ceylon and Malaysia. In Ceylon (now Sri Lanka) and Malaysia, large estates of rubber trees were planted. These were called **rubber plantations**.

The demand for rubber grew even more when John Boyd Dunlop invented the inflatable rubber tyre in 1888 and when Henry Ford produced a motor car which many people could afford. Figure 5.13 shows where the world output of natural rubber came from in 1984.

Rubber trees need temperatures between 24°C and 28°C and rainfall of 1800–2000 mm, evenly spread throughout the year. These conditions are found in equatorial regions. Look back at the map of world climate (Figure 3.18).

	'000 tonnes		
Malaysia	1 529	Other S. American	23
Indonesia	1 115	Ivory Coast	35
Thailand	600	Campouchia	22
China	190	Zaire	18
India	184	Cameroon	18
Philippines	80	Burma	10
Liberia	76	Ghana	1
Vietnam	55	Central African Republic	2
Nigeria	45		
Brazil	36	Other countries	180
Total world production			4 225

Figure 5.13 World production of natural rubber

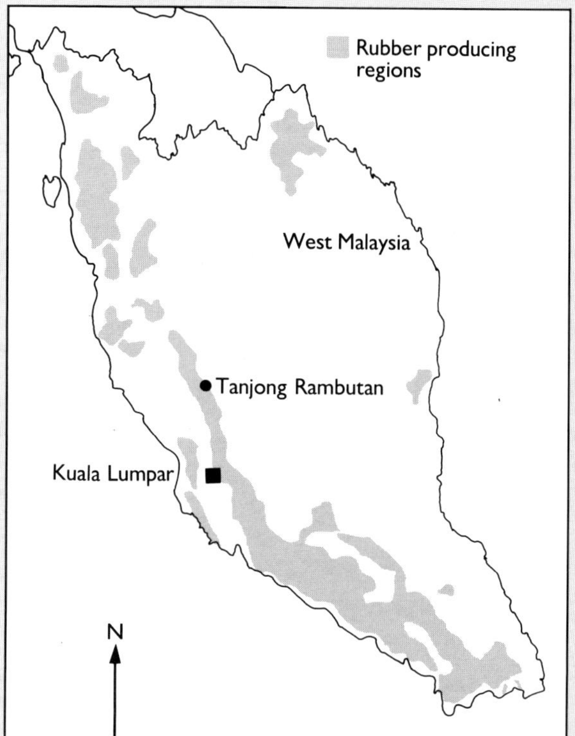

Figure 5.14 W. Malaysia

Figure 5.13 shows that Malaysia is the world's most important producer of natural rubber. Figure 5.14 shows the peninsula of West Malaysia and Figure 5.15 shows the area around the town called Tanjong Rambutan. The Tanjong Rambutan area is a typical area for rubber plantations.

West Malaysia has 1.88 million ha of rubber trees. They are mainly found to the west of the mountains. About half of Malaysia's rubber is grown on plantations of more than 40 ha. Most plantations are between 600 and 1200 ha. About 100 trees are planted on each hectare. Each plantation employs between 300 and 500 people.

The other half of Malaysia's rubber is grown on smallholdings. These are usually between 1.2 and 3.2 ha. The smallholdings are owned and run by separate families. The family will have a few hectares of rubber, an orchard or a rice field and a house on its land.

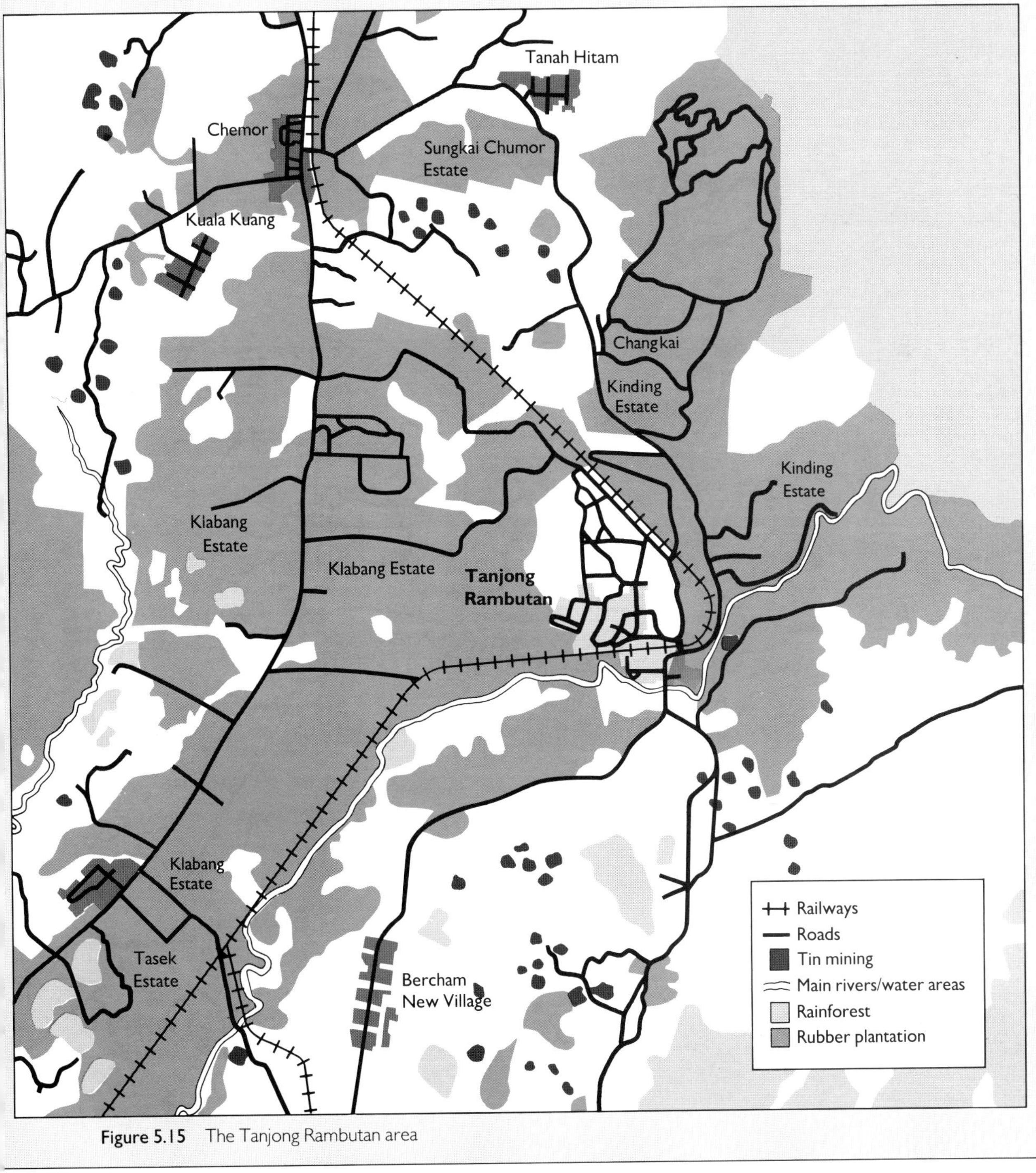

Figure 5.15 The Tanjong Rambutan area

Figure 5.16 A typical Malaysian rubber plantation

1 The rubber tapper cuts the bark and allows the latex to flow into a cup which is attached to the tree.

2 The tappers take the latex to a collecting centre from where it is sent to the processing factory by lorry.

3 At the factory the first task is to test the quality of the latex by measuring its dry rubber content (DRC).

4 At the factory the latex is concentrated by spinning off excess water in a huge centrifuge.

5 Some of the concentrated latex is packed straight into drums for export.

6 Some of the latex is sieved to remove dirt. Then it is coagulated by adding acid.

7 In some modern factories, the coagulated latex is made into crumbs of rubber by adding castor oil and passing it through rollers.

8 When this crumb rubber is made, it is dried by hot air at 100 °C.

9 Baling rubber. The dried crumb rubber is compressed into bales which are kept clean by being wrapped in polythene film.

10 Each bale weighs 33.33 kg. 30 of these bales are packed together on each 1 tonne pallet.

11 The pallets are packed into containers to be sent to the port for shipment.

12 Nursery of rubber tree seedlings. Carefully selected trees have been cross-fertilized to give modern high-yielding varieties.

13 Clearing old trees for replanting with the latest high-yielding varieties.

14 Plantation of young rubber trees. These are not tapped until about five years after planting when they can produce enough latex to make tapping worthwhile.

15 Estate village. The many workers employed on a large rubber plantation live in villages which may have shops, schools and hospitals.

16 A typical smallholding. A smallholder usually has a couple of hectares of land with rubber trees, an orchard or rice field and a small wooden house. He may grow other crops or keep animals between the rows of rubber trees.

Figure 5.16 shows the layout and work of the plantations and smallholdings. Figure 5.17 shows how the tree is cut so that the latex can drip into the collecting cup.

In recent years scientists have developed new types of rubber trees by crossing different species. The new trees produce more latex each day.

Rubber from Malaysia is exported to the countries of Europe, Japan, USA, USSR and the Republic of China. Almost half of Malaysia's total exports is made up of rubber. Rubber brings in one third of the country's earnings. One third of its workers are employed in the rubber industry. Since World War II synthetic rubber has been made from oil. This has taken away some of the uses of natural rubber. Natural rubber is still best for aircraft tyres which need to stand up to sudden high temperatures on landing and for rubber mountings for road bridges and buildings which must stand up to much vibration.

Figure 5.17 Tapping rubber in W. Malaysia

Activities

■ **15** Study Figure 5.13 which shows where the natural rubber grown in the world came from in 1984.

a On an outline map of the world, shade in the countries which produce natural rubber.

b Draw columns or circles on your map to show how much rubber each country produces.

c Describe the location of the countries which produce natural rubber. Mention:

i) the lines of latitude which enclose the rubber producing countries

ii) the climate of the areas where rubber grows

iii) the main types of natural vegetation in the areas where rubber grows (look back at Chapter 3).

d Draw a bar chart to show the proportions of the world's rubber production which come from:

i) SE Asia **iii)** South America

ii) Africa **iv)** Other areas.

▲ ■ ● **16** Study Figure 5.16.

a Describe the ways in which the rubber plantation is similar to natural equatorial rain forest.

b i) Explain how people have changed the ecosystem of the lowlands of Malaysia.

ii) Write a paragraph to describe the advantages of these changes for people.

iii) Write a paragraph to describe the disadvantages for people and for the ecosystem itself of these changes.

■ **17 a** Use each of the 4 pairs of words on page 100 to describe a rubber plantation.

b Draw a systems diagram like the one in Figure 5.4 to show the inputs, processes, outputs and feedback of a rubber plantation.

▲ ■ ● **18** Read back over Chapter 4 and the information on Malaysia in this chapter. Rubber accounts for half of Malaysia's foreign trade, one third of Malaysia's revenue and occupies one third of its labour force.

a Explain why this concentration on rubber may make long term planning for the Malaysian Government difficult.

b Explain what may happen if a type of synthetic rubber which was suitable for aircraft tyres were developed.

General features of plantations

Crops such as cotton, tobacco, cocoa, coffee, tea, sugar cane and bananas are also grown on plantations. All these plantations are very similar to rubber plantations. Most plantations were set up during the time when European countries were controlling other parts of the world as colonies. Money from the western countries was used to set up the estates and the managers were nearly always Europeans or Americans. When the colonies became independent countries, they took over the management of many of the plantations. Sometimes the European or American managers were kept on. Some people think that the plantation system has been good for the developing countries. Other people think the opposite. The following two activities will help you to decide your own views.

Activities

▲ ■ **19** Figure 5.18 lists pairs of phrases which describe farms. The phrases are separated by boxes. You have to choose the box which you think best summarizes what plantations are like. A score of 1 means that you think that the left-hand phrase describes plantations exactly, 5 means that you think that the right-hand phrase describes plantations exactly, 3 means that either of the phrases could be used; 2 or 4 means that you think that the phrase could be used to a certain extent, but not entirely.

a Copy Figure 5.18 and put rings round the scores which you think describe plantations best.

b Add up your total score. If your total is 24 or less, you have described plantations well.

c Use the phrases you have scored as 1 or 2 to write a description of plantations.

▲ ■ ● **20** Figure 5.19 gives two viewpoints on plantations. Read them both carefully.

a Decide on the advantages and disadvantages of plantations. Write two or three paragraphs explaining your own views on whether plantations are good or bad for developing countries.

b Organize a class debate on advantages and disadvantages of plantations.

Cover a large area	1	2	3	4	5	Cover a small area
Need capital investment	1	2	3	4	5	No capital investment needed
Are examples of intensive farming	1	2	3	4	5	Are examples of extensive farming
Use very little machinery	1	2	3	4	5	Use a lot of machinery
Grow mainly cash crops	1	2	3	4	5	Grow mainly subsistence crops
Employ a large labour force	1	2	3	4	5	Employ a small labour force
Export most of their produce	1	2	3	4	5	Their produce is mainly for home consumption
Specialize in one or two crops	1	2	3	4	5	Grow a large range of crops
Do not usually keep livestock	1	2	3	4	5	Frequently keep livestock
Are usually found in thinly populated areas	1	2	3	4	5	Are usually found in densely populated areas
Use a local labour force	1	2	3	4	5	Use mainly western labour
Use 'western' capital	1	2	3	4	5	Use local sources of capital
Do some basic processing on site	1	2	3	4	5	Do not do any processing on site

Figure 5.18 Phrases describing farming

Plantations viewpoint no. 1

North America and Western Europe act as key markets. They specialize in secondary and tertiary industry. They are like the cities in von Thünen's theory, but on a world scale. During the colonial period they 'developed' the farming of sub-tropical countries by establishing the large-scale production of crops in plantations. They supplied capital, employed managers, cleared the natural vegetation and provided employment for the native people. They improved transport by building roads, railways and ports. The standard of living was raised. Wages, health and housing were improved. Upon independence, the plantations were left for the newly independent nations to carry on as a source of income to purchase food, equipment and raw materials. Where required, western management would stay on. Western countries processed the plantation products and produced food and clothing which could be imported by the developing countries. Western people provided the drive, capital, expertise and technology. The host countries provided the labour and the land and benefited from the reorganization.

Plantations viewpoint no. 2

During the colonial period, less developed countries were exploited by colonizing powers. Their land and labour were used by the western world. Large areas of land were taken over for plantations. Peasant subsistence farming was destroyed to make way for the plantations. The cultivation of specific crops was forced on the traditional farmers. Local people provided cheap labour. Millions of people were involved in migration to form labour pools. Indians, for example, moved into Malaysia to work on the rubber plantations. American and European industry became rich by importing cheap raw materials and making them into items for sale at home and abroad. Manufacturing was limited in the developing countries. Upon independence, third world farmers keep plantations going as a source of income, though conditions of sale may not be favourable and they might be better off growing more food and developing their own industries. They should also grow a greater variety of crops. For example, sugar became the mainstay of the economy of many Caribbean countries because of the plantation system. The prices change from year to year. The sugar cane producers are in competition with sugar beet farmers. Beet is grown in the developed countries who first established the plantations and who originally depended upon the sugar cane for their imports of sugar.

Figure 5.19 Plantation viewpoints

The Green Revolution

> *'Famine is thriving. At the start of the third development decade, the food resources of several hundreds of millions of people are falling. At a time when the rich nations are mastering costly and often useful technologies and when science is regarded with religious fervour, the most elementary needs of men, women and children are not being satisfied.'*
>
> (*Jacques Grall*)

These words were written in 1980. They tell us that many people are underfed in the 1980s, even though the amount of food produced has been steadily increasing for the last 30 years.

The increase in the amount of food produced has been encouraged by the **Food and Agricultural Organization** of the United Nations (**FAO**). This organization was set up in 1945. FAO works with the governments of the world to try to increase food production and to improve the management of forests.

Population 684 million
70% of population engaged in agriculture
Half the total area of India is under cultivation
Principal cash crops: sugar cane, oil seeds, cotton, jute, cashew nuts, tea, tobacco, rubber
World's largest producer of groundnuts and tea
World's second largest producer of rice and jute
World's third largest producer of raw sugar, tobacco and cotton

Growth rate of agricultural production

1900–47	0.3%
1951–79	2.7%

Production of food grains (rice, wheat and other cereals) (million tonnes)

1950–1	55
1977–8	126.4
1978–9	131.4
1979–80	109.7

Average yields (kg per ha)

	1950–1	1977–8
Wheat	655	1480
Rice	668	1308

Land growing high yield varieties of crops (million ha)

1979–80	43
1985	56

Total irrigated area (million ha)

1950–1	22
1978–9	58.5
1985	68

Use of chemical fertilizers (million tonnes)

1961	0.3
1979–80	5

Figure 5.20 Fact sheet: The Green Revolution in India

Figure 5.21 A simple tube well in N. India (Punjab)

During the 1960s in particular there were many important new developments in food supply. These became known as **The Green Revolution**.

The Green Revolution has been successful in many countries. Figure 5.20 gives a summary of the improvements in India. The changes in India were organized in a series of five-year plans. The sixth plan began in 1980.

Four changes in the Green Revolution have been particularly effective. Firstly, new varieties of crops have been developed. This has been done by **hybridization** – cross-breeding plants. This can make varieties which produce high yields, are resistant to disease and grow quickly. There are hybrids of maize, wheat, rice and grass for animal fodder.

Secondly, many countries have built new water control schemes. Some schemes, like the Aswan scheme (Chapter 2), are large and expensive. Other schemes just involve drilling new tube wells and using more efficient pumps to pump water on to the fields. Figure 5.21 shows a simple tube well with a small pump in the Punjab of India.

Thirdly, more chemicals have been supplied as fertilizers and for controlling pests and diseases.

Fourthly, farmers have been helped to store, handle and sell their produce. Much of the food grown in the world is lost due to wastage in store.

Figure 5.22 shows just some of the successes of the Green Revolution as newspaper headlines. Headlines may attract attention, but they do not tell the whole story. We will describe the background to one of these headlines in more detail.

IR 58, the wonder rice of the 1980s

The International Rice Research Institute (IRRI) in the Philippines has done a lot of research into new varieties of rice. One of its best known new types of rice is **IR 8 miracle rice**. This is used on 10% of the **padi land** in India. Padi land is rice growing land which is flooded for the rice to be planted.

Although IR 8 has a high yield, many farmers found that it is not very resistant to diseases and pests. The IRRI tried to produce a better rice. In the 1970s they created **IR 36**. This rice could resist a long list of nasty problems such as bacterial blight, rice blast, grassy stunt, green leaf hopper, brown leaf hopper, stem borer and gall midge. However, even with IR 36, new

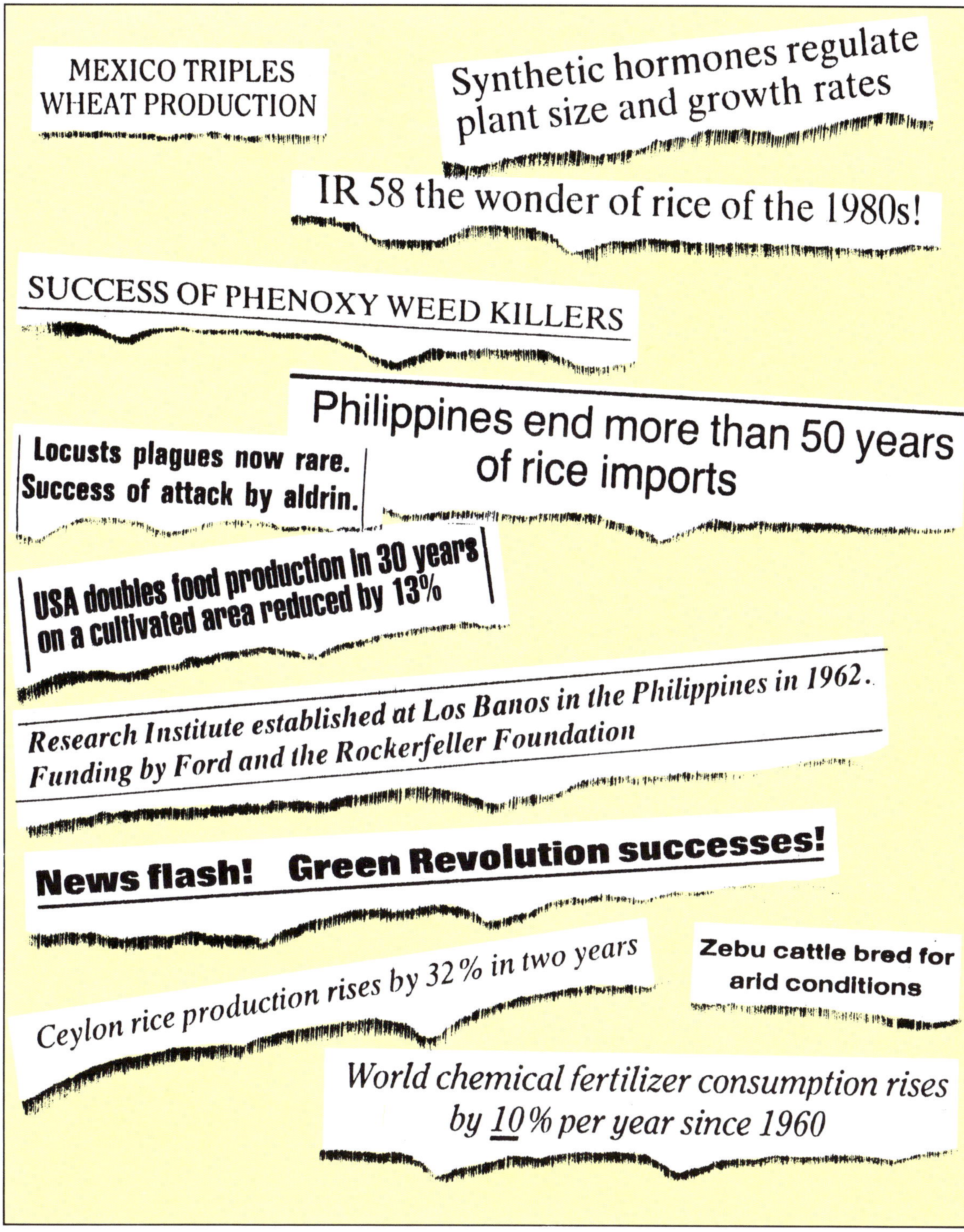

Figure 5.22 News Flash! Green Revolution successes

diseases and pests appeared. Two of these were virus diseases called ragged stunt and wilted stunt.

In October 1982, **IR 58** was introduced. IR 58 can resist these new diseases. It takes 10% less time than IR 36 to reach harvest time. It looks as if IR 58 is the high yield rice of the 1980s. The IRRI are now waiting to see what new disease will be discovered. They will then try to solve the next problem!

The Green Revolution has not been all success. There have been problems as well. The case study of the Green Revolution in the Punjab shows some of the successes and problems.

Case Study

Progress and problems in the Punjab

In the mid-1970s three British geographers visited the Punjab. The Punjab is known as India's 'bread-basket' state. Today it is a wealthy state and produces about a quarter of India's wheat. The farmers of the Punjab are hard-working and ready to try out new ideas and machinery.

One of the most important improvements in the Punjab was the increase in irrigation. This is done by using the canals and rivers and by new tube wells. A tube well is a narrow boring deep below the water table. The water is then pumped up by diesel pumps. Tube wells were a major technological advance for the Punjab. Figure 5.21 on page 112 shows a tube well in the Punjab.

There were other improvements. Many farmers owned their land in strips which were scattered around their village. These strips were brought together so that each farmer had land in a single plot. New high yield types of wheat, maize and IR 8 rice were introduced. Loans of money were made so that farmers could buy the chemical fertilizers, chemical pesticides and the machinery they needed to get the best out of these new types of seeds.

This quickly brought changes to the standard of living in the Punjab. In a few years the farmers stopped being traditional subsistence farmers. They became modern technological farmers and sold their goods for money. Some of them left their old baked mud houses and moved into new brick built houses. Many farmers could afford refrigerators, electric fans and transistor radios.

There is another side to this success story. Many of the small landowners were forced to give up farming because they could not afford to borrow money to modernize their land. By 1975, even the more successful farmers were finding it difficult to repay their loans. It was getting more difficult to find workers. Many labourers moved to the towns to get better wages. This added to the problems of the towns which we will explain in Chapter 7. The Indian Government was planning to introduce a new tax based on the value of the farmers' land.

Even more difficult problems were caused by the world economic situation. There was an oil shortage. This put up the cost of diesel fuel, electricity, fertilizers, pesticides and seeds. Fertilizers were polluting the ground water and upsetting the ecosystems of rivers. In some places the water supply for humans became polluted. In the rivers and lakes fish died. The fish often provided important protein for people to eat. Some farmers began to save the seeds from their own crops for the next year. Others used less and less fertilizer or pesticide. If farmers could not afford diesel fuel they could not irrigate their crops. All these things began to lead to lower and lower yields. Some of the new types of rice give even lower yields than the traditional types if they are not given the right fertilizers and amount of water.

Some experts have said that the successes of the Green Revolution in India in the early years were mainly due to a number of years of good farming weather. They are afraid that poor quality soils which have been ploughed up for intensive farming may become dust bowls during the next series of dry years. (Look back to the dust bowl of America, Chapter 2.)

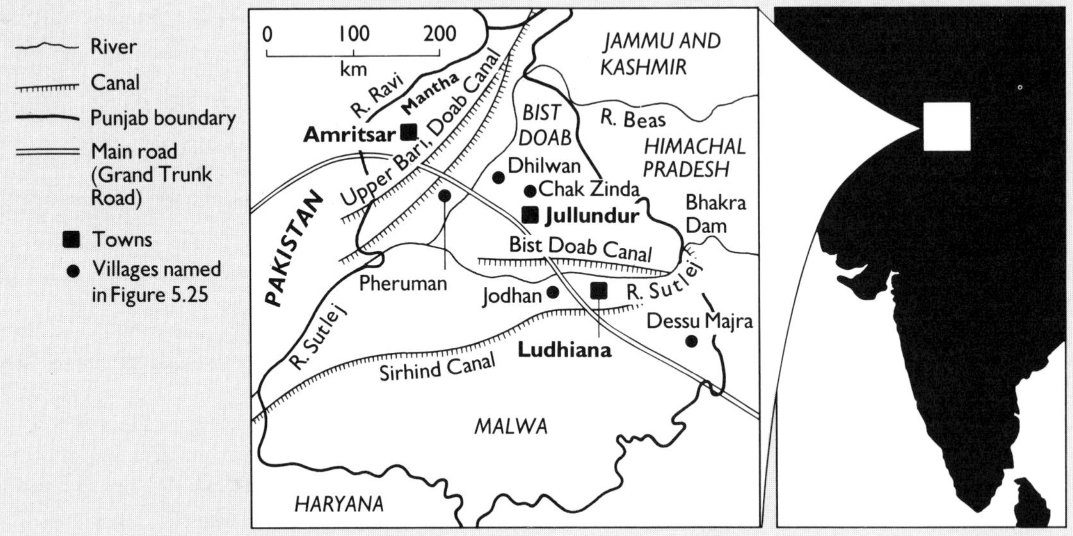

Figure 5.23 The Punjab, North West India

Activities

▲ ■ ● **21** Read the quotation which was given at the start of this section on the Green Revolution.

a Explain what 'the third development decade' means.

b Describe 4 'costly but useful technologies'.

c Explain what the writer means by 'the most elementary needs of men, women and children'.

▲ ■ **22** Study the fact sheet on the Green Revolution in India (Figure 5.20).

a Draw a series of graphs to illustrate the changes shown by the figures.

b Look at the information in your diagrams and at the top of Fig. 5.20. Describe how agriculture in India has changed.

■ **23** Look back at the case study of the Aswan scheme in Chapter 2 and the photograph of the tube well (Figure 5.21). Describe the advantages and disadvantages of each type of irrigation scheme.

▲ ■ **24** Figure 5.24 shows the climate of the Punjab and the farming activities during the year. Figure 5.23 is a map of the Punjab.

a Describe the location of the Punjab in India.

b Use the map of climate (Figure 3.18) and Figure 5.24 to help you to describe the climate of the Punjab.

c **i)** List the months when a drought is most likely.

ii) Explain why there can be a drought in these months even though the graph shows rainfall all through the year. (There are 2 possible answers to this.)

d **i)** List the crops grown in the village of Chak Zinda and Jullundur.

ii) Make a chart of the months of the year. Under each month write a list of the main jobs of the farmer in these villages.

iii) Describe the links between climate and farmers' jobs.

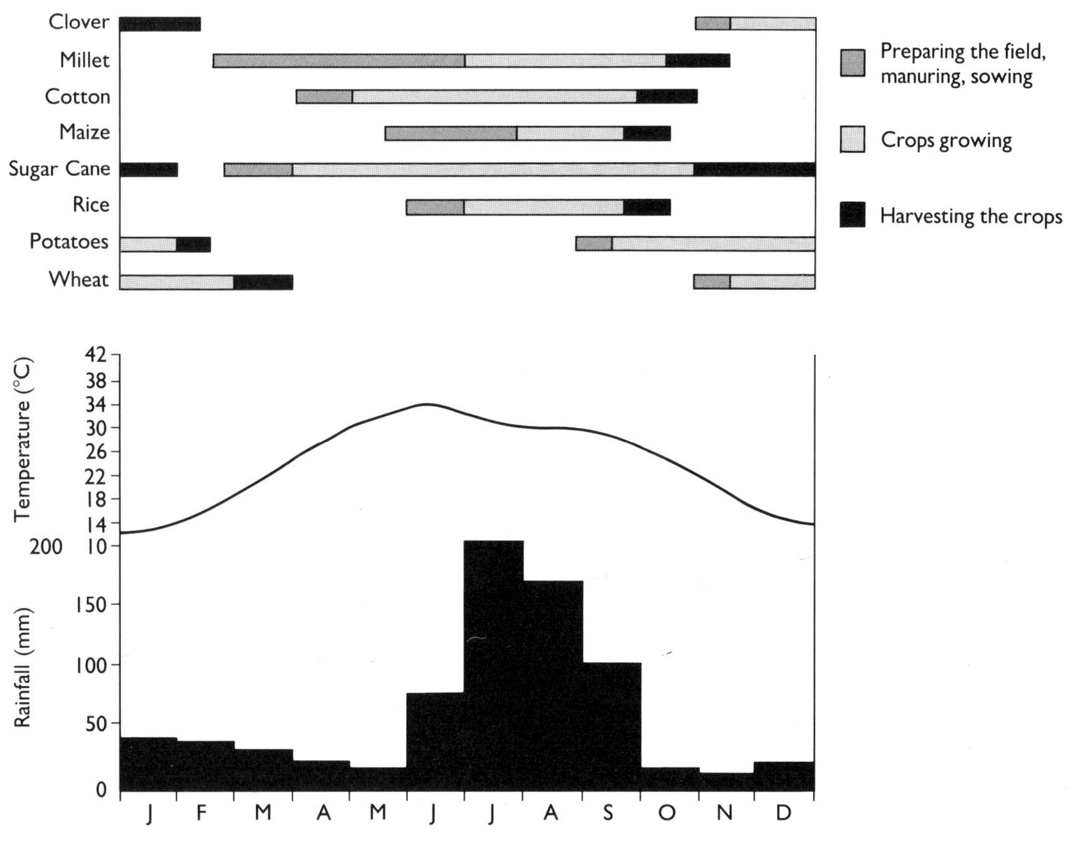

Figure 5.24 Farming activity and climate in the villages of Chak Zinda and Jullundur

Activities

▲ 25 Figure 5.25 shows how the amounts of
■ wheat, rice, maize and millet grown in the Punjab increased from 1950–1 to 1973–4. Figure 5.26 shows how irrigation was introduced in 5 villages.

a i) Draw bar charts to show how the production of the different grains has increased.

ii) Write a paragraph to explain what your bar charts show.

b Use the information in Figures 5.26 and 5.24 to help you describe the irrigation in each of the 5 villages. You should describe where the water comes from and how much land of each village is irrigated.

▲ 26 a Make 2 lists. In one, list the successes of the
■ Green Revolution in the Punjab. In the
● other, list the problems caused by the Green Revolution in the Punjab.

b i) For each of the problems you have listed, suggest one way in which that problem could be overcome.

ii) Write a final paragraph to explain how likely you think it is that your answers to the problems will be tried. Explain all the things which might prevent your answers being successful.

Crop	Area ('000 ha)	Production ('000 tonnes)	Yield (kg/ha)
Wheat			
1951	1137	1024	901
1973–4	2336	6000	2408
Rice			
1951	120	107	892
1973–4	335	1125	2045
Maize			
1950	252	142	565
1974	558	838	1610
Millet			
1950	220	83	383
1974	145	171	1180

Figure 5.25 Food grain production in the Punjab 1950-57

Village	% of land irrigated	Approx no. of wells tube	open	Date of 1st tube well	Use of canal for irrigation
Dessu Nājra	85	40	60	1962	–
Pheruman	100	50	10	*	Upper Bari Doab
Dhilwan	*	200	–	1965	–
Chak Zinda	100	10	–	1963	–
Jodhan	80	200	–	1964	Sirhind

*not recorded.

Figure 5.26 Irrigation in five Punjabi villages

Farming in the future

Farming began only about 12000 years ago and it has developed very quickly, particularly in the last 300 years. There are no signs that the speed of development will slow down. A crystal ball would probably show that agriculture will continue to develop in three main ways. Firstly, farming will become even more efficient by using new types of technology. Many processes will be controlled by microchips. Secondly, new ways of growing, storing and selling crops will be developed which can be used by poor people as well as rich people. Thirdly, agricultural products will be used in new ways.

There are already many examples of developments like these. Here are some of them.

New technology: Remote control on the farm and the use of satellites

Scientists at the National Institute of Agricultural Engineering in Bedfordshire think that the tractors, ploughs and combine harvesters of today will be in museums by the early 21st century. They may be replaced by gantries like the one described in Figure 5.27.

Satellites are already providing a lot of information which is useful to farmers and governments. They could provide much more information. **Landsat** is a satellite specially made to provide information on land use. It was used in an American experiment called **LACIE**. LACIE stands for **Large Area Crop Inventory Experiment**. Landsat used infra-red cameras to record the Russian grain crop in 1977. From the results, the scientists forecast a total yield of 91.4 million tonnes. Later, after the harvest, the Russians announced that the actual yield was 92 million tonnes. Satellite photographs can also show areas where the crops are not getting enough water and where forests are suffering from diseases.

Exit tractor enter gantry: a field of crops in 2030

Farming by remote control

FIFTY years from now, the typical British farmer will have seen a plough or a combine harvester only in a museum. He will cultivate his fields from the cab of a 60-foot wide gantry that will till the soil, sow seed, spray and irrigate growing crops, and harvest them when they are ready.

This picture of mechanized farming in the year 2030 was outlined to the British Association for the Advancement of Science in York by John Matthews, of the National Institute of Agricultural Engineering. It is, he says, "based very much on today's technology and that which a research engineer can see to be not far away."

In many fields of growing cereals today, well-defined "tramlines" can be seen, along which tractors drive to spray and fertilize the crop.

A gantry spanning a wide strip is an obvious improvement. A farmer near Stratford-upon-Avon is already experimenting with such a system for spraying and irrigating. For the year 2030, Matthews envisages a gantry spanning 60 feet or so guided automatically by cables laid under the trackways.

Its job will include:

Cultivation: Weed control will be chemical. With a gantry, tillage to a depth of only a couple of inches should be sufficient, instead of eight inches or so at present. The power required may be as little as 10 per cent of today's levels.

Planting: Cereal seeds will be planted automatically, singly and at optimum spacing. With the help of a soil moisture meter, they might also be planted automatically at the optimum depth. Planting might even take place before the previous crop had been harvested, when the soil structure is at its best.

Spraying: Fertilizers and other sprays will be applied from the gantry at a height of only a few inches to minimize drift and wastage.

Harvesting: The gantry will not thresh the grain as it cuts it, like a combine harvester. Instead, it will harvest the whole crop, chop it up, and deliver it to remote-controlled carrying vehicles at the edge of the field. Threshing might be done ultrasonically, and grain drying by microwave.

Bryan Silcock

Figure 5.27 Gantries like this may replace tractors by the 21st century

New methods for feeding rich and poor

Today the world produces enough food to give every person on Earth 3000 calories and 65 grams of vegetable protein each day. In fact human beings can live quite happily on 2200 calories and 13 grams of vegetable protein. In spite of all this 'spare' food, many people on Earth are underfed or starving.

A lot of food is lost by being stored badly. Some food is eaten or spoiled by mice and rats. Some is eaten by insects. Some gets damp and rots, or is spoiled by fungus and mildew.

In the rich countries one third of all grain crops grown are used to feed animals for meat or milk production. A lot of food which could be used for humans is used to feed pet animals in richer countries. In the poor countries the farmers are often encouraged to grow crops for export rather than food for home consumption. Farmers are also put off growing food crops because their governments keep prices low so that the poor people in towns can afford to pay for food.

Food which is imported from the developed world is often used by the rich people in the developing countries. The poor people cannot afford to buy it.

The world economic system needs to be changed so that everyone can be fed properly. In Chapter 4 we explained how important it is that the developed world pays fair prices to developing countries for their agricultural and other primary products.

In the meantime various ways of producing more cheap protein for the starving people of the world are being developed. Here are five of them.

More protein would be available for human beings if

1 Animals were fed on things which people can't eat, like grass, waste foods as in pigswill, algae which grows in sewage and chemically-treated straw. This would increase protein for humans by between 5 and 10 times.
2 Fish farming could produce a lot of protein and need not take up any land! In the Antarctic Ocean there are large shoals of tiny fish called krill. If these shoals were harvested it could double the world's annual fish catch.
3 Scientists can convert waste materials such as fish waste into protein suitable for human consumption by changing the taste, smell and texture.
4 Scientists can also 'knit' vegetable proteins like soya beans into foods which seem like meat. This is already on the supermarket shelves and in school lunches as **tvp (texturized vegetable protein)**.
5 The Welsh have made laver bread from seaweed for many years and the Japanese produce several different dried seaweeds and vegetables. The idea of eating algae is being taken further in Israel. Shallow, salty ponds in the desert are used to grow algae. The algae are then collected, dried and converted to food.

Figure 5.28

With modifications, a vehicle can run entirely on alcohol fuel
Alcohol fuel is ethyl alcohol
A car can run on 10% alcohol and 90% petrol with no modifications
There are 315 million cars in the world
1400 million people in the world are underfed
It is estimated that in 1985 the US used $\frac{1}{5}$ of its maize (corn) surplus for alcohol fuel
$\frac{1}{5}$ of the US grain production would feed 100 million people for a year
Brazil planned to produce $\frac{1}{3}$ of its fuel needs from sugar cane in 1985
It would take 3 million ha of sugar cane to produce $\frac{1}{3}$ of Brazil's fuel needs
$\frac{2}{3}$ of Brazil's people are undernourished
The rich people of the world use 5 times as much of the world's food-producing resources as the poor people
In USA, more fuel could be saved by fixing only manual gears in new cars than that produced by 20 million tonnes of grain
A small car would take 7 tonnes of grain to run for a year on alcohol fuel
In the Third World, a subsistence diet uses $\frac{1}{4}$ of a tonne of grain in a year
A car needs 3.2 ha of cropland to provide it with fuel
A poor peasant farm requires 0.8 ha of land to produce enough food for the farmer and his family
Experiments with alcohol as a fuel began in the 1920s
Work expanded rapidly after the fuel crisis of 1973
In the 1980s, the true cost of alcohol fuel is hidden by government subsidies
Alcohol is a renewable resource – petrol is not

Figure 5.29 Fact sheet: Gasohol and people

New uses for agricultural products: Gasoholic automobiles

Drinking and driving are two things which should not mix, but drivers in some parts of the world are now running their cars on alcohol. Alcohol can be made by fermenting many plants including sugar cane and cassava. Large amounts of money have been poured into these attempts to find a cheap alternative to petrol. The Brazilians have estimated that they could supply all their fuel by planting 0.3% of their land with alcohol-producing crops. They would need 500 new distilleries and these would create 500000 new jobs.

This all seems too good to be true. Figure 5.28 hints at just one of the problems. Figure 5.29 is a fact sheet on 'Gasohol and people'. The fact sheet suggests several other problems.

For better or worse?

Finally, we should all think about the effects of these developments on our quality of life. Many people are already unhappy about the way animals are treated on farms. For example, chickens are kept in half light in broiler houses and calves are kept in boxes so small that they cannot turn around. Many people are concerned about the way our food is being processed before we eat it.

These things seem to be lowering the quality of life so that those who live in the richer countries can keep a high standard of living. What are your views about this?

Activities

■ ● **27** Study Figure 5.27. Make lists of the advantages and disadvantages of using a gantry for:

a The economy of the country
b An individual farmer
c The ecosystem of the farm
d The standard of living of everyone
e The quality of life of everyone.

▲ ■ ● **28** Study Figure 5.28 and Figure 5.29.

a Write an account of the advantages and disadvantages of using alcohol as a fuel for vehicles.
b Petroleum is a **non-renewable resource**. Alcohol is a **renewable resource**. Write a paragraph to explain the difference between these two terms.
c Explain why producing alcohol fuel might be particularly good for tropical countries. You should mention the climate, the terms of trade and the needs of developing countries.

6 Factories and offices

The distribution of manufacturing industries

There are three main questions which can be asked about the distribution of manufacturing industry. Firstly, do some countries have more industries than others? Secondly, do all parts of any single country have the same amount of industry? Thirdly, where are the factories located in the 'industrial' parts of a country?

Let's start by looking at the distribution of industry in the world. There are far too many industries to show them all on one map. We will therefore look at one example – the steel industry. Figure 6.1(a) shows the distribution of the world's steel making. Figure 6.1(b) shows the distribution of the countries which use most steel. Figure 6.2 shows the production of crude steel for the most important steel producing countries in the world, as a bar chart.

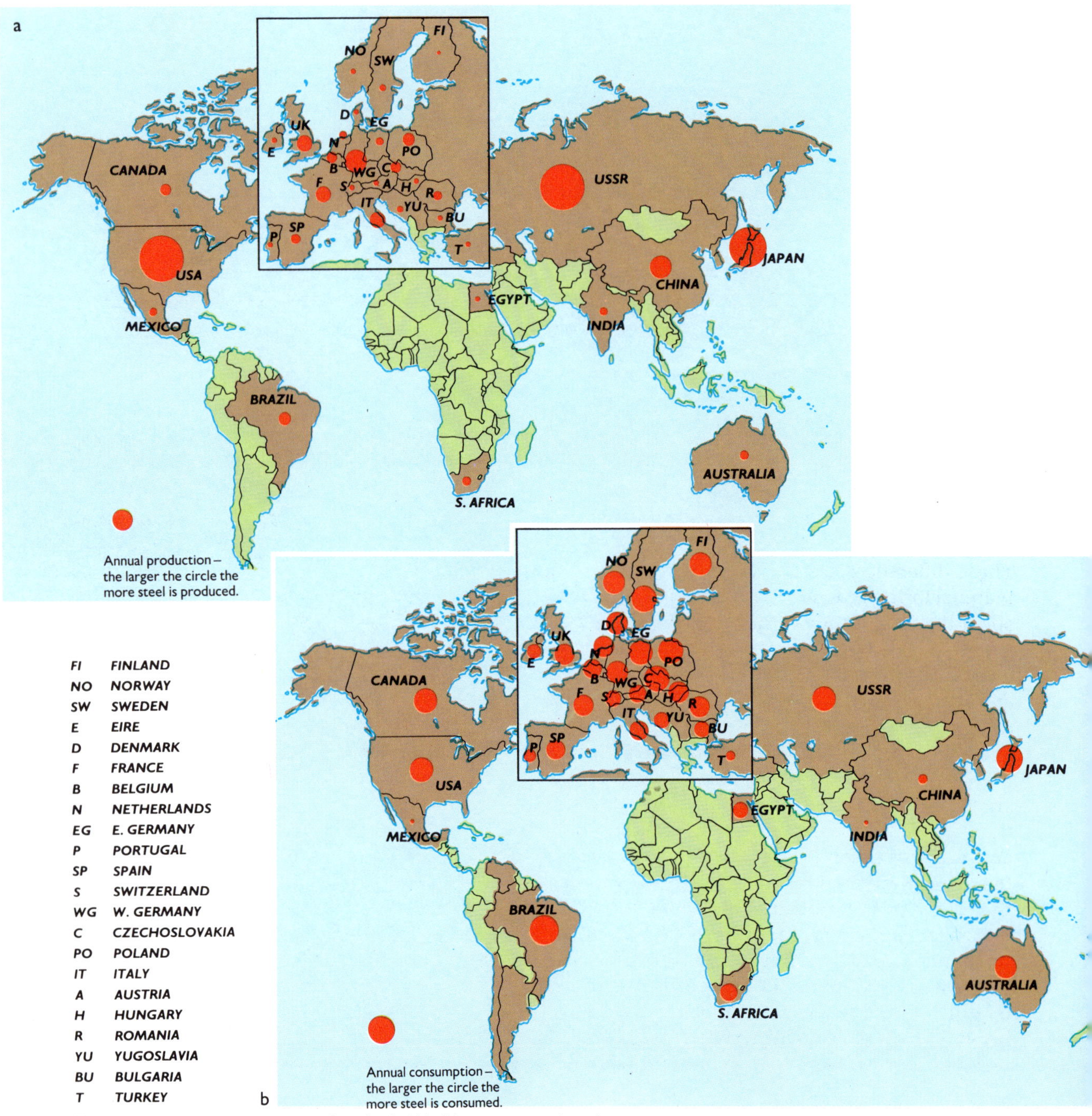

Figure 6.1 a World producers of steel b World consumers of steel

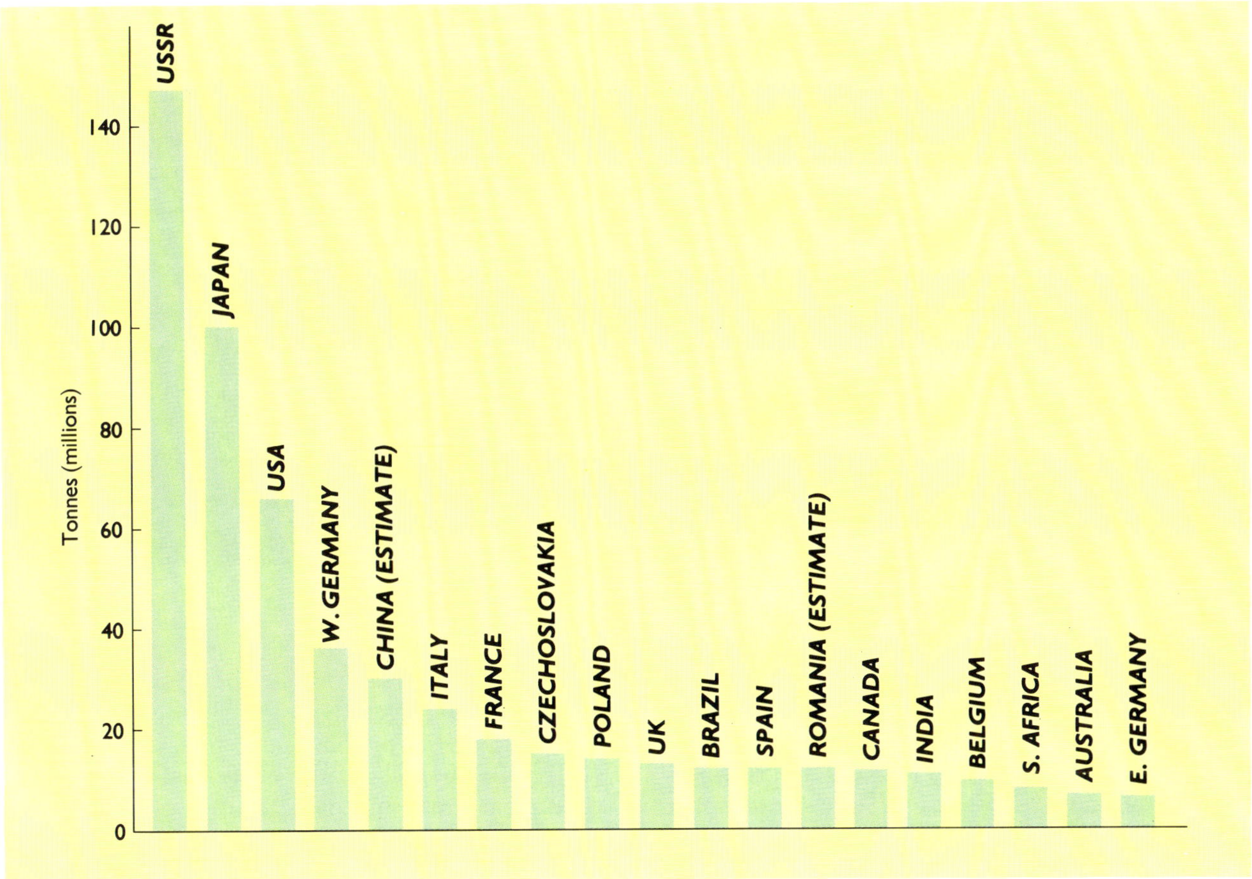

Figure 6.2 Production of crude steel

The maps and the bar chart show important differences between the countries of the world. Some countries produce large amounts of steel and also consume large amounts. Others produce little or no steel, but among them some are great consumers and some use very little. These differences are similar for almost all manufacturing industry. There is a very uneven spread of industry over the world as a whole.

Let's look at the distribution of industry in one area. Figure 6.3 shows how the people employed in manufacturing industry are distributed between newer and older industries in the Republic of Ireland and Northern Ireland.

The pattern of the divided circles in Figure 6.3 shows two differences. Firstly, it shows that there is more manufacturing industry in the east and north of Ireland. Secondly, it shows that the larger industrial centres have more jobs in the *older* types of industries and the smaller industrial centres have more jobs in the *newer* types of industries. There is another difference which is not shown on the map. This is that the older industries are usually concerned with heavy industries like shipbuilding and cloth making. The newer industries have usually

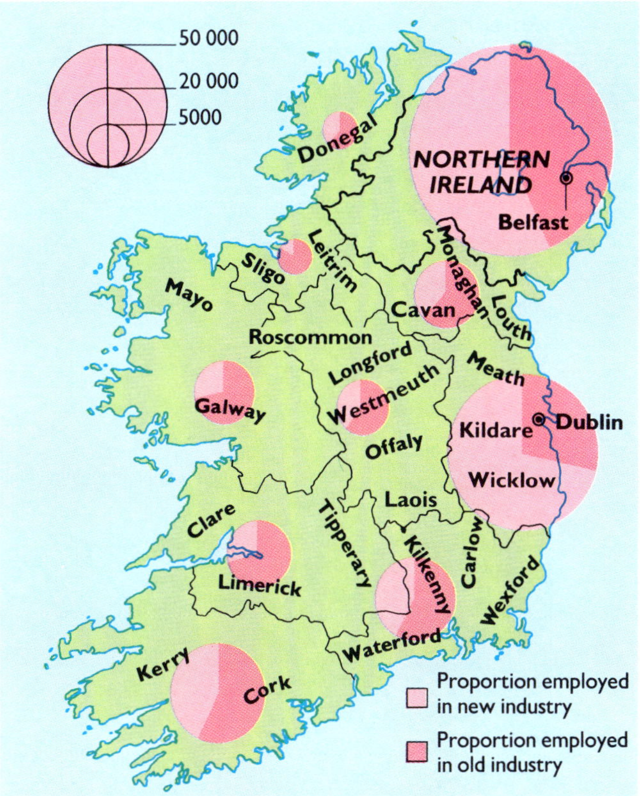

Figure 6.3 Manufacturing industry in Ireland

Figure 6.4 Two pottery factories belonging to the Rosenthal company in Selb, West Germany

started since 1960 and are light industries. One example of a new light industry is the medical appliance industry in Limerick. Other examples of light industries are making electric drills, microcomputers, bookbinding and furniture.

The overall pattern of industry in Ireland is that the old, heavy industries are **concentrated** in a few large centres. The new, light industries are more spread out. Geographers say that they are **dispersed**. The pattern of concentrated older industries and dispersed newer industries is found in many countries in Europe and North America.

The pattern of industry in an industrial area is not so easy to show on maps. However, most people have seen factories, like the ones in Figure 6.4, in towns. These are two Rosenthal factories in Selb (in the north-east of Bavaria, West Germany). Rosenthal makes high quality china. Not all factories in towns are as colourful or as well designed as these two, however. Newer factories are usually found on the outskirts of towns. Figure 6.5 shows the Solmer iron and steel works in southern France. Not many steel works are in the middle of a field like this one.

Figure 6.5 The Solmer iron and steel works, Fos-sur-Mer, Southern France

Activities

▲ ■ 1 Study Figures 6.1(a) and (b) and 6.2 which show the world steel industry.

a Describe the distribution of the countries which make most iron and steel in the world.

b Describe the distribution of the countries which use most steel in the world.

c Explain why there seems to be a link between the countries which make and use steel and the developed countries of the world.

▲ ■ 2 Figure 6.2 is a bar graph which shows the main steel producing countries of the world.

a Suggest why the USSR and USA produce so much more steel than any of the countries of Europe.

b Suggest why Japan produces so much steel even though it is a fairly small country.

c Suggest why China, which is a large country with a large population, only produces a fairly small amount of steel.

▲ ■ 3 Study Figure 6.3 which shows the manufacturing industry in Ireland.

a i) Describe the distribution of all manufacturing industry in Ireland.

ii) Describe the distribution of older and newer industries in Ireland.

b Write a paragraph to explain why there is this pattern of distribution.

▲ ■ ● 4 Study the photographs of the two Rosenthal porcelain factories in Selb, West Germany (Figure 6.4).

a Describe the evidence in the photographs which suggests that one of the factories is older than the other.

b Suggest why one of the factories has been painted with rainbows.

c What is your opinion of the look of the two factories?

▲ ■ ● 5 Study the photograph of the Solmer iron and steel works (Figure 6.5).

a Describe the effect of the works on the landscape.

b Suggest how the works could be camouflaged.

What influences the location of industries?

Once upon a time nearly all manufacturing industry was small and evenly spread among the population. In the Middle Ages, and up to the 18th century in western Europe, manufacturing workshops made things which the people nearby needed for their homes or their farms. If possible they were made from materials found locally. Most of the power was hand or foot power so fuel supply was not a problem. It is true that iron could only be made where there was iron ore and plenty of wood to make charcoal. However, in the Middle Ages much of Europe was covered in forest and many areas had enough iron ore for local purposes.

Before the 18th century, roads were very poor. This made transport difficult and costly. It did not make sense to make something in one part of the country and send it to another part to be used.

When new machines were invented to make cloth or to hammer iron, the situation began to change. Instead of going into **'cottage' industries**, the new machines were put into large factories. The new machines were larger and more expensive. They needed more power to drive them. At first, this power was provided by running water. The factories were built beside streams. Later on, the power was supplied by steam engines. Then the factories were built on coalfields. By putting them on coalfields the cost of transporting coal to the factories' boiler houses was kept down. The introduction of water and then steam power, which led to industries being concentrated on the coalfields, is known as the **Industrial Revolution**. It first happened in England on the coalfields of Northumberland and Durham, Lancashire, Yorkshire, Derbyshire, Nottinghamshire, and Staffordshire. Industry then developed in France on the Nord coalfield. Development on the Ruhr coalfield of Germany and the Appalachian coalfield of the USA followed. Later there was industrial development in Russia on the coalfields of Tula and in the Don river basin. In countries where there is no coal, factories were usually set up in ports so that coal could be imported easily.

The iron and steel industry in particular needed to be on a coalfield. This is because the raw materials and fuel for making iron are all heavy and expensive to transport. Even today, 4 tonnes of raw materials are needed to make 1

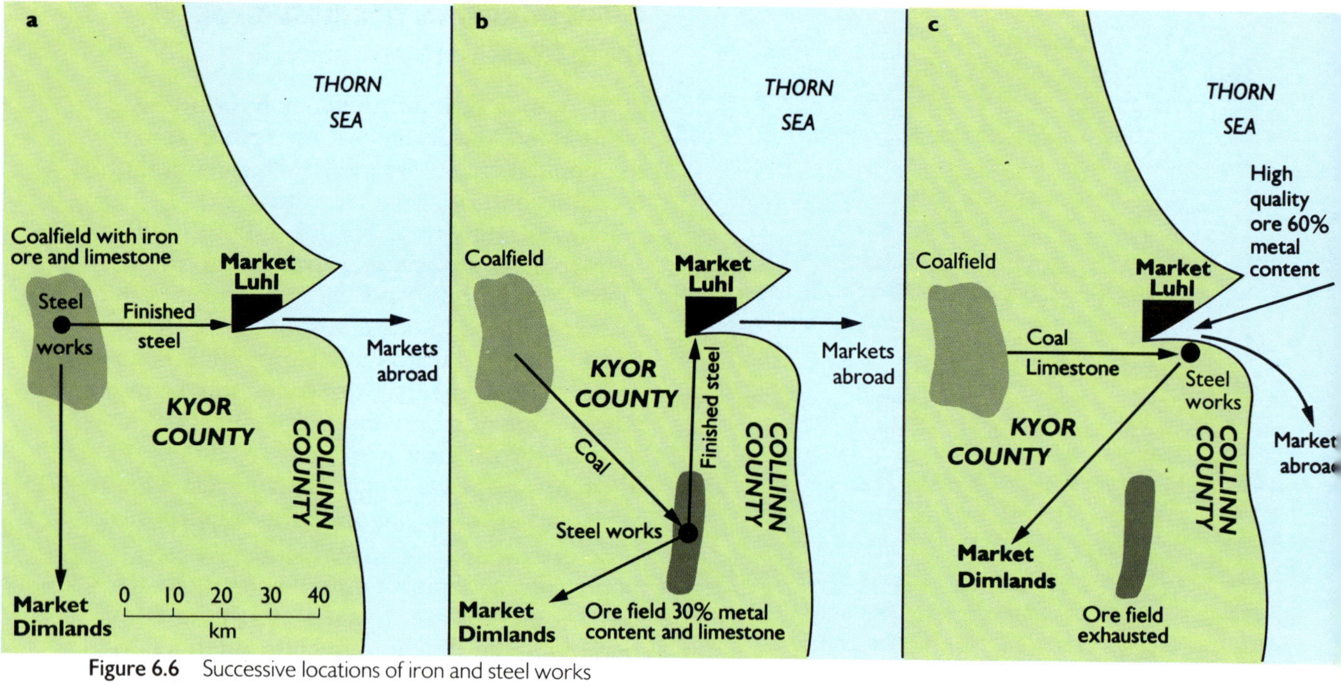

Figure 6.6 Successive locations of iron and steel works
a early 19th century **b** late 19th century **c** late 20th century

tonne of steel. This means that 3 tonnes out of the 4 tonnes of raw materials are 'lost' during the manufacturing process. A tonne of steel is worth much more than a tonne of iron ore, coal or limestone. The cost of transporting a tonne of steel is more or less the same as the cost of transporting a tonne of one of the raw materials. So this means that the proportion of the price of a tonne of steel taken up by transport costs is much less than the proportion of the price of a tonne of raw materials. Figure 6.6 shows how the relative costs of transporting the raw materials and the steel affects the best place to build a steel works.

The iron and steel industry is an example of an industry which is usually located either close to its raw materials, or near a port so that it can import its raw materials easily and cheaply. It is known as a **resource orientated industry**. Cement-making, brickmaking and heavy engineering works are other examples of resource orientated industries. In these industries, it is the inputs which are important when deciding where factories should be located.

There are other industries, like the soft drinks industry and the brewing industry, which are usually located near their customers. This is because most of the costs involved are not in the raw materials but in delivering the product to the market. In the case of soft drinks and beer, the heaviest raw material is water. Soft drinks factories and breweries are usually located in or near the towns where the drinks and beer are to be sold. This keeps the cost of transporting and delivering them low. Industries which make items which are bought frequently tend to be located near large populations. They are called **market orientated industries**. Bread, canned foods, frozen foods and clothing are often market orientated. In these industries, it is the outputs which are important in deciding where they should be located.

Industries which are resource orientated are usually found concentrated near their resources. Market orientated industries are usually scattered or dispersed among the centres of population of a country.

Some industries which were once resource orientated have become more market orientated. When coal was the main source of power, many industries were concentrated on, or near, coalfields. Now, electricity is used by most factories. Electricity is available wherever there are power lines. In western and eastern Europe there are power lines to all parts of the countries. But this is not always true in larger countries like the USSR, Canada or even the USA. For example, in Canada there are large areas with no power lines. This would make it difficult for industries to set up in these areas. Power lines often only serve certain parts of developing countries. Nigeria is an example, where the electricity power lines only serve part of the country. Figure 6.7 shows the electricity grid in Nigeria.

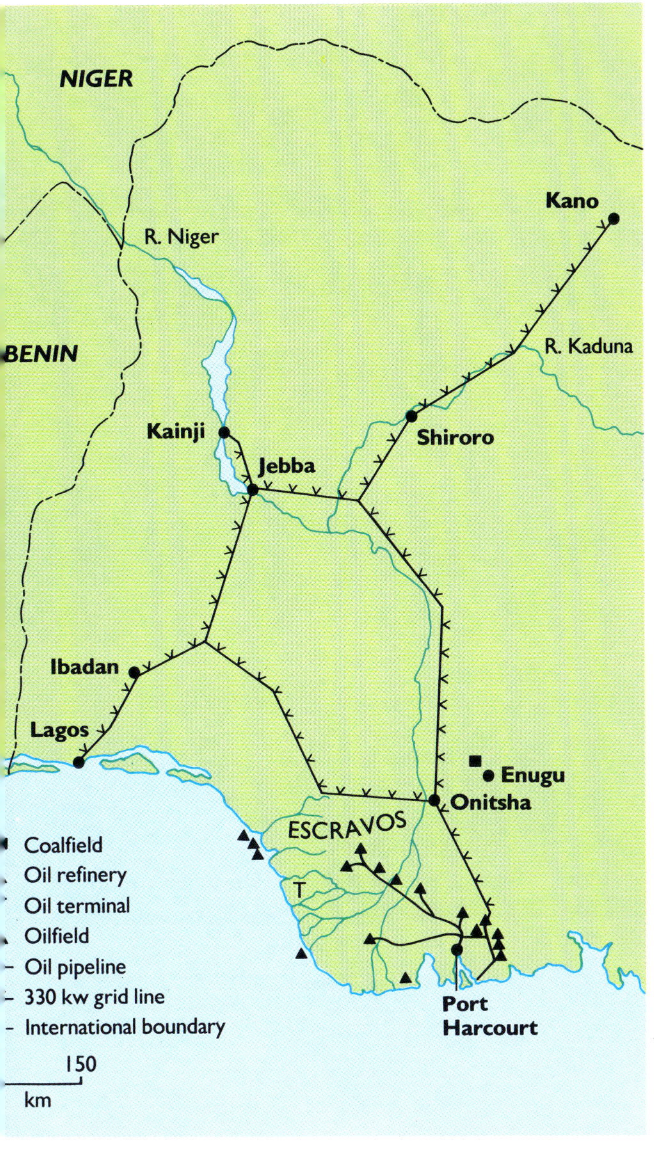

Figure 6.7 The electricity grid in Nigeria

Activity

▲6 ■ Study Figure 6.6 which shows maps of the relative position of steel works in three different circumstances. The maps represent the changing location of the British Iron and Steel Industry in the 19th century, early 20th century and late 20th century.

a Describe the reasons for the location of the steelworks in each of the three circumstances.

b Explain why new iron and steel works have been built in new locations on two occasions.

The advantages of industries being concentrated in one area

Although some industries may have become concentrated because they were resource orientated, the concentration often led to other advantages.

Firstly, factories usually need services such as a water supply, waste disposal, electricity or gas supply, and a road and rail network. Where there are a lot of people in the same industry, local technical colleges can run special training courses. It is cheaper to provide these services for an area with many factories than for an area with just a few factories.

Secondly, where there are a number of factories, tertiary firms can set up to provide the services the factories need. Tertiary firms include road transport firms, technical services such as installing and maintaining new machinery, and professional services such as accountancy and legal advice.

It is much cheaper for all these services to be provided for a number of factories than for just a few. The savings which can be made by each factory by being located near other factories are called **agglomeration economies**.

Agglomeration economies are so important that once a group of industries has been set up in an area, they attract other industries to them. The new industries attracted to the area may be similar to the early ones. They may supply either materials or services to the early industries. They may use some of the products of the early industries.

The links between the industries in an area can be seen very well in the Ruhr area in West Germany (Figures 6.8 and 6.9 overleaf). The Ruhr is a huge industrial area 70 km long and 10 km wide. It began to develop in the 19th century on the coalfield in the valley of the river Ruhr. When the coal in the Ruhr valley was worked out, coal was mined further north in the valleys of the rivers Emscher and Lippe.

The coal was first used to make coke for iron and steel making. The by products of the coke ovens were used to make dyes for the textile industries in Wuppertal (which is south of the Ruhr). The steel industry led to the growth of the engineering industry. The engineering industry supplied machinery for the textile industry, as well as many other industries which grew up in the Ruhr.

This example shows that industrial regions grow because more industries choose to be located in an area which was first developed by

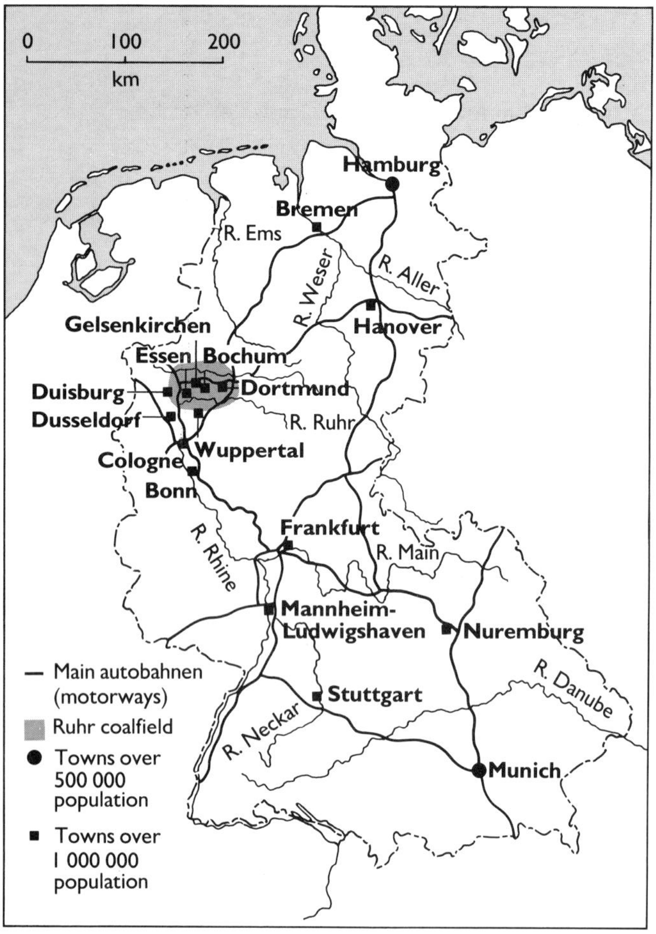

Figure 6.8 The Ruhr industrial area

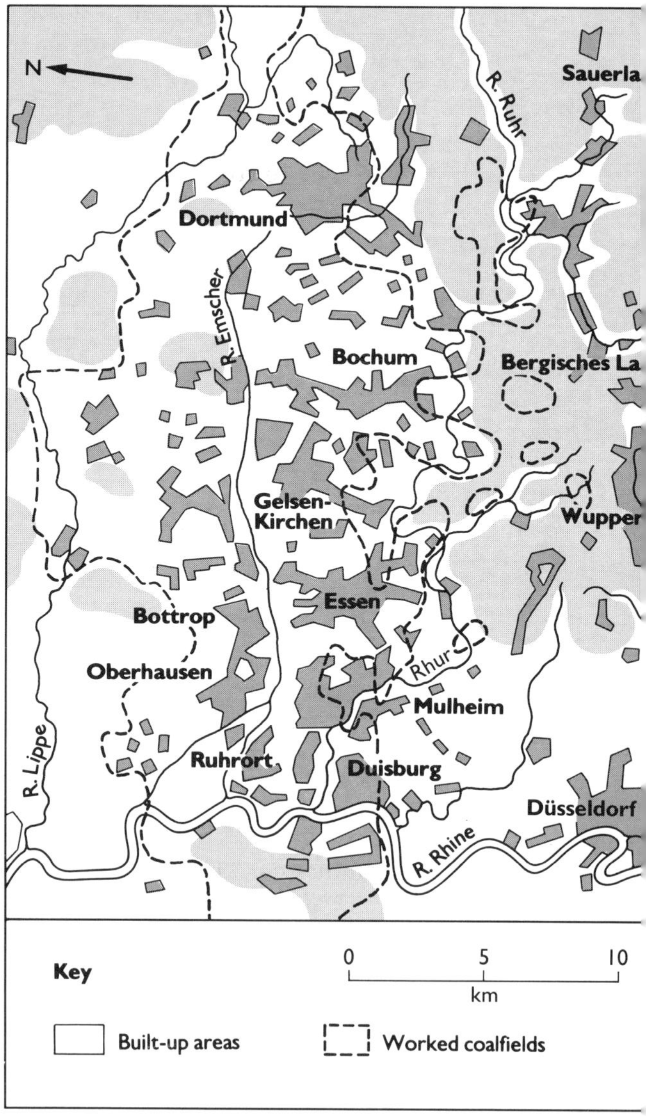

one or two industries. The output of one industry, e.g. steel, becomes the input of another industry, e.g. engineering.

These links between industries are also one of the reasons why an industry tends to stay in the area where it was first established. For example, the textile industry, which is still important in the Wuppertal area, was originally established there in the 18th century. This is known as **geographical momentum**.

Problems caused by industrial concentrations

The growth of industry in the Ruhr area has led to a conurbation of nearly 6 million people. Although the industries provide jobs and incomes for people, there are also problems. In Chapter 4 we explained that there is a difference between the standard of living and the quality of life. The jobs and incomes can give people a high standard of living. The quality of life is affected by the environment in which people

Figure 6.9 The Ruhr

live. Heavy industry can lower the quality of life in three main ways.

Firstly, it is unfortunate that when there is a concentration of heavy industries, there is usually **pollution** as well. For example, in an iron and steel works, the coke ovens, blast furnaces and steel furnaces give out fumes which pollute the atmosphere. Chemical works release waste which may pollute streams and rivers. Towns often empty sewage into rivers without treating it first. The river Rhine is already very polluted before it reaches the Ruhr industrial area. Pollution is bad for various reasons. Whether it is in the air or in the water, pollution kills or damages life. Human lungs are damaged by carbon monoxide and sulphur dioxide in the air. The sulphur dioxide causes the acid rain which is killing the forests and lakes of northern Europe. (Look back at Chapter 3.) Pollution in the rivers kills the fish and plants.

Secondly, atmospheric pollution also lowers the quality of life by cutting out sunlight. It can become impossible to wear light-coloured clothes because of the dirty air. In areas where smoke pollution is controlled, the amount of sunlight has increased.

Thirdly, large industrial works are often very ugly to look at and spoil the beauty of an area. This is even more true when there are smoke and fumes hanging over the works. This is often called **visual pollution**.

Many of these different types of pollution can now be controlled. Waste gases and liquids can be filtered out so that they do not go into the atmosphere or rivers. It has been estimated that 2000 different chemicals are dumped into the Rhine. Many have been dumped by chemical companies. In recent years many of these companies have spent a lot of money in filtering equipment. Bayer, for example, filters 122 000 tonnes of sulphuric acid each year from the waste from its factory at Verdingen.

Some old industrial areas are being improved by new buildings and new parks. The Ruhr valley is no longer a coalmining area. The old pit head buildings have been demolished and the valley has been changed back into a recreational area with woods, lakes and fields.

Another problem of old industrial areas is unemployment. This is a problem in most of the old industrial areas in the UK, Europe and the USA. There are two sides to this problem. Firstly, as an industry becomes more advanced it uses fewer people and more machines. For example, coalminers used to dig coal with picks and shovels. Then pneumatic drills were introduced. This meant that each man could dig more coal in a shift. Now the modern mines use a mechanical coal cutter called a **trepanner**. The job of a coalminer has changed from digging coal to operating a machine.

The job is more skilled, but there are fewer jobs. In motor car assembly plants, machines now do many jobs which used to be done by hand. These machines which have taken the place of human beings are often called **robots**. In the car industry, there are now fewer jobs for skilled welders, but there is a smaller number of new jobs for highly skilled machine setters for the robots.

Secondly, the heavy industries usually make machinery and other types of capital goods. These industries are much more affected by changes in the economy than light industries. The light industries usually make goods for consumers. If there is an economic depression, people spend less on holidays, clothes, cars, washing machines, etc. As soon as the manufacturers notice this, they stop any plans they may have had for expanding their factories or buying more machinery. This means that the capital goods industries cannot sell their products, so they cancel their orders for steel. A small fall in the demand for consumer goods can cause a large fall in the demand for heavy engineering, steel and coal. This will cause unemployment for engineers, steel workers and miners.

When there is a depression, these two causes of fewer jobs can combine to cause high unemployment in the areas of heavy industries.

One way of preventing this is for governments to encourage a wide variety of different industries in the areas which have concentrated only on heavy industries. For example, in the Ruhr, lighter industries such as those making clothes and electrical goods have been encouraged. A new university has been set up at Bochum to encourage professional employment.

There are always changes going on in an industrial area. Some industries are growing while others are declining. In an ideal world the workers made unemployed by the declining industries would find jobs straight away in the expanding industries. Unfortunately this does not often happen. There are three main reasons for this. Firstly, newer industries are often more mechanized than the old industries. This means that the total number of jobs may go down. Secondly, it is not always possible for people

Figure 6.10 **a** Making silicon chips
b The position of 'Silicon Valley' in California, USA

trained in one industry to move to another. For example, a steel worker may find it difficult to learn the skills needed to make micro-chips. This may be even more of a problem for older workers. Thirdly, the expanding industries may not be in the same area as the declining industries. Many expanding industries are in the sunnier parts of the world where highly skilled workers often prefer to live. The French Aerospace industry is at Toulouse in southern France. In England, many computer firms have moved to the south coast. Most micro-chips are made in California. Figure 6.10(a) shows micro-chips being made and Figure 6.10(b) shows the area of California which has been nicknamed **Silicon Valley**. Industries like these are neither market orientated nor resource orientated. They do not even need large amounts of electricity. They are usually located where they can attract highly qualified workers by offering a high standard of living and a high quality of life.

Activities

▲ ■ 7 Study Figure 6.8 which shows the position of the Ruhr industrial area in West Germany and read the description of the Ruhr.

a The towns marked on the map are the most important towns in West Germany. Describe the distribution of important towns in West Germany.

b 'The river Rhine is already very polluted before it reaches the Ruhr industrial area. Explain where the pollution could come from.

c i) Describe the motorway network of West Germany.
ii) Which areas are best served by the motorway network? Explain why.

▲ ■ 8 a From Figure 6.8 and the description of the Ruhr, draw a diagram to show how the industries of the Ruhr are linked together. (*Hint*: start with the *output* of the coalmining industry.)

b Figure 6.9(b) shows that the Ruhr industrial area is not completely covered with buildings. If you travelled through the Ruhr by road you would see very little empty land. Explain why this is so.

c Figure 6.9(a) is a cross-section of the rocks in the middle of the Ruhr coalfield.
i) Why were the first coalmines dug in the south?
ii) Describe which part of the coalfield is most broken up by faults.
iii) Why has the area of working coalmines grown towards the north?
iv) Describe the problems faced by the newer coalmines in the Lippe valley part of the coalfield.

▲ ■ 9 Explain, in your own words the meaning of the following terms.

a Geographical momentum
b Agglomeration economies
c Resource orientated industries
d Market orientated industries
e Heavy industry
f Light industry
g Consumer goods industry
h Capital goods industry
i Depression
j Unemployment

▲ ■ 10 Look at Figure 6.10(a) and 6.10(b) and the maps of climate in Chapter 3 (page 57). Why is California a good place for making microchips? List as many advantages as you can.

Case Study

The Solmer iron and steel works at Fos-sur-Mer in France

This case study shows the kind of factors that the management of an iron and steel company had to take into account when they were planning a new works in France.

After deciding that a new iron and steel works was needed, the management had to decide how much extra steel would be needed in the future. They decided to build the new works in stages. The first stage would have a capacity of 3.5 million tonnes of steel per year. Later on it could be expanded to 7 million tonnes.

Next, they had to decide whereabouts in France the new works should be built. In the past, most steel works were built either on a coalfield such as the Nord coalfield, or on an iron-ore field such as the Lorraine iron-ore field. Figure 6.11 (overleaf) shows that the Nord and Lorraine are in the north and north-east of France.

In the case of this new works there were two new factors to take into account. Firstly, the best and cheapest iron ore does not come from Europe any more. It is imported from Africa, the Middle East and Australia. Coal is also imported from the USA and Australia. This means that the best site for a new steel works had to be on the coast. Secondly, the French Government wanted to encourage new industry in the south of France. Because of these two factors it was decided to build the new steel works on the south-east coast of France, on the Mediterranean Sea.

The third decision was to choose the actual site along the coast. An iron and steel works takes up a lot of room. This one needed 1500 hectares. The French Government had already set aside a huge area for the development of a new port and industrial area to the west of the village of Fos-sur-Mer. This area already had docks, electric power, an oil refinery and good communications by road and rail. It seemed an obvious choice for a new works. The position of the industrial area at Fos-sur-Mer and the new Solmer iron and steel works is shown in Figure 6.12 (overleaf). (The works themselves are shown in Figure 6.5 on page 122.)

Figure 6.11 The regional division of France showing the location of Fos-sur-Mer, near Marseille

Activity

▲ 11 Study Figure 6.12 which shows the site of the
■ Solmer iron and steel works and the map of France (Figure 6.11).

a Make lists of the advantages and disadvantages of this site and situation in France for an iron and steel works.

b From Figure 6.12, describe the possible linkages between the industries at Fos.

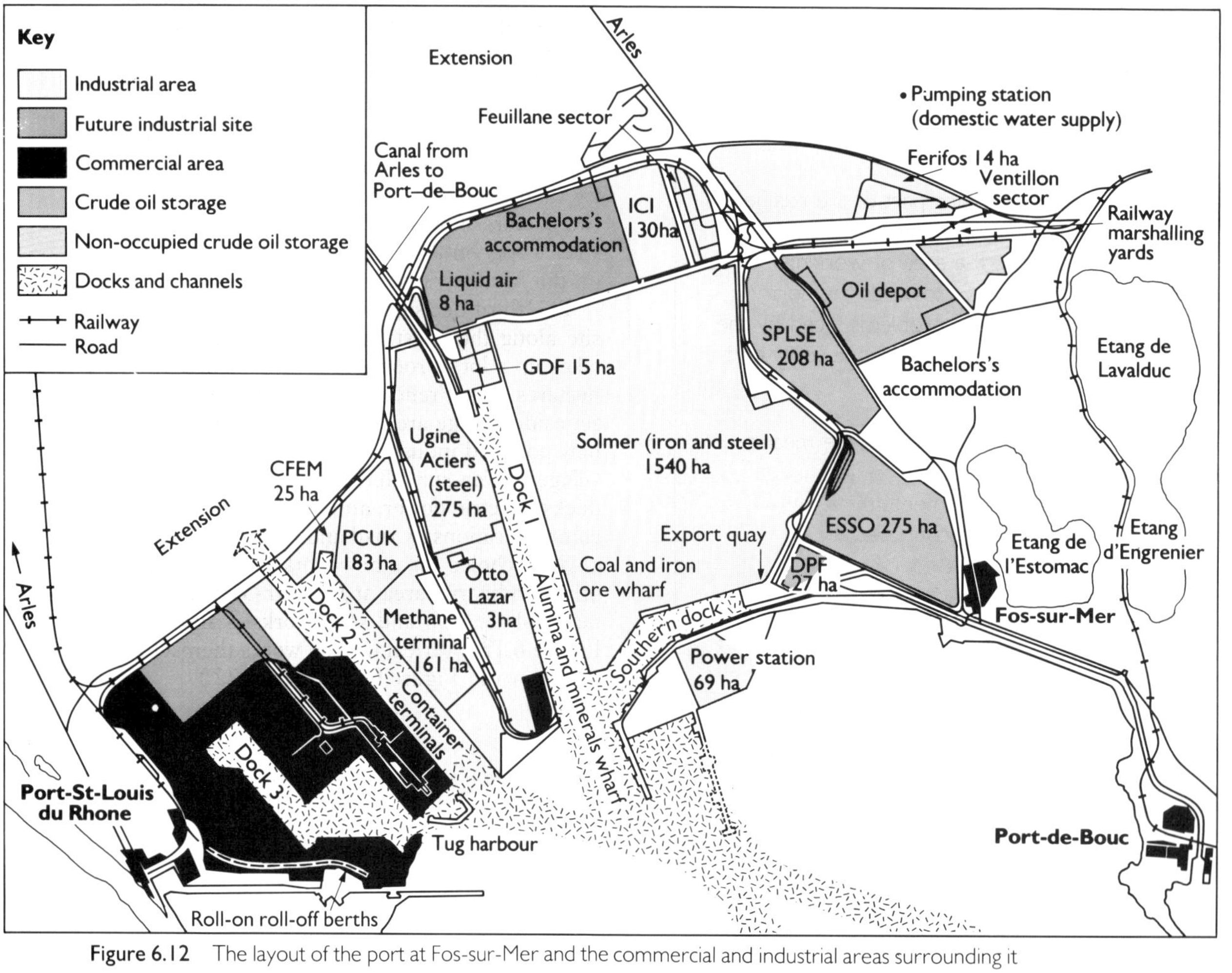

Figure 6.12 The layout of the port at Fos-sur-Mer and the commercial and industrial areas surrounding it

The Philips electrical works at Eindhoven in the Netherlands

The Philips company makes electric light bulbs, radios, televisions, cassette recorders, calculators and so on. This is a very different industry from the iron and steel industry. It is called a light industry because the value of its output is much greater than the value of all the raw materials which go in. The extra value is in the skill of the designers and the assemblers. Also, there is no loss of weight. The weight of a completed tape recorder is about the same as the total weight of all the parts used to build it.

For these reasons, a firm like Philips is more likely to think about closeness to its market than closeness to its raw materials when it is looking for a site. However, this is not the only reason for the location of the Philips factory. Accident is also important.

The original founders of the firm were the Philips brothers. In the 1880s they were making electric light bulbs in a small workshop in a village 32 kilometres from Eindhoven in the Southern Netherlands. Figure 6.13 shows the position of Eindhoven.

The demand for light bulbs grew. In order to expand, the Philips brothers looked for a factory. They found a factory in Breda. However, in 1891 two textile factories in the village of Eindhoven closed and many people, especially women, were unemployed. Philips cancelled the Breda factory, which would have been more expensive, and bought one of the factories in Eindhoven. This was the main reason why the factory was founded in Eindhoven and not in Breda. There was another advantage for a light bulb factory being located in the south of the Netherlands. Most of the people in the south were Catholics. The Catholics did not mind women working in factories such as textile mills or light electrical goods. In the north the people were mainly Protestants who did not approve of women working. The factory started with 10 workers in 1891 and by 1900 it employed 400. The changes in the size of the firm are shown in Figure 6.14. The factory grew rapidly. From electric light bulbs the factory grew to make radio valves. During World War I it was difficult for Philips to get supplies of the components and accessories they needed, such as glass and cardboard. They therefore began to make their own. This led to further growth. As the Philips factory grew, so the village of Eindhoven grew to be a town.

However, the growth of the town is not just due to Philips. Cigar making, textiles and car

Figure 6.13 The Netherlands, showing the position of Eindhoven

Year	No. of employees	Important events
1891	10	Factory started in Eindhoven
1900	400	
		First university-trained employees
1909	1200	
1916	3700	
		1917 First radio valve made 1914–18 War; Philips started making some of their own components e.g. glass
1927	10000	
1929	23000	
1933	11000	World economic depression
1936	15000	
1940	19000	1939–45 War
1944	7000	
1974	17000	Post-war economic boom
1985	14000	Automation

Figure 6.14 The number of employees at the Philips factory at Eindhoven, 1891–1985

industries also grew. This is another example of agglomeration economies.

The town also grew because of the tertiary sector which developed to provide services for the population. These services include bakers, milkmen, shopkeepers, bankers, solicitors, teachers and so on.

Some geographers have divided the working population of towns like Eindhoven into two groups. The first group is the workers who provide goods or services for a market outside the town, e.g. the electrical, textile, tobacco and car industries of Eindhoven. These are called **basic activities**. The second group is the workers who provide goods or services for the workers who work in the basic industries. They include bankers, solicitors, teachers and so on. These are called **non-basic activities**.

The basic activities are the original creators of income in a town. Non-basic activities depend on the people who work in basic activities for their jobs. If the ratio between basic and non-basic activities can be worked out, it is then possible to work out how many new jobs will be caused altogether if a new basic activity moves into a town. For example, if the 108000 workers in Eindhoven can be divided into 36000 workers in basic activities and 72000 in non-basic activities, the ratio is 1:2. If a new firm which makes solar heating panels and employs 200 people sets up in the town, then another 400 jobs in non-basic activities should appear later. This would mean that the new factory would really create 600 new jobs.

This idea is called the **multiplier effect**. The wages paid to a worker in a basic activity work their way through the economic system of the town. As the money moves from one sector of the economy to the next, its effect is multiplied. The multiplier effect is not always as simple as the example above because some of the basic goods may be sold inside the town rather than outside.

Even though it is difficult to work out the effect of the Philips factory exactly, there is no doubt that Eindhoven has grown considerably since Philips started. Figure 6.15 shows how the town has grown. It was a small village of about 5000 people in 1895; it is now a city of about 200000 people, or 375000 if we include the suburbs. The way the town has grown up around the Philips works is shown in Figures 6.16 and 6.17.

The map and the photograph show how factories and houses have spread over what used to be open land. This means that there has been a loss of farmland and heathland. The village has become a large town where it is more difficult to get to know people. The buildings have become larger and less friendly to look at. There have also been advantages. There are now facilities which did not exist before. There is a technical school, a technical university, a theatre, a museum of modern art and a technical museum, which was built by the Philips company. These changes show yet again that there are both advantages and disadvantages in development.

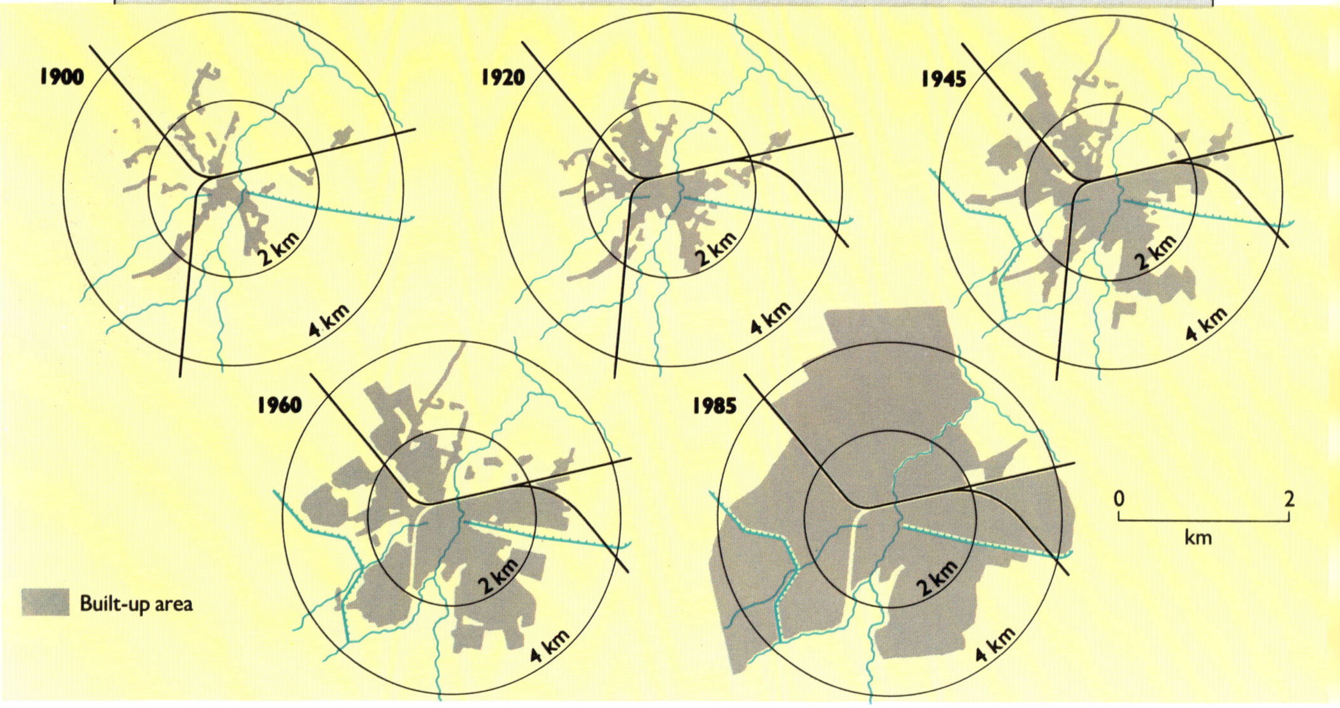

Figure 6.15 The growth of the built up area at Eindhoven 1900-1985

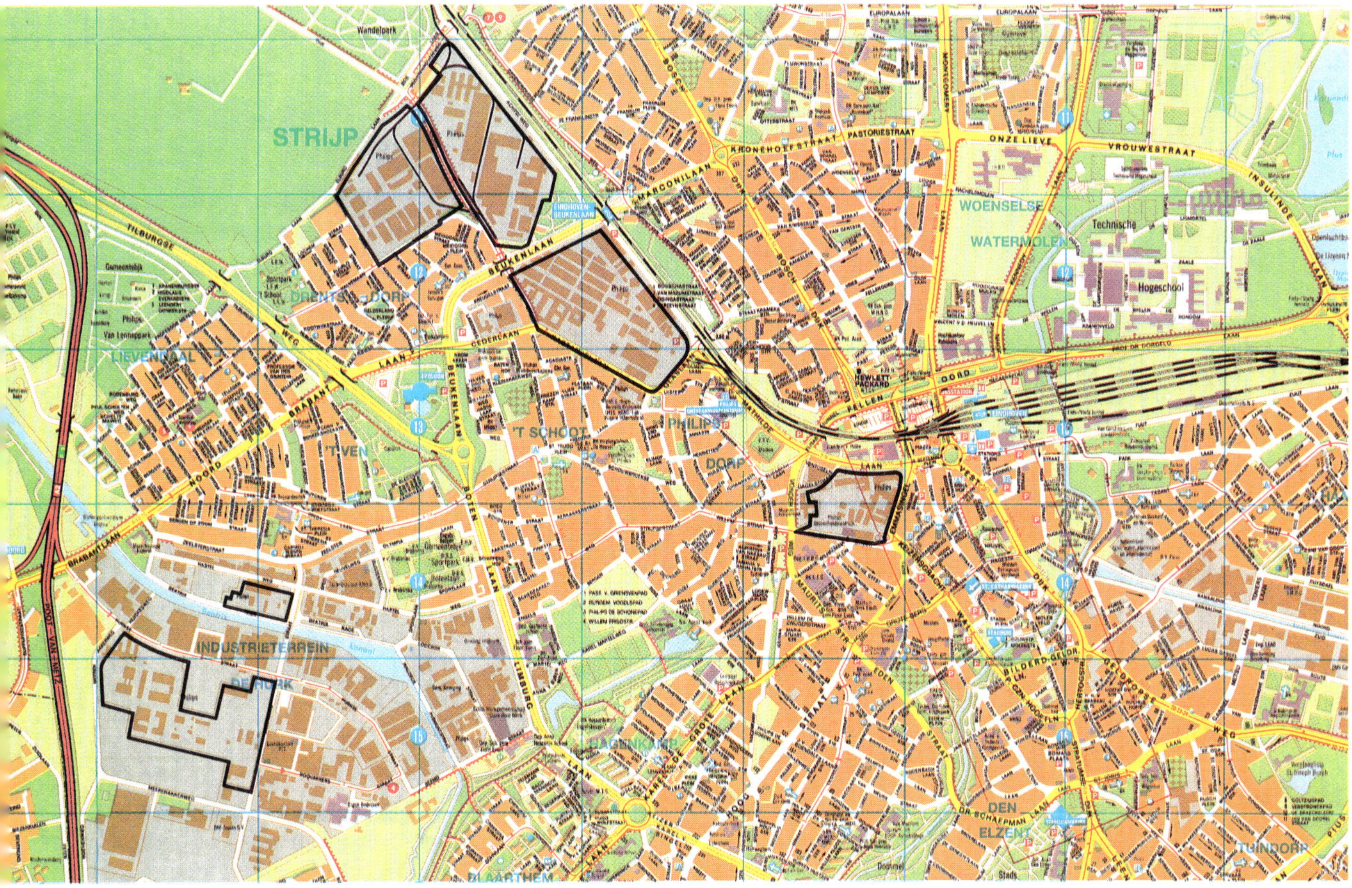

Figure 6.16 Part of Eindhoven showing the position of the Philips factory

Figure 6.17 The Philips factory, from the air

Activities

▲ **12** Read the description of this Philips factory.
■ Look at the population density map in Chapter 1 (page 15), and Figure 6.13. Explain the advantages of the location of the Philips works for making electrical goods. Use these headings.

a Inputs (space, raw materials, components, workers)

b Outputs (nearness to markets, ease of transport)

▲ **13** Use the example of Philips to explain what is
■ meant by 'geographical momentum'.

▲ **14** Study Figures 6.16 and 6.17.
■ **a** Use the map to name the features marked
● A, B, C and D on the photograph.

b i) Describe the site of the Philips works.

ii) Explain the advantages of this site for a factory.

c Explain the advantages of the newer industrial estate.

Case Study

The Ford works near Valencia in Spain

The Ford Motor Company has a works near Valencia in Spain. This works makes *Fiesta* and *Escort* cars. The story of how this factory came to be built starts in 1970.

The Ford Motor Company thought that by siting a factory in Spain they would have access to the markets of southern Europe and possibly Latin America. After they chose Spain, the first problem they faced was Spanish law.

The law in Spain said that, firstly, new factories should be owned mainly by Spanish people, secondly, that 95% of the parts should have been made in Spain. The Ford Motor Company negotiated with the Spanish Government to get the law changed. The Ford Motor Company wanted to control production and to import components from other countries. The Spanish Government wanted to have as many jobs for Spaniards as possible and to bring money into the Spanish economy. In the end Ford and the Spanish Government reached a compromise. Ford promised to create thousands of jobs; to export ⅔ of all the cars made from Spain to other parts of Europe and to the rest of the world; and that ⅔ of the components would be made in Spain. The Spanish Government then agreed to reduce customs duties on the rest of the components which were imported, so that the cost of the finished car would not be too high.

The next problem was where to build the new works. Richard Holmes was the man who led the search for a new site. He had to find out:

1 What sites were being offered by the various cities and councils.
2 Whether the cities and councils would make any special conditions for the new factory.
3 What roads, railways, ports, power supplies and other services were available at each site. (These services are called the **infrastructure**.)
4 Whether there were plenty of workers looking for jobs in the area or whether there was a shortage of workers for factories.

Richard Holmes investigated all the sites shown in Figure 6.18. He rejected Barcelona because it had the Spanish SEAT car company. He also rejected Valladolid which had the Renault works, and Pamplona which had a British Leyland works. He rejected Seville, Cadiz and Algeciras in south-western Spain because they were too isolated from the rest of Europe. Eventually the choice fell between Zaragoza and the village of Almusafes, 16 kilometres from Valencia. In September 1973 the Valencia site was chosen.

The next problem was to buy the land from 636 different peasant farming families. The Ford Motor Company was able to reach an agreement with all but 11 of these farmers. The last 11 were forced to sell their land by compulsory purchase.

In January 1974 bulldozers could start to level the ground ready for building the factory. On 18 October 1976 the first *Fiesta* car rolled off the assembly line. By 1977 thousands of *Fiestas* had been produced and had been sold in Spain, France, Italy and the UK. Figure 6.19 is an aerial photograph of the site near Almusafes near Valencia, and Figure 6.20 (page 136) is a plan of the site.

In the 6 years between Ford deciding to build a new works and the first car being produced, about 3½ years were taken in deciding where to build, negotiating with the Spanish Government and in finding a site. Only 2½ years were spent in building the factory and getting it working.

Figure 6.18 Location of suggested sites for the Ford Motor Company factory in Spain

Figure 6.19 Aerial view of the Ford Motor Company at Almusafes

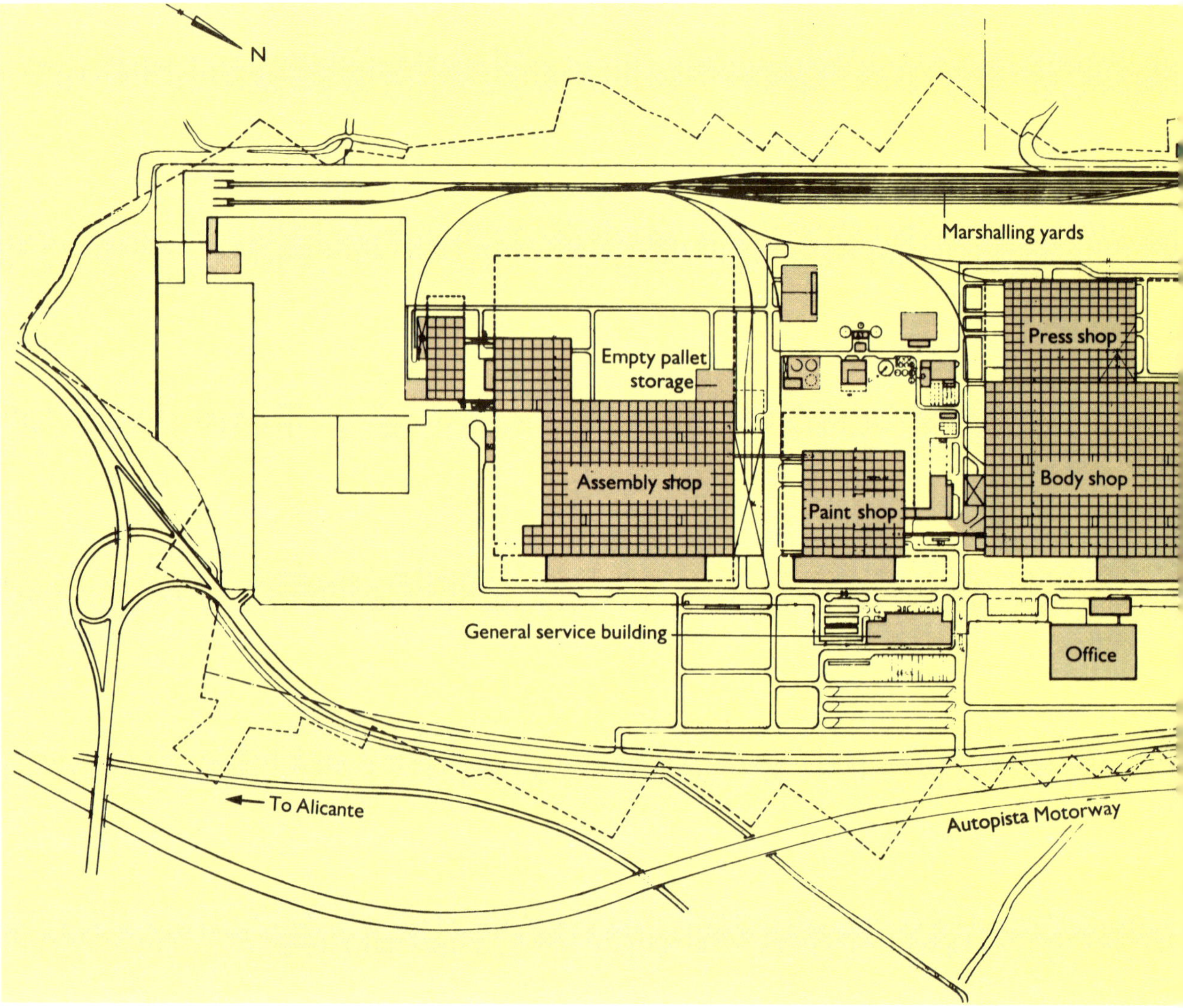

Figure 6.20 Plan of the Ford works at Almusafes

The Ford Motor Company claims that the Spanish Government, the local authorities and most of the local people were in favour of the project because it created a lot of jobs and wealth for the Valencians. Ford also think that the effect on the environment was not bad since the factory does not cause any pollution.

The result of all the decisions about the best place to make cars is that Ford have a factory in Spain far away from the main industrial areas of Europe. Their decision seems to have been influenced by the potential of a growing Spanish market for cars, by the relative cheapness of labour and the absence of tradition and restrictive practices.

Activities

■ **15** Study Figures 6.18, 6.19 and 6.20. Describe the location and site of the Ford car plant near Valencia.

▲■● **16** Explain how the Spanish economy would gain from the following facts.

a Thousands of Spaniards would be employed by the new Ford factory.

b ⅔ of all the cars made in Valencia would be exported

c ⅔ of the components would be made in Spain

▲■● **17** What are the advantages to the Ford Motor Company of having car plants

a All over the world

b In several countries of Europe?

Give reasons.

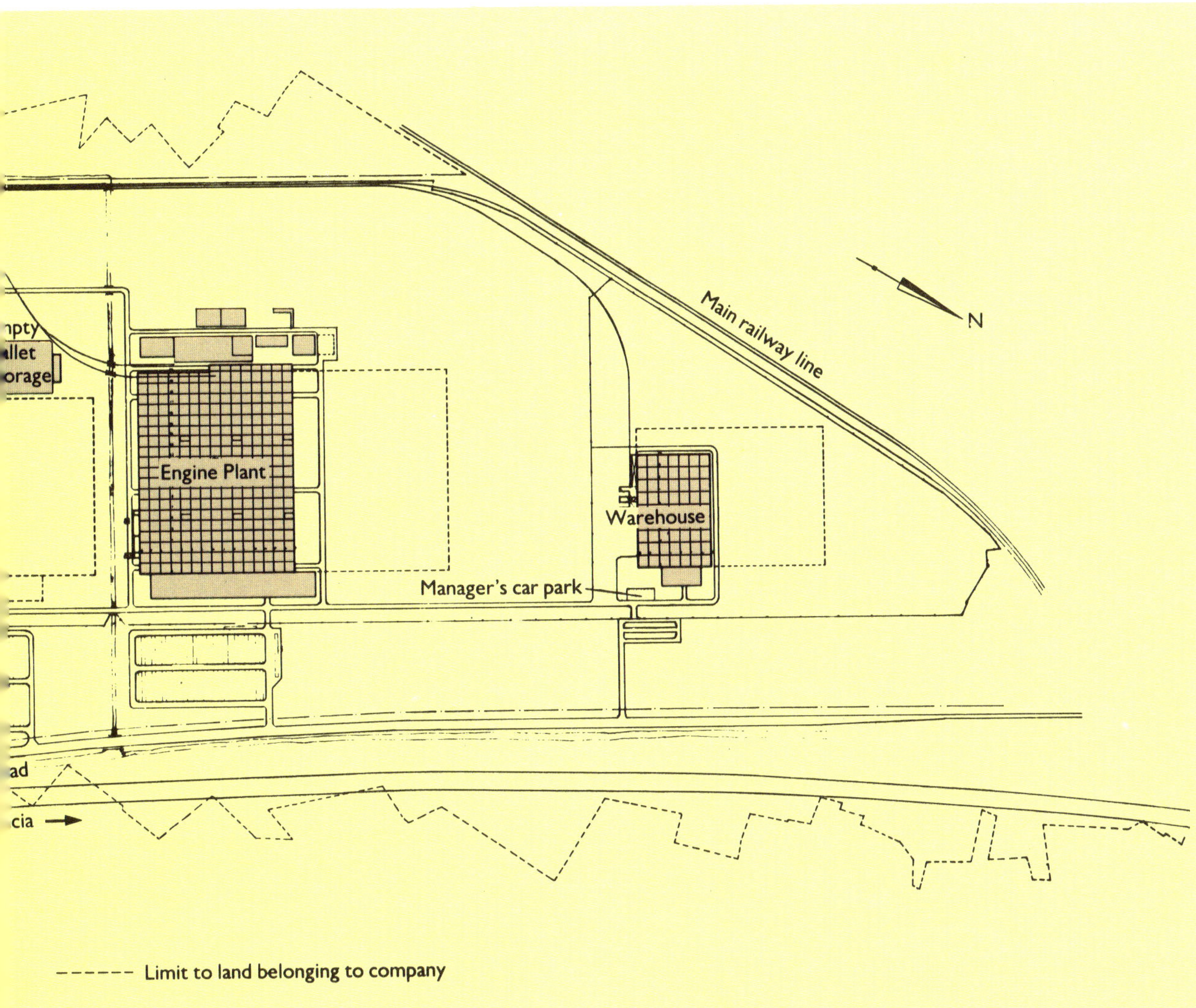

The location of industry in the USSR

In the case study of the Ford works in Spain, we explained that the Spanish Government wanted some control over the way the new car works is organized. In most countries the governments try to have an effect on the location of industries. Governments can also affect the prices of raw materials and finished products by charging taxes and customs duties.

In some countries, such as the communist countries, the governments make all the decisions about industries. They believe that they can plan the factories to produce the goods their country needs, to give jobs where they are needed by their people and to do the least damage to the environment. However, they also have to think about providing raw materials, power supplies and the costs of transporting the goods to the market.

For example, the Government of the USSR would like industry to be distributed more widely. Most of the older industries were built in the European part of the USSR, particularly around Moscow. The Government would like new industries to be developed in Siberia, Soviet Central Asia and the Far East. The Government would like a wider spread of industries for many reasons. Here are some of them.

Firstly, many of the resources needed by industries are found in Soviet Central Asia. There are large deposits of coal, iron ore and oil. There are also deposits of scarce but very valuable minerals such as titanium, molybdenum, gold, tin and copper. There are rivers which can be dammed to produce hydroelectric power. The Government of the USSR is encouraging the development of these resources by building whole industrial regions

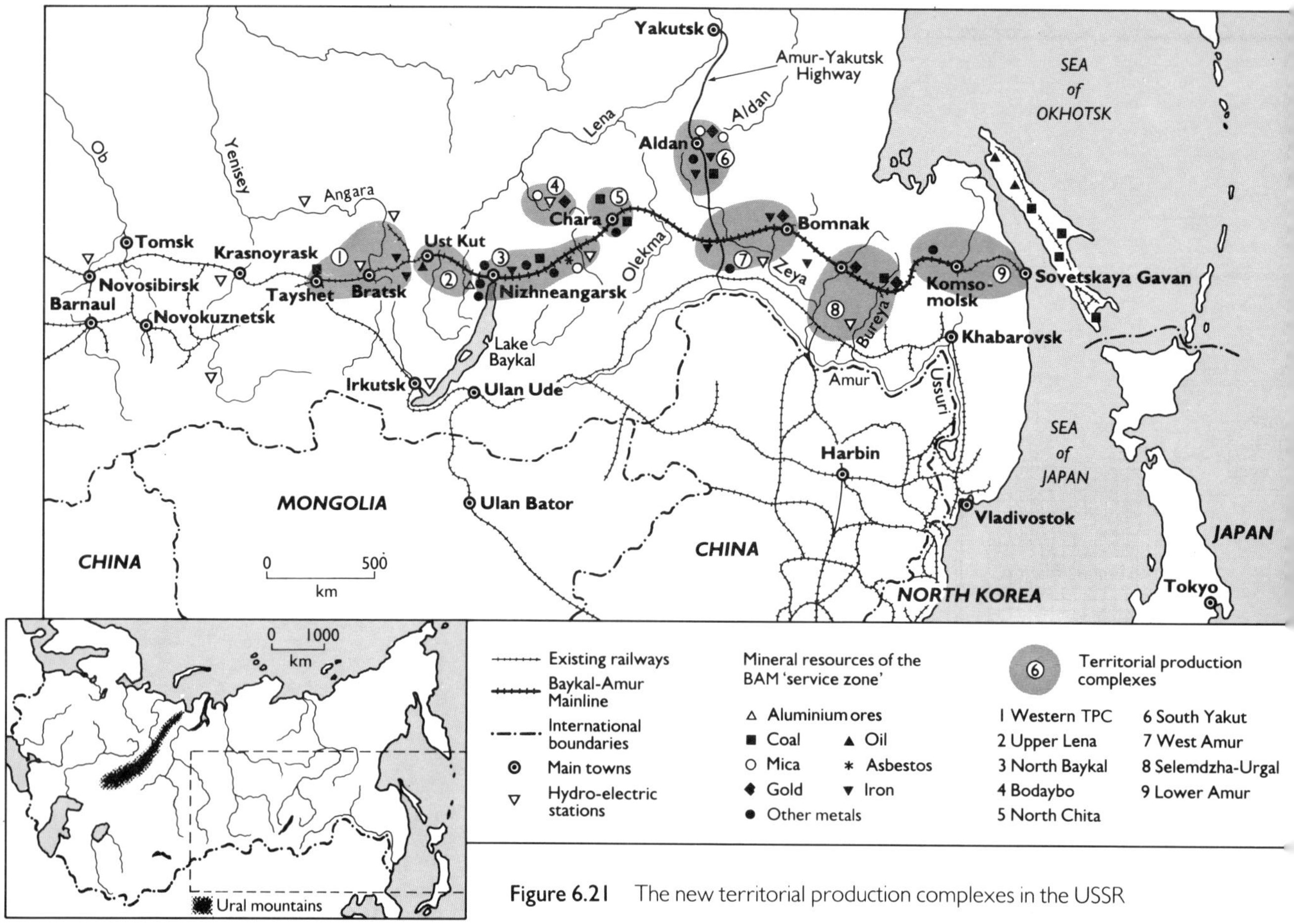

Figure 6.21 The new territorial production complexes in the USSR

called **territorial production complexes** or **TPCs**. The railway network in Figure 6.21 shows the difference between the amount of industry in European USSR and the eastern USSR. It also shows the new industrial areas which have been planned by the USSR Government.

A second reason why the Government of the USSR may want to develop industry and population in the east is to do with defence. Most of the industry of the USSR is in the western part of the country near to western Europe. In the same way that many western European countries have joined together in NATO in case they need to protect themselves from a Soviet attack, the Government of the USSR is afraid that the USSR could be attacked. They think that industries and people further east would be much safer than industries near to the borders with NATO countries.

The USSR is also worried about China. As we explained in Chapter 1, China is a very crowded country. The eastern part of Russia has a very low density of population. The USSR is worried that China might try to take some of its land and resources. This would be less likely if there were more USSR citizens living in the Far East.

To the east of the USSR lies Japan. Japan has developed its industries very rapidly, but has a shortage of natural resources. There are plans for Japan to buy coal and other minerals from the USSR. The new railway line north of the old Trans-Siberian Railway should make this easier.

Finally, countries wanting to increase their GDP need to develop all their natural resources. Natural resources include land area as well as minerals, soils and timber. The USSR needs to develop its huge land area.

Activity

▲■● **18**

a Study the map of the USSR (Figure 6.21), and the maps of population density (Figure 1.17, page 15) and climate (Figure 3.18, page 57). Make a list of the problems which the Government of the USSR is likely to find in developing industry in the far east of the country.

b Describe the kinds of industries which are most suitable for the new industrial regions to start with. Explain why these types of industries are most suitable.

c Describe where the main markets for the goods produced in the far east of the USSR will be.

d Explain how more market orientated industries will be encouraged to develop in the far east of the USSR.

The distribution of industry in developing countries

So far we have described some of the reasons why various industries were located where they were. The separate decisions which led to the final location of each factory or group of factories were made by single people, by companies, and by governments. Most of the decisions were made for one of four reasons: economic reasons, political reasons, social reasons, and, sometimes, personal reasons. The Philips electrical works are at Eindhoven because of a decision made by two brothers in 1891. Fords are near Valencia in Spain because of a series of decisions negotiated with the Spanish Government. The locations of the new industrial areas of the USSR are the result of strategic, economic and political decisions by the Government of the USSR.

The same kinds of reasons for industry can be found in developing countries today. However, because the developing countries have to operate in a world economic system which is dominated by the richer countries, their industries need more help to develop than, for example, the Philips brothers did.

Small workshops

Most villages in the developing countries have small workshops where people make pots or simple farming tools. These workshops supply what the local people want and use the raw materials which are available nearby. They could be described as market orientated. Very little machinery is used and so we can say that they are labour intensive.

One of the greatest problems which faces developing countries is a shortage of jobs so that people can earn their living. In many developing countries there are schemes to develop small workshop-type industries to provide jobs.

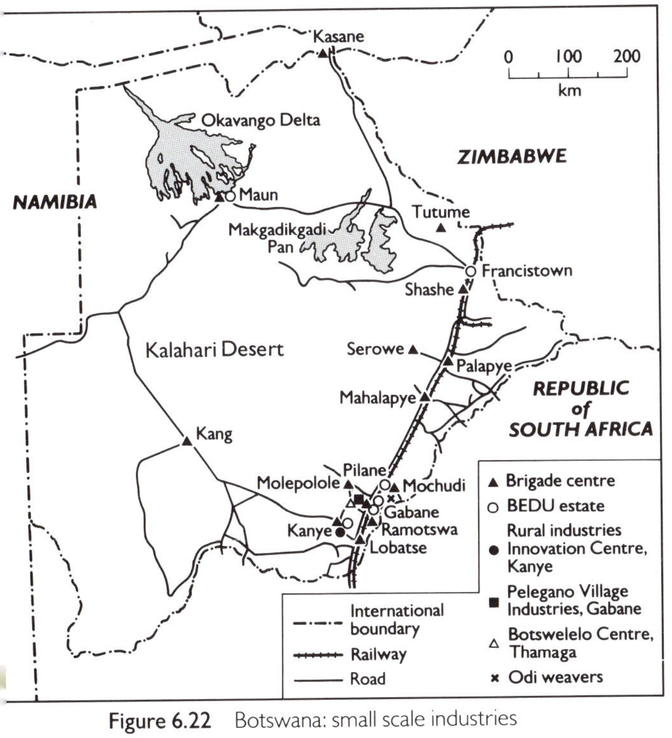

Figure 6.22 Botswana: small scale industries

Case Study

Small-scale industries in Botswana

Figure 6.22 shows that Botswana is a small country on the borders of South Africa. Most of its land is part of the Kalahari desert. Until 1966 Botswana was dependent on South Africa. Botswana provided labour and South Africa provided manufactured goods. The total population of Botswana is just under 1 million. The capital is Gaborone which has a population of about 50 000. Since 1965 the Botswana Government has tried to encourage more industry and jobs.

Firstly, the Government set up **brigades**. These are groups of young people who have left primary or elementary school. They are taught to do various jobs and pay for their training by selling what they produce. They can be trained in building, carpentry, welding, dressmaking and other trades. This scheme has only been partly successful. One problem has been a shortage of good instructors. Another problem has been that the goods made by the trainees have been difficult to sell in competition with South African imports. However, some brigade trainees in welding and draftsmanship have got jobs in the mining industry.

The Botswana Government has also set up **nursery estates**. These are small industrial estates with 10–20 workshops organized by the **Botswana Enterprises Development Unit (BEDU)**. Each estate has a manager and advice centre. The problem for these industries is that Botswana is very short of natural resources so all raw materials have to be imported. Also, the towns are small so there is a shortage of markets for the goods.

The BEDU estates are in the towns but there is a similar scheme at Kanye called the **Rural Industries Innovation Centre**. Here there are workshops which make mesh fences, handcarts, farm tools and equipment for tanning leather. They also make windmills and simple solar energy equipment. All these workshops concentrate on simple methods. Because they do not need the complicated linkages of western industries, the methods are called **alternative technology** or **appropriate technology**. Figure 6.23 shows some of the workshops.

Private charities have also encouraged simple industry schemes in Botswana. **Pelegano Village Industries (PVI)** was set up in 1975 in Gabane by European volunteers. Money was provided by various Christian charities and the Canadian and German Embassies in Gaborone. PVI has tried to help the poorest families by encouraging work which can be done at home. There are 15 different farming and industrial projects including chicken and rabbit breeding in broiler houses, sorghum milling, metal and carpentry workshops, and making corn dollies. It has been worked out that in its first 4 years, PVI raised the cash income of Gabane by 30%. Most of this money went to the poorest families. The multiplier effect has meant that most families in Gabane have benefited from the PVI scheme.

Other schemes which have been set up by charities include the Botswelelo Centre at Thamaga, and a weavers' co-operative at Odi. There is also a rug-weavers' brigade in Lobatse. These schemes have concentrated on crafts for export to Europe. The pottery, clothing and rugs provide work for men and women. However, their raw materials are imported. The goods are high quality, expensive and obviously designed for Europeans. The goods are not bought by Botswana families so the multiplier effect cannot work. These kinds of industries are not so useful for Botswana because although they provide some work, they use imported raw materials and do not save the country from having to import goods for its own people.

For a country like Botswana, industrial development seems to be most useful when it:

a Is small scale
b Involves as many people in the town or village as possible
c Produces goods and services for the local people
d Uses appropriate types of technology.

For these reasons the 1979–85 Development Plan of the Botswana Government concentrated on encouraging more small industries and linking industries with agriculture. The most important part of the plan is to provide production work for as many poor people as possible.

In Chapter 7 on Settlement you will find information on a similar scheme at Arumbakkam in Madras, India.

a

b

c

d

e

Figure 6.23 **a** Workshop units on the BEDU industrial estate at Pilane
b The front of a leatherware workshop and showroom on the BEDU industrial estate at Pilane
c A knitware workshop at Pilane
d A carpentry workshop at the Mochudi brigade centre
e A training course at the Rural Industries Innovation Centre (RIIC) at Kayne; the women are learning to make ovens so that they can earn money by baking bread

Activities

▲ ■ **19 a** Compare Figure 6.22 with the maps of climate and soils (Figures 3.18 and 3.25, pages 57 and 63).
i) Where are the main towns and villages located in Botswana?
ii) Explain why the population of Botswana is mainly concentrated in this area.
b Explain why most of the industrial schemes in Botswana are near Gaborone.

▲ ■ **20** Study the photographs of workshop units and brigade work in Botswana (Figure 6.23 (a) and (d).
a Describe the design of the workshop units and the materials of which they are made.
b Write a few sentences to explain why this type of design and building materials were chosen.
c Describe your conclusions about the type of people who are most likely to buy the goods produced in the leatherware unit. Look carefully at the shopfront display and the customer in the shop.

▲ ■ ● **21** Study Figure 6.23 (b), (c) and (e).
a i) Describe the organization and the type of technology being used in photographs (b) and (c).
ii) Write a paragraph to explain how suitable the organization and types of technology shown in the photographs are for a developing country. You should think about productivity, unemployment, amount of training needed and the cost of the equipment being used.
iii) Write a paragraph to explain why the products are not really suitable for a developing country.
b i) Describe the organization and types of technology being used in photograph (e). (Don't forget to mention the instructor.)
ii) Write a paragraph to explain the advantages of this type of technology for a developing country.
iii) Write a paragraph to explain the advantages and disadvantages of the kind of scheme shown in Figure 6.23(e) compared with the schemes shown in Figure 6.23(b) and (c), for the people of Botswana.

Case Study

Zambia's cotton production and textile industry

Cotton has been grown in Zambia for at least the last 60 years. Until 1965 most of the cotton was grown by a few European farmers on large farms. When Zambia became an independent nation in 1964, many European farmers started to leave the country. The new government increased the minimum wages for agricultural workers and so the European farmers who were left changed over to crops which needed fewer workers. By 1971 no cotton was planted by European farmers. It was all grown by 10 000 Zambian farmers on small plots of land. Figure 6.24 shows the cotton growing areas, the main clothing manufacturing centres and main markets.

The cotton seeds are sent to **ginneries** (factories where cotton lint is separated from the seeds) in Lusaka or Chipata. Before 1969 all the cotton was then exported and much of it went to Rhodesia. (Rhodesia is now called Zimbabwe.) In 1969 a new cotton textile mill for spinning and weaving cotton cloth was opened at Kafue, about 45 km south of Lusaka. This mill needs 8 million kg of seed cotton a year. Zambia could not provide this amount of cotton itself until 1971. The Zambian Government encouraged farmers to grow more cotton by offering high prices for hand picked cotton.

The cotton mill is also helped by the Zambian Government. No clothing manufacturer is allowed to import cloth which can be produced at Kafue. This guarantees the cotton mill a market for its cloth with no competition. The mill at Kafue produces about a quarter of the cloth needed by Zambian clothing manufacturers. The rest of the cloth needed can be imported.

The Government also protects the clothing industry in Zambia. Before Rhodesia left the Commonwealth and became Zimbabwe, Zambia did not have a clothing industry. Since 1969 imports of clothing have been restricted and the number of clothing factories in Zambia has increased. By the early 1980s there were over 100 factories, employing about 22 000 workers.

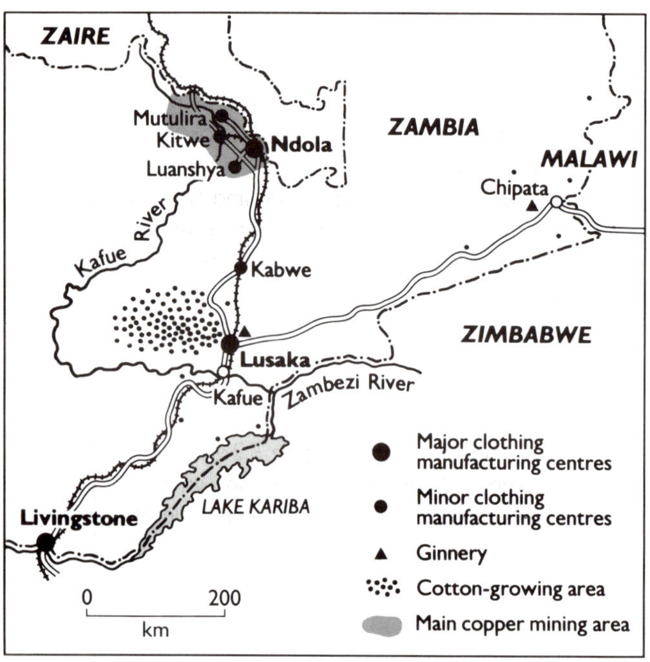

Figure 6.24 Location of cotton-growing areas in Zambia

Activities

▲22 Study Figure 6.24 and the description above.

■ a Suggest reasons why the two ginneries are
● located at Lusaka and Chipata.

b Describe how cotton seed production in Zambia changed after independence.

c Explain the advantages of Kafue for a new industrial town and cotton textile mill.

d i) Describe the location of the clothing manufacturing centres in Zambia.

ii) Explain why the clothing factories have been built in these areas.

iii) Do you think Livingstone is likely to stay a major clothing manufacturing centre? Give reasons for your decision.

The third type of industrial development in developing countries is the type where multinational companies build western-style high technology factories.

Brazil's economic miracle

Figure 6.25 The Fiat car plant at Betim Belo Horizonte, Brazil

During the late 1960s and early 1970s Brazil was able to borrow a lot of money from richer countries. At the same time Brazil exported more primary products. Foreign multinational companies wanted to build new factories in Brazil. Industry in Brazil grew between 8% and 10% each year from 1968 to 1980.

Figure 6.25 shows one of the new industries. It is the Fiat car plant at Betim in Belo Horizonte. Belo Horizonte is the capital of Minas Gerais State. Fiat joined forces with the Minas Gerais State Government to build the new factory. It opened in 1978. It is one of the most modern Fiat factories in the world. It produced more than 150 000 cars a year and employed about 10 000 workers. Thousands more people worked in the nearby factories which produced components.

Although this was the first Fiat factory in Brazil, other large multinational vehicle makers such as Volkswagen, Ford and General Motors already had factories there. These other firms expanded the factories they already had.

The growth of the car industry and other industries increased the demand for steel and oil-based products. The Brazilian steel and petroleum industries, owned by the Government, were also expanded. A new steel works was started at Ouro Branco in Minas Gerais. Two new petro-chemical refineries were started. This boost to the steel industry led to a growth in Brazil's shipbuilding industry. Brazil became one of the world's great shipbuilders.

Other large schemes which were encouraged by the boom in the Brazilian economy included a new hydroelectric scheme in the Amazon. Another one on the borders of Brazil and Paraguay (the Itaipu scheme) was planned to be the largest in the world. A nuclear power station, an underground railway system for Rio de Janeiro, and thousands of new distilleries for distilling sugar into alcohol for fuel (see Chapter 4) were also included.

In 1979, however, things began to change. Industry began to decline due to the world recession. Foreign companies began to cut back their factories in Brazil. In 1983 car workers in São Paulo protested in the streets about redundancies. The Government had to cancel some of the large schemes before they were finished. The nuclear power station, the steel mill and plans to open up huge iron ore and bauxite fields in Amazonia were cancelled.

There are many reasons why Brazil's modern industrial growth stopped and the country found itself badly in debt. Here are some of them:

First, the rise in world oil prices in 1973 made Brazil's bill for importing oil and goods which have oil as a raw material go up by more than the price of its exports. Also, the increase in oil prices put up the prices of almost all the goods and machinery which Brazil imported from richer countries.

Second, international banks put up their interest rates, so that Brazil had to find more and more money to pay the interest on what it had borrowed.

Third, the recession in the developed countries meant that Brazil could not export its products. This made it difficult for Brazil to earn money to pay the interest on its loan.

Fourth, the war between Argentina and the UK over the Falklands/Malvinas Islands made international banks and companies wary of lending or investing more money in South America.

Fifth, industry in Brazil had expanded so rapidly that the Government could not keep check on the country's whole economy. The Brazilian exchequer did not appreciate what was happening to the economy.

Finally, the world recession and Brazil's economic problems meant that foreign companies gradually began to run down their factories in Brazil.

This example shows the problems which can happen when a country bases its industrial growth on foreign companies and borrowed money. Brazil developed high-technology industry but the rest of the economy and many of the people could not support these industries by providing a large market. This meant that changes outside Brazil upset the Brazilian economy. It also suggests that the factories built by multinational companies may not be the most suitable type of industrial development for developing countries.

Activity

▲ ■ ● 23 a Write lists to show the advantages and disadvantages of the new Fiat works in Brazil to
  i) The Fiat company
  ii) The Brazilian Government.
b Explain why the Ford works in Valencia would be less likely to be closed than the Ford works in São Paulo.
c Suggest ways in which the Brazilian Government could have developed industry without the country suffering so badly from the world recession.

Power for industry

All industry needs power of some kind. Originally this was human power but long before the Industrial Revolution other forms of power such as the power of running water and the wind were used. Today, most machinery in factories is driven by electric motors. Most transport is powered by petroleum products or electricity, although there are still some steam engines. Most of the energy needed in the modern industrial world comes from electrical power or from fossil fuels like petroleum or coal. However, electric power has to be generated by a source of energy.

Figure 6.26 shows the sources of our energy. These sources can be divided into **renewable** sources and **non-renewable** sources. Renewable sources are those which are not used up by human beings. Non-renewable sources could be used up in time. For example, the world is not likely to run out of wind, so this is a renewable source. On the other hand, the large amounts of coal and oil which are taken from the Earth, once they are burnt, are lost for ever, so coal and oil are non-renewable sources. Let's look at some of these energy sources in more detail.

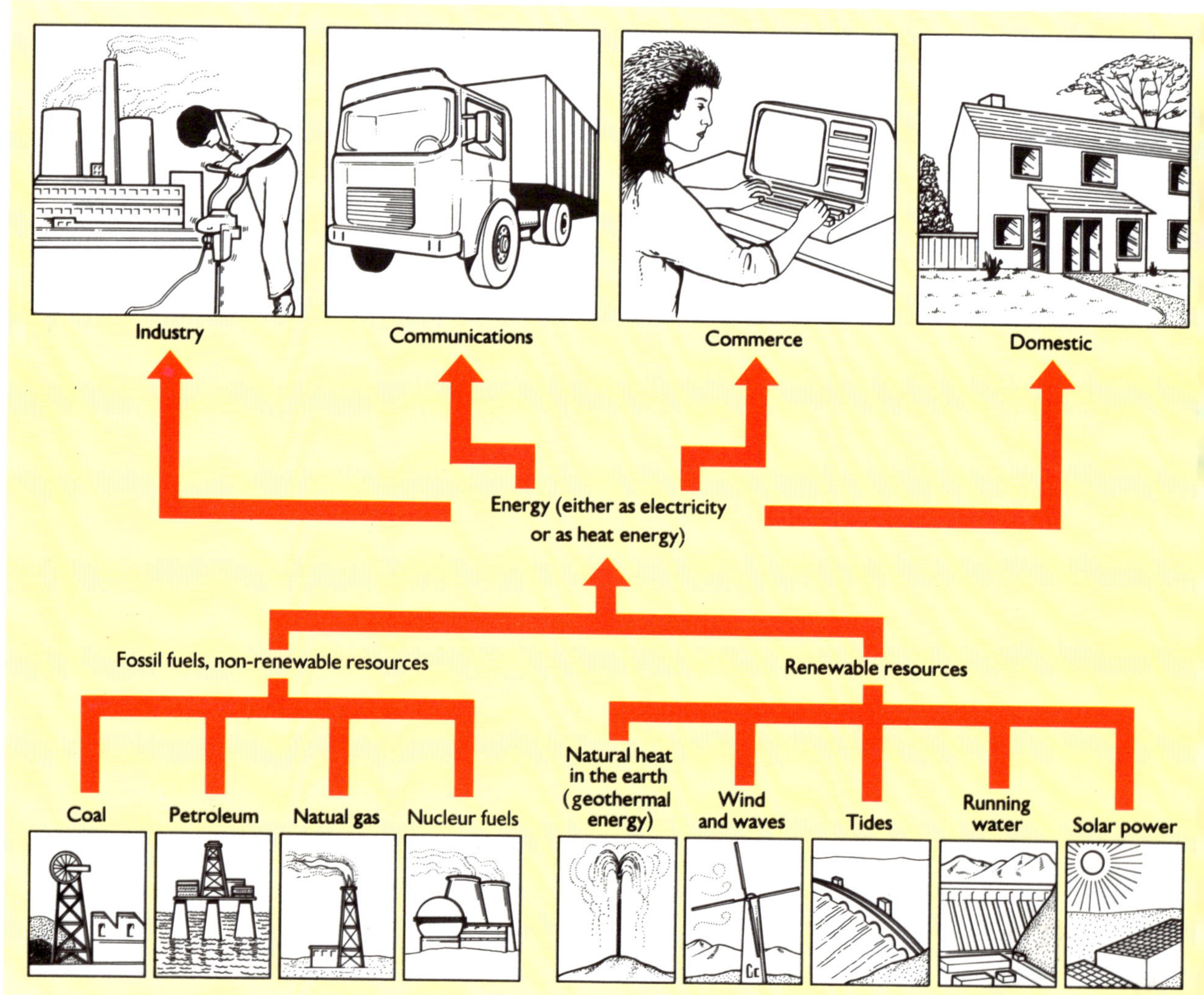

Figure 6.26 Sources of energy for industry, transport, commerce and the home

Fossil fuels

Coal, oil, natural gas and radioactive fuels are called **fossil fuels**. Different substances in the Earth's crust have changed over many years to make these fuels. Coal is the remains of trees and other vegetation which have changed to carbon. Petroleum and natural gas have been made from tiny organisms which have decomposed to form hydrocarbons. Nuclear fuels are made from rocks which contain large amounts of natural radioactivity in the Earth.

Petroleum and natural gas

The word 'petroleum' means 'oil from rocks'. It is found in porous sedimentary rocks like sandstone. The oil and gas drift upwards through the porous rocks until they reach an impermeable layer. If the rocks are folded upwards then enough oil or gas may collect to be worth drilling for. Figure 6.27 shows how the rocks are folded upwards (an **anticline**) and oil and gas have collected in the top of the anticline underneath the impermeable rocks.

The art of oil prospecting is to find oil traps like this. Figure 6.27 shows how oil explorers can use explosions to work out the depth and lie of the rocks. The noise of the explosion is reflected back differently by each type of rock. Many hundreds of measurements are taken to draw accurate geological maps. Even when anticlines in porous rocks are found, there is no guarantee that they contain oil. This makes oil exploration very expensive because only a few of the holes drilled actually contain oil. Drilling in rocks under the sea is particularly expensive.

Figure 6.28 shows the geology of the North Sea. Even though this is a simplified diagram, it is much more complicated than the simple anticline in Figure 6.27. The biggest difference is that the rocks have many faults in them. The names on Figure 6.28, such as *Cretaceous* and *Jurassic*, show the ages of the rocks. Figure 6.29 shows the ages of the rocks in the North Sea.

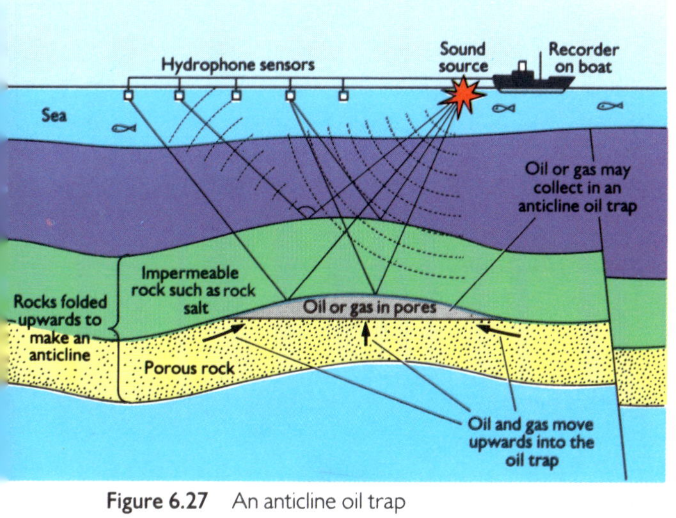

Figure 6.27 An anticline oil trap

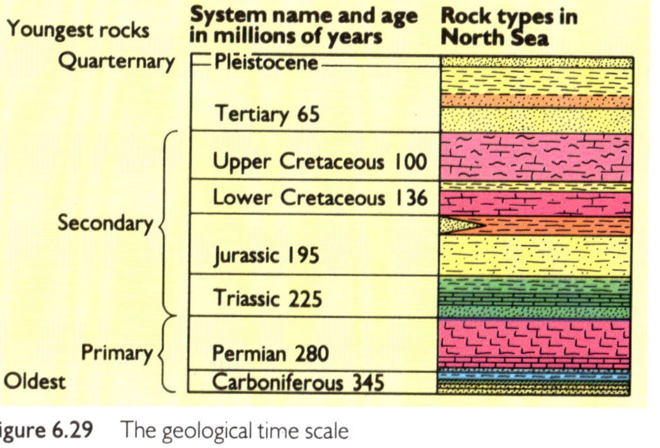

Figure 6.29 The geological time scale

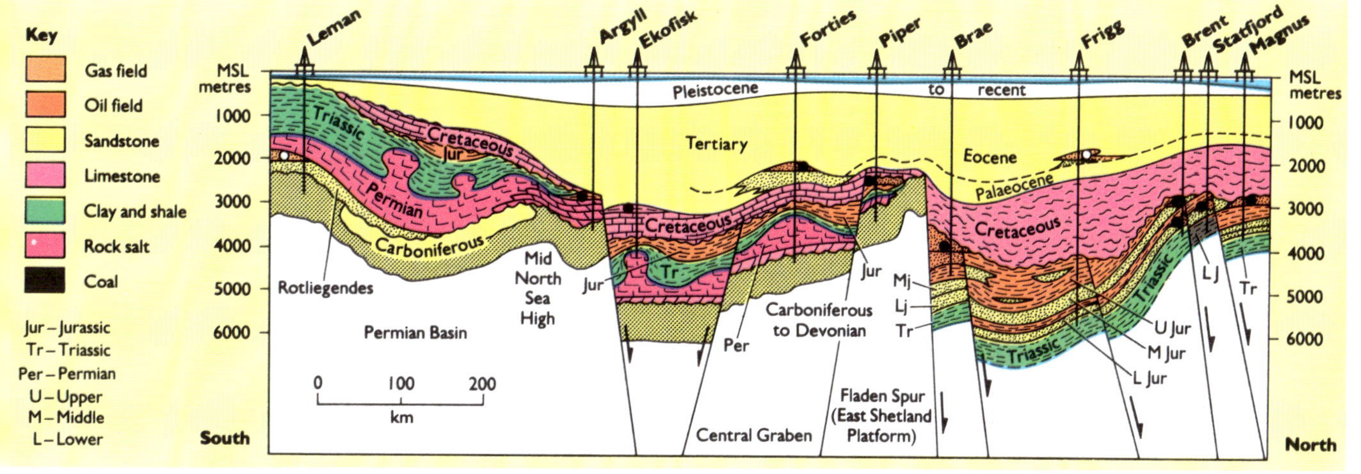

Figure 6.28 The geology of the petroleum and natural gas fields beneath the North Sea

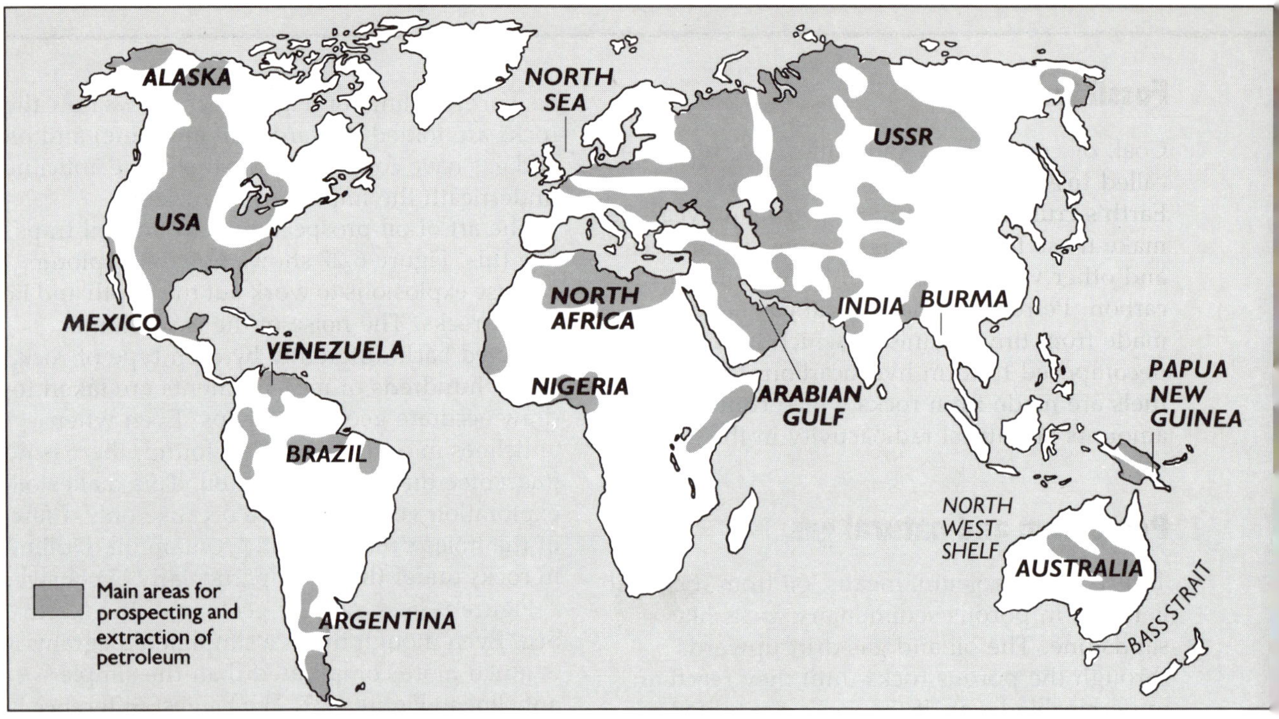

Figure 6.30 Main areas of the continents where petroleum can be found

Most of the oil and gas in the world are found in rocks of secondary age or younger. Coal, on the other hand, is often found in rocks laid down in the carboniferous period of the primary era.

Figure 6.30 shows the main areas of the world where petroleum can be obtained, on land. As we know, much petroleum is now obtained from areas beneath the sea, such as the North Sea. The output of the main producing countries is shown in Figure 6.31.

Different oilfields produce different qualities of crude oil. This quality depends on whether the crude petroleum contains more heavy or light oils. The lighter the oil, the easier it is to refine it into petrol. Figure 6.32 shows the quality of some of the world's oilfields and Figure 6.33 shows how different qualities of oil can be refined into different types of fuel. You can see that the light crude oil can be refined to give more petrol, diesel fuel, jet fuel and petrochemicals than the heavy crude oils. The heavy oils provide more fuel for power stations.

Because oil is a non-renewable resource and only collects in certain kinds of geological structure, all oilfields have a limited life. Figure 6.34 shows what happens to the output of an oilfield over about 20 years.

This may make it look as if the UK will almost run out of oil by the end of this century. However, the estimates of oil reserves are constantly rising. The reserves may be increased for two reasons. Firstly, new oilfields may be discovered. Secondly, new methods of extracting oil may be developed which make it economic to exploit oil which at the moment would be uneconomic. Figure 6.35 shows various estimates of UK oil reserves. Another factor which affects oil production is price. Thus in the mid 1980s the price of petroleum decreased owing to a fall in demand, and the incentive to extract and sell it was reduced.

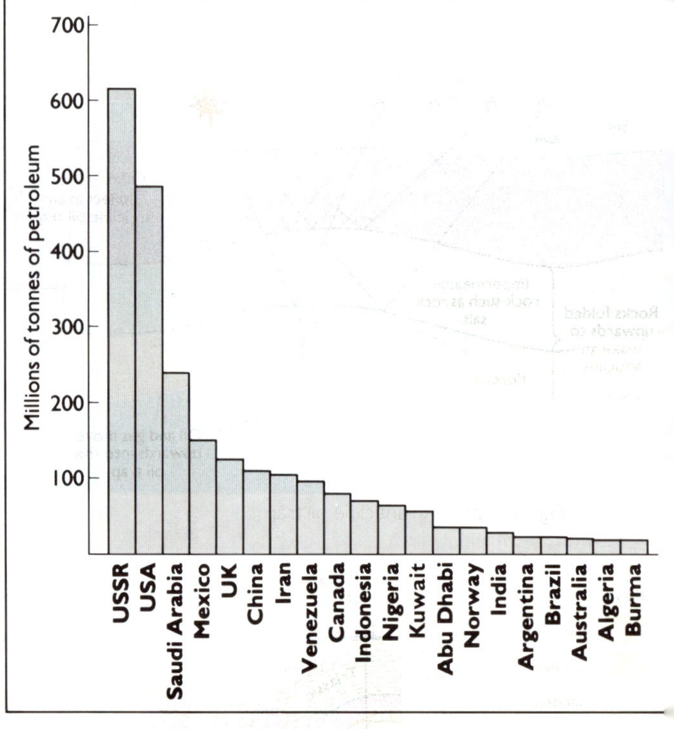

Figure 6.31 Production of crude petroleum

Origin	Crude	American Petroleum Institute Gravity Number (1–100)
North Sea	Piper	37
	Claymore	30–31
	Ekofisk	42–44
	Thistle	37
North Africa	Algeria	44
	Libya-Brega Zueitina	40
	Es Sider	37
	Amna	36
Arabian Gulf	Arabian Light	33
	Arabian Heavy	28
	Kirkuk	36
	Basrah Heavy	23
	Murban	39
Venezuela	Range	15–31
USA	Average	34
	Range Chief	22–44
Worldwide average		34

Figure 6.32 American Petroleum Institute (API) gravity numbers for typical crude oilfields around the World

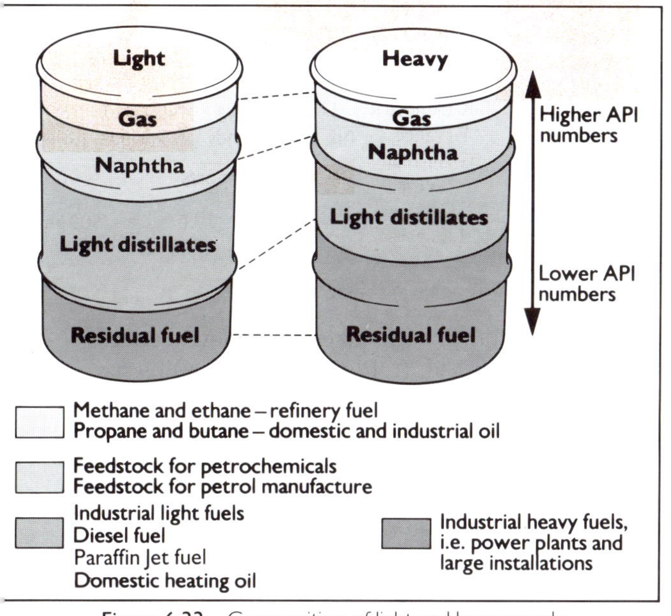

Figure 6.33 Composition of light and heavy crude petroleum

Activities

▲ ■ **24** a Explain why the costs of oil prospecting and drilling are going up and will probably continue to go up (apart from the increases due to inflation).

b The organisms which gave off natural gas may have been alive in the carboniferous period, but natural gas is usually found in secondary age rocks. Explain why this is the case.

▲ ■ **25** Study the map of oil bearing areas in the world (Figure 6.30).

a Write a list of the countries which have sedimentary rocks but which have not yet opened oil and gas fields.

b Since oil is found beneath the North Sea, what kind of rocks must be found below the sea bed?

c Explain why the continental shelf areas of the world could be important oil producing areas in the future.

▲ ■ ● **26** Study Figure 6.30. What kind of difficulties do you think oil companies face when they drill for oil in

a Alaska
b Libya
c The Niger Delta
d The North Sea
e Western Australia?

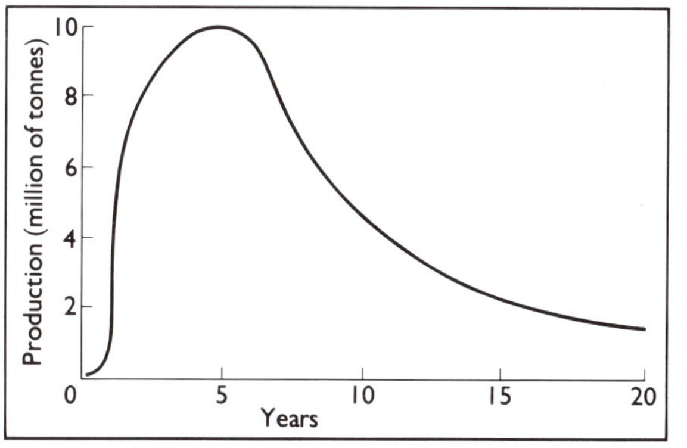

Figure 6.34 Typical output in an oilfield over 20 years

	Proven	Probable	Possible	Possible total
1 Oil fields in production or under development	1070	110	80	1260
2 Other significant discoveries not yet fully investigated	310	460	470	1240
Total present discoveries	1380	570	550	2500
Expected discoveries	–	350	350	700

Notes

Proven: oil reserves which are almost certain to be technically and economically suitable for production

Probable: oil reserves which are thought to have a better than 50% chance of being technically and economically suitable for production

Possible: oil reserves which are thought to be important but which at present have a less than 50% chance of being technically and economically suitable for production

Figure 6.35 The make-up of estimated oil reserves in the UK licensed areas in the North Sea

Activities

▲ ■ 27 a Study Figure 6.31.

i) Explain why the USA buys oil from abroad even though it is a large oil producer. (The population of the USA is 232 million. The standard of living is very high.)

ii) Explain why most of the oil in international trade comes from the Middle East (population 68 million).

b Study Figure 6.32 which shows the different qualities of oil in different oilfields, and Figure 6.33 which shows how the oils are refined. Explain why the UK still needs to import some oil from the Arabian Gulf.

▲ ■ 28 a Draw bar charts of 'oilfields in production or under development' and 'other significant discoveries' divided into the proven, probable and possible reserves of the UK given in Figure 6.35.

b Describe any ways you can think of which could change the *possible* reserves into *probable* reserves.

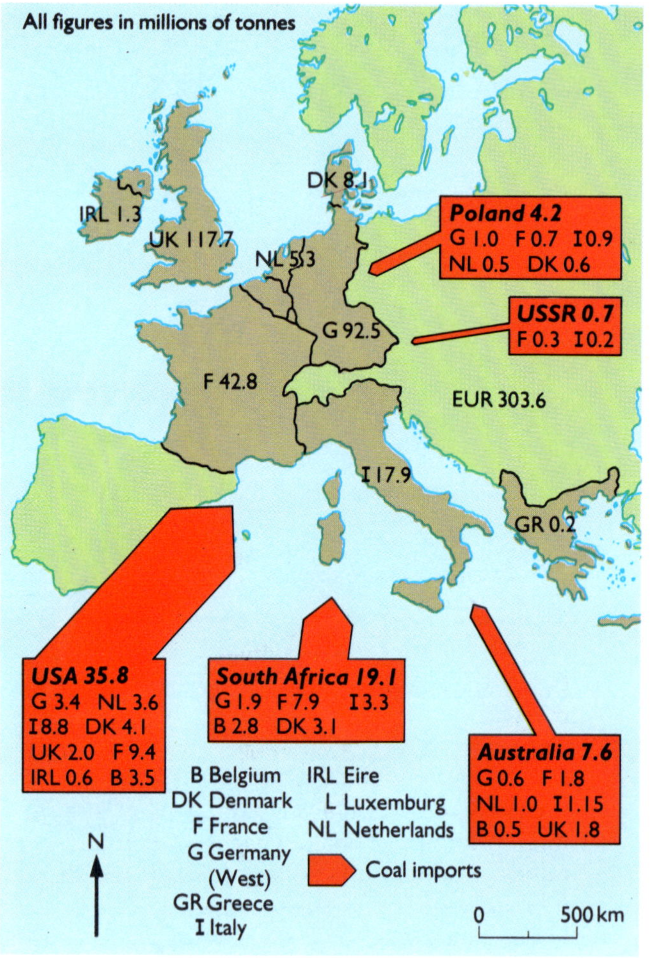

Figure 6.36 Coal imports into EEC countries

Coal and other fuels

We explained at the start of this chapter that the Industrial Revolution began in Europe and that coal was the main source of power for most of the new factories. After World War II, oil became much cheaper than coal and the demand for coal became less. The amount of coal mined in western Europe dropped from 467 million tonnes in 1955 to 279 million tonnes in 1972. In 1955 the hard coal mined in western Europe was 29% of world production. In 1972 it was only 14% of world production.

During the 1960s the coal industry of Europe was run down. Many pits were closed. The coal industry in Europe became concentrated in the UK and West Germany. In 1981 these two countries produced almost 90% of all western Europe's coal output.

During this period of time, oil became much more important in supplying western Europe's energy. In 1960 only 29% of western Europe's energy came from oil. In 1972 60% of the energy came from oil.

In 1973 the price of oil started to rise due to the Arab–Israeli war. The price rises continued as the **OPEC** countries realized that they needed to conserve their oil. (OPEC stands for Oil Producing and Exporting Countries.) In 1980 the revolution in Iran caused more price rises. All these price rises made coal much more competitive as a fuel.

This meant that the use of coal in Europe did not go down as fast as the production of coal. In fact the amount of coal used went up from 281 million tonnes in 1975 to 304 million tonnes in 1981. 59% of the coal in Europe was used in electricity generating stations. In the UK 74% of all coal was used for electricity. In West Germany only 50% of coal was used for electricity.

The cut-backs in the coal industry in the 1970s have led to a shortage of coal in the EEC. The shortage has had to be met by importing coal from other parts of the world. In 1970 only about 9% of the coal used in Europe was imported. In 1981 23% was imported. Figure 6.36 shows where the coal came from and where it was used.

	1970	1973	1974	1975	1976	1977	1978	1979	1980	1981
Coke ovens	32.6	34.5	36.2	36.7	33.8	31.1	28.9	28.2	28.0	28.1
Power stations	39.3	45.0	43.5	45.2	50.6	52.6	55.7	56.7	58.6	59.0

Figure 6.37 The use of coal for coke ovens and power stations in the EEC

Production (million tonnes)	**W. Germany**	**France**	**Belgium**	**UK**
1973	103.65	25.68	8.84	130.15
1984	84.86	16.59	6.29	49.55 (coal miners' strike)
Number of mines				
1973	53	35	18	261
1984	35	20	6	183

Figure 6.38 Changes in coal production and number of mines since 1973 in the EEC

There have been great changes in the way coal is mined in Europe. For example, the amount of coal mined in the UK has stayed roughly the same from 1973 to the present, but the total number of mines has fallen drastically. New coalfields have been opened at Selby and the Vale of Belvoir. It is thought that these coalfields have reserves of coal which will last for 300 years. The important change in the UK coal industry is in the size of the mines. For example, at Selby, 4000 workers will produce 10 million tonnes of coal a year from 6 linked mines. In the South Wales coalfield, which is much older, 22 700 workers produced 6.9 million tonnes of coal from 33 mines in 1983. The average price of mining coal in South Wales is much greater than in Selby.

The changes in the coal industry can be summed up as follows:

1 In Europe, and particularly in the UK, there are large reserves of coal in newly discovered coalfields. Coal is important in generating electricity and has become more competitive with oil once again.

2 Despite this, the coal mined in Europe in deep pits still remains more expensive than imported coal. For example, the average price of a tonne of British coal at the pithead in 1979 was USA $57. A tonne of coal could be shipped and delivered to the same pithead for $41 from the USA, $38 from Australia and $31 from South Africa.

3 The price advantage of coal over oil since 1973 has encouraged the use of coal in Europe, but European mines cannot produce sufficient coal cheaply enough to satisfy the demand. The shortage of cheap coal is likely to be met from imports from other continents. In the mid-1980s however, the price of petroleum has slumped and competition with coal is important.

Activities

▲ ■ **29** Study Figure 6.37 which shows the percentage of coal used for coke and electricity power generation from 1970 to 1981.

a Draw a graph to show how the use of coal changed between 1970 and 1981.

b Write a paragraph to describe the change in use and to explain why this change has occurred.

▲ ■ **30** Study Figure 6.38 which shows the changes in coal production and number of mines in the EEC between 1973 and 1984.

a Draw a graph to show how coal production and the number of mines changed between 1973 and 1984.

b **i)** Write a few sentences to describe the changes in production and number of mines.

ii) Explain the conclusions which may be drawn from these changes.

▲ ■ **31** Study Figure 6.36 which shows the amount of coal used in the countries of the EEC in 1981 and where the coal came from.

a List the countries of Europe in order of the amount of coal they use.

b Draw up a table to show the countries which receive coal from outside the EEC and where it comes from.

c **i)** Describe the pattern of coal imports into the EEC.

ii) Why do some countries import more coal than others?

iii) Why do EEC countries get their coal from different parts of the world?

Nuclear energy

In nature, uranium is a dense, hard, white element. It is the eighth most plentiful mineral in the world.

Uranium originally became part of the Earth's crust in granite magma formed over a subduction zone. (This is explained in Chapter 2.) Granites made in this way only contain 0.001% uranium so they are not worth mining. Uranium mining takes place where the uranium ore has become concentrated. The average concentration of the ore which is mined is 0.15%. This means that 670 tonnes of ore are needed to give 1 tonne of uranium.

Although uranium is so common in the world, whether or not it is exploited depends on the total costs of mining and processing. Figure 6.39 shows uranium production in the world.

In Western countries about 10% of all electricity is produced by nuclear power stations. There are already over 180 nuclear reactors. Although it was hoped that electricity generated by nuclear power would be very cheap, the nuclear power stations which have been built have turned out to be much more expensive than expected. For example, the power station at Wylfa on Anglesey was intended to produce 1180 MW of electricity but can only actually produce 840 MW (megawatts) due to design problems. The Dungeness B power station should have been working by 1971 but was still not finished in 1986.

If uranium is used as a fuel on its own, it has been estimated that there will be a world uranium shortage some time between 1995 and 2000. This problem could be solved by using nuclear reactors which, through fast atomic reactions, produce or 'breed' plutonium. Plutonium is a much more powerful fuel but it is very dangerous. At the moment plutonium is mainly used for nuclear weapons. The Central Electricity Generating Board is planning to build some fast breeder reactors. The programme to build advanced gas reactors was originally estimated to cost £419 million. The latest estimate is that they will cost at least £1500 million.

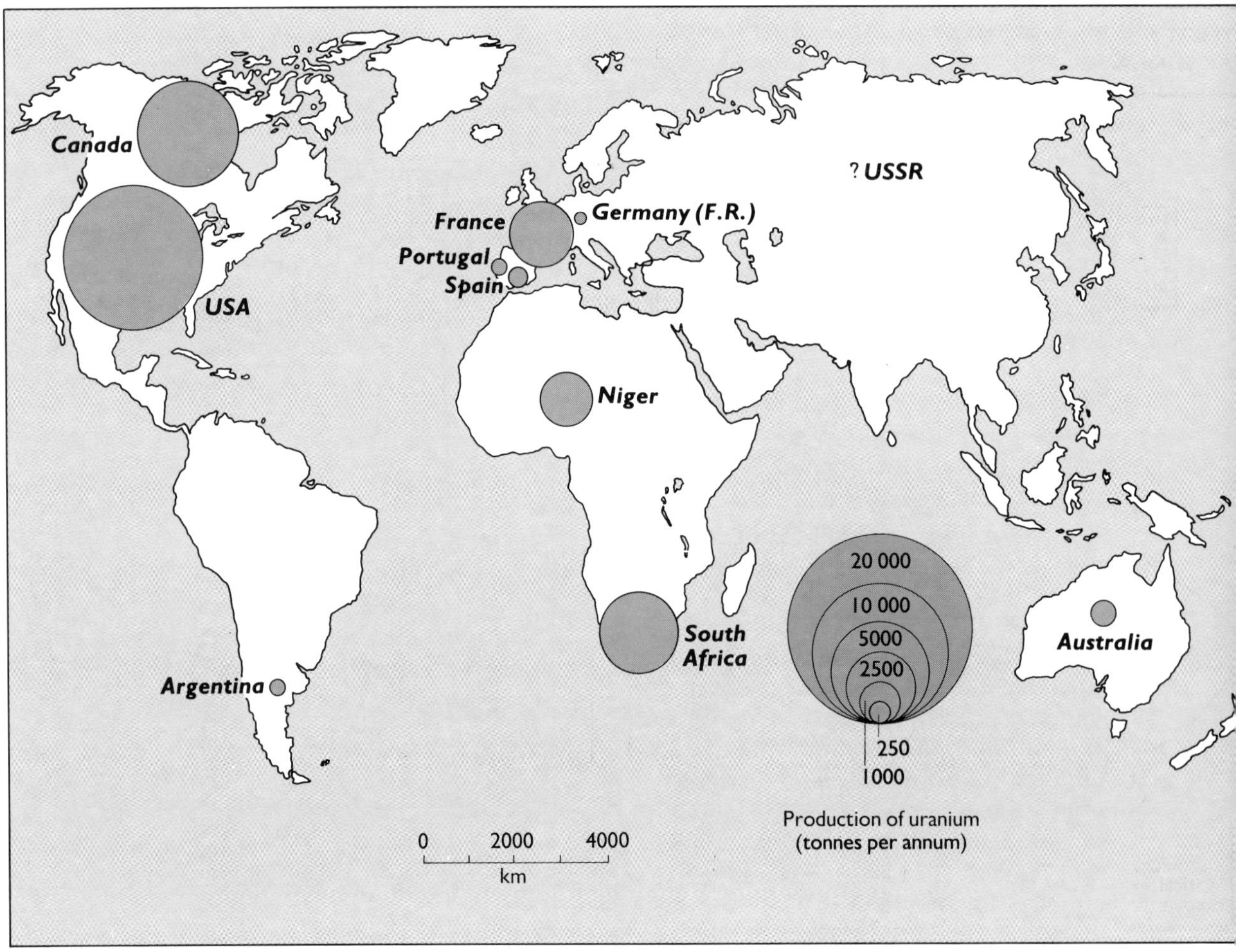

Figure 6.39 World distribution of uranium production

Mining uranium and producing power for nuclear energy are both difficult activities. This is because they are dangerous to health and are politically 'hot'. We will briefly describe some of the problems of mining uranium and processing the used uranium.

In South Africa, which possesses 18% of the non-socialist world's uranium resources, uranium is mined as a by-product of gold mining. Only a quarter of the miners come from South Africa. The rest come from the surrounding countries. Political relations between the black nations of Africa and South Africa are not very good, so this source of uranium could be blocked at any time.

In Australia much of the uranium is under the traditional lands of the Aborigines. This land is sacred to Aborigines. The Aborigines have fought to protect their land from being torn up by uranium mines.

In the USA it has been proved that the health of uranium miners is at risk from the dust in the air. Also, waste from the mines has been washed into the Colorado river and carried downstream. Some of the waste has been used to make materials for house building in Salt Lake City, Durango and Grand Junction.

In Canada the Government stopped exporting uranium to EEC countries and Japan because it was afraid that the uranium would be re-processed into material for nuclear weapons.

Finally, Figure 6.40 shows some of the problems which have occurred at the Windscale/Sellafield uranium re-processing plant in Cumberland. These problems have resulted in the Irish Sea becoming the worst area of water in the world for radioactive pollution. The British Government has warned people to stay clear of large areas of the beaches in Cumberland.

Although nuclear energy is so difficult and dangerous to produce, one writer has suggested that we may have to choose between either having our countryside spoiled by new coal-mines, like the ones in the Vale of Belvoir, or putting up with nuclear advanced gas reactor or pressurized water reactor power stations.

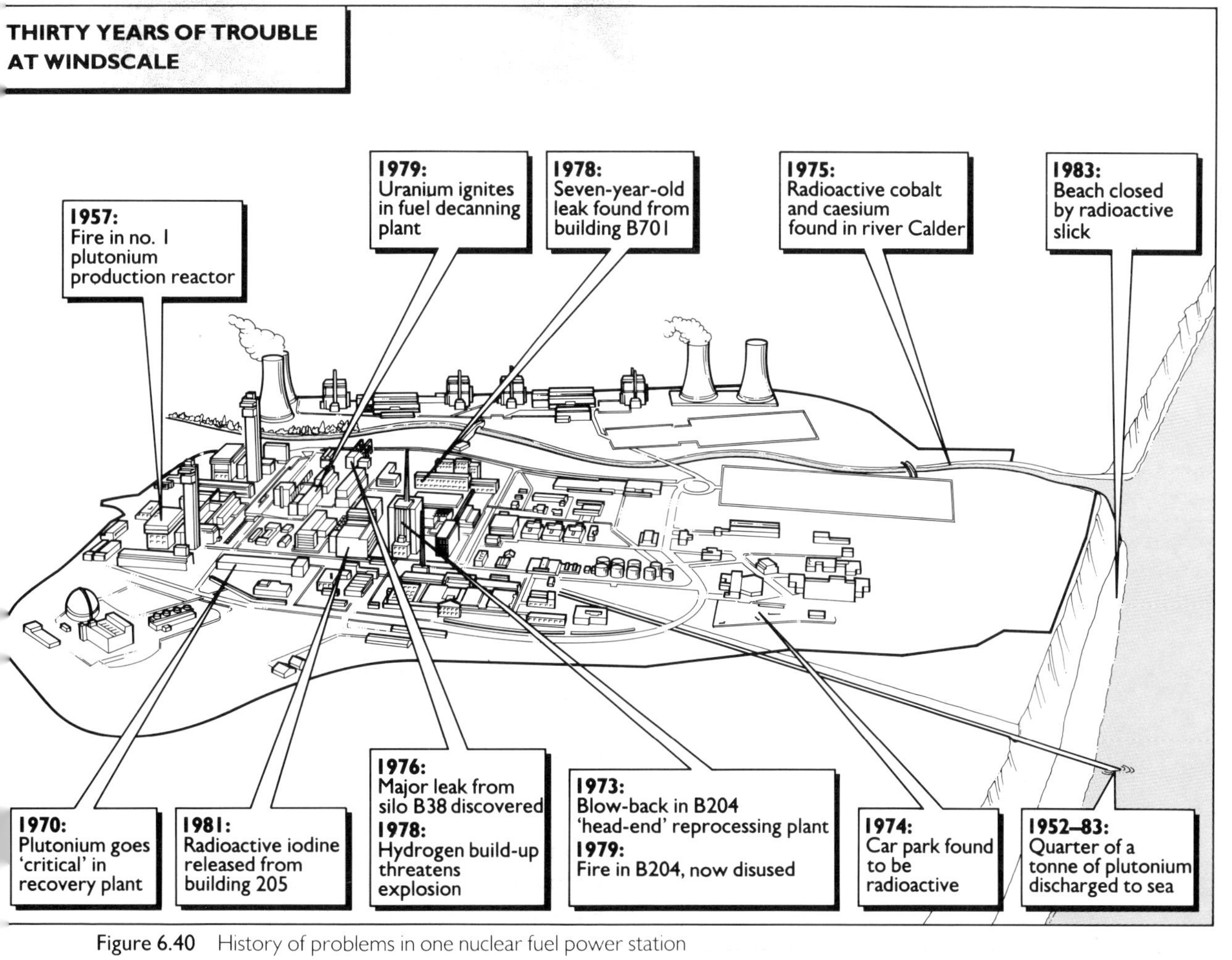

Figure 6.40 History of problems in one nuclear fuel power station

Activities

▲ ■ ● **32** Suggest why no information is available on the resources and production of uranium in the USSR and China.

▲ ■ ● **33** **a** Study Figure 6.39. Describe the location of uranium resources in the world.

b **i)** Suggest reasons why there seems to be so little uranium in the developing countries.

ii) Is there any evidence that the reason why the uranium resources of the USA are high is that the Americans have looked harder for it?

c **i)** Explain why there is so much waste material from uranium mining.

ii) Write a paragraph to explain how the problem of radioactive mining waste could be solved.

d **i)** Sweden has 80% of western Europe's uranium resources but actual production is very small. Explain why this might be.

ii) Look back at Chapter 2. Why do gold and uranium occur together in South Africa? Give reasons.

■ **34** Make a table to show the advantages and disadvantages of each of the fossil fuels. You should mention

a Cost
b Availability
c Difficulty of extraction
d Safety
e Effect on the environment.

▲ ■ **35** Study Figure 6.40 which shows some of the problems found in the Windscale/Sellafield nuclear fuel re-processing plant.

a Briefly describe the two main causes of the problems.

b Find Windscale/Sellafield on an atlas map of the British Isles. Describe where the pollution from Windscale is most likely to be carried.

i) by ocean currents
ii) by the wind.

Water power

Figure 6.41 Small hydroelectric power station at Quebec

In the previous sections we saw that all fossil fuels are non-renewable resources. This means that sooner or later they are going to run out. Because of this, governments are trying to develop forms of energy which will not run out. We have already mentioned the schemes in Brazil for making fuel-alcohol from sugar cane (Chapter 4). Other forms of energy which will not run out are water power, tidal power, wind power and solar power.

Water power has been used for many years to drive mill wheels. Now it is mainly used to drive electricity generators. Figure 6.41 shows a small hydroelectric power (HEP) station in Quebec. Figure 6.42 shows the Dinorwig pumped storage HEP station in North Wales. The small HEP plant could probably provide electricity for a small town. The Dinorwig scheme is the largest pumped storage scheme in Europe. It has the same generating capacity as a large coal burning power station – 1800 MW.

Although HEP stations are found in many parts of the world they are unevenly distributed. This is shown in Figure 6.43 which lists the percentage of the total power supply generated by water power.

Figure 6.42 Dinorwig Pumped Storage Scheme, North Wales

Country	% HEP	Country	% HEP
USA	11	Poland	3
USSR	14	Spain	21
Japan	16	India	39
West Germany	6	East Germany	2
Canada	70	Australia	18
China	21	Norway	99
UK	2	Netherlands	0
Sweden	58	Switzerland	70
France	26	Greece	0
Italy	25	Denmark	0
Brazil	92		

Figure 6.43 Percentage of electricity generated by HEP

Activities

▲ 36 a Write a list of the physical conditions
■ needed for HEP generation. Chapters 2 and 3 will help with this.

b Explain the problems of building HEP stations in areas where the conditions for HEP are best.

▲ 37 Study Figure 6.43.
■ a With the help of an atlas, explain the physical reasons why the Netherlands, Denmark and East Germany have little or no HEP.

b What are the economic reasons why West Germany, UK and Poland have so little HEP?

c Describe and explain the reasons why Norway, Switzerland and Brazil get such a high proportion of their power from HEP stations.

Tidal power

Another form of water power is tidal power. In this case sea water is made to flow through a turbine which revolves and generates electricity. The principle is the same as for HEP.

The first tidal power station was built in the Rance Estuary in Brittany, France, in 1966. Figure 6.44 shows the location of the Rance scheme.

Figure 6.44 Location of the Rance Tidal Power Station, Brittany, N. France

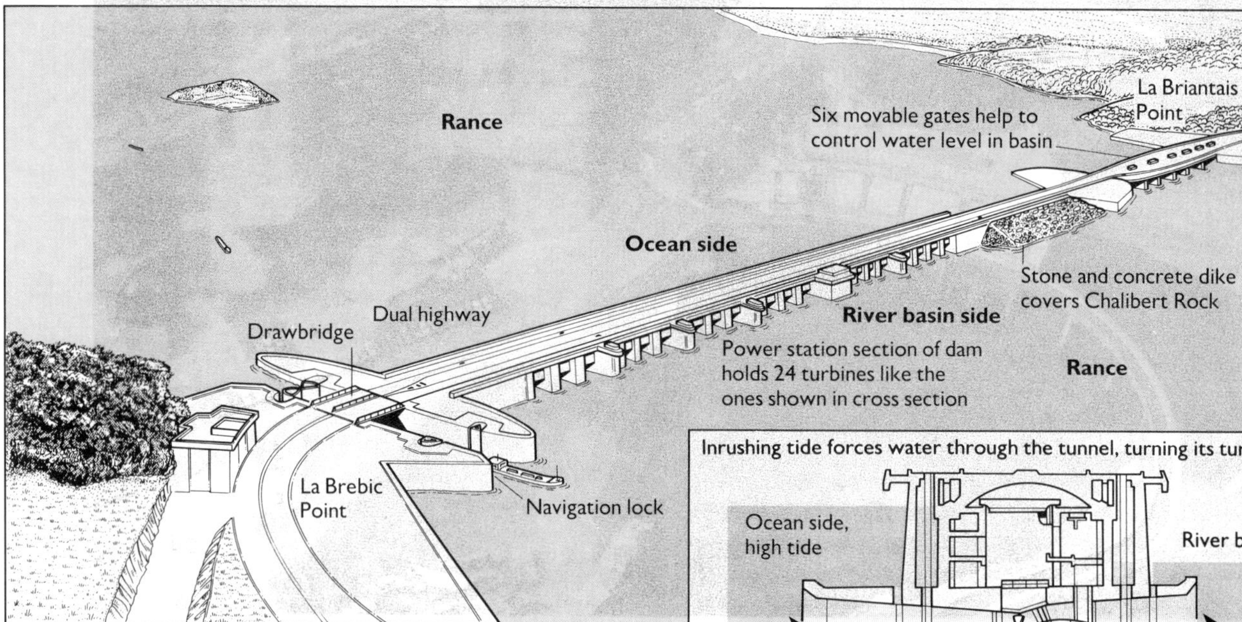

Figure 6.45 The Rance Tidal Power Station

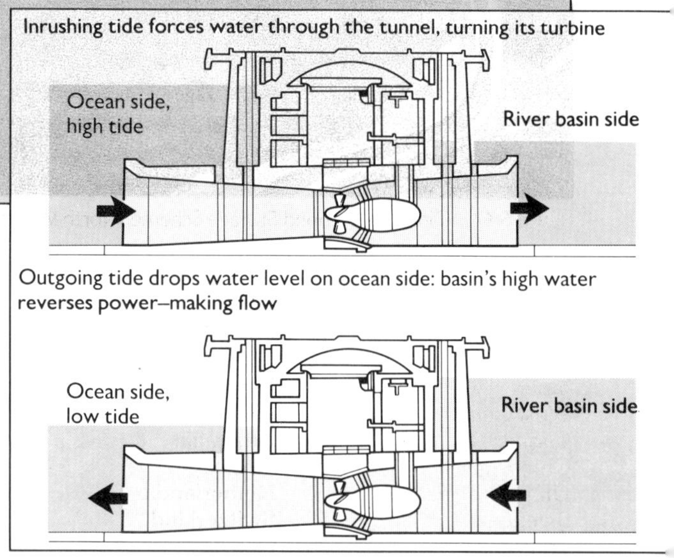

Figure 6.46 How electricity is generated in the Rance Tidal Power Station

Figures 6.45 and 6.46 show how the power station works. The Rance Estuary is a **ria** (a drowned river valley). The estuary narrows between the Pointe de la Brebis on the west and the Pointe de la Briantais on the east. A dam 750 metres long has been built across the estuary at this point. Inside the dam there are 24 tunnels. Each tunnel has a turbine. The turbines are turned one way when the tide rises and water rushes into the estuary, and the other way when the tide falls and water rushes out. The average difference between high and low tide is nearly 10 metres. The Rance power scheme can produce 240 MW. This is small compared with, for example, the 1320 MW capacity of the gas-fired power station at Peterhead in Scotland. However, there are plans to build a 3800 MW tidal power station in the Bay of Fundy between Nova Scotia and New Brunswick. There are also some plans to use the power of the tide in the Severn Estuary in England. If it were built, the Severn scheme could produce 10 000 MW as well as a new Severn bridge.

Activity

▲ ■ ● 38 a Study Figures 6.45 and 6.46 and the description above. List the advantages of the Rance Estuary for tidal power.

b What are the advantages and disadvantages of tidal power stations?

c Why have very few tidal power stations actually been built in the world?

Wind power

Wind power has been used, on a small scale, to generate electricity for single houses or farms in remote areas, for some time. More recently, a 125 kW wind generator was built in Aldborough in North Yorkshire, which feeds current into the local electricity grid or network of power lines. The Central Electricity Generating Board is also planning to build 4 MW wind generators at Richborough in Kent and on Orkney. A 3 MW wind generator was completed at the mouth of the river Elbe in West Germany in 1983.

So far, however, the capacity of wind generators is fairly small.

Activity

▲ ■ ● 39 Give as many reasons as you can why so few wind generators have been built to feed electricity into a country's electricity grid.

Solar power

Solar power is used to generate electricity in various ways (Figure 6.47). The best known way is by using photoelectric cells. These produce small amounts of electricity when sunlight falls on the cells. They are used for watches and calculators and for providing the electricity needed by space satellites.

Another way is to use the differences in temperature between two layers of water which have been heated by the sun. This method is used in Israel in an experimental station at the south-western end of the Dead Sea. The Israelis hope that by the year 2000 all of Israel's electricity could be provided by solar power. Figure 6.47 shows an experimental solar powered electricity generating station in White Cliffs, New South Wales, Australia. It was opened in 1983 and supplies electricity for the town's hospital, post office, school, community hall and church as well as some houses and street lights. The power station consists of 14 dishes which concentrate direct sunlight on to absorbers. Water passes through the absorbers and is heated to superheated steam at over 400°C. The steam is used to drive an electricity generator. The electricity is used directly in the town and is also stored in a bank of batteries to be used at night. The dishes are rotated so that they always face directly to the sun. This movement is controlled so that they are on target even after cloudy periods.

Figure 6.47 White Cliffs solar powered electricity generating station

Activity

▲ ■ ● **40** Solar power is more likely to be used for space and water heating than for electricity generation in the near future. Explain briefly the problems of large scale solar power schemes.

Energy policy by governments

In the first 70 years of this century, the use of coal, oil, electricity, nuclear energy and so on depended mainly on their price and whether they were available.

During the 19th century, coal was the main source of energy partly because it was available and partly because most machinery was driven by steam. In the second half of the 20th century, oil took over. Again this was partly because it became available in large quantities and partly because ships, aircraft, lorries and cars used oil products as fuel.

In the last part of the 20th century, governments have realized that they need to use fuels carefully to avoid them being used up. For example, in 1973 the **Organization of Oil Exporting Countries (OPEC)** increased the price of oil to increase their income and also to encourage countries to economize on oil. In the UK the Government decided to raise the price of natural gas to discourage people from using it.

Governments can also encourage people to use one fuel rather than another by taxes. For example, if oil is taxed, firms and people may use more coal. Governments could also encourage the development of new sources of renewable energy such as solar energy and wind power. They could do this by giving subsidies to this type of energy, or tax relief on the equipment needed. They could encourage research into these methods. So far, however, most money for research has gone into nuclear energy.

The type of energy used is no longer a matter of simple economics. It has become a political matter just like the location of industry.

Activity

▲ ■ ● **41** a Make two lists, to show the advantages and disadvantges of
  i) Fossil fuels
  ii) Renewable sources of energy.

b Write two or three paragraphs to explain the different decisions which have to be made by any government which is deciding how to supply electricity to its country.

Tertiary activities

We explained in Chapter 4 that tertiary activities include the parts of the economy which buy and sell the goods produced by the primary and secondary sectors. Tertiary activities also include banking, insurance, entertainment and organizing. The head office for a large chain of shops may not see many customers, but it is still part of the tertiary sector.

The two questions which need to be asked in this section are, firstly, where do tertiary activities go on, and secondly, why are they located in those places?

In answer to the first question, most people would answer that most tertiary activities take place in town centres. Banks, shops, libraries, estate agents, building societies, solicitors, dentists and public houses gain customers if they are located where people congregate. This is also the reason why shops tend to be close to one another rather than distributed throughout the town. We will now look at the location of tertiary activities in a small town (Epsom in Surrey) and a new way of dealing with large scale tertiary activity in Hamburg, West Germany.

Figure 6.48 Epsom town centre

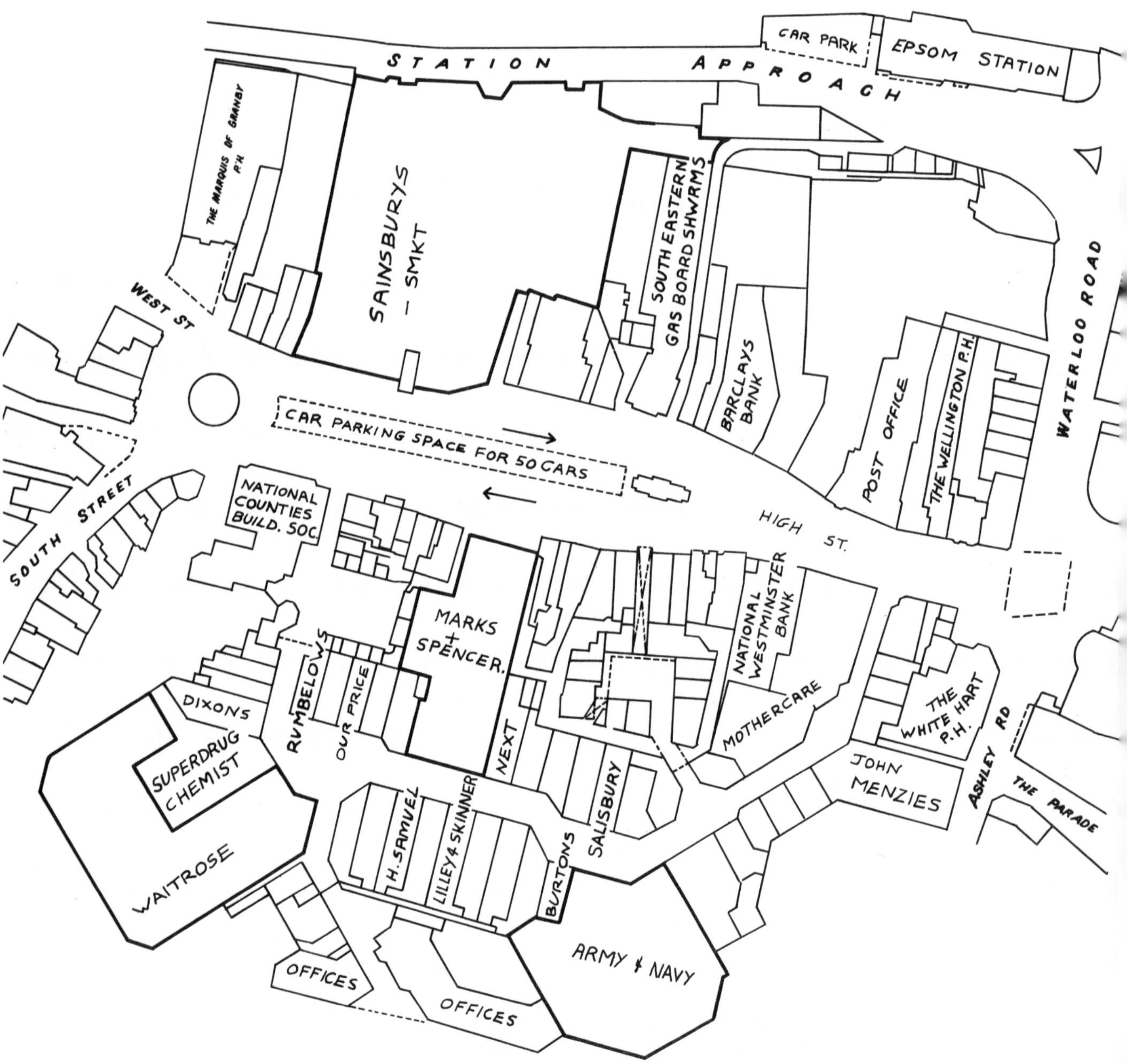

Case Study

A new shopping centre for Epsom

Figure 6.48 shows part of the centre of Epsom and the use of some of its buildings. Originally, Epsom was a market town and it still has a street market on Saturdays. In the 18th century Epsom became a spa town. Epsom salts are still famous. There is a memorial to them by the Clock Tower in the High Street. In the 20th century Epsom has become a **dormitory town**, that is, a town housing people, most of whom work in London, although it still remains an important shopping centre for its local area.

A new shopping centre was planned and built for Epsom. It is called the Ashley Centre. It is a mixed development of supermarkets, larger stores like Marks and Spencer and Army and Navy, a number of smaller shops, offices, a car park, some meeting halls and a theatre. Although the architects were asked to change some details to improve the look of the scheme, the plan was approved by the Epsom and Ewell Borough Planning Committee in 1980 and the buildings were finished in 1983. Figure 6.49 shows a plan of the new development and photographs of the new centre. There is a multi-storey car park within the centre.

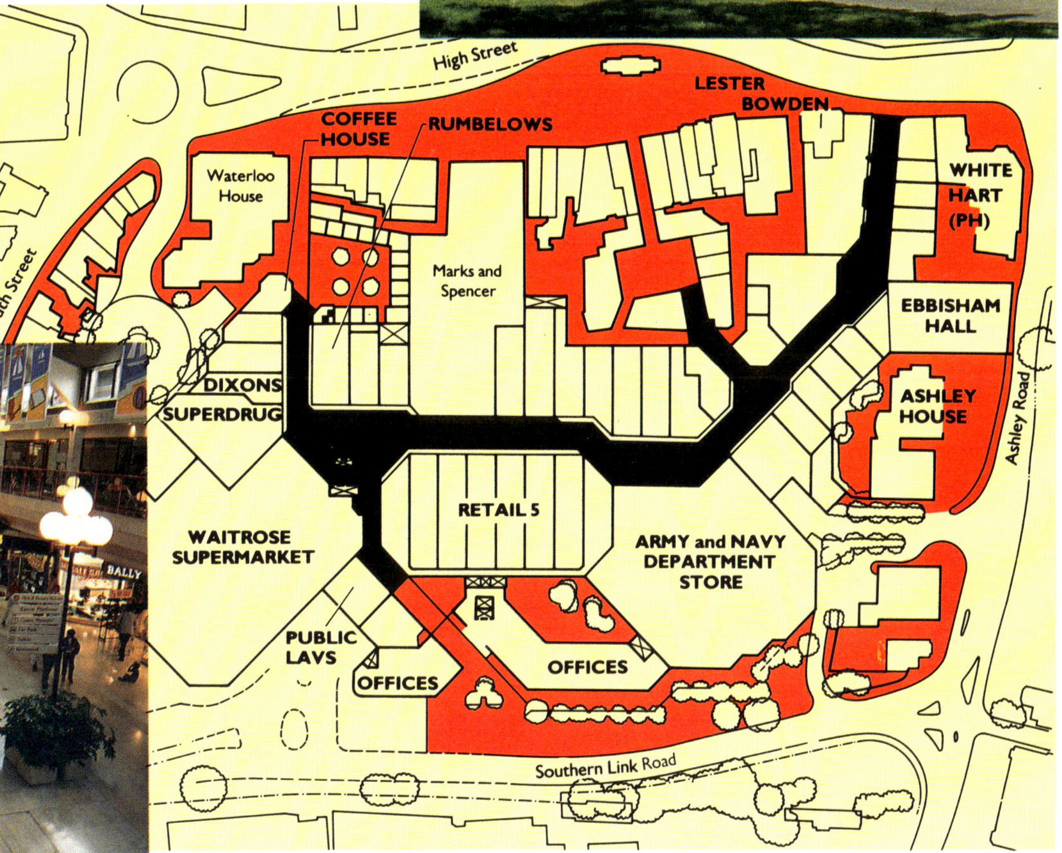

Figure 6.49 Ashley Shopping Centre

Activities

▲ ■ ● **42** Study Figure 6.48 which is a plan of part of Epsom town centre. What indications are there that this is the shopping centre for Epsom?

▲ ■ ● **43** Examine the plan of Epsom shopping centre. (Figure 6.49)

- **a** Write two or three paragraphs to describe the new style of town centre for Epsom.
- **b** What advantages are there to this type of shopping centre?

▲ ■ **44** Study Figure 6.48.

- **a** Where do you think the market is held on Saturdays? Why is it held in that area?
- **b** How could Epsom town centre be made into a pedestrian precinct?

▲ ■ ● **45** What do you think are likely to be the difficulties faced by shoppers coming to the Ashley Centre from outlying areas?

Case Study

Offices in Hamburg

Although small office blocks can be included in new developments in small towns, cities have had great problems in providing enough space in their city centres.

In the past, most European cities have made the extra space for offices in two ways. Firstly, they have allowed high rise office blocks to be built and secondly, they have allowed their central areas to spread outwards into the suburbs. This growth in offices has provided many new jobs, but it has also caused a less pleasant environment. These problems will be described in more detail in the next chapter. Here we will describe how Hamburg has solved the problem of where to put some of its growing office blocks.

Although many shops and offices need to be right in the centre of the city, other offices need to be near the city but not necessarily in the centre.

To solve this problem, the Hamburg Council decided to build an office park. They chose 95 ha of land, 6 km from the city centre, which had been allotments and temporary housing. They called the new office park City Nord. Figure 6.50 shows the location of City Nord.

The idea behind the park is to create a 'town in the country'. A third of the land was set aside for landscaped open space. A third of each plot sold to businesses must be made 'green'. The open spaces and the view across the Stadtpark makes the office park seem very spacious. The layout of City Nord is shown in Figure 6.51.

One of the problems in the centre of Hamburg had been that the office buildings were spoiling the views of the city. In the office park, firms have to hold architectural design competitions before they can start building. This has meant that the standard of architecture and comfort for the workers is very high.

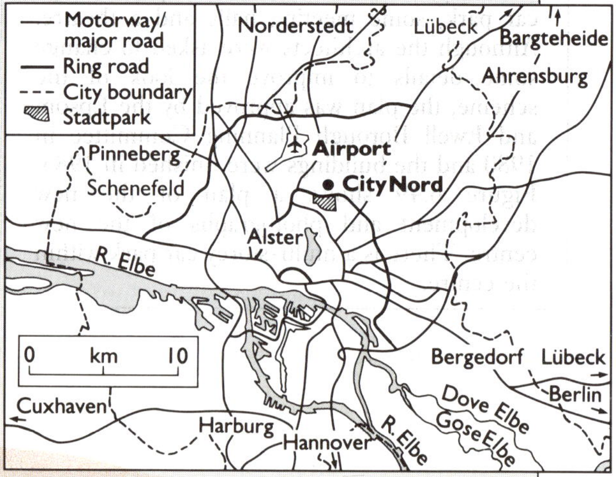

Figure 6.50 The location of City Nord, Hamburg

The everyday needs of the workers are met by a central shopping precinct with banks, restaurants and a post office. The park is well served by underground railways, suburban railways, buses and roads. The office park is close to Hamburg's airport. Inside the park there are footpaths and bridges to separate pedestrians from motor traffic.

The office park has made it possible for firms to have their headquarters all in one place instead of scattered across the city. For example, Esso and BP left 27 different buildings in Hamburg centre to go to City Nord. These buildings can now be used for activities which need to be in the city centre. Some offices have even been converted back to houses and flats. The advantages to large firms have attracted several to move their main headquarters here.

This section is about the tertiary sector of industry. Another name for the tertiary sector is the **service sector**. A service can only be performed if the person or company providing the service can be contacted easily by the person or company who requires the service. In other words, service industries must be accessible.

In the case of the shopping centre, it is important that customers can get to the shops easily. This is why shopping centres are usually in the centre of town, or sometimes outside towns but on main roads and with lots of parking space for cars.

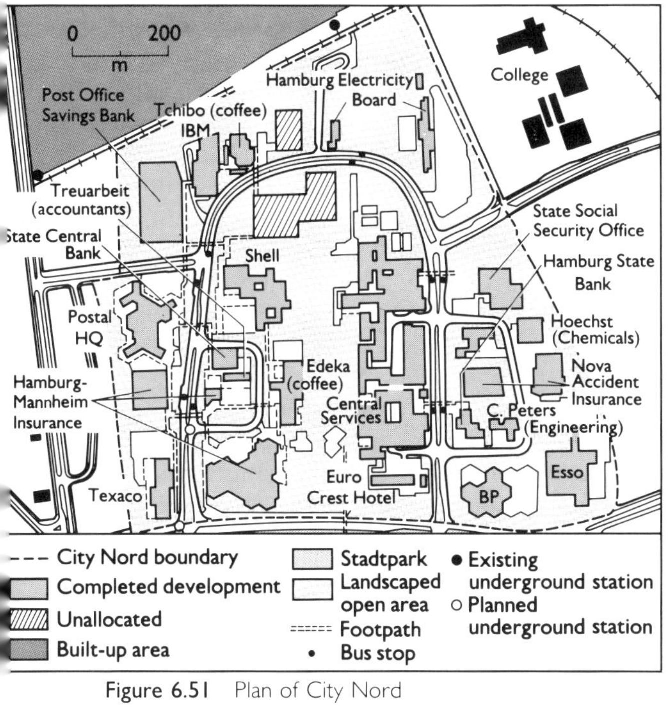

Figure 6.51 Plan of City Nord

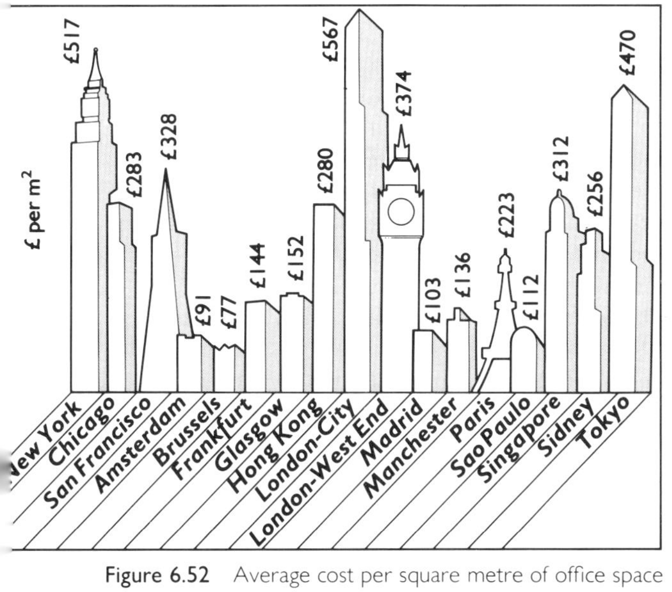

Figure 6.52 Average cost per square metre of office space in different world cities

In the case of the office park, accessibility is also important. Offices, however, can provide their services to customers or clients who contact them in a number of ways. It may be that the office needs good communications by road or rail. Large companies with international connections may need good air accessibility. This means being near an international airport. Increasingly, companies need accessibility by telecommunications. These include telephones, telex and, increasingly, computers linked together. The telecommunications link is now so important that it is having an effect on the geographical location of offices. Many firms now decide where to put their offices by the quality of the telecommunications links available.

A fairly new office building in a 'good' area of a city may be left empty. An older building in an 'unfashionable' part of the city but which is served by good telecommunications links is in great demand. Figure 6.52 shows the average price for good office space in various world cities. Prices in the City of London are high because so many firms want to have offices there. One of the reasons for this is the British Telecom Tower which uses microwave dishes to give rapid telecommunication. (You will find more about the importance of communications in Chapter 8.)

Activities

▲ ■ **46** Study Figure 6.50 which shows the location of City Nord.

a Describe the location of the new office park in relation to

i) Hamburg and

ii) The rest of Germany and Europe.

b List the advantges of this location for the head offices of large companies.

▲ ■ ● **47** Study Figure 6.51 which shows the layout of City Nord.

a Which firms listed as having offices in the office park seem to indicate that Hamburg is a port handling international trade? State what the connection is in each case.

b Explain the differences in the kinds of locations most suitable for

i) Shops and other tertiary activities which need direct contact with the public and

ii) Offices which do not need direct contact with the public.

c Describe the advantages of office parks for the head office of a firm.

7
Settling down

Where do you live? If you live in the UK, more than three-quarters of you will answer 'in a town'. The rest will say 'in the country'. People who live in towns are called the **urban population**. Those who live in the country are called the **rural population**.

You may have answered the question with the name of the place in which you live. If you were then asked to describe the place, you would probably use one of these descriptions.

1) a city
2) a hamlet
3) a large town
4) a small village
5) a small town
6) a large village
7) a house on its own

Most people in the world live together in some kind of group like the first 6 of these. Only a few people live on their own. These 6 groups are different types of **settlement**. Some types of settlement may be grouped together and described as **rural settlements**. Other types are definitely **urban**.

Many of us find it difficult to decide whether some places are large villages or small towns. A large village would probably be described as rural. A small town would be described as urban.

Settlements can be divided up according to their size. One geographer has suggested that the population figures in Figure 7.1 might help. This system of classifying settlement by size works reasonably well in the UK. Most people would agree that a settlement with less than 2000 people is probably a village. A settlement with more than this is probably a small town.

It is not so easy to use the system in other countries. In Denmark, for example, a town officially must have at least 250 people. In France, the official figure for a town is 2000. In the USA the official figure is 2500. In Japan it is 30 000.

There are other ways by which we could separate towns from villages. We could use the area of land covered by the settlements. Towns are usually larger than villages.

We could use the size of the buildings. Villages do not usually have buildings of more than three storeys.

We could use the occupations of the people. We might assume that agriculture is the main occupation in a village. Industry and commerce are the main occupations in a town.

Finally, we could examine the different services such as shops, banks and hospitals or clinics found in the settlements. All villages will have at least one shop. Only a large village will have a bank. A small town will probably have branches of several banks and may have a cinema.

Using some of these ways we could probably agree on some of the main differences between a village and a town. Cities are more difficult to define. In earlier times in the UK, a city was a settlement containing a cathedral. This meant that it was the administrative centre of a church diocese. Some cities like Winchester and St. David's were quite small settlements. Now, in the UK, cities are created by a Charter from the Queen. On a worldwide basis, cities are usually very large towns with a wide range of services and industries.

Where towns have grown so much that several separate towns have merged together, the whole settlement is called a **conurbation**.

The population density map of Japan (Figure 1.20) shows that Osaka and Kobe have grown together to make one conurbation. The Osaka–Kobe conurbation has a population of about 16 million. In West Germany the cities which grew on the coalfield north of the river Ruhr have become the Ruhr conurbation (see Chapter 6). The problems caused by the growth of the cities of Holland into the Randstad conurbation will be described later in this chapter.

In the USA, some conurbations have grown so rapidly that they themselves have started to merge. An area where conurbations have merged is called a **megalopolis**. The first true example of a megalopolis has developed along the east coast from Boston to Washington. The megalopolis also includes New York, Philadelphia, Baltimore and many smaller cities. This vast urban sprawl, 650 km long, has been given the unofficial names Bosnywash or Boswash. Its total population is over 40 million. Look again at Figure 1.17 but remember the warnings in Chapter 1 about the differences in population density which can be hidden by world maps.

Activities

▲ 1 a Make a copy of Figure 7.1.
■ b Write the name of the place where you live beside the correct description. Make it stand out either by writing it in a different colour or drawing a box around it.
c Write in the names of the settlements nearest to your home which correspond to each of the other sizes.

Population	Description of settlement
1 – 10	Isolated house
11 – 100	Hamlet
101 – 500	Small village
501 – 2000	Large village
2001 – 10000	Small town
10001 – 100000	Large town
100001 and more	City

Figure 7.1 Classification of settlements

▲ 2 Figure 7.2 gives a list of services which most
■ people expect to find available in the western world.
a Make a copy of the table.
i) For each type of settlement, place a tick in the correct column beside each service you would expect to find.
ii) Include any other services you feel are needed at the end of the list.
iii) Add up the number of services you have ticked for each type of settlement.
b Write a paragraph to explain the differences between the different types of settlement.

	Isolated house	Hamlet	Small village	Large village	Small town	Large town	City
mains water							
mains power (gas or electricity)							
mains drainage							
weekly rubbish collection							
public house							
church							
chapel							
cathedral							
synagogue							
mosque							
post office							
general store							
primary school							
secondary school							
village school							
butcher							
grocer							
baker							
hardware store							
supermarket							
department store							
chain store (e.g. Marks & Spencer)							
polytechnic							
university							
bank							
solicitor							
building society branch office							

	Isolated house	Hamlet	Small village	Large village	Small town	Large town	City
cinema							
bus station							
railway station							
taxi							
hospital							
clinic							
theatre							
farm							
factory							
docks							
leisure facilities (playground, park)							
public conveniences							
garage							
newsagent							
tobacconist							
confectioner							
shoe shop							
clothes shop							
furniture shop							
jewellers							
Total number of services							

Figure 7.2 Services in settlements

Factor	Details and examples
Sites	
WATER SUPPLY – essential for drinking and sometimes for industry, e.g. flour milling.	Settlements found near rivers and streams, wells, springs or oases. Sometimes aqueducts may be needed.
DRY SITE – protection from flooding.	On well-drained land, e.g. limestone or sandstone areas. On 'dry points' above flood plains, e.g. the terraces of the Rhine and Elbe, or the slightly raised areas of the Tigris–Euphrates valley. On 'terpen', or mounds above the polders in the Netherlands. On people-made banks in Bengal, where land has been drained.
GOOD AGRICULTURAL LAND – for grazing and crop production.	In Europe, the rich Paris Basin and parts of the North German Plain have more settlements per square kilometre than the Central Massif or the Black Forest. Alluvial plains of major rivers are very important.
DEFENCE – especially important in early times.	Use of hills, rocky outcrops, cliffs, rivers and coasts as natural aids to defence, e.g. the hill top settlements of parts of central Spain and the Hopi Indian villages on the tops of mesas in New Mexico. (A mesa is a flat-topped hill.)
ASPECT AND SHELTER	Settlements avoid exposed sites largely in shadow. In mountainous areas in the northern hemisphere, villages are found on the northern slopes of valleys, since these face the sun in the south.
Situation	
ACCESS – ease of communication with other villages.	Common sites are at entrances to mountain passes; where rivers meet; where rivers are easy to ford or bridge; where roads are easily constructed, e.g. on a low-lying ridge.
SERVICES – special sites for particular purposes.	Some villages were built next to castles, cathedrals or monasteries. The villages received protection and helped to supply food. In France, Amiens and Chartres are examples.
BUILDING MATERIALS	Availability of building materials, wood, reeds, stone or clay, may influence the sites of villages.

Figure 7.3 Major factors influencing the sites and situations of settlements

Settling in: choosing a village site

Even if you have never been camping, you can imagine the sorts of things you need to look for when you are deciding where to pitch your tent. Ideally, you need a fairly flat site with enough slope to drain away the rain. You would also probably try to find a place sheltered from the wind, close to the toilets, near drinking water and perhaps with a good view. You would choose your site carefully.

Early settlers took the same care when they chose the places for their settlements. Many settlements were founded in western Europe before AD 1000. People slowly spread westwards across the northern lowlands of Europe. As groups moved further west, just like the early settlers of the American West, they looked for suitable places to live.

These settlers had to think about two things. Firstly, they had to look for a suitable **site** on which to build. The site is the actual land on which a settlement is built. The early settlers also had to think about their **situation**. This

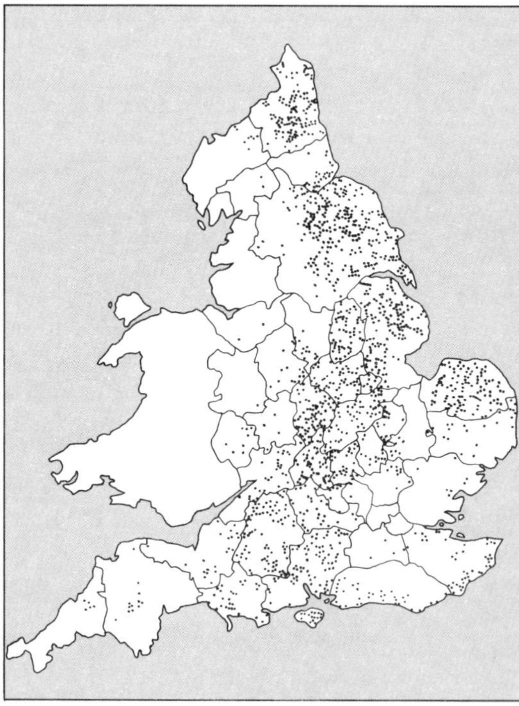

Figure 7.4 Distribution of deserted medieval villages in England

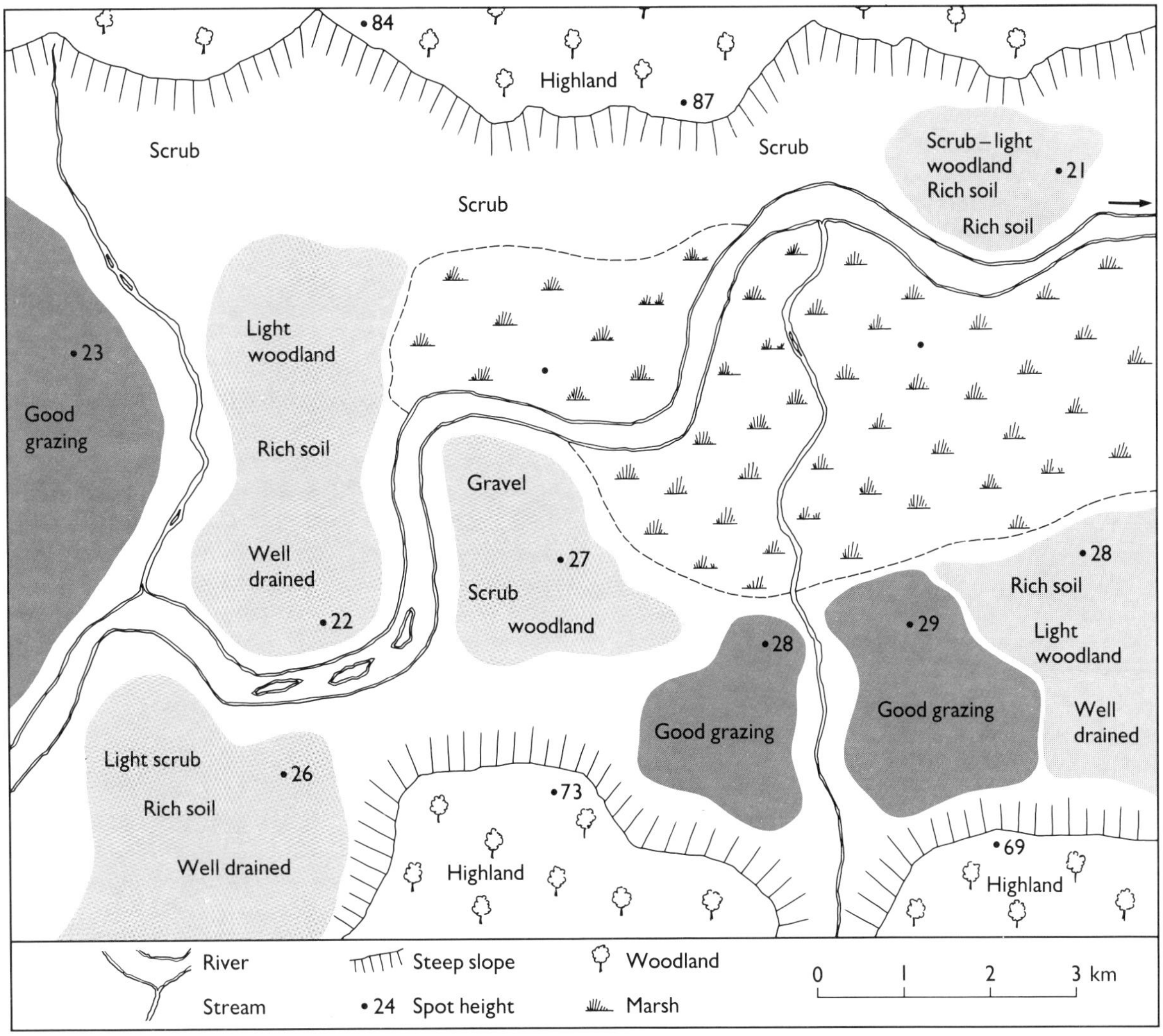

Figure 7.5 Choosing a place to build a village; choosing the site

means where the settlement is, compared to the resources of the area around it.

All those things which had to be taken into account are called the **location factors**.

Figure 7.3 gives you a summary of some important locational factors which influenced the choice of sites and situations for permanent settlements. Usually a combination of factors helped settlers to decide on a particular site. Sometimes one particular factor was most important. If that particular factor ceased to be important, the site might have been abandoned. Figure 7.4 shows some of the sites of medieval villages which were deserted. Some of these villages died because the people who lived in them died from the Black Death. Some villages died because people moved away from them to live in towns engaged in industry and trade. Many died because their farmland was given over to sheep grazing by the land owners so that there was no longer any work for the villagers.

Many settlements have died in the past but many have survived. In the Nile Valley, many

Activity

▲■● 3 Figure 7.5 is a map of an area in which some settlers would like to build a village.

a Decide where you think the best place would be to build a village.

b Write some notes to explain your reasons for choosing your site.

c Discuss your decision with others in your class. They may not agree with your choice or your reasons for making your choice.

d After your discussion, add to your list any new factors which you have learned from your class colleagues.

c Write a description of the best site for a village in the area shown on the map. Carefully explain all the reasons why your chosen site is the best to build a village.

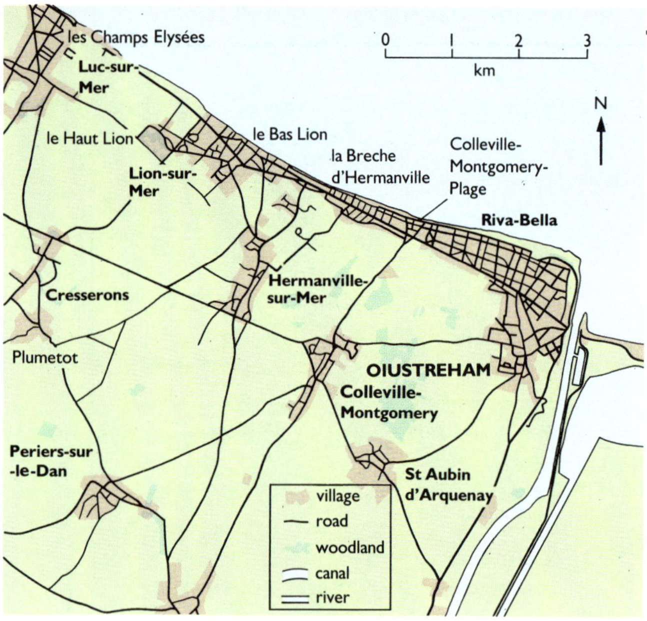

Figure 7.6 Nucleated villages north of Caen

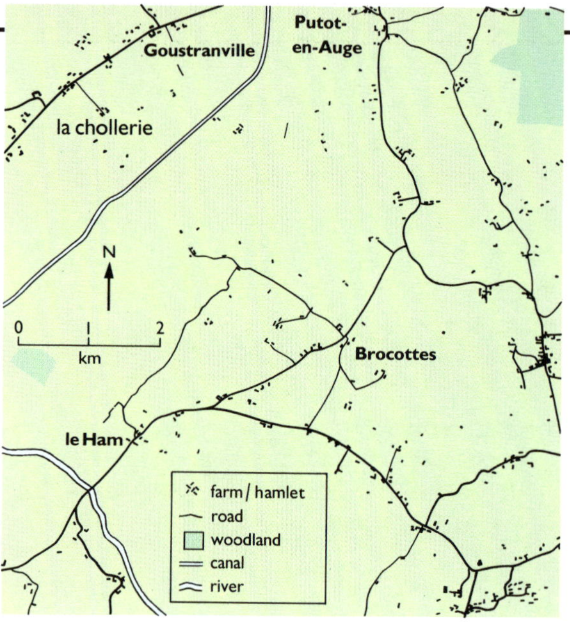

Figure 7.7 Dispersed farms and hamlets east of Caen

of the present settlements are on sites first built on over 6000 years ago.

We have looked at the reasons why particular places were chosen for settlements in early times. However, some settlements were isolated houses and hamlets, while others were villages where people gathered together to live.

These two patterns of settlement are given special names. Where the houses and farms are spread out over a large area, the pattern is called **dispersed settlement**. Where the houses and farms are clustered together, the pattern is called **nucleated settlement**. Figures 7.6 and 7.7 show examples of nucleated villages and dispersed settlement near Caen in Northern France.

Activity

▲4 Study Figures 7.6 and 7.7.

■ a Name the nucleated villages in Figure 7.6.

b Estimate the average number of people living in these villages. First you will have to suggest an average number for each dwelling, then count the dwellings in one village. Do this for several villages to obtain your average.

c What is the average distance between the villages in Figure 7.6? Are they regularly spaced?

d Name the dispersed farms in Figure 7.7.

e Name 1 village and 3 hamlets in Figure 7.7.

f Comparing the numbers of dispersed farms, villages and hamlets in Figure 7.7, would you agree that it is an area of dispersed settlement?

Patterns of settlement

The pattern of settlement in an area was usually decided by two factors. Firstly, the physical features of the land (the relief, drainage, soil and rock type) can influence the settlement pattern. Secondly, the way the people live and work on the land, and how the land is owned, can have an influence.

Nucleated settlements, which we usually call **villages**, grew up for a variety of reasons. Most village sites can be explained by one or more of the following reasons.

1 Where the land was owned by all the villagers and was worked in strips, the obvious place for the people to live was in a village in the middle with the 'open fields' around it.
2 Where the people needed a good site for defence they would live together on the top of a hill or on the inside of a meander, or even together in the centre of flat land.
3 Where there was a shortage of water, a village may have grown up around a natural spring.
4 Where the land was very swampy, villages may have grown up on the 'dry point sites'.
5 In areas where there was a shortage of building materials, villages may have grown up near a supply of wood or stone or clay for making bricks.
6 Where the people wanted to use land on either side of a natural barrier, such as a river or a line of hills, they would probably gather together near an easy way through the barrier, such as a ford across the river or a gap in the hills.

7 Where new villages were planned or built by governments or landowners, they were usually built in a nucleated form.

The reasons why an area has dispersed settlement usually have more to do with the history of the people and the type of farming they practise than the land itself. The following reasons may explain the pattern of most areas of dispersed settlement.

1 When open fields were enclosed, each farmer fenced in his own land instead of having a share of two or three 'open fields' owned by the whole village. This made it logical for each new farmer to build his own farmstead in the middle of his land.
2 Where soils were very fertile and suited to a specialized type of farming, farmers often lived in the middle of their land.
3 In areas where the main type of farming was looking after livestock, the farmers often lived near their animals.
4 People often lived in dispersed settlements in areas with very low densities of population. This may have been in upland areas, or along coasts where people divided their time between farming and fishing.
5 Where very large estates were broken up into smaller farms, the farmhouses were often built on the farms.
6 Dispersed farms are often found where woodland has gradually been cleared or heathland has been removed for farming.
7 Farms may be dispersed where marshland has been drained.

Case Study

Villages in Germany

To understand the village shapes of northern Europe, we must first know a little about the early history of this area. Up to about AD 1000 there were two main groups of tribes in northern Europe. To the west of the rivers Elbe and Saale there were tribes who spoke languages which have become modern German. To the east of these two rivers, there were tribes who spoke Slav languages.

The German tribes in the west were the first to set up permanent settlements. Where the soils had been made from materials blown by the wind (**loess** soils) the land was very fertile. This good land was farmed by the open field system where each farmer had strips in each of the large fields owned by the village. The houses and farm buildings were clustered together in the centre of the farm land, to form nucleated villages.

In the north and west of what is now West Germany, the land was very wet and well-suited to cattle farming. The settlements in this area grew as small hamlets and isolated farms.

The Slav tribes who lived east of the river Elbe and the river Saale lived mainly from cattle herding, hunting and fishing. They usually lived in temporary huts and moved on to fresh land from time to time when their cattle needed new grazing land.

After about AD 1200 the Germans started to move east of the river Elbe, into the lands of the Slav tribes. This led to trouble between the Slavs and the Germans. Raiding parties from each side attacked the other. Both Germans and Slavs found that they needed villages which could be defended against attack. They each planned their villages by putting their farmsteads in a roughly circular pattern around an open space. They left only two or three entrances between the buildings which could easily be defended. When there was an attack from the other side, the villagers and their animals would gather in the centre of the village and fight off the raiders.

Eventually the German tribes beat the Slav tribes and took over the organization of what is now East Germany and Poland. The Germans gave the job of organizing the farming in their new colonies to overseers called **lokators**. These lokators planned the villages carefully. In some they built the farms face to face across a wide green. These are called **green villages**. They built other villages with the farm on either side of a road. These are called **street villages**. In forests and marshy areas the farm buildings were arranged like beads on a string either along a road or a drainage ditch. Figure 7.8 (overleaf) shows where these village types are found today. Figure 7.9 shows the soil types of northern Europe.

The largest farm in any village was always the one owned by the lokator. Over the centuries, the families of these lokators became richer and bought more farmland until they became the owners of large estates. Some of these estates continued until 1918. In 1918 many of them were confiscated, divided into smaller farms and given to the tenants. This led to some dispersed settlements developing again. However, by 1960 all the farms of East Germany had been re-organized into the communist system of collective and state farms.

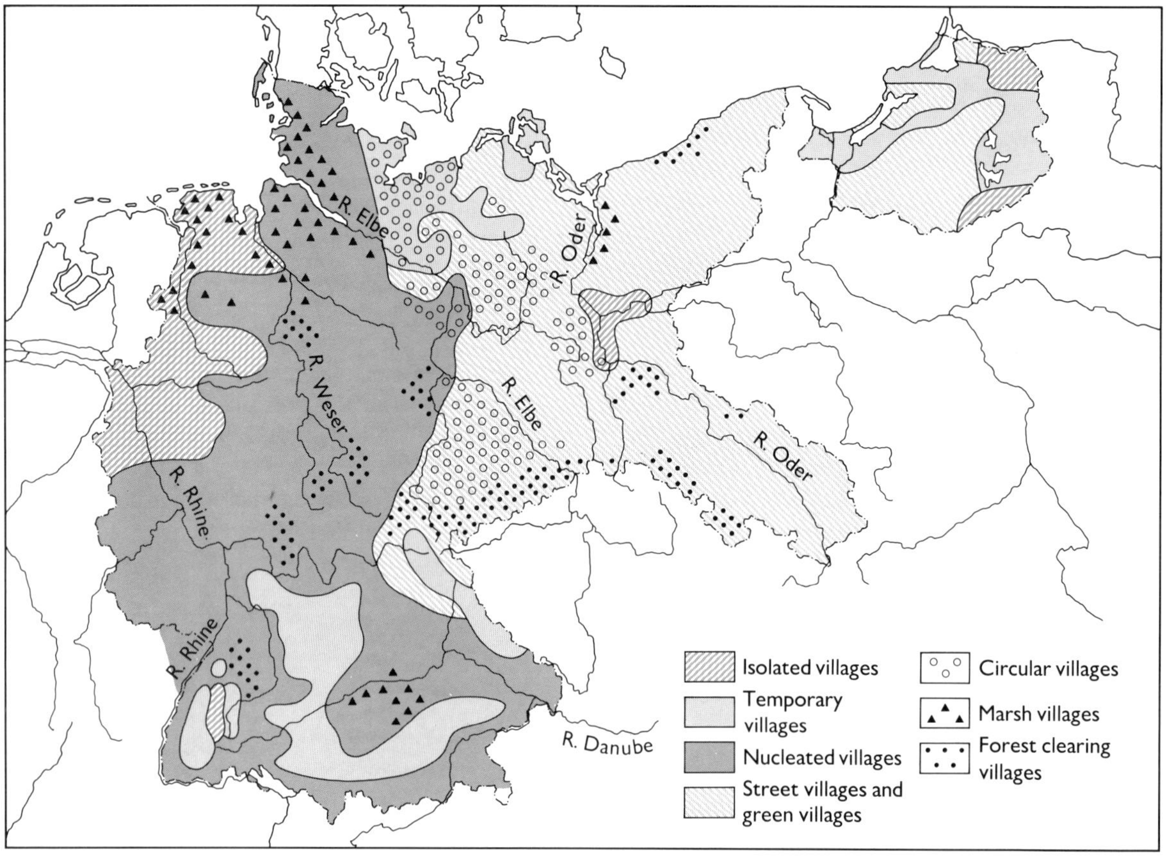

Figure 7.8 Types of village in Northern Europe

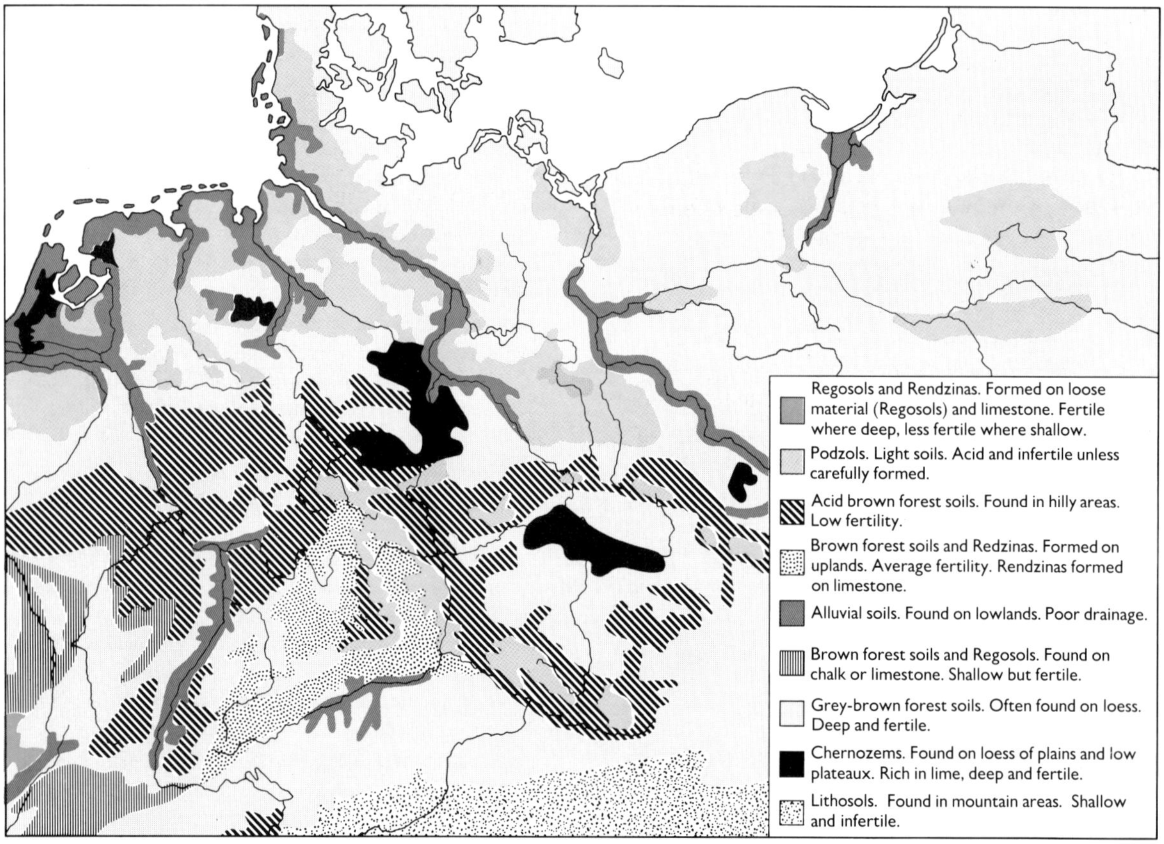

Figure 7.9 Soil map of Northern Europe

This German example shows how the present pattern of settlements is the result of events which took place over a thousand years ago. Some of these villages, especially the ones with large churches or markets, grew to be more important than others. Some villages grew to be the towns of today.

This does not mean that all villages are old. In East Germany, new villages were built in the 19th century. Some were built for workers in the coal-mining industry. Others were built for farmers working on new land which was reclaimed from the broad and damp river valley floors of the northern lowlands.

Most countries of the world have a mixture of traditional villages and planned villages.

In England, factory owners built villages such as Port Sunlight near Liverpool and Bournville near Birmingham for their workers to live in. In Durham and Northumberland many villages of miners' cottages grew up around pit-heads. Some were added on to old farming villages.

In other countries villages have been built by governments to encourage some types of co-operative farming.

In China, the village commune committees decide everything for their people from where they should work to when they should have the one child they are allowed.

Activities

▲5 ■ Look at the case study on villages in Germany, together with Figures 7.8 and 7.9.

a List the types of village described.

b For each type of village you have listed, draw a sketch map to show the layout of the village and the kinds of landscape which surrounded it. Label your sketch to explain why each village was built in this way.

▲6 ■ Study the map of the location of the different types of village (Figure 7.8) and the map of the soil types of northern Europe (Figure 7.9).

a Make a list of all the different factors which have affected the type of village layout found in northern Europe.

b Draw up a table. Put the different types of village down the side of the table and your list of factors across the top. For each type of village, mark your table to show whether each factor was 'very important', 'of some importance' or 'not important'.

c Use your table to help you to write a brief account to explain the distribution of village types in northern Europe.

Growth of towns

Figure 7.10 shows some early centres of town development. In southern Europe, the Greeks and the Romans founded the first cities. Our word **civilization** comes from the Latin word for a city – *civis*. The Greek writer, Plato, thought that it was important for everyone to live in a city and play a full part in city politics. He wrote that a man who does not play a part in the life of a city-state is as much use as a finger which has been cut off from a hand!

Even in those days, some people had mixed feelings about city life. The Roman poet, Horace, complained about the noise, the traffic and the crowds and called it 'that bit of hell known as big city life'.

The Greek and Roman towns were places where people could meet to exchange goods. The Greek city-states had trading links all along the Mediterranean coast in about 800 BC. Greeks set up new towns in the places where they wanted to trade. One of these new towns in southern France grew to become the modern city of Marseille. By 500 BC there were towns set up for trading from the west coast of Spain to the Ganges valley in India.

The Roman Empire was even larger than the Greek Empire. By AD 200 the Romans had built towns and roads right across Europe and into Britain. Many large present-day towns, like

Area	Location	Civilization
Middle East	Nile Valley	Egyptians (3000 BC)
Fertile Crescent	Tigris and Euphrates Valleys	Sumerians (2700 BC)
East Asia	Indus Valley Hwang Valley Mekong Valley	Indus (2500 BC) Shang (1300 BC) Khmer (AD 1100)
South Europe	The islands in the Aegean Sea Greece	Greeks (2000 BC)
	The Italian Peninsula	Romans (400 BC)
America	Yucatan Peninsula Central Mexico Peru	Mayan (AD 500) Aztecs (AD 1400) Incas (AD 1500)
West Africa	Niger Valley	Yoruba (AD 1300)

Figure 7.10 Early centres of urban development

York, London, Paris and Lyon were originally Roman towns.

In AD 500 the Roman legions left western Europe. This began the period known as the Dark Ages. There was much less trade than before and only a few English towns such as York, Canterbury and London carried on trading. Many towns became just like villages again, with most people linked to farming.

Trade and industry started to grow again after about AD 1000 and towns began to expand. By AD 1100 Norwich had about 4000 or 5000 inhabitants, York had over 8000 inhabitants and London probably had over 12 000 inhabitants. At this time about a tenth of England's population lived permanently in towns.

In the 16th and 17th centuries trade between the countries of Europe and between Europe and Asia and America grew quickly. Because of this, towns in Europe which were trading ports grew as well. By 1700, Amsterdam, Antwerp, Lisbon, Rome and Seville had populations of over 100 000. Paris had 180 000 and London had 250 000. Spain, Portugal, France and England set up colonies in North and South America. These colonies traded with their home countries and this led to the growth of towns in the Americas.

Most of the towns mentioned so far grew because they were important for trade. However, the greatest growth in the size and number of towns was caused by the Industrial Revolution (see Chapter 6).

The Industrial Revolution is the name given to the period of time, beginning in about 1750, when new inventions in industry and transport led to the building of many new factories. Many of these factories were built on the coalfields because coal was the main source of power for the steam engines which turned the machines. Vast quantities of coal were also needed to smelt iron.

Many of the new inventions were British and so the Industrial Revolution began first in Britain. Industry and towns also grew in other parts of western Europe and North America, but not until later in the 19th century.

Towns grew rapidly to house the workers in the newly opened mines and factories. Some of the towns grew from old agricultural villages. Other towns grew up around newly opened mines.

The growth of towns was helped by other new developments. Improvements in agriculture made it possible for farmers to provide food for all the town dwellers. Canals, railways and improved roads were built. This made it easy for the food to be transported to the towns and for the products of the mines and factories to be distributed around the country. As towns grew bigger, the roads and railways made the growth of **suburbs** possible. People could live on the outskirts of the town and travel to work near the centre each day by train.

The houses built for the new townspeople were often very poor. A letter to *The Times* newspaper which described the conditions in one area of London was quoted in Chapter 1 (Figure 1.5). However, not all the terraced houses built for factory workers led to such poor living conditions. Many people found better conditions in the towns than they were used to in the countryside.

By 1860, half the people of England and Wales were living in towns. By 1900, this had risen to three-quarters.

In Scandinavia, southern Europe and in much of Africa, Asia and South America, the main

growth of industry and towns occurred this century.

The growth of towns was continued in many countries of the world. This has resulted in three important trends.

1 The number of towns and cities in the world is increasing.
2 There is an increasing number of very large towns and cities.
3 The proportion of the world's population who live in towns and cities, rather than in the countryside, is increasing.

These trends are shown in the tables and maps. Figure 7.11 shows how rapidly the proportion of the world's population living in towns with more than 20000 people increased between 1900 and 1970 . Figure 7.12 shows how the number of cities with over a million people has increased since 1800. Figure 7.13 shows the location of all the cities in the world with over 2 million people.

Year	%
1900	9.2
1950	20.9
1970	30.0

Figure 7.11 Proportion of World's population living in towns with more than 20 000 people

Year	No. of 'million' cities	
1800	0	(London 959 310)
1850	2	(London, Paris)
1900	11	(London, Paris, Berlin, Vienna, Moscow, St. Petersburg, New York, Chicago, Philadelphia, Tokyo, Calcutta)
1920	20	
1940	51	
1960	80	
1970	162	containing a total of 416 million people
1985	273	containing a total of 805 million people

Figure 7.12 Growth of 'million' cities

Figure 7.13 Major world cities

At the beginning of this chapter we described how some cities have grown together to form conurbations and how in the USA, conurbations have grown together to form megalopolises. Some geographers have said that if the world's population and cities continue to grow, there may be a huge world-city stretching around our planet by the end of the next century. They have called this possible world-city **ecumenopolis**.

Activities

▲ ■ **7** Study Figures 7.11, 7.12 and 7.13.

a The description of the growth of towns suggests that there are three main trends in town growth in the world. Decide whether the evidence given actually supports these suggestions.

b Write a paragraph to support each of the trends for which you can find adequate evidence in Figures 7.11, 7.12 and 7.13. Describe the evidence you can find.

c Have any of the suggestions been made without providing you with adequate evidence? If so, explain what kind of evidence is missing and suggest ways in which you could test the truth of the statement.

▲ ■ ● **8** Some geographers have suggested that the world's cities and conurbations may grow together to form megalopolises and eventually an 'ecumenopolis'.

a Study Figure 7.13 and decide which cities could grow to form a band around the world to form an ecumenopolis. Draw this band lightly in pencil on an outline map of the world.

b Use an atlas to find any physical features (such as mountain ranges or deserts) which might create breaks in an ecumenopolis. (The oceans will obviously create breaks.)

c Would your ecumenopolis cross any countries which may result in breaks for political reasons?

d Change your drawing to take these physical and political factors into account.

e Do you think that a world-city is likely ever to develop?

Patterns inside towns and cities

In the last section we described how many towns in the western world originally grew up as trading centres. Later, many of them grew further with the development of factory based industries. Although some towns or cities are famous for one particular industry, most larger cities have a wide range of occupations. For example, Oxford is famous for its University, but it also has a huge Austin Rover motor vehicle works. There are, however, four things which most towns have in common.

1 They provide housing for their people.
2 They provide services such as shops and offices for the people who live in them as well as for people who live in the area around them.
3 They act as route centres.
4 They usually have a range of different industries.

These different features of towns are studied in geography because they form patterns on the Earth's surface. Geographers have studied the patterns made by towns and cities in three main ways.

1 Some geographers have studied the patterns made inside towns by the ages of the buildings and by the use of the land.
2 There are only a few really large cities, but many more towns and even more villages. Some geographers have tried to find whether there is a relationship between the size of a town or village and the number of settlements of each size.
3 Some geographers have tried to find a pattern in the way cities, towns and villages are spread across the landscape.

Think of the town that you know best. Is it changing? Many towns have areas in the centre which are being demolished to make way for new buildings or a new road. Many towns have new houses being built on the outskirts. Some towns have estates of factories being built.

As a city grows and changes, so it develops certain patterns. Some parts concentrate on offices and shops. Some parts are mainly houses. Factories are often found together. Houses, shops and offices, and factories are three of the many different ways in which the land in a town or city is used. Other land uses include parks, schools, hospitals, roads and car parks. The pattern made by these things is called the **land use pattern**.

Housing, shopping and manufacturing can

also be described as three of the **functions** (or purposes) served by the town or city. Since buildings which supply these different functions are often found clustered together, the clusters are called the **functional areas** of a town or city.

Four researchers have tried to explain how the patterns of land use in a town have developed (Figure 7.14). Burgess studied a number of towns in the USA and thought that towns grew outwards as a series of rings around the town centre (Figure 7.14(a)). The centre of the town is called the **central business district** (**CBD**). It is occupied by businesses such as shops, banks, insurance companies and other offices. These businesses want space in the centre because it is the easiest place to get to from all directions. There is competition for space in the CBD and so tall buildings are often built. The tallest office building in London is the National Westminster Bank tower in the City of London.

There is often an area around the CBD where landowners expect to be bought out by companies who want to build more shops and offices. Some of the old buildings in this zone have already been demolished and their sites have been redeveloped. Other old buildings such as old factories and houses are left to decay because their owners expect to sell them for demolition. The houses may quickly become slums used by the poorest people in the city. In times of economic growth, this area may not have long to wait to be redeveloped. When the economy is stagnant, the area may not be required for redevelopment for a long time. It is then left to become an even more unpleasant place for people to live. Sometimes this gives a chance for government or local authorities to redevelop the area with housing schemes. An area waiting for redevelopment is sometimes called a **transition zone** or **twilight zone**.

Outside the transition zone is a zone of working-class homes. Some of the families here may have moved out from the transition zone. These people often work in the CBD and need to live close to their work because they could not afford to travel long distances each day.

Further out from the centre, there is a ring of middle-class homes with some high-class houses. On the edge of the city, where the city meets the countryside, there is often a zone of commuter housing. People here can afford long journeys into the city centre each day. They put up with the long journeys because they like to live near the countryside.

Sometimes there is a **green belt** between the commuter belt and the rest of the city. To prevent the city sprawling further and further, new buildings are not usually allowed in the 'green belt'.

The second model for land-use patterns in a town was put forward by Homer Hoyt. Hoyt suggested that towns did not simply grow in rings. He thought that new developments were more likely to grow outwards in wedges or sectors (Figure 7.14(b)).

Imagine that a group of factories is built where a main road, or canal, enters a town. The next factory to be opened will probably be built further out along the same road or canal. If more factories are built like this, the result will be a wedge or sector of factories pointing towards the town centre. In the same way, new high-class houses will probably be built on the same side of a town as the existing high-class

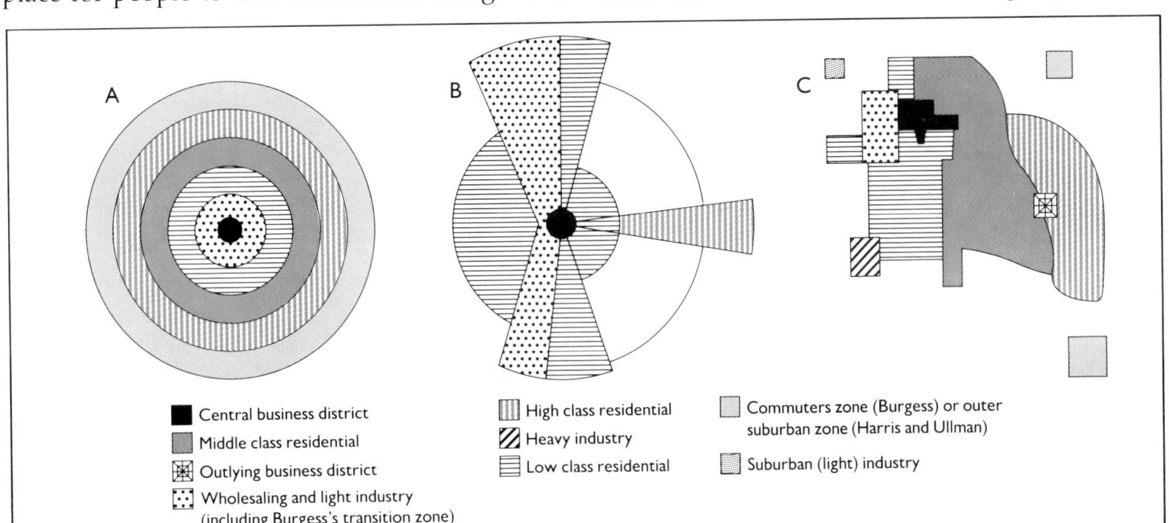

Figure 7.14 Urban models
a Concentric model (after Burgess) b Sector model (after Hoyt) c Multi-nuclear model (after Harris and Ulmann)

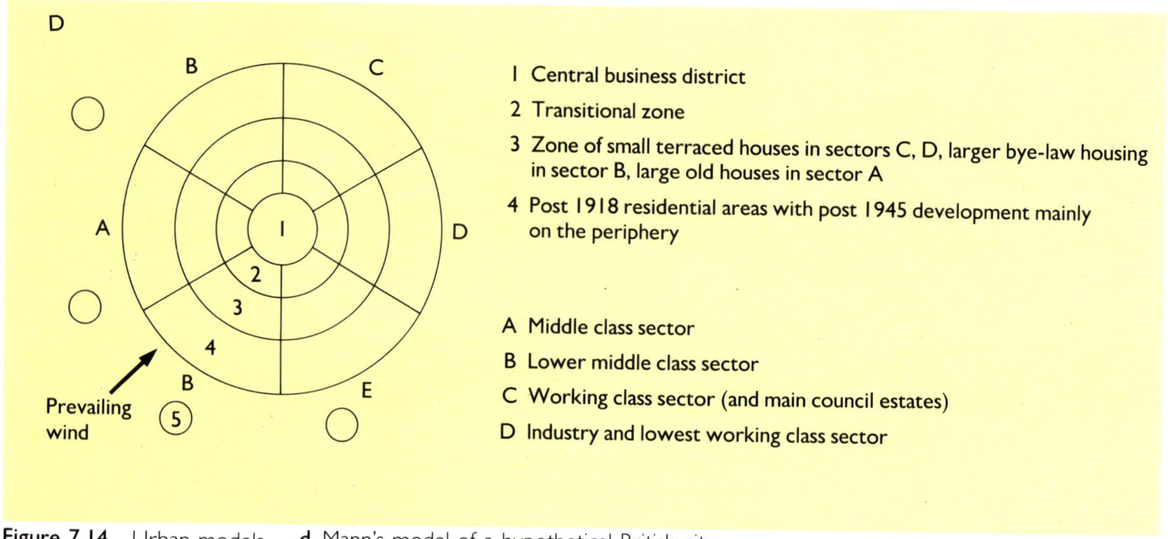

Figure 7.14 Urban models **d** Mann's model of a hypothetical British city

areas. This theory shows how important routeways can be for the growth of a town.

Harris and Ullman, also American, disagreed with the two ideas just described (Figure 7.14(c)). They said that towns do not just grow outwards from a centre. Instead, they suggested that any important place around the edges of a town can cause the growth of houses, shops and offices. People may choose to build new houses near the centre of an old village. In time, the village will become part of the town.

When railway stations were built on the edge of old towns, the towns often grew more quickly on that side than others. In time, the area around the station became part of the built-up area of the town.

On a larger scale, Heathrow Airport was built well away from London. Since it was built, new houses, factories, warehouses and hotels have been built around it. Today, Heathrow Airport is a part of the built-up area of London.

Because large cities have many important places which act as **nuclei** (centres) for growth, this model is called the **multiple-nuclei model**.

These three models were suggested by American geographers. A British geographer, Peter Mann, studied Sheffield, Nottingham and Huddersfield. From these cities, he suggested that towns grew in a mixture of concentric zones and sectors. Mann noticed that industry is usually found to the east of the CBD. Since the prevailing winds blew from the west, the smoke and fumes would be blown away from the town. This idea is supported by the fact that high-class houses are usually found in the west and south-west of the town. This means that they are up-wind of the smoke (Figure 7.14(d)).

These theories are all based on cities in the western world. They assume that land uses are decided by the people who are willing to pay most for the land. The high price of land in the CBD can be seen in the high-rise buildings found near the most important places. These 'important places' are either the CBD or some of the other growth points suggested by Hoyt. Most towns and cities in western countries show something of all these theories.

Activities

▲ ■ **9 a** Draw each of the models of land use in towns and cities in the centre of your page.

b Read carefully through the descriptions of each model and write brief labels around each diagram to explain the different areas of the town.

▲ ■ ● **10 a** Obtain a street map of your own nearest town or city.

b Use different colours to mark on the map the main areas of

i) Shops and offices

ii) Factories and warehouses

iii) Cheaper, medium priced and expensive houses.

c Stand back from the map and decide whether the town's land uses form circles, sectors or have grown around a number of different centres.

d i) Make a list of the land uses in the areas you have not yet coloured on the map.

ii) Could these uses of land be decided by competition with other land uses? Write a paragraph to explain how you think these non-competitive land uses should be decided.

Cities outside the westernized world

In the introduction to this section, we said that early western towns and cities grew because of trade. The Industrial Revolution led to many of them becoming industrial centres. Many countries of the world still have cities which are mainly trading centres. These kinds of cities are sometimes called **pre-industrial cities**.

Because there is less competition between housing, businesses and factories, pre-industrial cities often have no clear CBD. Their land use pattern is not as clear as in industrialized cities. Shops, houses and small workshops are often mixed together. Less competition for land also means that most of the buildings are the same height. The scattered land uses have often meant that roads have remained narrow and winding. In some towns, there are separate areas for people of different classes. People of the ruling class may gather around a temple, castle or palace in the centre of the town, while poorer people live on the outskirts.

In other towns, people from western countries who invaded the country built their settlements beside the original towns. These cities today have an 'old town' and an 'old colonial town'.

Many cities are becoming westernized. Large companies from the more developed nations set up offices and factories in these old cities so that they can sell their goods to more people. This means that new western-style areas are added to the old cities.

This growth in the number of functions of the cities has led to a growth in population. Most of the cities in the developing world are growing rapidly. This is because many poor people from rural areas are moving to the cities in search of work. When these people arrive in the cities, they have nowhere to live. The only way they can find a home is to join other squatters on the outskirts of the city and to build their own shelter. The part of the city where the squatters live is often called a **shanty town**, although each country has its own name for it. A shanty town is called a 'bustee' in India, a 'favela' in Brazil and a 'ghourbi' or 'bidonville' in Tunisia.

Even from this short description you can imagine how the pattern of even these old cities is becoming more complicated.

Activity

■ **11** Study the map and photographs of the Nigerian city of Ibadan (Figures 7.15 and 7.16 overleaf).

a Draw up a table to show the kinds of land uses which are found
  i) inside and
  ii) outside the original town wall of Ibadan.

b For each of these areas, write brief statements to describe each of these:
  The height of the buildings
  The materials of which the buildings appear to be made
  The street width
  The street pattern
  The kinds of activities which are occurring in the streets

Figure 7.15 Ibadan

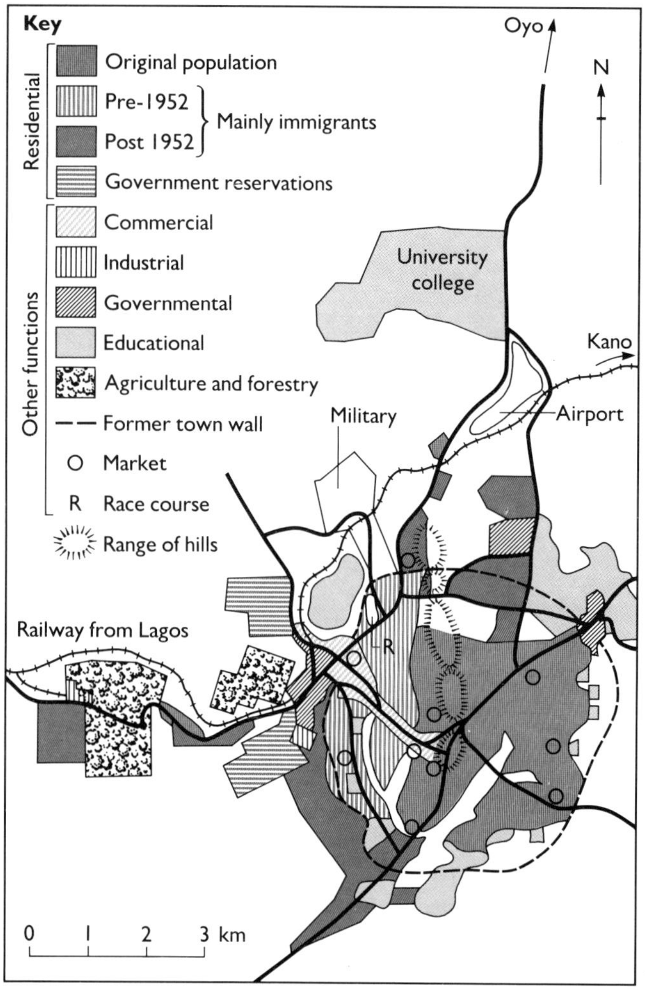

Figure 7.16 Ibadan, street plan

Activity

▲ ■ ● **12** Figure 7.17 lists in rank order the largest cities in the UK and Australia.

In Figure 7.18 both scales show logarithmic values. Using logarithms of population sizes and rankings helps us in two ways. Firstly, large differences in population between cities can be shown accurately without using very large graphs. (Imagine trying to plot cities which have populations of 100000, 120000 and 15000000 on a piece of ordinary graph paper!) Secondly, a graph which shows a perfect application of the rank size rule will appear as a straight line.

You will need sheets of tracing paper the size of Figure 7.18 for each country you graph.

a Place one sheet of tracing paper over the graph outline in Figure 7.18, and trace the two axes of the graph paper. Plot the size of London as the largest city in the UK.

b According to the rank size rule, the second city's population should be one-half that of the largest city. The third city's population should be one-half that of the second city, and so on. This means that the third city's population should be one-quarter that of the first city. From the population of London, work out what the population of the third largest city should be if the rank size rule is applied. Plot this figure on your graph and draw a line which extends from the largest city, through the third city and off the bottom edge of the graph.

c Now plot the *actual* sizes of the second to the twentieth cities in the UK.

Patterns in the number of settlements of different sizes

In any region there are usually a few large cities, several medium sized towns, a large number of small towns and many villages.

Some services provided by settlements are needed more often than others. For example, many people use a newsagents or a sweet shop every day. They may use a supermarket once a week. But most people use a hi-fi or television shop only occasionally. This means that a fairly small village will have enough people to keep a village shop in business. It will take the people of a small town plus several villages to keep a supermarket in business. A large hi-fi store will need the people of several small towns and many villages to provide enough customers, since each family will probably visit it very occasionally.

There seems to be a pattern to the sizes of towns in a region. If the towns are put in order of size, the second largest town often has half the population of the largest town. The third largest town has a third the population of the largest town; and so on. This is called the **rank size rule**.

Although it often seems to work, many countries have one city where the population is more than double that of the second city. London has more than three times the population of Birmingham, which is Britain's second city. A city which is more than twice the size of the second city in a country is called a **primate city**. As countries become more developed, the number of very large cities often increases.

This idea is useful when we are looking at the towns and cities of whole countries or large regions like the states of the USA or Australia.

d Write a few sentences describing how the actual sizes of the cities of the UK relate to the theoretical sizes of cities according to the rank size rule.

e On another sheet of tracing paper, draw the theoretical and actual sizes of the cities of Australia.

f Describe the relationship between the theoretical sizes and the actual sizes of the cities in Australia.

cities in each of these countries.

g Think back over all you know about the countries for which you have drawn graphs. Write a list of reasons why these countries do not obey the rank size rule.

Australia (1981)		UK (1981)	
Sydney	3205000	*Greater London	6696000
Melbourne	2723000	Birmingham	920000
Brisbane	1029000	Glasgow	762000
Adelaide	932000	Liverpool	510000
Perth	899000	Sheffield	477000
Newcastle	389000	Manchester	449000
Wollongong	223000	Leeds	449000
*Canberra	220000	Edinburgh	419000
Hobart	168000	Bristol	388000
Gold Coast	155000	Coventry	314000
Geelong	137000	Bradford	281000
		Leicester	280000
		Cardiff	274000
		Nottingham	271000
		Hull	268000
		Wolverhampton	252000
		Stoke-on-Trent	252000
		Plymouth	244000
		Derby	216000
		Southampton	204000

*Capital city

Figure 7.17 The rank size rule

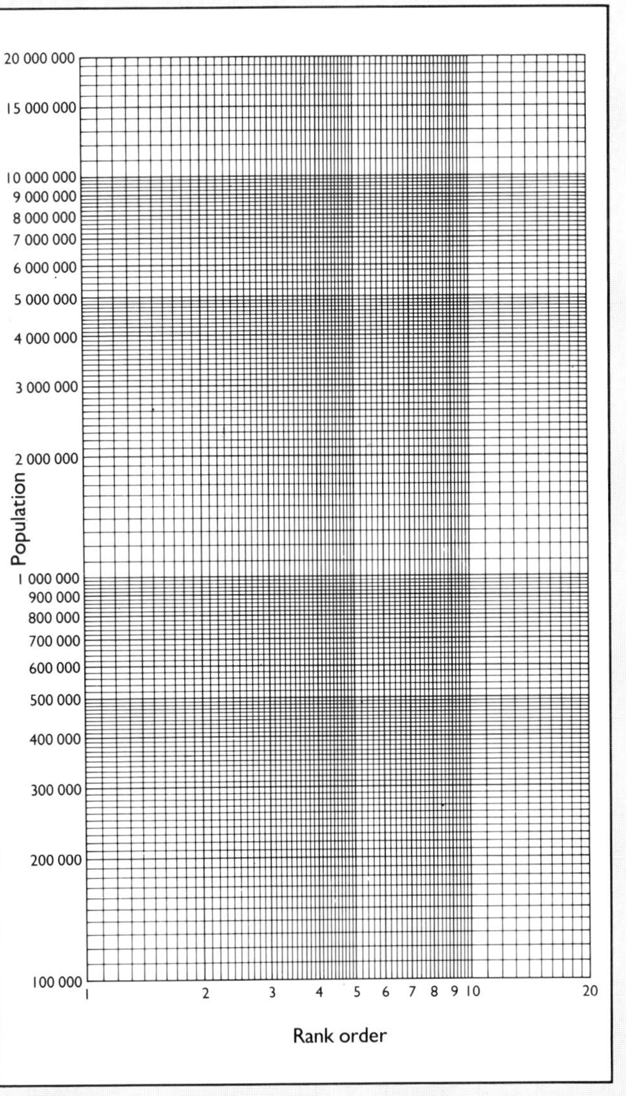

Figure 7.18 The rank size rule (graph)

Patterns in the way settlements are spread across the landscape

In the previous section we saw that people go to different sized settlements to buy different goods. Most people will go to the nearest settlement large enough to provide the shops and services they want. This means that each settlement will be visited by people from a circular area. Settlements which provide shops and services for the people around them are called **central places**. In theory, central places which are the same size and which have the same number of shops and other services should be spaced regularly across the landscape. The early ideas about this were put forward by a German called Walter Christaller.

Christaller worked out his theory by imagining settlements on a plain, with no differences in relief, soil types or population density. Transport would be just as easy in any direction. If each settlement had a circular area around it, though, there would have been gaps, so Christaller built up his theory with each settlement serving a hexagonal area. This is shown in Figure 7.19.

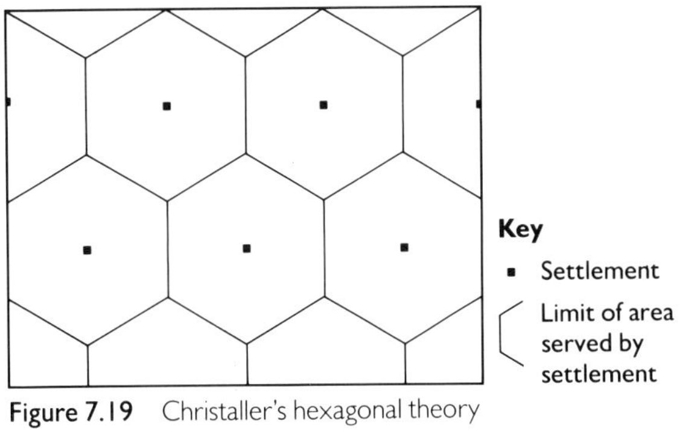

Figure 7.19 Christaller's hexagonal theory

Activity

▲ ■ **13** This activity is designed to show you how a pattern of villages, towns and cities of different sizes would develop on a plain settled mainly by farmers. Like Christaller, we have to imagine a large plain with no differences in soils, availability of water or barriers to easy travel in any direction. We will assume that the area is a part of the prairies of North America.

You will need a copy of Figure 7.20, 3 different coloured pencils and a ruler to do this activity.

a During the 19th century, pioneers moved westward taking all their possessions in covered wagons. When they reached the flat, fertile plains, many of them decided to settle. In time villages developed. The villages were spaced evenly over the land so that farmers could travel from their farm to the village store and back easily in one day. A farmer who lived exactly half way between two villages could go to either village. These villages are shown in Figure 7.20 as dots.

During the early years of the 20th century, settlers continued to arrive in the area. This increased the demand for goods and services, and some villages grew into small towns. The towns could support stores which sold goods which were needed only occasionally. This meant that they had to attract people from the surrounding villages. However, since farmers only needed to visit the towns occasionally, they were prepared to travel further.

Villages X, Y and Z on Figure 7.20 grew to be three of these towns. They each served a hexagonal area and each one served a third of the people living in the six villages around it. (You can assume that a third of the people in each village use each of the three towns because they are the same distance away.)

Decide which other villages shown on the map would grow to be towns. Mark these villages by drawing a small circle around the dot with a coloured pencil. Use the same coloured pencil to mark in the hexagonal areas they would serve.

b After World War II, the population of the area continued to grow. Several of the towns grew into cities. Because the cities could support a greater range of shops and services than the towns, they served a much larger area. Each city could attract a third of the population in the areas of the six towns around it.

On the map, town C grew to be a city. The area it served has been drawn in for you as a dotted line. Use a different coloured pencil and mark the towns which would become cities with a circle. Use the same coloured pencil to mark in the service areas of all the cities on the map.

c In recent years, one city in this area grew more than any other. This city was in the best location to serve most of the region. It is called a **metropolitan city**. It provides a very wide range of services for the people who live in its region. A third of the people who live in the areas of each of the six ordinary cities around it use the metropolitan city. The metropolitan city is marked on the map as MC. Use the third coloured pencil to draw a ring around it. Mark on the boundaries of its service area.

d You should now have completed a map of the various settlements in this region. The villages are still shown as dots. The towns are shown as dots with a ring around them. The cities are shown as dots with two rings around them. The metropolitan city is shown as a dot with three rings.

The rings remind us of how the different types of settlement provide different types of shops and services. Figure 7.21 shows different types of settlements.

A village is the smallest central place. It may contain a village store, a public house and a primary school.

A town has all the types of shops and services provided by a village, plus restaurants, banks, a secondary school and a wider range of shops.

A city has all the shops and services of a village and a town and will also have department stores, a college, a hospital and government offices.

A metropolitan city is the largest urban centre. It has all that villages, towns and cities have, but more of them. It will also have specialist shops and services such as a university, a large teaching hospital, theatres, expensive jewellery shops and perhaps a daily newspaper.

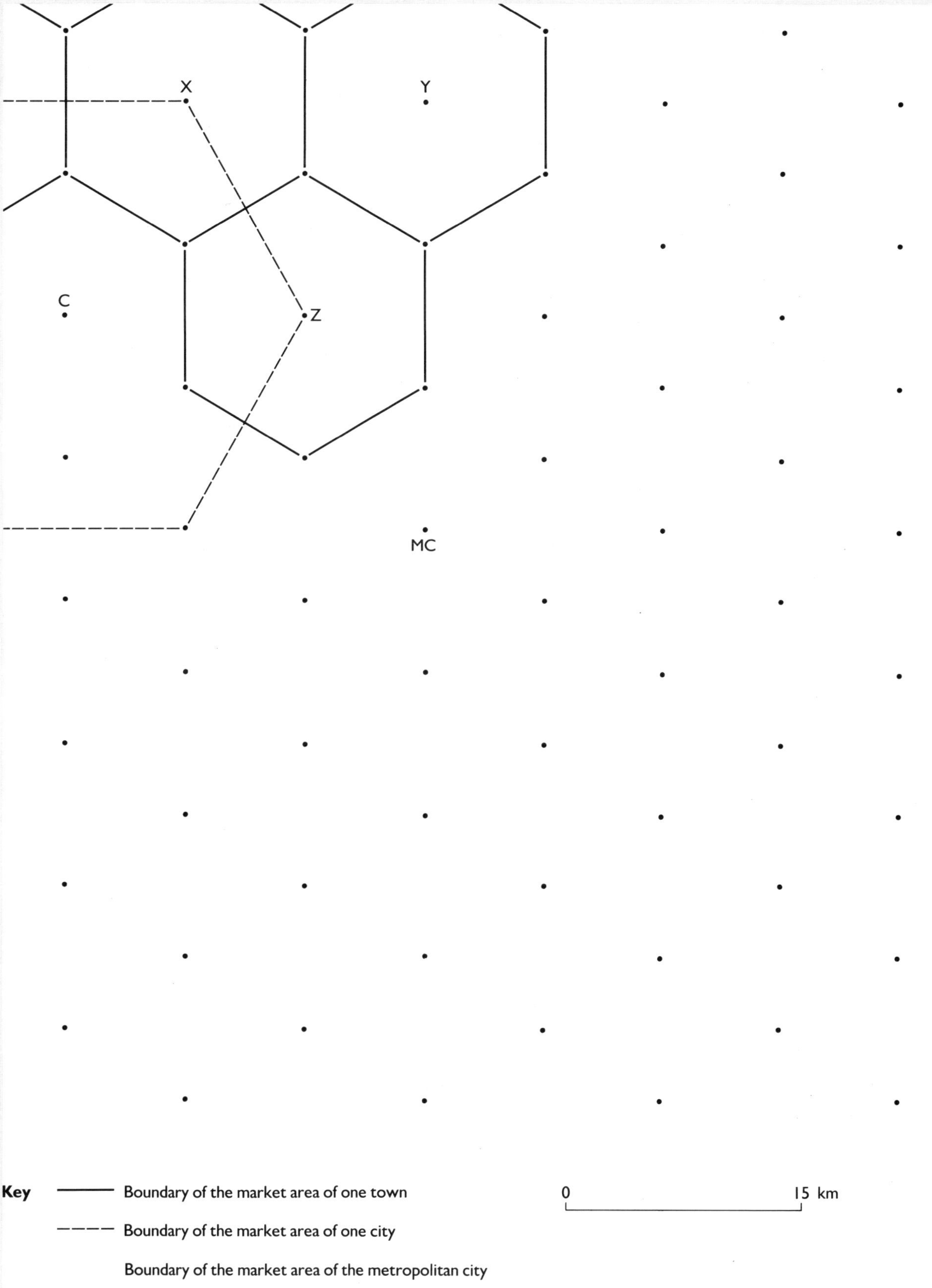

Figure 7.20 How market areas grew in part of the American West

Figure 7.21 Settlements: village, town, city, metropolitan city

We must remember that the word 'city' in the UK still has its old meaning of a town with a cathedral. The summary list above makes more sense in the UK if we think of the 'city' as a 'large town' and the 'metropolitan city' as one of our 'cities'.

From your completed map, work out how far (in a straight line) someone who lives in village Z would have to travel to find the following shops or services:

i) Petrol station iii) Furniture store
ii) Chemist iv) Theatre

e Look at the area served by the metropolitan city.

i) Work out the total number of city market areas which are included in the metropolitan city area.

Remember to add in all the parts of the city hexagons.

Remember that the metropolitan city provides all the shops and services of an ordinary city for the people who live in its city-sized market area.

ii) Work out the total number of town market areas which are included in one of the city market areas.

Add in all the parts of town hexagons.

Don't forget that each city provides the shops and services of a town for people who live in its town-sized market area.

iii) Work out the total number of village market areas which are included in one of the town market areas.

Remember that the people of each village can go to any one of three nearby towns, so assume that a third of the people in each village visit the town you have chosen.

Don't forget that each town still acts as a village for the people who live nearest it.

You will now see why Christaller called this a **K-3 network**.

f You have worked out the number of cities in the area of a metropolitan city. Now work out

i) The number of towns in a metropolitan city area

ii) The number of villages in a metropolitan city area.

Christaller's **central place theory** suggests that these numbers of villages, towns and cities should be the same in each metropolitan city area. In reality, some rich agricultural plains, such as southern Germany and the American Midwest do show patterns like this. However, even in these areas, the pattern is not perfect. If you look back to the beginning of this section, we explained the assumptions Christaller made for his theory. This should help you to understand why this precise pattern is never found exactly in the real world. It is because the assumptions Christaller made are never found to be true in reality.

The growth of towns...and the problems

Over the past 200 years, probably the most important change in the way human beings live has been the increase in the number of people who live in towns. In 1800, only about 1 person in every 40 in the world lived in a town. By the end of this century, 1 person in every 2 in the world will live in a town. Over 60 nations already had over half their people living in towns in 1980. Change in the percentage of a country's population living in towns is called its **rate of urbanization**.

The rate of urbanization increases for 2 reasons: Firstly, people may move from the countryside to the town. This means that the number of people in the towns goes up and the number of people in the countryside goes down. Secondly, more children may be born in the towns than in the countryside.

Urbanization started in western countries when the Industrial Revolution began. In developing countries it began later.

In both developed and developing countries, the move to the towns was due to two groups of reasons. The first group includes all the reasons *pushing* people out of the countryside. The second group includes all the reasons which *pull* people towards the towns.

People may be *pushed* out of the countryside by changes in their way of life. This may be because they are unable to grow enough food to feed their larger families. It may be because farms have been split among heirs so many times that many farms are no longer large enough to support a family. It may be because the landowners have modernized their farming methods and thrown their tenant farmers off their land.

People may be *pulled* towards towns by the possibility of finding jobs and houses.

In the UK during the Industrial Revolution, people moved to the towns in search of jobs when mines, factories and shipyards were expanding and needed more workers.

People in developing countries today may be forced to leave their village life to search for jobs and houses in the towns. However, they are less likely to succeed in finding either jobs or houses than people were in the UK in the last century.

The factories in many developing countries are not expanding fast enough to provide enough jobs. The industries which are expanding may use high technology which depends on machinery rather than human workers. Often, the countries of the developed world put import tariffs on manufactured goods from developing countries to protect their own industries from competition.

Because of these limits on the growth of jobs, many towns and cities in the developing world cannot collect enough taxes to have enough money to build roads, drains, houses and hospitals.

Although the reasons for increasing urbanization in developing countries today may be very similar to those which once affected the developed countries, the effects on the people are much worse. Many of the people moving into the cities of developing countries today are likely to be poor, unemployed and starving, with nowhere to live when they arrive.

On the other hand, the houses and factories built for the people who moved into the towns of the developed world last century are causing problems for people here today. Look at Figure 7.22 (overleaf).

Solving the problems of cities

Although the growth of cities has brought many advantages, it has also brought many problems. The question now is 'what can be done?'.

In the western world, the main line of attack has been to try to stop urban sprawl by creating **green belts**. A green belt is an area of land around a city which is kept as open space or farmland. Only very little new building is allowed in the green belt. People or firms who want to move to the edge of the cities where there is more room are persuaded to move to towns outside the green belt. In some cases, whole new towns have been built. In other

Figure 7.22 Problems in the towns of the developed and developing countries

cases, old towns have been expanded by building new houses and factories to cope with the extra people.

In the UK this approach has been almost too successful. So many people have left the centre of some cities, that only a few are left actually living there. Now, much more effort is being put into redeveloping inner city areas. In the 1960s and early 1970s this redevelopment often meant knocking down the old houses to build tower blocks of flats. Urban motorways were built to speed the flow of traffic into the centres of cities.

More recently, it has been realized that tower blocks and fast roads also cause problems. People living in tower blocks can be very lonely and find it difficult to make friends. The urban motorways encourage more traffic in the city centre. The cars and lorries increase the amount of pollution in the atmosphere. The traffic jams in the centre waste much time.

This has led to another change in the cities. In many cities it is becoming fashionable for better-off people to buy old workers' houses near the centre. This means that they can then live closer to their jobs and entertainments. The old houses are improved with inside toilets, bathrooms and central heating. Sometimes two small houses are knocked into one. This process of improvement by a change of fashion is called **gentrification**.

Although some changes in cities do come about on their own, most changes are planned. The following three case studies show how some city problems have been attacked.

Preserving the green heart of Holland, Zoetermeer in the Netherlands

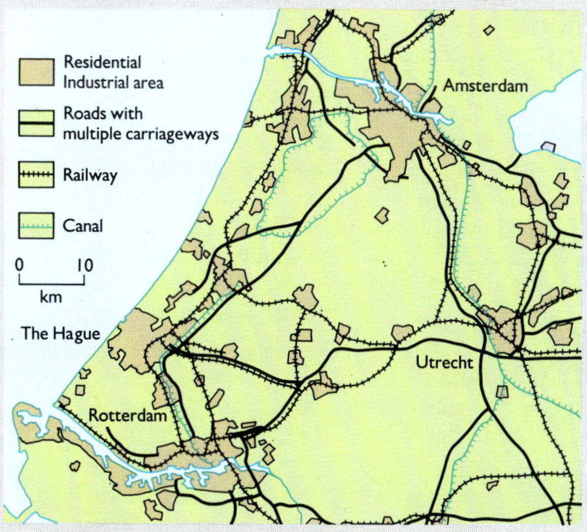

Figure 7.23 Randstad, Holland

The major cities of the Netherlands are located around the edge of an area of good agricultural land. Figure 7.23 shows how these cities have grown together to form a huge conurbation in the shape of a horseshoe. The conurbation is called **Randstad** which means 'Rim city'.

Figure 7.24 shows how the cities grew from 1850 onwards. As the towns and cities which make up Randstad grew, they suffered from all the problems of cities everywhere. The density of population rose. There was a shortage of houses. There were traffic jams. There was more pollution of the air, soil and water. Noise pollution increased.

Many people moved out of the cities to live in the villages of the green heart, the countryside. These villages began to grow into suburbs of the towns. Rush hour commuter traffic into the cities increased even more.

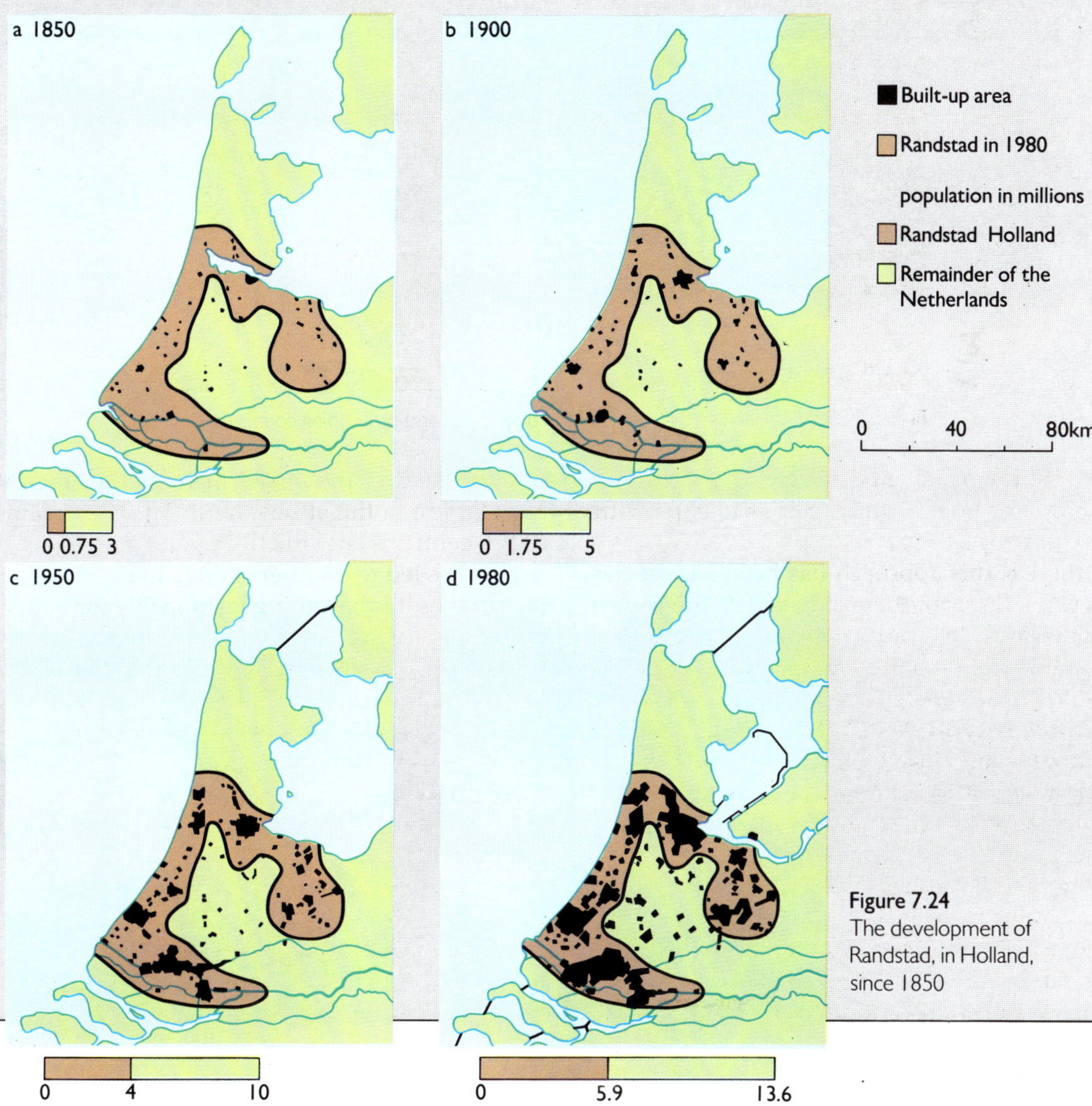

Figure 7.24 The development of Randstad, in Holland, since 1850

At first, the Dutch planners had three main problems. Firstly, they wanted to reduce the number of people in the cities. Secondly, they wanted to prevent the cities from growing even more and taking over the countryside. And thirdly, they wanted to prevent the villages from growing into suburbs of the towns and causing even more commuter traffic.

In the early 1960s the planners tried to tackle these problems by persuading people to leave the towns and cities of the Randstad and go to other parts of the Netherlands. They encouraged people to go to the southern and eastern parts of the country.

In the 1970s, the planners found that things were in danger of going too far. If people had continued to leave Randstad, there would have been too few people left to support the shops and services of the cities. The planners then had to find ways to slow down the migration from Randstad but at the same time they wanted to protect the green heart. This time they decided to improve the urban areas and allow carefully controlled overspill into some satellite towns.

Zoetermeer is an example of an expanded town in the green heart. In the 18th century, there were two separate settlements called Zoetermeer and Zegwoert on the old polders, 12 km east of The Hague.

Zoetermeer was the wealthier of the two villages. It had gained many hectares of new fertile meadowland in 1618 and again in 1669 when large lakes and marshlands had been drained. Figure 7.25 is a view of Zoetermeer and Zegwoert in 1766. Many Dutch towns at that time would have looked something like this. The population grew steadily and in 1935 both villages merged to form one community – Zoetermeer.

In the 1960s, the population of Zoetermeer was expanding rapidly. In 1966 the first piles were sunk for the foundations of new homes to take even more overspill population from Randstad. This growth had to be carefully planned in case Zoetermeer became just another suburb of The Hague. It was important to try to make it a *centre of growth*, not just an extension of The Hague.

The first part of the plan was for four large areas of housing. The first housing neighbourhoods are numbered 1 to 4 on Figures 7.26 and 7.27. Figure 7.26 shows the types of housing built in each area. Figure 7.27 is a map of the expanded town of Zoetermeer. Each neighbourhood was planned to house 20 000 to 25 000 people. A fifth neighbourhood, called Seghwaert, was developed later. A sixth neighbourhood is now planned. It will be built south of the RW12 motorway which leads to

Figure 7.25 View of Zoetermeer and Zegwoert, 1766

The Hague and Gouda. The town was planned so that each neighbourhood should have schools, shops and snackbars. The town centre was expanded to include department stores, supermarkets, restaurants, offices and a hospital. Figure 7.28 shows the expanded town of Zoetermeer in 1986.

The planners wanted to limit the number of people commuting from Zoetermeer to The Hague to work. To do this, they built an industrial estate. Even so, in 1978 Zoetermeer had 23 500 working people, but could only provide 10 000 local jobs. In order to provide more jobs, new factories are being encouraged and several Government Offices are being moved from The Hague to Zoetermeer. This will ease the pressure on office space in The Hague. It will also result in some workers travelling out from The Hague to Zoetermeer.

To help with this commuting both into and out of the capital city, a new railway to The Hague was completed in 1979.

You can see from Figures 7.26, 7.27 and 7.28 that Zoetermeer has grown rapidly in recent years. It is one town where the planners have had to give up trying to prevent growth in the green heart. They are now trying to limit growth to just a few chosen centres.

Neighbourhood	Year of Construction	High rise	'Stacked low rise'	Low rise
1 Palenstein	1966/1975	70	6	24
2 Driemanspolder	1967/1975	60	20	20
3 Meerzicht	1968/1978	50	7	43
4 Buytenwegh de Leyens	1974/1982	10	30	60
5 Seghwaert	1978/1982	0	33	67

Figure 7.26 High rise and low rise housing in the residential neighbourhood of Zoetermeer (in percentages)

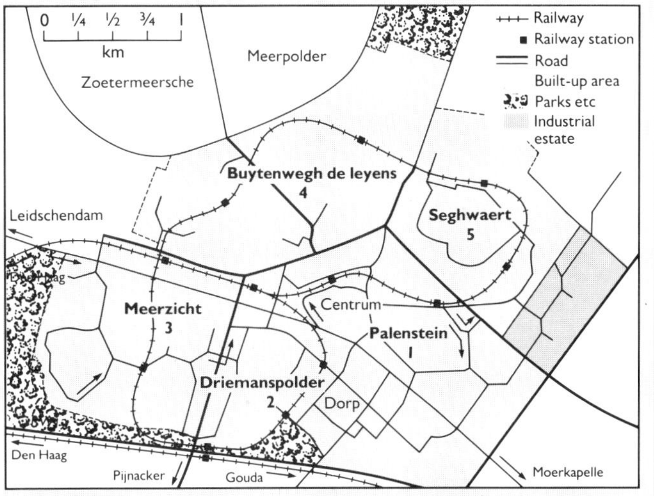

Figure 7.27 Zoetermeer: planned town for Randstad, Holland

Figure 7.28 The expanded town of Zoetermeer, 1986

Activities

▲ ■ ● **14** Figure 7.29 shows the population growth of Zoetermeer.

a Draw a line graph to show these figures.

b Read the account of the growth of Zoetermeer again (p. 182) and label the main events on your graph. For example, for 1966 you could add the label 'Foundations for new overspill homes'.

Year	Population	Year	Population
1960	8440	1976	45480
1970	17130	1978	52910
1972	24130	1980	63825
1974	36570	1990	95500*
			*Estimate

Figure 7.29 Population growth in Zoetermeer

▲ ■ ● **15** Look at Figure 7.26 which shows the different types of housing built in the five neighbourhoods of Zoetermeer.

a Draw divided bar graphs to show how the proportion of houses built as tower blocks, medium height blocks of flats, and one or two storey houses changed between 1966 and 1982.

b Write two or three paragraphs to explain the advantages and disadvantages of each type of building. Think of the buildings from the point of view of the planners, the builders and the people who will live in them.

Activity

▲ ■ ● **16** Look at the map of Zoetermeer (Figure 7.27).

a i) Explain why the industrial estate was built on the edge of the town.

ii) Explain why the industrial estate was built to the east of the town.

b i) Count the number of railway stations on the branch lines which run through the town of Zoetermeer.

ii) Roughly how far apart are the railway stations in Zoetermeer?

iii) Explain briefly why the railway is regarded as so important in Zoetermeer.

iv) Explain what this number of railway stations suggests about the future of Zoetermeer as an independent town with its own jobs and people.

Case Study

The Arumbakkam self-help scheme, Madras in India

The problems caused by urbanization are found in the developing world too. India had about 670 million people in 1981. Twenty million of the people lived in the four largest cities. These are Calcutta, Delhi, Bombay and Madras.

Madras is the capital city of the State of Tamil Nadu. Its population was estimated to be 4289000 in 1977. The location of Madras is shown in Figure 7.30.

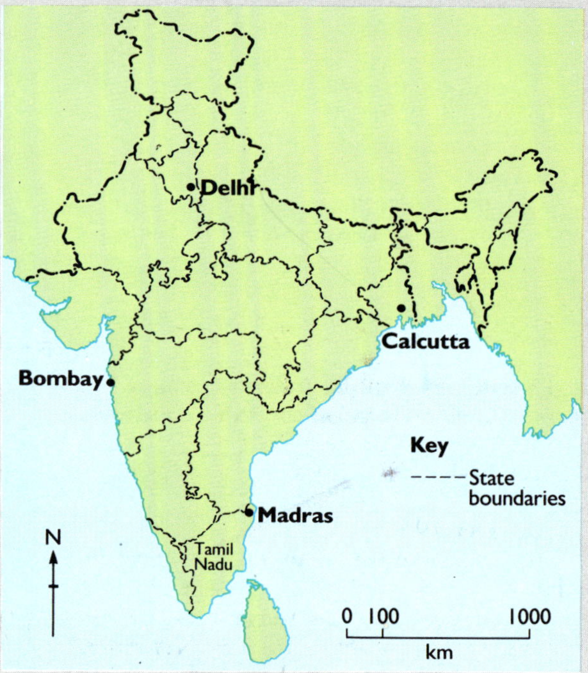

Figure 7.30 Location of Madras

The early growth of Madras

The modern city of Madras was once a number of separate villages. The villages were built along a sandy ridge and each village had grown up around a temple.

When the British East India Company built Fort St. George in 1639, a new town began to grow up around it. By 1746 the town's population was 19000. Fort St. George is now used for the State Government Offices. The town officially became a city in 1798.

In the 1860s railways and the port were built. This led to the growth of the trade and industry of Madras. A larger, artificial harbour was built in 1896.

Because Madras had a good harbour and railway links with other parts of India, new industries began to grow. These new industries included timber sawing; leather tanneries and metal works.

By 1941 Madras had a population of just under a million. As well as having a variety of industries, it was a 'central place' and supplied goods and services to its local area.

The city was a pleasant place to live in. It had a good water supply and sewerage system. It had an efficient public transport system of trams and electric trains. The roads were wide and shady. The city was still centred around the fort, but suburbs had grown out along the roads and railway lines which led to the city centre. Figure 7.31 shows the central area of Madras.

Figure 7.31 Central Madras

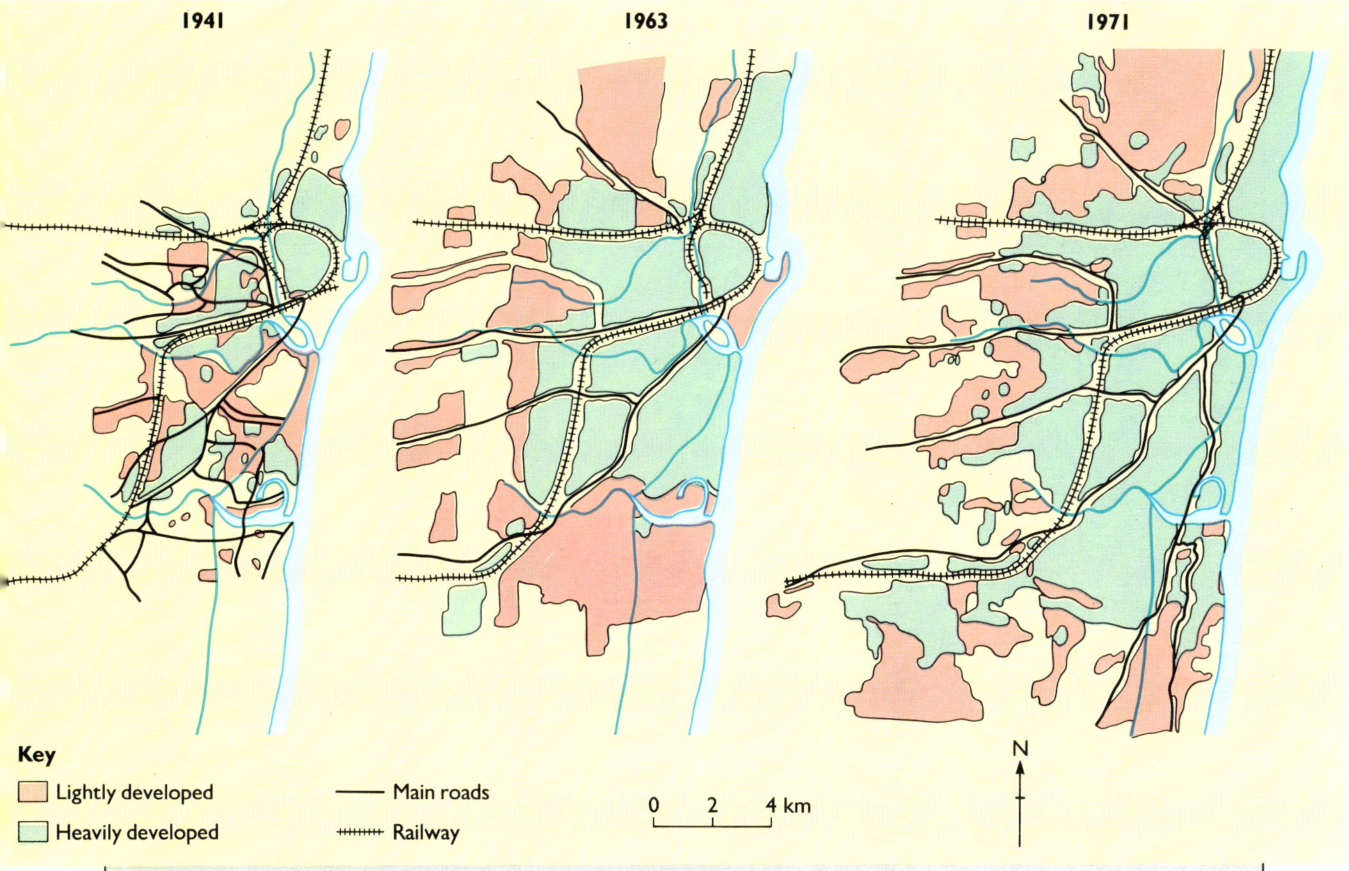

Figure 7.32 Growth of Madras since 1941

Despite its growth, Madras remained a centre for administration and trade. Its skyline had the low profile which was typical of many Indian pre-industrial cities.

Madras since 1941

Since 1941 there have been many changes in Madras. When India became independent of the UK in 1947, the new Indian Government encouraged the growth of industry. New areas of factories were built on the outskirts of the city. Today, Madras' factories produce many things including cars, bicycles, cotton cloth and cement. The growth of industry led to the growth of trade in the centre of the city and more suburbs around the outskirts. Figure 7.32 shows how Madras grew between 1943 and 1971. Figure 7.33 shows the land use pattern of Madras as it had developed in the 1970s.

Problems caused by the growth of Madras

Figure 7.34 (overleaf) shows the changes in the Indian population from 1901 to 1982. Figure 7.35 shows the growth in the population of the city of Madras in the same period. You can see that Madras has grown rapidly. Growth in the wealth and population of a city can be a good thing if they grow together. In Madras, however, the population grew faster than the wealth.

Figure 7.33 City land use, 1970

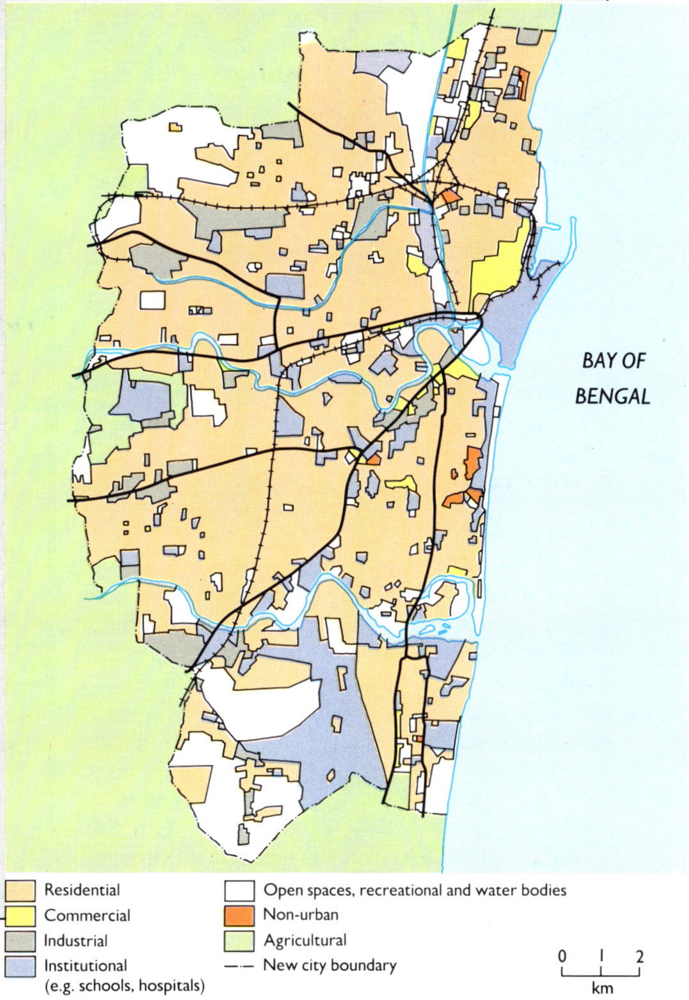

Census year	Total population (millions)	Urban population (millions)	Urban population as a percentage of total population
1901	235.3	25.7	10.9%
1911	252.1	26.6	10.6%
1921	251.4	28.6	11.4%
1931	279.0	33.8	12.1%
1941	318.7	44.3	13.9%
1951	361.1	57.5	15.9%
1961	439.2	78.8	18.0%
1971	546.9	*109.0	10.0%
1978	634.7	133.3	21.0%
1982	688.0	144.5	21.0%

*Estimate

Figure 7.34 Urbanization in India 1901–1982

Census year	Population	Census year	Population
1871	397000	1931	734000
1881	406000	1941	886000
1891	453000	1951	1416000
1901	553000	1961	2469000
1911	576000	1978	3401000*
1921	592000	1981	4289000*

*Estimate

Figure 7.35 Growth population in Madras 1871–1981

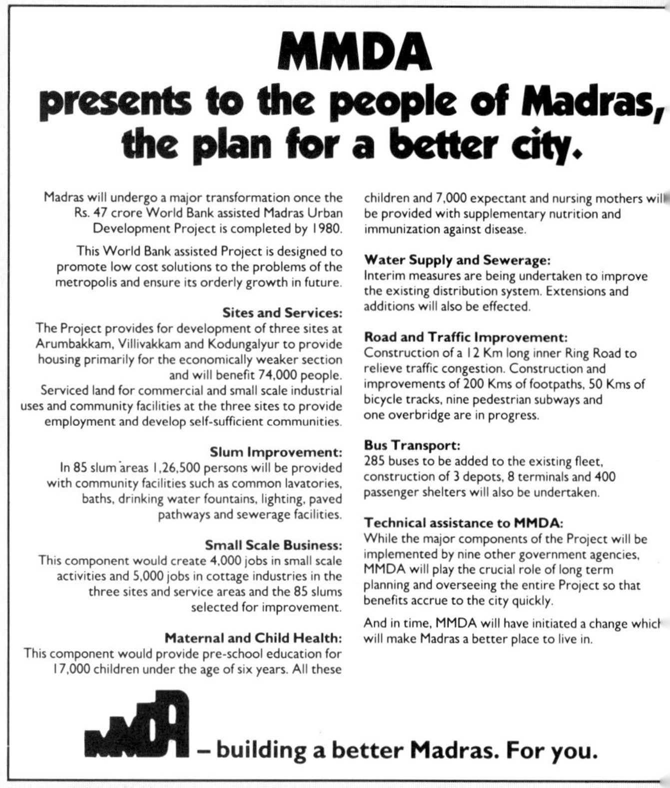

Figure 7.36

In June 1980, the planners of Madras produced a report called *The Structure Plan for Madras Metropolitan Area*. The report described the problems which were facing the city and suggested ways for overcoming them in the future.

The report showed that the population of Madras had increased on average by 130000 a year through the 1970s. The growth rate for the 1980s is likely to be more than 220000 a year. In the city, 1280000 people were earning too little money to pay taxes. This meant that 40% of the population could not pay towards the cost of basic urban services such as water supply, public transport and drains. Because so many people could not pay taxes, the city's services had deteriorated.

The report said that major improvements were needed in transport, water supply, flood control, sewerage, electricity supply and housing. It suggested that the problems should be attacked by a number of different schemes. These schemes were to be organized by the **Madras Metropolitan Development Authority** (known as the **MMDA**). Figure 7.36 is an advertisement issued by the MMDA to explain the plans to the people of Madras.

Of all the problems facing the city, the most serious was the shortage of houses. In 1980, 225000 families were living in slum huts and another 361000 families were living in overcrowded housing in old parts of the city. These families included about 3.2 million people. They made up more than 75% of the total population of Madras.

When the planners looked into the future, they could see that the situation would only get worse. They estimated that between 22000 and 32000 more families would be looking for homes each year throughout the 1980s. They could not think of building enough good quality homes for all the people who need them. Because of this, the MMDA's first suggestion was that the slum houses should be accepted and then the slum areas should be improved. Improvements could be made by providing water supplies, drains and sewers, street lighting, health centres and schools. They hoped that this would encourage the slum dwellers to improve their surroundings themselves.

Secondly, the planners wanted to encourage self-help schemes like the one at Arumbakkam which began in 1977. The idea of the self-help schemes is that people still build their own houses, but instead of building them at random, there is an overall plan to help them. The overall plan is shown in Figure 7.37.

Madras planners can encourage new experiments like this because there is space on the fringes of the built-up area. This could be seen as encouraging the urban sprawl of Madras.

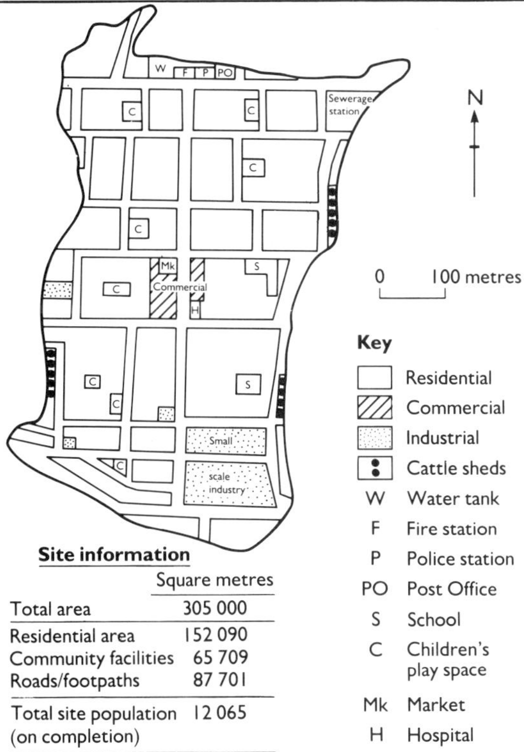

Site information

	Square metres
Total area	305 000
Residential area	152 090
Community facilities	65 709
Roads/footpaths	87 701
Total site population (on completion)	12 065

Figure 7.37 Arumbakkam, Madras: 'sites and services' scheme

Figure 7.39 The authorities have provided concrete platforms, walls, shower/toilet facilities and two rooms, with scope for expansion

However, at present this is probably a small price to pay for improving housing conditions.

Arumbakkam, which is to the west of the Madras city centre, is becoming a lively new township. 13 470 building plots have been laid out. Each plot is linked to water supplies, drains and sewers and is served by a road. Different types of plot are available. Depending on the type of plot bought, the families must build all or part of their homes themselves. Although modern building materials can be bought cheaply, many of the houses are still built like the other slum dwellings by using thatching, packing cases and other waste materials.

In the centre is an area for small shops. In the south are workshops for small scale industries. The only rules for the workshops are that they should employ people rather than machines wherever possible and that they should not pollute the environment.

Type A: A plot 430 sq. ft. (40 sq. m.) with a bath room and lavatory plus Rs. 500/- worth building materials. Cost Rs. 2,200/-.

Type B: A partially built house with two side walls and roof, bath room and lavatory, in a plot of 500 sq.ft. (46.5 sq.m.) plus Rs. 125/- worth of building materials the total cost being Rs. 3,300/-.

Type C: A complete house with Verandah, living room, kitchen, bath and lavatory in a plot of 500 sq.ft. (46.5 sq.m.). Cost Rs. 7,000/-.

Figure 7.38 Types of plot in the MMDA sites and services programme

Figure 7.38 shows the types of plot being offered in the Arumbakkam scheme. Figures 7.39 – 7.43 (above and overleaf) are photos of the scheme.

Unfortunately the Arumbakkam scheme and others like it have their problems. For example, they are on the outskirts of the city, far away from the city centre. Some of the poor people for whom the scheme is planned earn their living by selling goods and begging on the streets of the city centre. They are not always willing to move so far away from their work.

The problems of Madras are fairly typical of the other large Indian cities. The populations of all the cities are increasing, due both to natural increase and people moving to the city to look for work. Most of the poor people in the cities live in bad conditions (Figure 7.44 overleaf). There are not enough houses and the water, sewerage and transport services can no longer cope. In Bombay, for example, there is simply not enough space for 7 million people. The pressure is too great and the poor people get 'squeezed out' on to the pavement.

There are more than 50 new towns in India. Most of these towns are to cope with the overcrowding in the older cities. However, new towns are expensive to build and the number of people needing homes is growing very rapidly. It is likely that more self-help schemes like the one at Arumbakkam will be needed in the future.

Figure 7.40 View across the Arumbakkam 'sites and services' site, showing remnants of monsoon water lying on the site

Figure 7.42 Looking down one of the streets of the new Arumbakkam township; a family is already inhabiting a unit

Figure 7.41 A plot with walls and roof: traditional 'squatter housing' material is being used to complete the dwelling

Figure 7.43 The central community shops and facilities of Arumbakkam already beginning to look busy, with children in the street

Figure 7.44 Existing 'squatter' low income settlement, using traditional materials, overcrowded on a poorly drained site with no paving and no facilities; this is situated west of the city on the edge of the built-up area

Activities

▲ ■ **17** Look at Figure 7.31 which is a photograph of part of Madras. Use the evidence from the photograph to help you with the following exercises.

a Describe the site of this part of Madras.

b What do the number of trees suggest about the climate of Madras?

c What functions of this area of Madras can you identify from the photograph? In other words, how is this part of the city used?

▲ ■ **18** Look at Figure 7.34 and Figure 7.35.

a Draw two graphs.

i) In the first graph show the growth of the urban population of India as a whole between 1901 and 1982.

ii) In the second graph show the growth of the population of Madras.

b From your graphs, describe the similarities and differences between the growth of the population of Madras and the growth of the total urban population of India.

▲ ■ **19** Study Figure 7.33.

a Draw a simplified sketch map of Madras. On it, mark and name:

i) The Bay of Bengal

ii) The Central Area of commerce and government

iii) The harbour

iv) The main roads and railways

v) The main industrial areas.

b Explain the location of:

i) The Central Area of commerce and government

ii) The main industrial areas.

▲ ■ ● **20** Study Figure 7.36. The advertisement says that the project is designed to promote low-cost solutions to the problems of Madras.

a Explain which of the schemes put forward you think are 'low-cost solutions', and which are likely to be rather expensive solutions.

b Can you suggest other ways of improving the 7 problem areas of public service which would cost less?

▲ ■ ● **21** Examine the photographs of the Arumbakkam housing scheme and their captions carefully (Figure 7.39 to 7.43) and study the descriptions of the plots (Figure 7.38). Describe the advantages and disadvantages of each type of house site:

a To the people who are going to live in the house

b To the MMDA.

▲ ■ ● **22** Look at the plan of the Arumbakkam housing scheme (Figure 7.37).

a Describe the way in which each of the following are distributed in the area.

i) The houses

ii) The children's play areas

iii) The industrial units

iv) The cattle sheds

b For each land use, describe the advantages and disadvantages of planning the scheme in this way.

c Design your own scheme to overcome the disadvantages you have described in b.

Case Study

Brasilia: a planned capital, Brazil

From 1763 until 1960, the capital city of Brazil was Rio de Janeiro. Rio was an important port before 1763 and was also convenient for the goldfields inland. Once it became the capital, its importance and size grew and it is still the most important city in Brazil.

Rio is, however, in the south of Brazil. It is a long way from the huge areas of Brazil in the centre and north. By the 1950s it was clear that one of Brazil's biggest problems was that most of her economic development was going on along the coast, especially in the south around Rio and São Paulo.

Many people from the country districts were attracted to these cities. Just as in Madras, the city could not cope and shanty towns, called **favelas**, grew up. The regions and cities of Brazil are shown in Figure 7.45, (overleaf).

The Brazilian Government realized that they needed to develop the centre-west and northern regions if they were to solve these problems and make Brazil more wealthy. They decided to build a new capital city inland to act as a centre for new industries, farming and transport.

For 8 years studies were carried out to decide where to build the new city. Eventually the planners decided to put the new capital

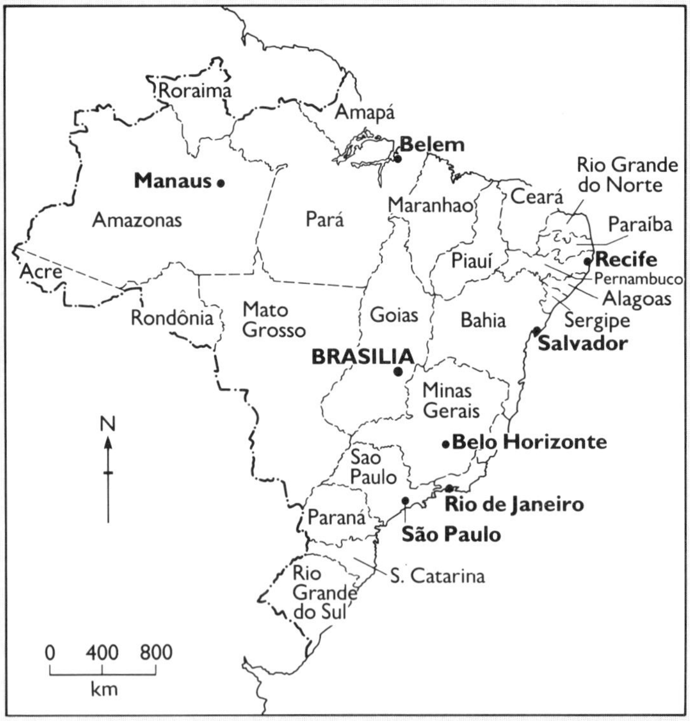

Figure 7.45 Main towns and regions of Brazil, to show the position of Brasilia

900 km inland from Rio, 1070 m above sea level on the Central Plateau.

A competition was held to decide who would design the city. Professor Lucio Costa won the chance to design the city and Oscar Niemeyer was made chief architect.

Costa planned a city in the shape of an aeroplane. The 'fuselage' area is occupied by government buildings, banks, theatres, cinemas and broadcasting stations. The 'wings' are blocks of flats, hotels, churches and embassies. Figures 7.46 is a map of Brasilia and its 8 satellite towns.

Niemeyer designed the buildings with great imagination. Figure 7.47 shows some of the buildings in Brasilia.

By 1974 all the government departments of Brazil had been moved from Rio to Brasilia. Today over a million people live in the city and its 8 satellite towns.

Brasilia was planned to achieve two main aims. The first aim was to help with the development of the north and centre of Brazil. The planners hoped that Brasilia would do this by becoming a major route centre by attracting a wide variety of industries and by providing a market for new farms.

Figure 7.46 Federal district of Brasilia

Figure 7.47 Buildings in Brasilia

The second aim was to make another centre to attract people away from the south-east coast. In particular, it was hoped that fewer country people would move into the cities of the south-east such as Rio, São Paulo and Belo Horizonte.

However, there is a major difference between Brasilia and most other cities in the world. Most cities start as small central places serving the local area. They then grow to serve a larger and larger area. Brasilia was built to serve a whole country, without ever having had to serve its own region.

To decide whether or not the idea has been a success, we must look, firstly, at the structure of Brasilia, and, secondly, at Brasilia as a central place.

The structure of Brasilia

Brasilia was planned to fulfil the functions of a national capital, but it was not planned for poorer people to live in. The description of Brasilia by Simon Hoggart, in the *Observer* newspaper, explains many of the problems the design of the city causes for people (Figure 7.48, overleaf).

The industries of Brasilia are so far not varied enough to provide jobs for the growing population. By the mid 1960s, for every 2 people living in planned houses or flats, 1 person was living in a shanty town (favela). One area in which the favelas are especially large is around Taguatinga, south and west of the city.

Brasilia as a central place

As a central place, Brasilia's greatest problem is that it is designed for the whole country and not for a region. Some people have argued that the plateau of centre-west is not the region with the greatest problems. They think that the new capital should have been built in the north or north-east.

Brasilia has been linked to Belem by a new 2276 km hard road. Some farming settlements have grown up along this road.

The number of country people moving into Rio and São Paulo has been reduced a little. However, Brasilia has not yet developed the same range of functions as, for example, Rio. Rio still has the most important stock market in Brazil. Rio's international airport is the busiest. Rio is the centre of Brazil's printing and publishing industry. The majority of tourists who visit Brazil, visit Rio.

Earlier we said that all settlements change over time. Only time will tell whether Brasilia's structure will change to suit the people who live there. In the meantime the Brazilian Government is still hoping that their new central place will result in the growth of a more prosperous service area.

Simon Hoggart takes to the streets of Brasilia, which he finds a particularly hazardous pastime

The city where people fear to tread

BRASILIA has just celebrated, if that is the word, its twentieth anniversary. When it was established as the capital of Brazil in 1960, to replace Rio which had entirely run out of land and resources, it was greeted as a triumph of modern architecture and planning. And so, I suppose, it still is. It must be a marvellous place to be if you are a building or a motor car, for this is a city masterfully designed to cater for everything except people. Twenty years on, I found it terribly depressing.

The place still looks extraordinary and, from some angles, magnificent. There is virtually no pollution, no traffic jams and unlike Rio, 700 miles away, very little crime. It is cool, on top of a plateau 3,000 feet up, and the sky around it is unimaginably vast.

It ought to be perfect but I found nobody in three days who actually liked living there. "You get used to living anywhere in time" was the warmest praise anyone offered.

For a start, there is nothing to do – none of the teeming night life of other Brazilian cities, no pavement cafés for the excellent reason that there are no pavements. If you are not in a residential quarter, and need a packet of fags or a battery for your radio there is simply nowhere you can get them. All the shops are concentrated in two bustling malls above the bus station. Here, with relief, you can find people walking and shouting and arguing. Yet 100 yards away, looking towards the ranks of ministerial buildings lined up like glass dominoes, you see a landscape as barren of life as the moon.

Suppose you want to go from the bus station to the cathedral, a distance of perhaps a quarter of a mile. Though it is the very centre of Brasilia you can see no humans in the intervening space. Your journey inevitably takes you a distance of more than a mile, involving the hazardous crossing of six lane highways on which drivers honk at your insolence.

The handful of Brasilians who dare to cross the road have developed brains like computers – skipping in front of a car in lane 1, they can arrive just after the car in lane 3 and so dodge the truck in lane 6.

If you have the bad luck to live in Brasilia, you will almost certainly inhabit one of the near identical tower blocks which spread in two great wings from the centre.

Each block of four has its official allocation of shops, services and schools. At least the shops and the odd bar have a pleasantly grubby look, and occasionally the shouts of children provide a reminder of the vigour and life of the rest of Brazil.

If you are really lucky you live in one of the great "favelas," huge towns erected at top speed on the outskirts, row after row of identical brick huts built to cope with a growth rate much faster than the planners expected. They stretch up to 30 miles from the city and the menial workers who live in them may spend four hours a day travelling to and from the capital.

Yet still Brasilia draws peasants from hundreds of miles around; sometimes you can see them in the bus station, clutching their belongings in cardboard boxes, with no idea where to go or what to do. Some do not even leave the bus station and remain to beg from travellers.

When you fly in at night it looks sensational, a swirling geometric pattern picked out in brilliant lights. Yet it has been dry here recently and the sky is lit by the orange glow of the bush burning, a hint or threat that nature may return one day to take over again this most grandiose and arid of cities.

Figure 7.48 The city where people fear to tread (*Guardian* 1980)

Activities

▲■● **23** Study the maps, photographs and descriptions of Brasilia (Figures 7.45–7.48).

a Describe the ways in which Brasilia is different from unplanned cities in developed countries.

b Describe the ways in which Brasilia is different from unplanned cities in developing countries.

▲■● **24** Look at the map of Brasilia (Figure 7.46).

a Calculate the average distance that poorer people have to travel from the centre of the satellite towns to the centre of the city (e.g. the bus station).

b Calculate the average distance the wealthier people in the city blocks have to travel to the centre.

c In what ways is this arrangement different from the way people are usually spread out in western cities?

d Describe the problems this spread causes for Brasilia and its people.

Activity

▲ **25** Read the newspaper article (Figure 7.48).

■ **a** List the functions served by Brasilia.

● **b** Make a list of the problems caused by the land-use pattern of Brasilia for the people who use the functions you have listed.

c All settlements change over time. How does Simon Hoggart think that Brasilia may change? (*Hint:* see his last sentence.) Suggest the changes you would make which could make Brasilia into a city more likely to serve the needs of all people living there.

Conclusion

In this chapter we have seen how people like to cluster together to settle in villages, towns and cities. Over the years, more and more people have sought the attractions of city life. This has led to overcrowding in cities and the emptying of the countryside. Now planning is necessary if the advantages of both city and country life are to be preserved and put to the best possible use.

8 Moving around

The ways in which the different parts of the world are linked together are mentioned many times in this book. Links between different parts of a drainage basin are described in Chapter 2. The links between the climate zones of the world are explained in Chapter 3. Trading links between countries which concentrate on primary industries and countries which concentrate on manufacturing industry are described in Chapter 5. The location of industries between their sources of raw materials and their markets and the links between them are described in Chapter 6. The links between the different parts of towns and cities and their surrounding areas are described in Chapter 7.

All these types of links, except the links in our natural environment, depend on people communicating with one another. Communication includes all forms of transport. People and goods are carried from one place to another in many different ways. Communication also includes all the ways in which information can be sent from one place to another. It includes letter post, telephone, telex, facsimile transmission, computer links and radio and television. All these means of communication can be two-way. People in one place can give information or goods to people in another area and receive information or goods from them. This exchange of information or goods can make things change in both areas. The exchange is sometimes called **spatial interaction**.

Figure 8.1 is a European food map. In 1973 the UK joined the European Economic Community (EEC). Many customs duties between the UK and other members of the EEC were reduced. This meant that the amount of

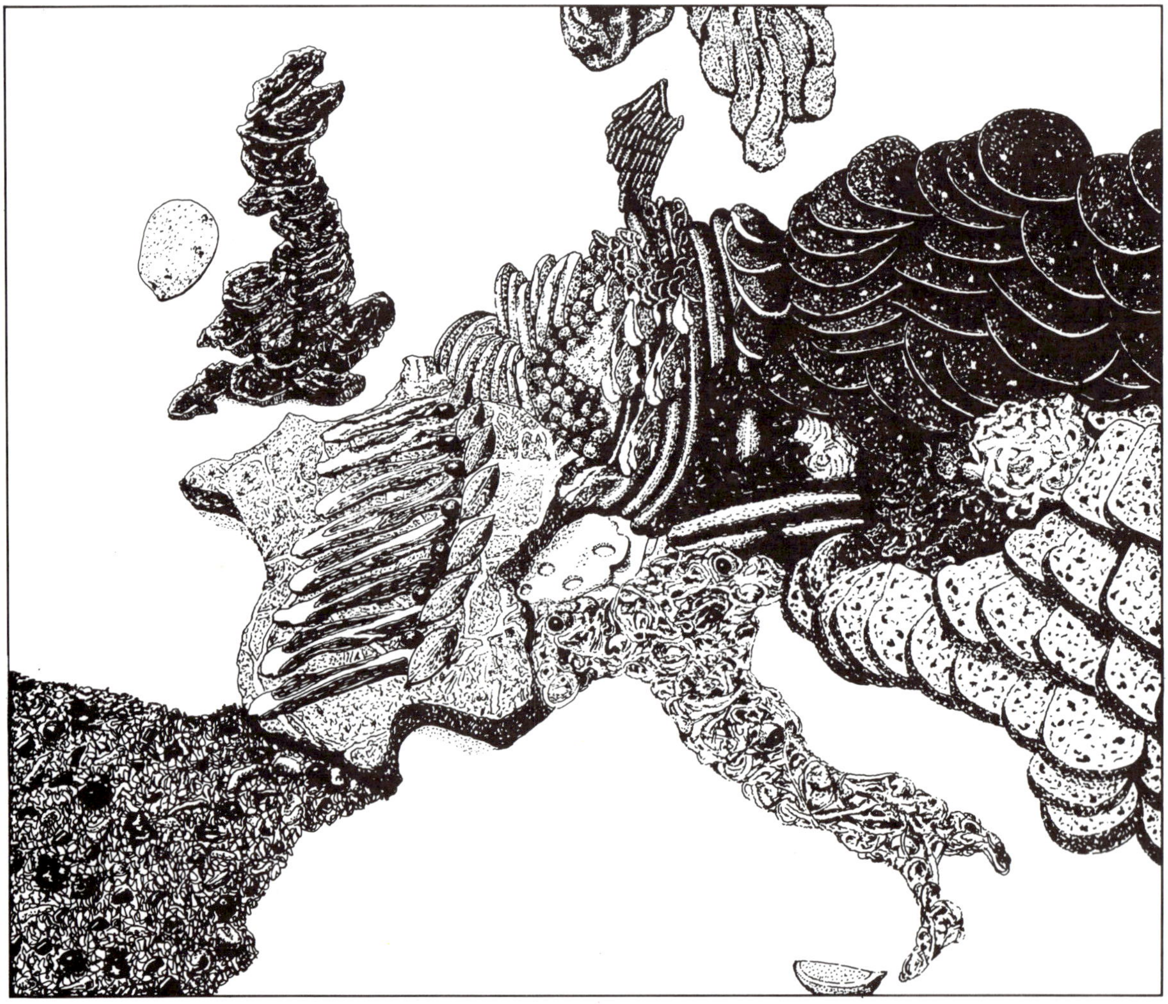

Figure 8.1 European food map

trade between the UK and the other countries increased. The UK began to import large quantities of goods from Europe, and one result was that continental foods and wines were easier to buy. More and more people from the UK travelled to European countries for their holidays, and came to like continental foods. The result has been a change in British eating and drinking habits.

Today it is common to travel abroad, make telephone calls to Europe and buy continental foods in supermarkets. These changes have come about because British people have come into contact with continental goods and continental ideas. There has been spatial interaction between the UK and Europe.

In the rest of this chapter we will describe some of the causes and effects of spatial interaction.

The effects of communication on spatial interaction

We have described how new goods and new ideas have been introduced into Britain by increased and improved communications.

One of the authors had a grandfather who lived his whole life within 10 kilometres of where he was born. He had neither telephone nor television. For this man there was little spatial interaction outside a 10 kilometre radius. The same author's parents moved much further and lived much of their lives over 100 kilometres from where they were born. The author himself has travelled to all the continents of the world, except for Antarctica, in the course of his career.

These different patterns of movement have been made possible by improvements in transport and increases in the incomes of most people. In the 1920s and 1930s only the rich went to the USA for a visit and if poorer people went they would have had to save up to emigrate. They would have travelled by train to Southampton and then by ship to New York. The journey took over 4 days. Today many people can afford a holiday in America. Most of them go by air and the journey takes 7 hours. If they are better off they can fly in *Concorde* in half that time.

Very few people in developed countries will spend their whole lives in a small area. The extent of spatial interaction is much greater than it was. The spatial interaction is made stronger by electronic communication such as television. People are aware of what is happening in the world much more quickly than they were 50 years ago. Reactions to some events are so fast that they can occur while the event is still taking place. This means that the reaction can actually affect the event. One example of this is the way the conflicts in Northern Ireland are reported all over the world soon after they occur. The reactions of some people in North America to the news are reported back to Ireland. The reactions may make matters worse by giving support to one side and antagonizing another. It is said that when the American public saw colour television pictures of American soldiers being killed and injured in Vietnam, they insisted that their Government pulled out and ended the war.

Fast communications had a double effect during the coalminers' strike in the UK in 1984–5. Firstly, the striking coalminers could travel long distances to persuade miners at other pits to join the strike. They were called **flying pickets**. In this way the ideas of the striking miners could be communicated to miners in other areas.

The second aspect of the picketing was that television showed the arguments between striking miners and those who stayed at work. This communicated the ideas of both sides to people who lived in areas where there are no coalmines.

Activities

▲ ■ **1 a** Describe the ways in which you have been influenced by ideas or goods from other areas. It may be in the areas of politics, food, fashion, music or any part of your life.

b Try to remember how these new ideas or goods reached you. Make a list of the forms of communication which were involved in giving you the idea or knowledge of the goods in the first place.

▲ ■ **2 a** Make a list of the means of transport and communication which you have used and another list of those which you have not used.

b Explain why you have not used some forms of communication.

▲ ■ ● **3** List the advantages and disadvantages of

a Rapid methods of transport

b Rapid methods of communication.

The development of transport networks

Roads, railways and air routes link places together in a complicated pattern. These patterns are called **networks**. Networks develop as more and more links are added. Figure 8.2 shows the motorway network of France as it was in 1972. Figure 8.3 shows the network in 1985. The motorway network is not finished. It will continue to develop.

Various geographers have tried to discover if networks develop in any fixed pattern. It seems that the way networks develop depends on two main factors. Firstly, it seems to depend on whether the network is to do with road, rail or air. Secondly, it depends on whether the networks are in a developed industrialized country or in a developing country.

We will begin by describing road patterns. Roads, or at least footpaths, are the oldest form of transport system.

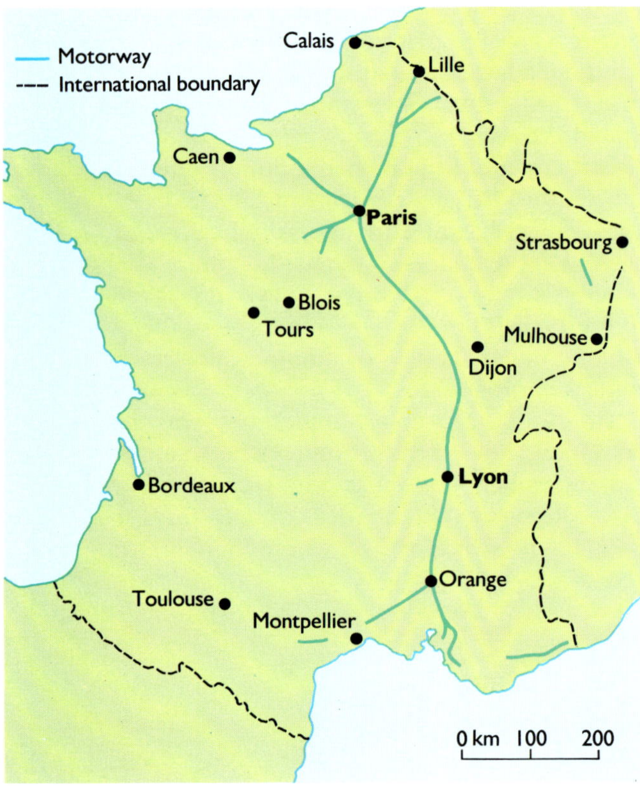

Figure 8.2 French motorways 1972

Figure 8.3 French motorways 1985

Case Study

The road pattern near Orgeval, west of Paris

Figure 8.4 shows the routeways around Orgeval, a small town west of Paris. Originally people walked from one village to another along footpaths. As more and more people used the same route the footpaths became better marked. The little lines of dashes on Figure 8.4 show some of the original footpaths. In the area south of Orgeval, one footpath goes south-eastwards to le Poult. Another footpath goes south-westwards towards the Radio Station. Many footpaths were eventually converted to small country roads. Orgeval is linked to Morainvilliers and Chambourcy by the D69 and to les Alluets-le-Roi by the D45. Some of these country roads became main roads because they linked places which grew in size. The N13 which runs just north of Orgeval became the main link between Paris, Rouen and Le Havre. The traffic along this route became so heavy that the motorway A13 was built. Paris, Rouen and Le Havre had become much more important than St. Germain-en-Laye. Because of this, the A13 was built well to the west.

The basic road pattern gradually grew and developed as more and more traffic used the routes between the towns. The motorway pattern was planned. Deliberate decisions were taken to by-pass towns so that local traffic did not clog up the motorway.

The map also shows how local features affected the routes of the roads. Old roads joining villages tend to twist and turn to follow field boundaries or to avoid steep slopes. The roads also concentrate where there are bridges over the river Seine. This happens at Meulan and Poissy. The newer roads were built from scratch with modern earthmoving equipment. They tend to sweep through the countryside in fairly straight lines and smooth curves, so that traffic may travel fast.

The road pattern is much denser in areas where there is more settlement. For example, the network is denser around Orgeval than it is to the west of Verneuil. Even more important, the road network in the whole area of the map is denser than that in many other parts of France because this area is so near Paris.

Figure 8.4 Michelin map of the area west of Paris

Figure 8.5 Dempster Highway, Yukon, Canada
a Highway with earthmoving equipment

b Notice seen on the Highway

c The country through which the Highway passes

The road pattern in France is typical of a developed country. The amount of road traffic is high and the country has fairly dense settlement. Even in developed countries, however, roads are not always like the ones you know in Europe. Figures 8.5(a), (b) and (c) show the Dempster Highway in the Yukon, Canada. This road is surfaced with gravel rolled flat. In this area the amount of road traffic is not high and the settlement is very sparse. Compare the Dempster Highway with the road in India, shown in Figure 8.6.

We will now describe the road pattern of Nigeria.

Figure 8.6 A road near a village in southern India

Case Study

The road network of Nigeria

Figure 8.7 shows the road network of Nigeria. Nigeria is a much larger country than France. It also has a larger population. Despite this, Nigeria still has far fewer roads suitable for road traffic. The reason for the sparse network is that until recently there was a limited amount of internal trade in Nigeria. The money being earned from selling oil is helping Nigeria to develop and new roads are now being built.

The road network of Nigeria has developed in a similar way to the road network in western Europe and for similar reasons. The difference is that the network in Nigeria has developed later. There was only one motorway in 1982, linking Lagos and Ibadan. Other extensions to this motorway are planned.

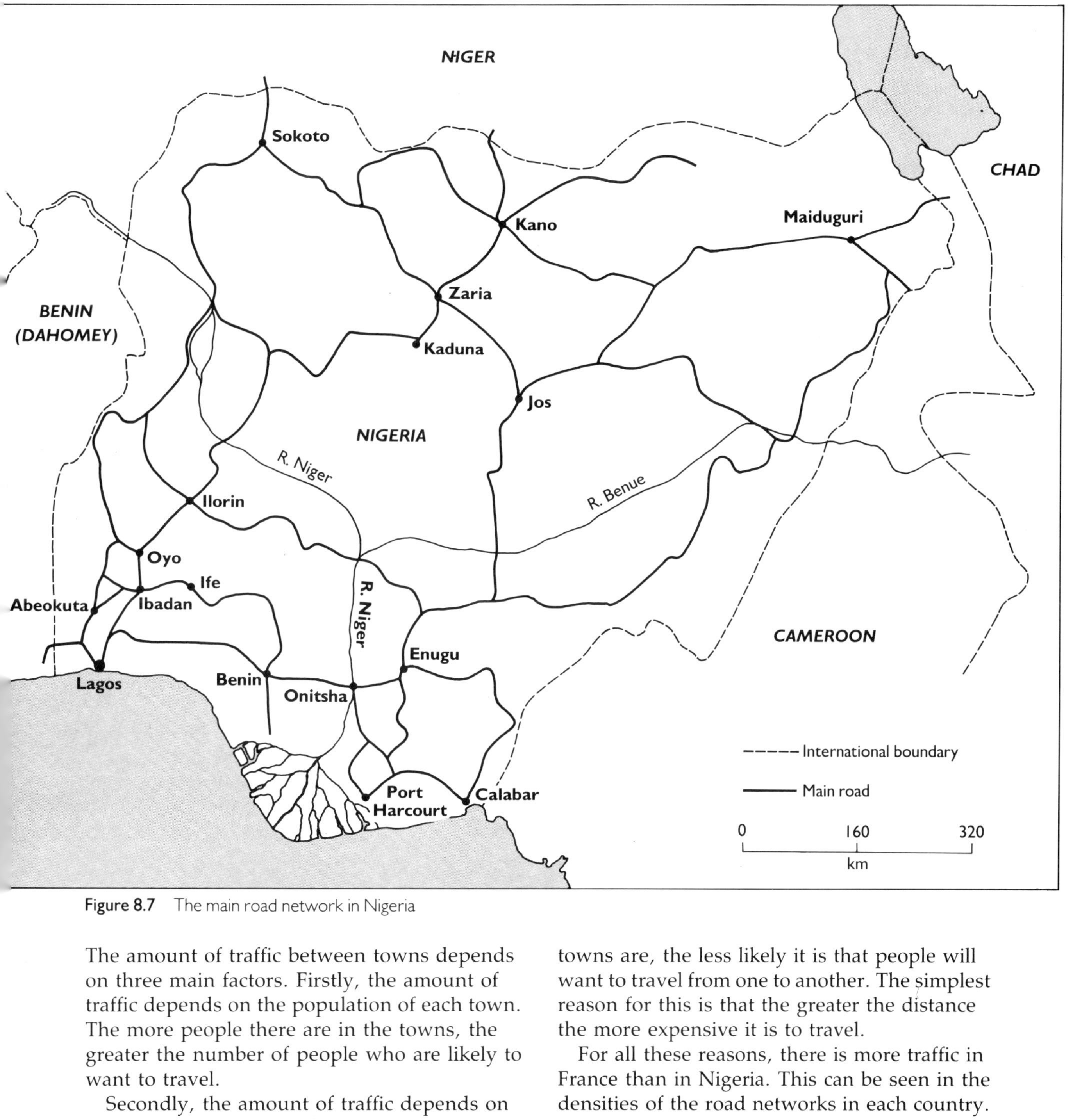

Figure 8.7 The main road network in Nigeria

The amount of traffic between towns depends on three main factors. Firstly, the amount of traffic depends on the population of each town. The more people there are in the towns, the greater the number of people who are likely to want to travel.

Secondly, the amount of traffic depends on the amount of economic activity there is in the towns. If a town has a large number of industries, many warehouses, lots of offices, banks, insurance companies and so on, it will generate more traffic than a town of the same size with very few industries or offices. This is one of the main differences between towns in developed countries and towns in less developed countries.

Thirdly, traffic depends on the distance between the towns. The further apart two towns are, the less likely it is that people will want to travel from one to another. The simplest reason for this is that the greater the distance the more expensive it is to travel.

For all these reasons, there is more traffic in France than in Nigeria. This can be seen in the densities of the road networks in each country.

Measuring the differences between networks

The differences between the road networks of France and Nigeria are easy to see on a map. It is much more difficult to compare more complicated networks 'by eye'. There are various ways of measuring networks. Two of these are the **Beta Index** and the **Accessibility Index**.

Figure 8.8 **a** The East African railway system, 1914

b The East African railway system, 1963

The Beta Index

The **Beta Index** measures the extent to which parts of a network are linked together. The ends of each route or junction along a route are called **nodes**. Each connection is called a **link**. The Beta Index is worked out by dividing the number of links by the number of nodes.

The Beta Index can be used to describe how the railway network of East Africa developed. Figures 8.8(a), (b) and (c) show the East African Railway network in 1914, 1963 and 1981.

In 1914, the railways were single lines built to bring goods to the coast for export. At this time there were 4 links (Kisumu to Nairobi and Nairobi to Mombasa count as 2 links). There were 7 nodes. The Beta Index was $4/7 = 0.57$.

By 1963, the original lines had become linked together at certain points. There were 27 links and 29 nodes. This gave a Beta Index of $27/29 = 0.93$. The Beta Index rose from 0.57 to 0.93 between 1914 and 1963.

By 1981 the linkages had become even more complicated. Although the differences between 1963 and 1981 can be seen on the maps it would be difficult to describe them in words. The Beta Indices for the two dates show the improvements clearly.

c The East African railway system, 1981

	Dunkerque	Lille	Paris	Caen	Rennes	Bordeaux	Strasbourg	Dijon	Mulhouse	Lyon	Grenoble	St. Gervais	Orange	Toulouse	Marseille	Toulon	Nice	Accessibility Index
Dunkerque	0	1	2	3	3	3	3	5	5	4	6	6	5	6	7	8	8	75
Lille	1	0	1	2	2	2	2	4	4	3	5	5	4	5	6	7	7	60
Paris	2	1	0	1	1	1	1	3	3	2	4	4	4	4	5	6	6	48
Caen	3	2	1	0	2	2	2	4	4	3	5	5	4	5	6	7	7	62
Rennes	3	2	1	2	0	2	2	4	4	3	5	5	4	5	6	7	7	62
Bordeaux	3	2	1	2	2	0	2	4	4	3	5	5	4	5	6	7	7	62
Strasbourg	3	2	1	2	2	2	0	4	4	3	5	5	4	5	6	7	7	62
Dijon	5	4	3	4	4	4	4	0	2	3	5	5	4	5	6	7	7	72
Mulhouse	5	4	3	4	4	4	4	2	0	3	5	5	4	5	6	7	7	72
Lyon	4	3	2	3	3	3	3	3	3	0	2	2	1	2	3	4	4	45
Grenoble	6	5	4	5	5	5	5	5	5	2	0	2	3	4	5	6	6	73
St. Gervais	6	5	4	5	5	5	5	5	5	2	2	0	3	4	5	6	6	73
Orange	5	4	3	4	4	4	4	4	4	1	3	3	0	1	2	3	3	52
Toulouse	6	4	4	4	4	4	4	5	5	2	4	4	1	0	3	4	4	62
Marseille	7	6	5	6	6	6	6	6	6	3	5	5	2	3	0	1	3	76
Toulon	8	7	6	7	7	7	7	7	7	4	6	6	3	4	1	0	2	89
Nice	8	7	6	7	7	7	7	7	7	4	6	6	3	4	3	2	0	91
															Total = Gross Accessibility Index			1136

Figure 8.9 Accessibility matrix for the French motorway network, 1981

The Accessibility Index

Another aspect of transport networks is the extent to which they make particular places easily accessible. The accessibility of a town can be measured simply by counting the number of road or rail links (or both) that enter the town. For example, in Figure 8.4, the village of Brezolles (north-west of Orgeval) has only 2 roads which enter the village. Orgeval itself has at least 6 roads entering the village from different directions.

Places in a network can be compared by drawing up an **accessibility matrix**. Figure 8.9 is an accessibility matrix for the French motorway network in 1981.

Figure 8.10 is a simplified version of the French motorway network in 1981. It shows the motorways of France as straight lines. The nodes (each town and motorway junction is a **node**) are shown as dots. The stretch of motorway between 2 nodes is called a **link**. This type of map is called a **topological map**. From this map it is possible to calculate the number of links which must be travelled between any 2 towns. Figure 8.9 shows that the journey from Dunkerque to Caen along the motorway networks uses 3 links. On the topological map, Figure 8.10, these links can be seen from Dunkerque to Lille to Paris to Caen.

The accessibility of a town can be worked out by adding up all the links between that town and every other town on the network. The most accessible place on the network will be the place which can be reached by the smallest number of links.

Paris seems to be the most accessible place in France from a glance at Figure 8.10. But the accessibility matrix in Figure 8.9 shows that Lyon was the most accessible town in France in 1981 with Paris a fairly close second.

If new links are added to the network, the accessibility of some towns will change. For example, a link between Bordeaux and Toulouse has been completed since 1981. This means that Toulouse is now 2 links from Paris and not 4 as in Figure 8.9.

The total of all links in the network between each town and every other town gives an idea of how well connected a network is. This is called the **Gross Accessibility Index**.

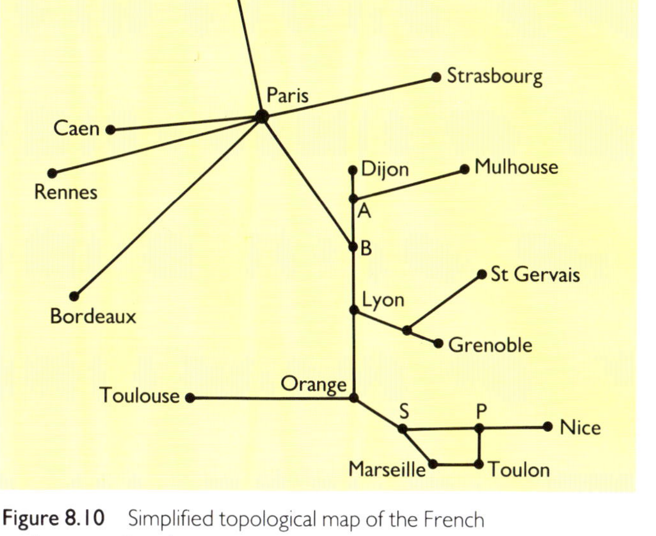

Figure 8.10 Simplified topological map of the French motorway network

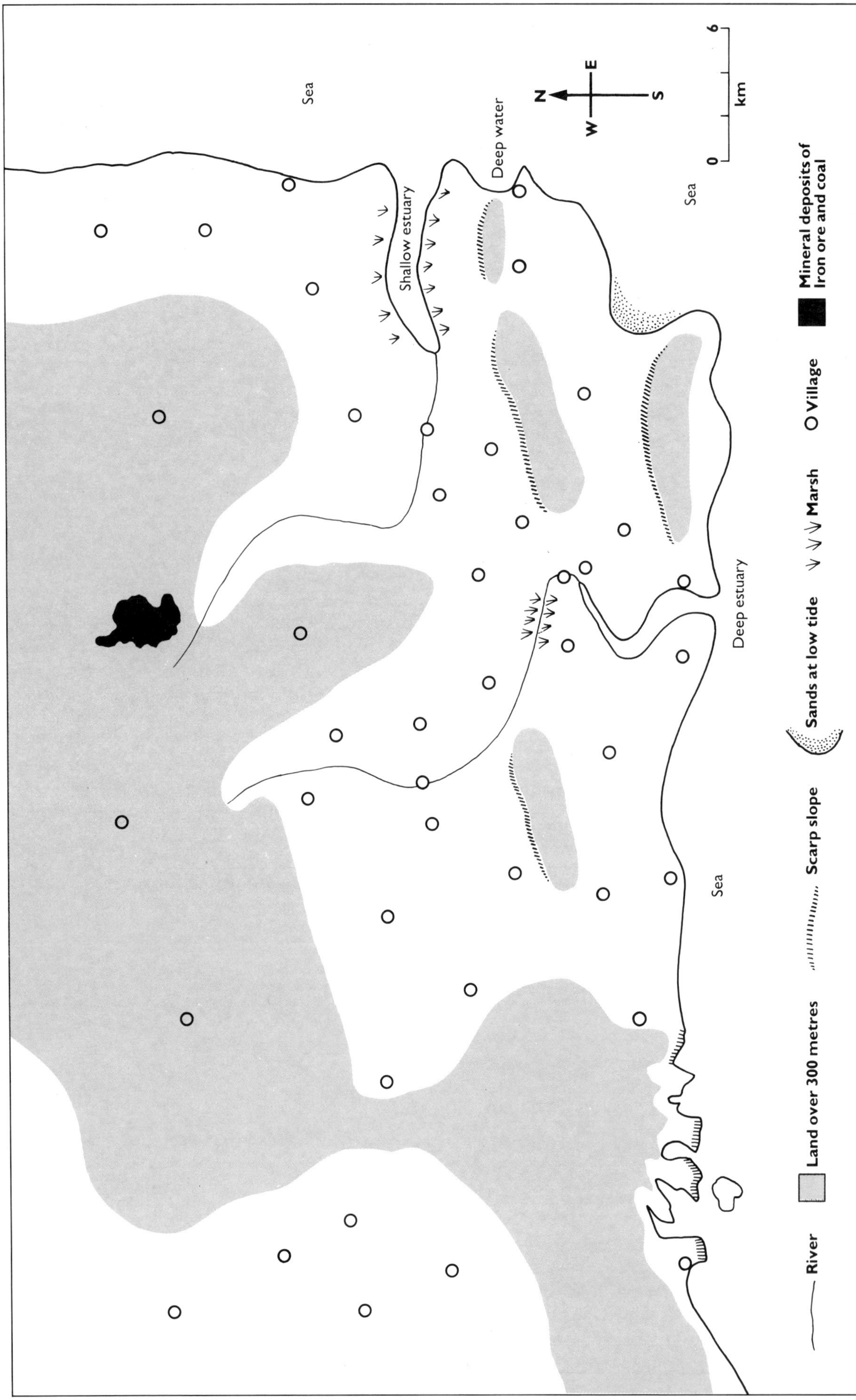

Figure 8.11 An imaginary area of western Europe

Activities

■ **4 a** Make a copy of Figure 8.11 which shows an imaginary area of western Europe in prehistoric times. There is a large number of villages in the area. The following instructions show how a road network could develop.

Stage one: simple tracks

i) Choose 8 villages which you think are well placed to develop into market towns. Mark these villages by filling in the dots.
ii) Use a light-coloured pencil (such as yellow) to draw in tracks to link each market town to 4 or 5 surrounding villages.

Stage two: a more general road network

i) Join all the villages, which were not linked in Stage one, to their nearest linked village with a dotted line in the same colour you used in Stage one.
ii) Link all the market towns together along existing tracks using a darker colour. Make sure that all these roads cross rivers at suitable points.
iii) Put a ring around 2 of the villages which are likely to have become ports and link these to the nearest market town in your darker colour. By this stage your network will be similar to real European networks in the 18th century.
iv) Choose 3 market towns which you think may have grown larger than others. Put a ring around these larger market towns in your darker colour.

Stage three

In the 19th century railways were built. Draw in railway lines in black to join the main market towns and the ports. One railway line will reach the mineral deposits of iron ore and coal. An industrial town will develop in this area. Mark it on your map. One railway line will link this area to the area to the north-east. The other railway line will link to the north-west.

Stage four

In the 20th century, motorways are built. The motorways link the main towns but do not go through them. Motorways are not usually built by enlarging existing roads but by using new routes.

You can now compare the network you have drawn with the network of the area of France shown in Figure 8.4.

b i) Draw a topological map of your road network to show the 8 market towns, the 2 ports and the industrial town. Each village and junction will be a node. Give each town a letter or a name.
ii) Draw up an accessibility matrix for your network
iii) Calculate the accessibility of each of the 11 towns.
iv) For the most accessible town on your map, describe its location and site on your map. Explain why it has become the most accessible town.
v) For the least accessible town on your map, describe its location and site on your map. Explain why it has become the least accessible town.
vi) Calculate the Gross Accessibility Index for your map. Is it the same for other pupils in your class? If not, explain why.

▲ **5** Study Figures 8.5(a), (b) and (c).

■ ● **a** Describe the road surface. Suggest the reasons why this kind of road surface was chosen. (There are several important reasons, ranging from cost to the likely effects of weathering.)

b Find the Yukon Territory on your atlas map. Explain why there is unlikely to be heavy traffic on the Dempster Highway.

c Describe the ways in which the routeways in Figures 8.5 and 8.6 are similar and how they are different. Think of
i) Their surface
ii) The traffic they will carry
iii) The areas they link together.

▲ ■ **6 a** Study the description of road networks again. Describe the three things which are most important in influencing the amount of traffic there is between two towns.

b On the journey from Lagos to Ibadan in Nigeria, the traffic was heavy on the outskirts of Lagos. It thinned out after a while, but became heavy again as Ibadan drew nearer. Explain the reason for this.

■ **7 a** Calculate the Beta Index for the French motorway network in 1985 (Figure 8.3).

b What would the Beta Index be if the following links were made?
i) Bordeaux to Clermont-Ferrand
ii) Strasbourg to Mulhouse
iii) St. Gervais to Grenoble
iv) Nice to Toulon
v) Caen to Rennes

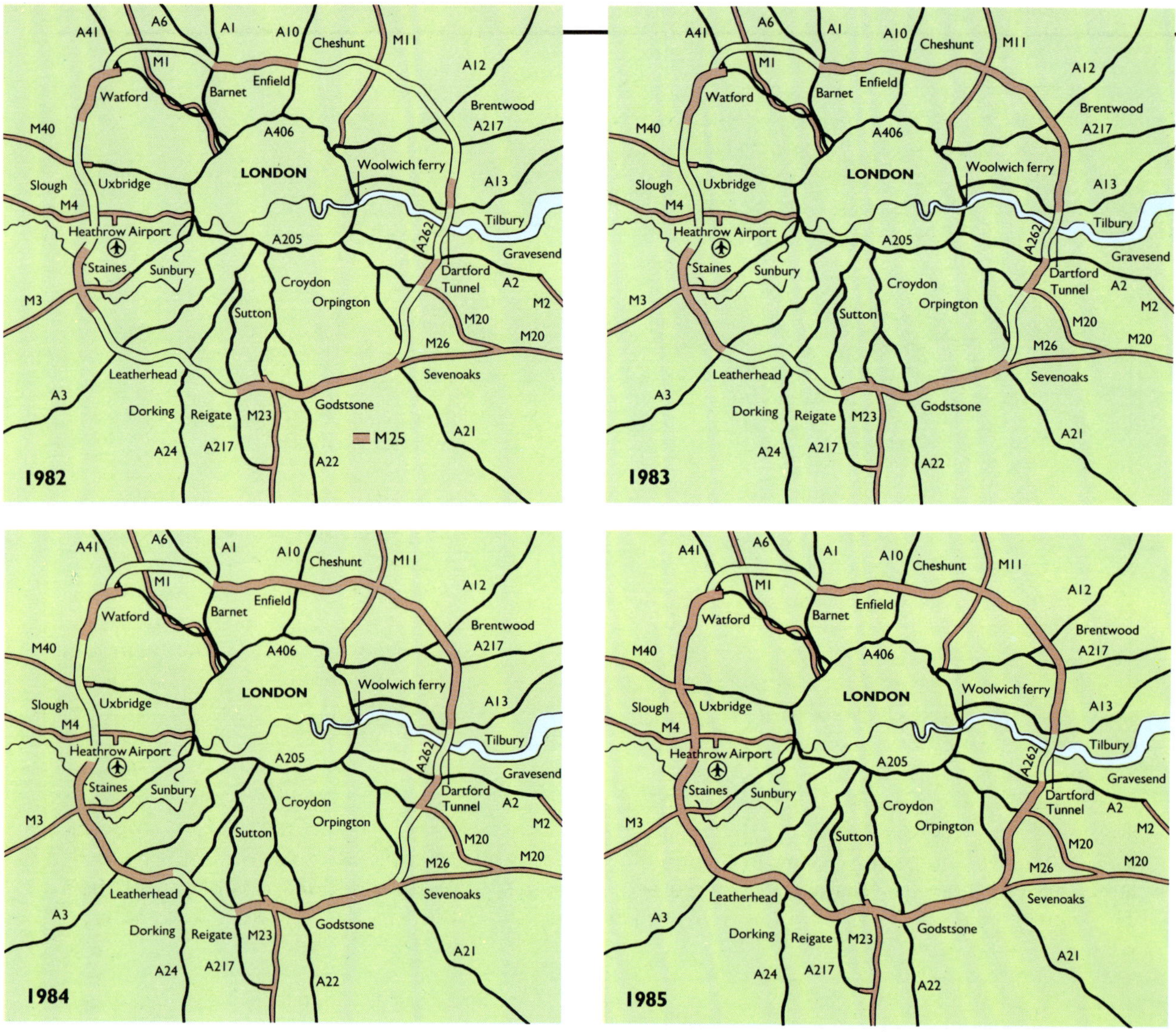

Figure 8.12 The developments of the M25 motorway around London 1982–6

The way a network develops depends partly on the history of the settlement or the development of a country or continent. In Europe, the road, rail and air networks were developed after the main settlement pattern. This meant that the transport networks were built to link existing towns. For example, the first main-line railway built in France linked Paris, Rouen and the port of Le Havre.

Where roads and motorways focus on a large town like Paris or London, the traffic can cause chaos. To ease the problems, ring roads or orbital roads are sometimes built. Figure 8.12 shows the stages in the development of the orbital motorway around London, the M25.

In countries which were not widely settled or colonized until the 19th century, such as the Prairies of Canada and the west of the USA, the railway networks were often the reasons why settlers went to particular areas. In the west of the USA the railway companies actually encouraged settlers by giving land along their routes to farmers.

Activity

▲8 Study Figure 8.12.

■ a Describe the ways in which the M25 will
● affect the British motorway network.

b List the advantages and disadvantages of the M25 scheme. You should consider its effects on
  i) Travellers from the south coast to the Midlands
  ii) Central London traffic congestion
  iii) Farmers on the outskirts of London
  iv) Towns and villages around London such as Leatherhead, Godstone and Sevenoaks.

Worldwide transport

Transport over very long distances is now very much more common than it used to be. Because worldwide transport is more common, the amount of spatial interaction between places far apart has increased.

There are four main means of long distance transport. These are railway trains, road trucks, ships and aircraft. Railway trains are usually most efficient for long journeys over continental land masses where no seas need to be crossed. There are transcontinental road and railway routes in North America, Europe, Asia and Australia. Because they have developed later, there are no transcontinental railway routes in Africa or South America.

Railways

When railways were the main form of rapid transport, railway companies often made good profits. Now that railways have to compete with airlines for carrying passengers and high value goods over long distances they can rarely make a profit. In the USA, the railway network was running down badly in the 1960s. The main use of railways over long distances was to carry bulky raw materials, which have a fairly low value, such as metal ores and coal. Because of this, the Government did not want the railways to close down. The Government set up the National Railroad Passenger Corporation (AMTRAK) to renovate some of the main long distance routes. This meant that the routes stayed open for freight traffic as well. Figure 8.13 shows the transcontinental railway routes run by AMTRAK.

These routes are subsidized by the American Government from taxpayers' money. Although it is costly to subsidize railways, most countries in the world have decided it is better for their quality of life and for their economies to keep their railways running.

Figure 8.13 Main transcontinental railways in the USA

Activities

▲ **9** Study Figure 8.13.
■ **a** Describe the general pattern of these
● routes.
b Compare Figure 8.13 with an atlas map of North America. How has the physical geography of North America influenced the routes of the railway?
c Work out the Beta Index for the main transcontinental railway routes of the USA.
d **i)** Compare the main railway route network of the USA with that of East Africa in 1963.
ii) Is this a fair comparison?

▲ **10** Study Figures 8.14(a), (b) and (c) which show
■ the railway network in the USA in 1860,
● 1884 and 1913.
a Describe the way in which the railway network developed from 1860 to 1913.
b With the help of an atlas map of North America and what you already know about the USA, explain why the network developed in this way.
c Compare these maps with Figure 8.13. Explain why the American Government had to help the railway companies in the 1960s.

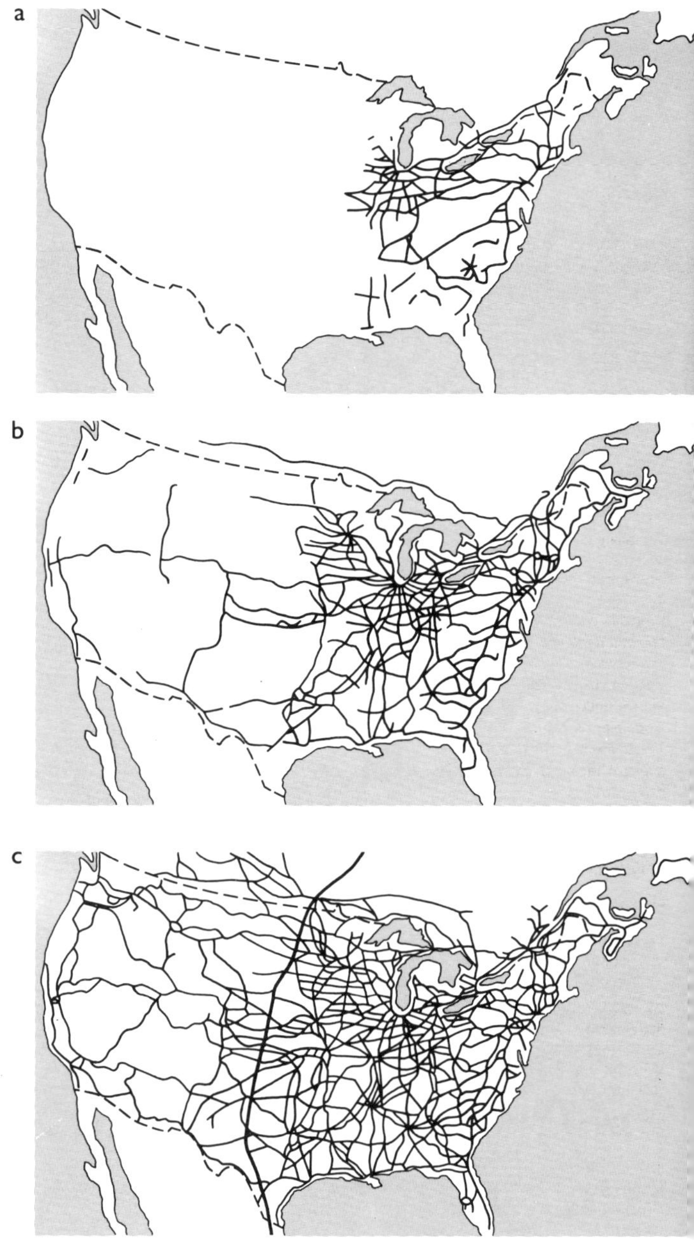

Figure 8.14 The development of railways in the USA

Shipping

Shipping routes are cheaper than railway routes because no tracks need to be provided. Most ships, except in socialist countries, are owned by private companies. The shipping business has changed greatly in the last 25 years. There are 3 major changes. Firstly, few passengers are now carried except on short routes such as those across the English Channel or to Ireland. This is because sea travel is slow compared with flying. It is also very expensive, because passengers need to eat and sleep for several days or weeks on board ship. The fare by sea to Australia is 4 times the air fare and it takes 28 times as long! Secondly, the single most important cargo now carried by sea is petroleum. Petroleum is carried in huge tankers. Because it is more important for there to be a constant supply of petroleum to the buying countries than for them to get a particular cargo of oil at a particular time, the tankers are large but slow. To save running costs, most of the supertankers only have one propeller and they are navigated automatically for most of their journeys. Thirdly, most cargoes other than oil are handled in containers. The containers can be carried by rail, road or ship, but need special cranes to move them from one type of transport to another. They also need special types of railway truck, lorry or ship to carry them.

The changes from general cargo ships to large tankers and container ships have meant that new types of ships have had to be built, and new port facilities are needed to handle the ships. Figures 8.15, 8.16 and 8.17 show how the port of Fos-Marseilles in Southern France handles containers.

The changes in the type of handling facilities have often led to new port developments being built in a different area from the original port. In

Figure 8.15 The container port at Fos-sur-Mer

Marseille, the new container port and new oil tanker terminals were built at Fos, 40 km west of the original port. In London, the new container port was built at Tilbury, 30 km east of the old docks. The oil tanker terminals are also downstream near the mouth of the Thames Estuary. The new port at Fos and the new docks and terminals at the mouth of the Thames were needed because the new ships are too large to enter the old docks.

In London, most of the old dock basins have been closed except for St. Katherine's Dock. St. Katherine's Dock and the 'Vieux Port' of Marseille are now used as marinas for pleasure boats and private yachts.

Caillard container gantry crane

Travelling gantry crane for ISO containers of 20 and 40 ft and sea land containers of 35 ft.
Lifting capacity: 40 tonnes - Weight: 660 tonnes approx.
(including 200 tonnes of concrete ballast)

Electrical power supply	380 V ± 10%
Maximum jib radius from front rail	36 m
From rear rail (15 m track)	8 m
Total horizontal travel of carriage	59 m
Height under rolling beam	30 m
Total pier height, sea side	52 m approx.
Lift, from spreader to quay	25 m
Vertical hook travel below quay	19 m
Passageway between oblique pier struts	16 m (average)
Maximum resistance per roller in the most unfavourable conditions of wind and load:	
SEA side	35 tonnes approx.
LAND side	42 tonnes approx.
Lifting speeds:	
Starting time	2 sec.
Working speed with 30 tonne load	0.75 m/sec.
Working speed with no load	1.65 m/sec.
(lifting control by Ward-Leonard equipment)	
Carriage speeds:	
Starting time	6 sec.
Stopping time:	6 sec.
Working speed with 30 tonne load	2m/sec.
(travel control by Ward-Leonard equipment)	
Carriage turning speed	90° in 30 sec.
Gantry speeds:	
Starting time:	6 sec.
Stopping time:	4 sec.
Working speed with 30 tonne load	0.75 m/sec.
Capable of working in winds of up to	15 m/s
Total time required to raise front jib	5 min.
Number of cycles per hour	20 approx. (i.e. 20 containers per hour)

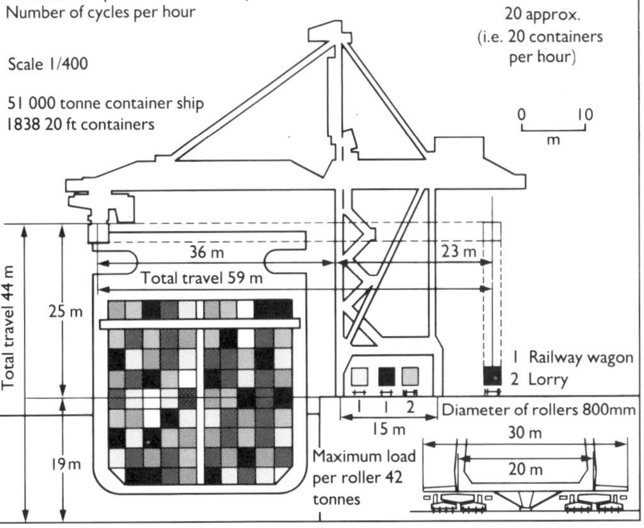

Figure 8.16 A container gantry

Activities

▲■● 11 Study Figures 8.15, 16 and 17 which show some of the ways ships are loaded and unloaded at Fos-Marseille.

a Describe the advantages of this type of cargo handling over older methods.

b i) Describe the kinds of port facilities which are needed to make this kind of handling a success.

ii) Describe the kind of port layout which is needed to make this a success.

c 'Modern methods of cargo handling save labour but waste space.' Explain whether or not this is true.

▲■● 12 Figure 6.12 showed the land use around the port of Fos-Marseille. The position of Fos is shown on the map in Figure 6.11.

a Describe the kinds of industries which have been located around Fos.

b Suggest why each of these types of industries has been located here.

▲■● 13 Fos is both an oil port and a container port. Are there any disadvantages in one port handling both kinds of traffic?

Figure 8.17 Roll-on roll-off cargo handling at Fos-sur-Mer

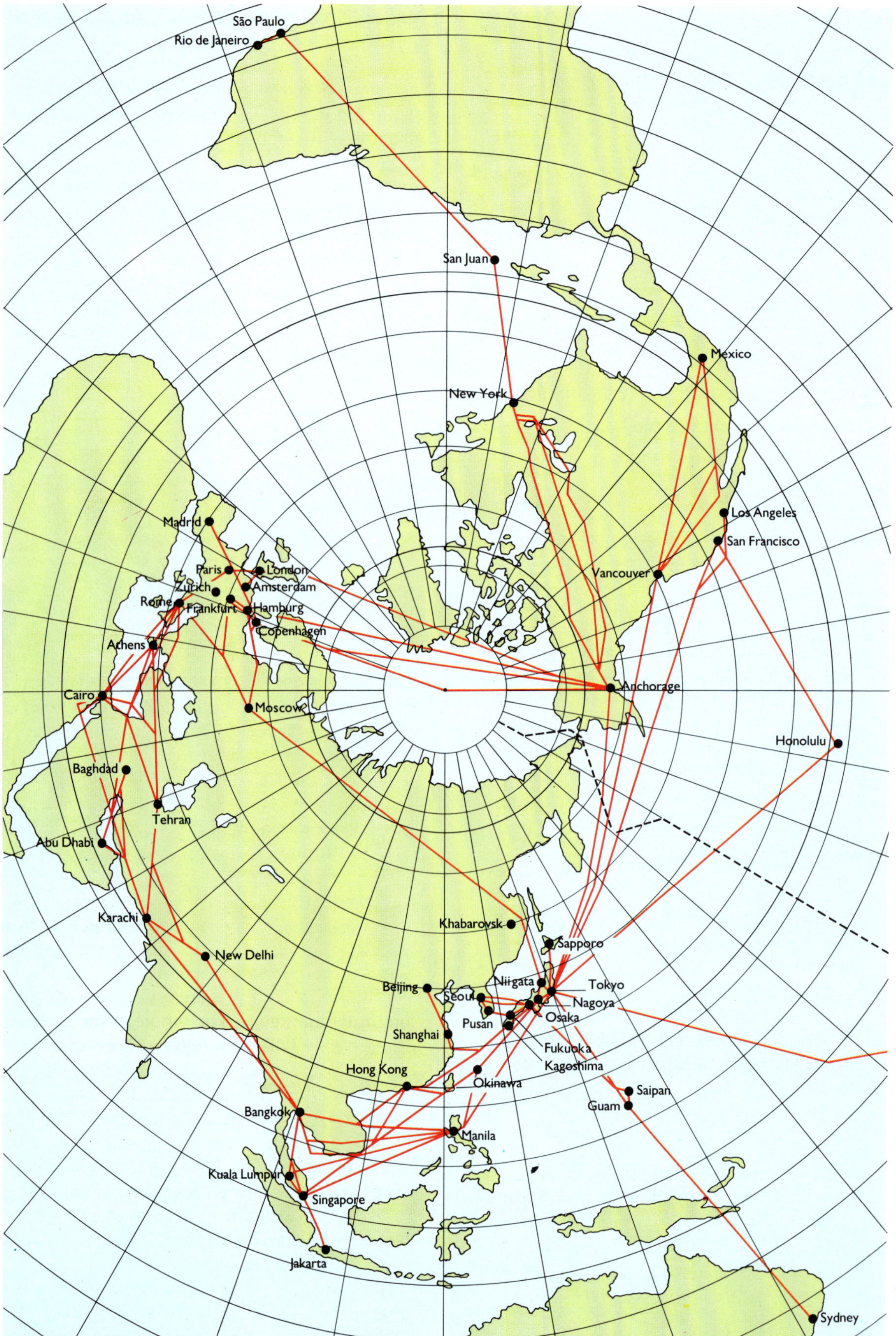

Figure 8.18 Japan Air Lines system

Air Travel

Air travel has expanded greatly since the 1960s. Today most long distance travellers go by air. The cost of air transport was steadily falling until the oil price rises of 1973. These rises pushed up the price of air travel. The price increases and the world trade depression have meant that the rate of growth of air transport has not been as fast in the 1970s and 1980s as it was in the 1960s.

Most airlines use wide bodied aircraft on long distance routes. These planes carry 300 to 400 passengers. Airlines are usually owned nationally rather than by multinational companies, so they are usually based on a country's capital city. Their routes fan out from that capital. Figure 8.18 shows the main routes of the Japan Air Line Corporation.

Air travel is very fast, but it does have some disadvantages. One of the greatest disadvantages is called **jet lag**.

One of the authors of this book recently went to Tokyo. This is how he described his journey back to London. You can follow the route on Figure 8.18.

'I left Tokyo at 2130 hrs on the Saturday night. The route was from Tokyo to Anchorage in Alaska, where we stopped for refuelling, and then on, over Greenland, to London. Although I left Tokyo at 2130 hrs on Saturday night, I arrived in Anchorage at 1000 hrs on Saturday morning. After an hour's stop, we left at 1100 hrs Saturday and arrived in London at 0500 hrs on Sunday morning.

My journey took only 7 hrs and 30 minutes if it is worked out by local times. In fact, I was travelling for 16 hours and 30 minutes. This is because of the 9 hour time difference between Tokyo and London.

Although I arrived in London early on Sunday morning, by 1400 hrs (2 o'clock in the afternoon) it was already 2300 hrs (11 o'clock at night) in Tokyo. My body was still working on Tokyo time, so I felt like sleeping. It took several days before I became readjusted to London time and woke and slept at normal times.'

You will have noticed that the traveller arrived in Anchorage at 1000 hrs on Saturday morning although he had not left Tokyo until 2130 hrs on Saturday night. This is because he had crossed the International Date Line between Tokyo and Anchorage.

Time zones and the International Date Line

Figure 8.19 is a diagram of the Earth divided into sectors 15° longitude wide. The Earth spins

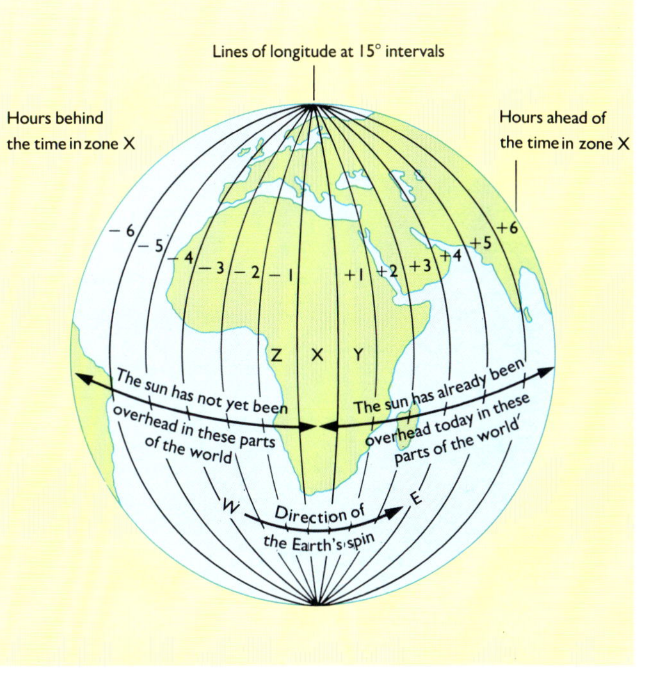

Figure 8.19 The Earth's theoretical time zones

from west to east. It turns on its axis once every 24 hours. This means that the Earth spins through 360° in 24 hours (or 15° every hour, or 1° every 4 minutes). Wherever the sun is directly overhead, the sun time is 12 noon. It would be inconvenient if places only 1 or 2 degrees of longitude apart kept different times, so the Earth is divided into zones roughly 15° wide and all places within one zone keep the same time. The zones are called **standard time zones** and the time in each zone is called **local time**.

Imagine the sun is overhead at the line of longitude marked X. The whole of the zone 7½° on each side will have noon at the same standard time. The zone with Y in it had the sun overhead an hour before. When it is 12 noon in zone X, it will be 1300 hrs in zone Y, i.e. 1 hour after noon (or, in Latin, *post meridian* – p.m.).

The zone with Z in it has not yet reached the point where the sun is overhead. This will happen in 1 hour's time. The time in zone Z is therefore 1100 hrs – 1 hour before noon, (or, in Latin, *ante meridian* – a.m.).

The zones do not work out as neatly on the map as they do on this diagram. Figure 8.20 shows the actual time zones of the world. On Figure 8.20, you will notice that the zone

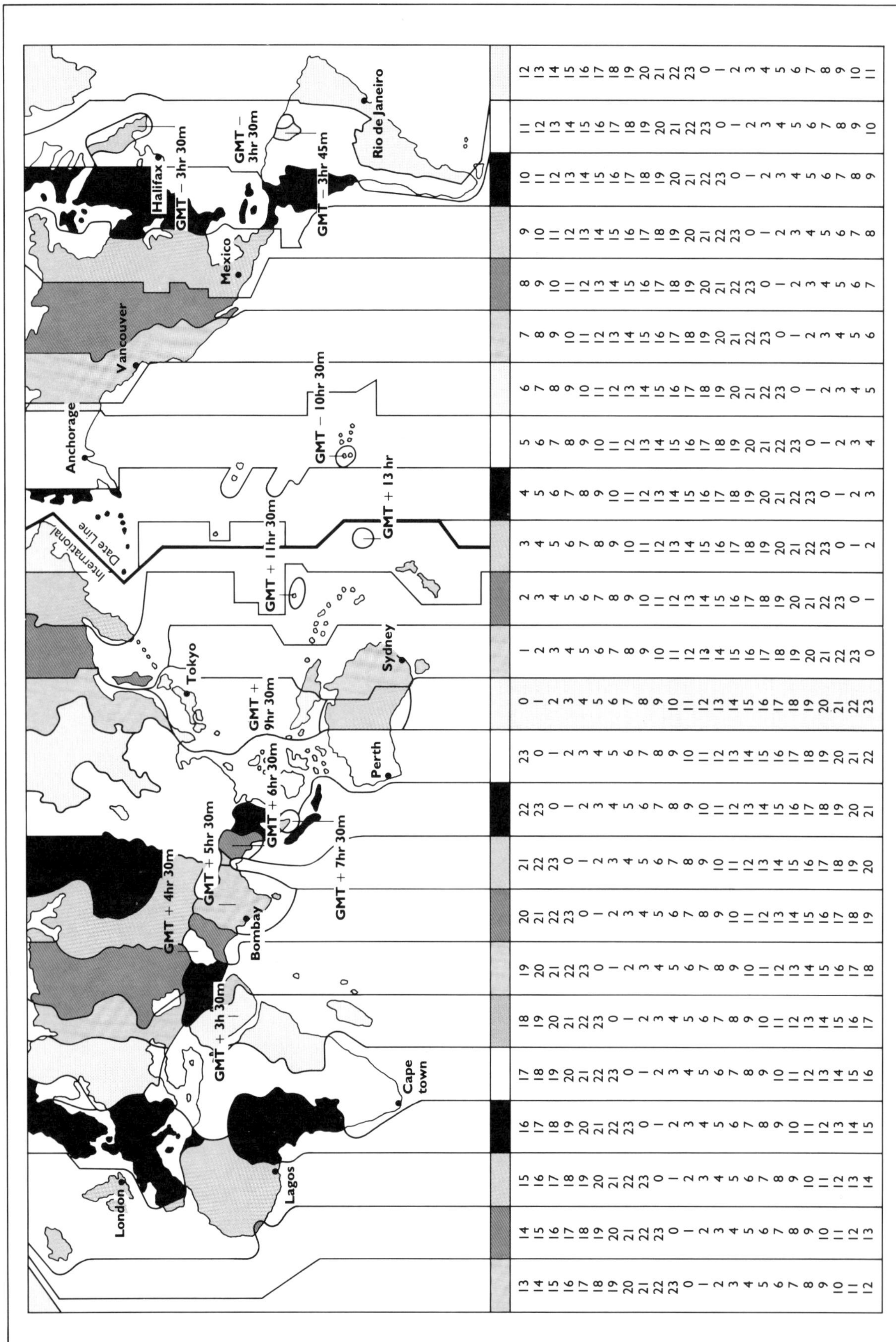

Figure 8.20 The Earth's standard time zones

boundaries are moved from their exact line of longitude so that smaller countries only have one time zone.

This system has its problems. Imagine two aircraft flying round the world from London. One goes eastwards and the other goes westwards. If they both reach 165°E and 165°W respectively at 1500 hrs Monday, London time, the local time for the plane flying eastwards would be 0200 hrs on Tuesday. For the plane flying westwards, the local time would be 0400 hrs on Monday. If they eventually passed one another at 180° longitude at 0300 hrs, one pilot would think it was Tuesday and the other would think it was Monday. To avoid this confusion, it was agreed that the 180° line of longitude would act as an International Date Line and people who crossed it by ship or by aircraft would change dates. When you cross the Date Line from west to east, you go back to the previous day. When you cross it from east to west, you go forward to the next day.

What happend to the Boeing 747 flying from Tokyo to London was as follows. By the time it had flown eastwards from Tokyo and reached the International Date Line, it was already 0430 hrs on Sunday morning by local time. When it crossed the Date Line, the calendar was put back to the same time on the day before, that is, Saturday. This made the time just over the Date Line 0430 hrs Saturday morning. By the time the aircraft reached Anchorage, it was 1000 hrs Saturday morning.

After a one-hour stop, the aircraft flew on eastwards to London. Each time it crossed a time zone, one hour was put on. This made the rest of Saturday and early Sunday go very quickly. When at last the aircraft landed in London at 0500 hrs on Sunday morning, the local time back in Anchorage was still only 1900 hrs Saturday.

For many people the effects of the changes in time is only an inconvenience. It makes them tired for a few days and causes them to wake up, perhaps hungry, at odd hours of the night. However, many businessmen and politicians fly long distances for important meetings which may affect all of us. In earlier chapters we have described the importance of negotiations between companies and governments, for example Ford in Spain and Fiat in Brazil. No one is yet quite sure what effect jet lag may have on the people who make important decisions. It would seem unlikely that someone who has flown a long distance in a short time will be as clear-headed as someone who has not.

Activities

▲■ **14** Study Figure 8.18.

a **i)** In which hemisphere do Japan Air Lines (JAL) mainly fly?
ii) Which continents are served least by JAL?

b In the list of routes below, some travellers leaving Tokyo at 1000 hrs on Monday would arrive at their destination on a different day. Describe the routes that each flight is likely to take and say on which day each flight is likely to land.
i) Tokyo to Bangkok
ii) Tokyo to Moscow
iii) Tokyo to San Francisco
iv) Tokyo to São Paulo
v) Tokyo to Karachi
vi) Tokyo to New York
vii) Tokyo to Sydney
viii) Tokyo to Honolulu
ix) Tokyo to Singapore
x) Tokyo to Mexico

c On the Tokyo–Anchorage–London route, in which direction will the plane be flying
i) Between Tokyo and Anchorage?
ii) Between Anchorage and London?

▲■ **15** Study Figure 8.20. If the time is 1500 hrs in London on Sunday, 3 February 1987, what time and day will it be at

a Cape Town
b Bombay
c Vancouver
d Mexico City
e Sydney
f Anchorage
g Tokyo
h Halifax
i Rio de Janeiro
j Lagos

▲■ **16** Figure 8.21 (overleaf) shows Japan Air Lines routes on a Mercator projection. Compare Figure 8.21 with the previous map in Figure 8.18.

differences between the two maps. (You should compare the direction of the lines of longitude and the sizes of the countries.) How does Figure 8.21 show routes over the North Pole to Anchorage?

b Write a few sentences to explain why most JAL routes in Asia go around the southern edge of the continent.

c On which map does the journey from Tokyo to London look further?
i) Via Anchorage **ii)** Via Moscow

d Use the distance chart on Figure 8.21 to calculate the distances between Tokyo and London.
i) Via Anchorage **ii)** Via Moscow

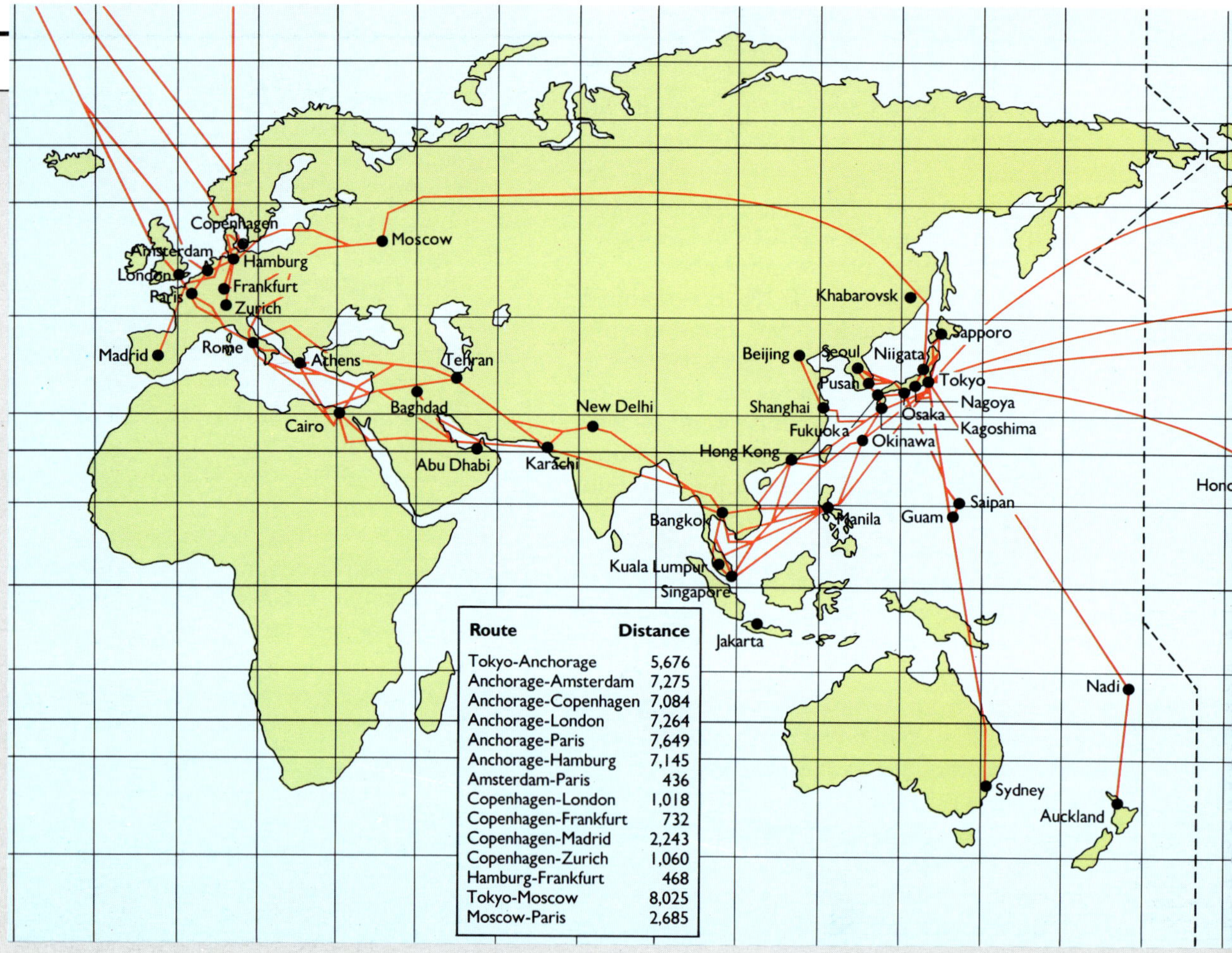

Route	Distance
Tokyo-Anchorage	5,676
Anchorage-Amsterdam	7,275
Anchorage-Copenhagen	7,084
Anchorage-London	7,264
Anchorage-Paris	7,649
Anchorage-Hamburg	7,145
Amsterdam-Paris	436
Copenhagen-London	1,018
Copenhagen-Frankfurt	732
Copenhagen-Madrid	2,243
Copenhagen-Zurich	1,060
Hamburg-Frankfurt	468
Tokyo-Moscow	8,025
Moscow-Paris	2,685

Figure 8.21 Japan Air Lines routes and distance chart

▼ **Figure 8.22** Air Canada flight chart

te	Distance
:ow-London	2,658
:ow-Rome	2,704
:ow-Frankfurt	2,234
ow-Copenhagen	1,676
.ta-Khabarovsk	1,525
e-London	1,484
ns-Rome	1,185
e-Paris	1,136
ns-Paris	2,206
o-Bangkok	4,898
Delhi-Tehran	2,234
:hi-Abu Dhabi	1,352
Dhabi-Cairo	2,763
:hi-Baghdad	2,688

Activities

e Write a few sentences to explain why several of the JAL routes to Europe go over the Arctic.

▲ ■ 17 Imagine you are going to make 2 journeys. One is from London to Lagos in Nigeria. The other is from London to Atlanta, Georgia, in the USA. Both these journeys will take about 9 hours.

a Use Figure 8.18 to work out on which journey you would be likely to suffer from jet lag.

b Write a paragraph to explain why you would suffer from jet lag on that journey.

▲ ■ 18 Figure 8.22 shows the flight path of an Air Canada Boeing 747 from London (UK) to Winnipeg (Canada).

a Winnipeg is almost due west of London, but the aircraft followed a north-westerly path, then a south-westerly path. Write a sentence or two to explain why this was the case.

b The aircraft left London at 1400 hrs Greenwich Mean Time and arrived at Winnipeg at 1700 hrs Central Standard Time. How long did the journey take? (See Figure 8.19.)

c The aircraft flew at an average speed of 800 kilometres per hour over the ground.

i) Work out the flight distance from London to Winnipeg.

ii) Work out the distance in a straight line from London to Winnipeg on a Mercator map in your atlas.

iii) Write a sentence or two to explain why there is this difference.

▲ ■ ● 19 In the 1980s there have been several incidents of hijacking international aircraft.

a Why are aircraft particularly liable to terrorist activities?

b Explain your view of hijackers. Are there any reasons which could make it right to hold an aircraft and its passengers to ransom?

c Write a paragraph to suggest ways in which:

i) Terrorist hijacking can be prevented.

ii) Governments and airlines should act if a plane is hijacked. (Should the governments give in to save the lives of the hostages, or should they refuse to negotiate with terrorists?)

Other forms of communication

Spatial interaction is made much easier by telecommunications. We are all used to radio and television broadcasts from all over the world. Business people can contact one another across the world very easily. New types of telecommunications are being developed all the time. Types of telecommunications in use in the mid 1980s include the following.

Telegrams and cablegrams

These were the first form of rapid communication for messages. The equipment for sending and receiving messages was originally at telegraph offices, along the telegraph wires. This meant that the sender had to travel to the telegraph office (which was often a post office) to send the message. At the other end, a messenger had to be sent to the receiving person's home or business. Today this is a costly and slow process. In the UK, telegrams are used to contact people overseas only when other types of telecommunication are not available or have failed.

Telex

The telex system is like the telegram, but it can link 2 people or businesses directly. Each person or business has a teleprinter. The teleprinters are linked directly by wires or radio through the telephone system. A message is typed in at one end and the teleprinter at the other end prints it out. The advantages of this system are speed and the fact that there is a written record of the message at both ends.

Telephone

The telephone system developed from the telegraph system. Today the links between telephone exchanges may be through cables, radio or microwave transmissions. Satellites are used to 'bounce' the messages around the curve of the Earth. The telephone system is now used for direct speech, pictures, written messages and computer links.

Fax

Fax is short for **facsimile transmission**. A fax machine is really a type of photocopier which can send pictures, diagrams or written messages through the telephone system to another fax machine which reproduces it on paper. However, fax machines can only link directly to each other, and the people at both ends must have the same type of machine.

Computers

Computers lie at the centre of most of the new forms of telecommunications. Since written messages, speech and pictures can all be stored as electronic pulses, computers can be used to store them and send them through the telephone system anywhere in the world. One of the problems of fast telecommunications is caused by the different time zones. A telephone call from Brisbane made at 9 a.m. Monday, Eastern Standard Time (Australia) reaches London at 11 p.m. Sunday night GMT. For this reason electronic mailing systems are becoming more popular.

A typical electronic mailing system includes a central 'postbox' computer connected to the telephone system. Each user has a personal mailbox number and a small personal computer. This can be wired to the user's telephone or linked to any telephone in the world by a modem. To send an electronic letter, the sender prepares the message on their computer. The message is then sent at high speed through the telephone system to the mailbox computer. When the person to whom the message is addressed next dials the system, he or she will be told that there is mail waiting to be read. The message can then be 'read' by the receiver's personal computer and either displayed on a monitor screen straight away or stored on disk to be displayed later.

There are several advantages of this system. Messages are sent very quickly and this saves money on telephone time. Messages can be sent and received at any time in the 24 hours. The system is also more secure than telex. A telex message can be left lying round for anyone to read.

Figure 8.23 shows the costs of sending a letter by the different methods in 1986.

Computers can also be used to gain access to public information. The British Telecom Prestel Service allows individuals to read on their television screens information held in a central computer.

All the developments in communication have created more spatial interaction. In other words, people in one part of the world can find out much faster what is happening in other parts. This is good for business and it can allow people to react to events in other parts of the world.

The approximate cost of sending a single page, 400 word letter from Edinburgh to London is

letter post:	18p (first class)
delivery time:	1–3 days
telex:	50p approx
delivery time:	8 minutes
FAX:	51p approx
delivery time:	30 s to 3 minutes, depending on machine
Telecom Gold:	18p
(British Telecom electronic mailing service)	
delivery time:	1 minute

Figure 8.23 Costs of telecommunications, 1986

Unfortunately, there can be a bad side. Any electronic communication from telephone to computer information store can be intercepted by government agents or others. The information could be used to harm individuals. Rapid communication can mean that information can be sent very quickly and perhaps before its truth has been tested. Before the age of rapid communication, a journalist abroad could spend time in preparing a report before sending it to the newspaper office. He or she would probably have time to check all the facts. Today people expect up-to-date information about new happenings within hours. This could mean that reports are made before all the facts are known. If people or politicians in other countries react to these reports too quickly, mistakes could be made.

Activities

▲■● **20** Look back at the section on office location in Chapter 6 (page 158). Explain why when deciding on the location of a new office block, access to a good telephone exchange and many telephone lines is becoming more important than a central location in a town.

▲■● **21** Telecommunication can improve business efficiency, particularly through computers. Write two or three paragraphs to describe ways in which computers could improve the quality of life for people.

Conclusion

In the 20th century there has been an enormous increase in spatial interaction. More people travel further more often than they used to. A greater variety of goods is available further from where they were made than ever before. This has happened because of improved technology.

There is also a greater exchange of information across the world than ever before.

For these reasons, people often say that the world is a smaller place than it used to be. Some people talk about 'Spaceship Earth'. By this they mean that we are all passengers on a spaceship which is isolated from the other planets. Although some people have travelled outside 'Spaceship Earth', they cannot escape permanently. This makes it important that we should all look after our environment on Earth. It is also important that everyone stays on good terms with the other passengers on 'Spaceship Earth'. One way to stay on good terms with people is to talk to them and listen to their views. This has been made easier by the development of telecommunications.

Unfortunately spatial interaction still occurs in a destructive way and wars can result. Communication may then be by war planes and missiles. The same technology which controls communication between business computers can be used to control the rockets and other missiles of war.

9
Caring for the Earth

Geographers study environments. These include the natural environments such as mountains, hills, rivers, valleys and the sea. Geographers are also interested in environments which have been created by human beings, such as farms, villages, towns and conurbations. Both the natural environments and the human environments are changing all the time. Geographers say that environments are in a **dynamic state**. Changes in both natural environments and in human environments are sometimes very slow and sometimes very fast. In Chapter 2 we described the slow movements of the tectonic plates of the Earth. We also described the faster changes which can occur during a volcanic eruption. In Chapter 7 we described the slow changes which led to the growth of many of our towns and cities. In Chapters 6 and 8 we described some of the effects of the extremely rapid changes in communications.

In the last chapter we described the increase in spatial interaction between different parts of the Earth. Because what is done in one area can affect other areas, we should think of the whole Earth as being our environment. We have given examples of the ways in which the different parts of the world affect one another in each chapter of this book. Here we will just mention a few of them.

Pollution of the Rhine in the Ruhr area of Germany affects the quality of the water which reaches the Netherlands.

If some countries of Europe use nets with small mesh and overfish the North Sea, then all the other fishing nations around the North Sea suffer from smaller catches.

If one of the richer nations decides to put an import duty on textiles coming from a developing country, this may cause unemployment in the developing country.

Migration of large numbers of people from one country to another may cause trouble between the native peoples and the immigrants. This has happened in many countries including the UK. Sometimes this trouble is kept alive for many generations as has happened in Northern Ireland.

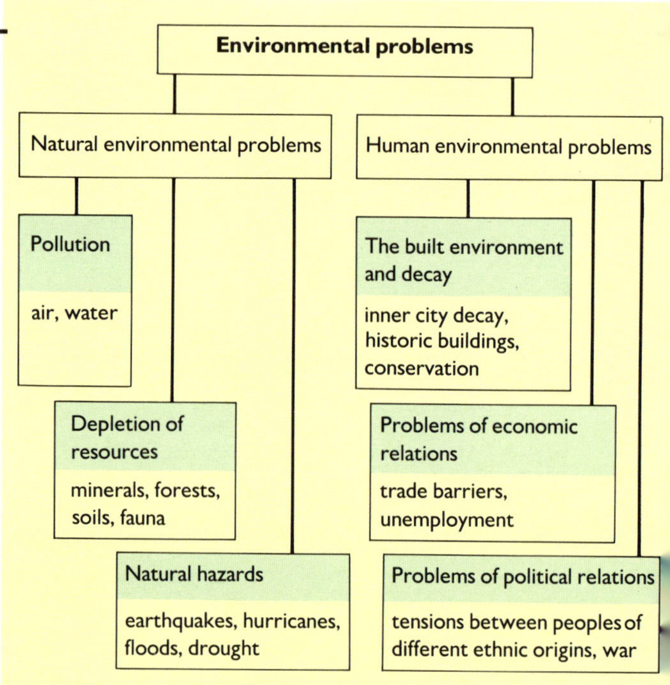

Figure 9.1 Types of environmental problems

Sometimes conflicts between different countries can develop into wars. Wars cause great suffering. They also do great damage to both the natural environment and the human environment. In Vietnam, for example, many people were killed, many cities were destroyed and the forests and soils were damaged by the chemical weapons which were used in the wars.

The ultimate catastrophe could be nuclear war. If you studied Chapters 2 and 3 carefully, you will realize that nuclear war would inevitably affect the whole planet.

Figure 9.1 summarizes all these problems which affect our environment.

Fortunately, our understanding of what went wrong in the past is improving. This means that ways of preventing damage to our environment and conserving natural resources can be developed. There is also the possibility of dealing with the economic problems and political problems of the world.

Protecting the natural environment from people and people from the natural environment

The effect of people in the world is so great that it is now difficult to know exactly what is meant by the term 'natural environment'. For example, an open stretch of ocean may seem to be completely natural. However, there may be

Figure 9.2 Mountains and logging roads in the Coast Ranges, British Columbia

many fewer whales living in that ocean than if people had left it alone. A mountain side may seem to be a natural feature, but it may have been stripped of its trees by lumberjacks. Figure 9.2 shows an area of the coastal mountain ranges of western Canada, north-east of Vancouver. The lines on the photograph are the logging roads built to get the trees which used to grow here down to the coast.

When the human population of the Earth was much smaller than it is today, the natural resources of the Earth could be exploited without anyone worrying about them. Most people assumed that what was being exploited would grow again (like trees). In the case of minerals (like coal) they thought that stocks were so large that mining would make little difference to the total amount in the Earth.

Today, the human population is so large and powerful that the effects of people on the natural environment cannot be ignored anywhere in the world. In fact, their effect is so powerful that in many places the natural environment has been badly damaged.

Even though people can do so much damage to the natural environment, there are still many occasions when the natural environment hurts people. Some of these were described in Chapters 2 and 3. It is just as important for us to protect ourselves from the natural environment as it is for us to protect the natural environment from our own actions.

We will describe the problems listed in Figure 9.1 one by one.

Natural hazards

In Chapters 2 and 3 we described the effects of volcanoes, earthquakes, storms and floods. When these affect people they are called **natural catastrophes** because they are caused by powers which human beings cannot control. Many people have tried to work out what could be done to avoid the great loss of life which is often caused by natural catastrophes. There seem to be three main ways of reducing the number of people hurt.

Firstly, if the processes which lead to the events in nature are understood, then people can be warned to stay away from where the catastrophe is likely to occur. In the example of Pallepallem in Chapter 3, a better forecasting system could have allowed people to move away from the area where the hurricane crossed the coast.

Secondly, the human environment can be planned to give protection against natural hazards as far as possible. Buildings in areas likely to suffer earthquakes can be built to withstand shocks without breaking up. The roofs of buildings in areas which suffer from typhoons can be firmly bolted to the walls. In areas which may be flooded, the buildings can have deep foundations and perhaps be raised up on stilts.

Thirdly, plans can be made so that once a catastrophe has occurred, the people who are affected are helped as quickly as possible. This kind of advanced planning is expensive and is usually organized by the richer countries. Most of the richer countries have their own emergency services, including well equipped militaries, which can deal with disasters. Developing countries are usually less well equipped to deal with large scale emergencies. The developing countries are often helped by international organizations such as the Red Cross and the United Nations. The richer countries of the world often help individually. The United Nations Children's Fund, and Oxfam are well known for their help in crises in all parts of the world.

Although the same type of natural catastrophes can happen in both developed and developing countries, the actual effects of the disasters are often different. A natural catastrophe can affect people in two ways. The primary effects of the disaster are those which occur immediately. The secondary effects are those which happen after the first strike of the disaster, but as a direct result of it.

The primary effects of a disaster can include

buildings falling down and killing people in an earthquake. People may be blown away or hit by flying debris in a hurricane. The number of people hurt in these kinds of ways may be greater in developed countries than in developing countries, because people may be living in high-rise buildings, made of bricks or concrete, or may be travelling at high speeds in cars or trains when the disaster strikes. On the other hand, people in rural areas of developing countries may be living in houses made of lighter materials which are less likely to cause such severe injury.

The secondary effects of a disaster may include epidemics of diseases such as cholera and typhoid. These diseases are spread if the water supply is polluted by sewage. People may also die because injuries cannot be treated. This could be because there are no doctors or equipment available. It can also be because the lines of communication are broken. Most developed countries are better able to cope with the secondary effects of a disaster than developing countries are.

This can be summed up by saying that in developed countries, most deaths and injuries are caused by the primary effects of a catastrophe. In developing countries, it is often the secondary effects which cause the most injuries and deaths.

Case Study

The earthquake in southern Italy, November 1980

This earthquake happened at about 7.30 p.m. on Sunday, 23 November 1980. It affected the area shown in Figure 9.3. The map also shows the intensity of the earthquake on a version of the Mercalli scale. This is another way of measuring the strength of an earthquake. The Mercalli scale goes from 0–12. (We mentioned the Richter scale for measuring earthquakes in Chapter 2.)

The area affected by the earthquake included a large number of small towns and villages as well as the city of Naples. Most of the damage was done to the small towns and villages. It is estimated that 3000 people died, 8000 were injured and 480 000 people lost their homes. The details of the disaster are given in Figure 9.4, which also shows the amount of damage which was done to the factories in the area. The table shows that in some areas nearly 80% of the workers lost their jobs at least for a while.

Help was arranged for the people who had lost their homes and their jobs. By 2 December 1980, 56 field kitchens, 7000 tents and 4000 caravans had been set up in the disaster area. 16 000 soldiers were sent to assist. However, there were still several important difficulties. Some of the villages which were affected were cut off by landslides across the roads. Some of the people who were sent into the area were so inexperienced that they were more hindrance than help. Some of the goods needed by the people were sent to the wrong places. Some families were split up and sent to different refugee camps. This kind of mistake added to the distress of people who had already seen their homes and belongings destroyed.

The Italian authorities could not possibly have known exactly when and where the earthquake would occur. However, they did know that southern Italy has had a long history of earthquakes. The previous earthquake hit the area in 1962. In addition, this area is not very far from the volcano, Vesuvius. It was, therefore, very likely that another earthquake would occur. The Italian authorities should constantly be on the alert for the next major earthquake because unless the organization of relief operations is really good, things can become chaotic.

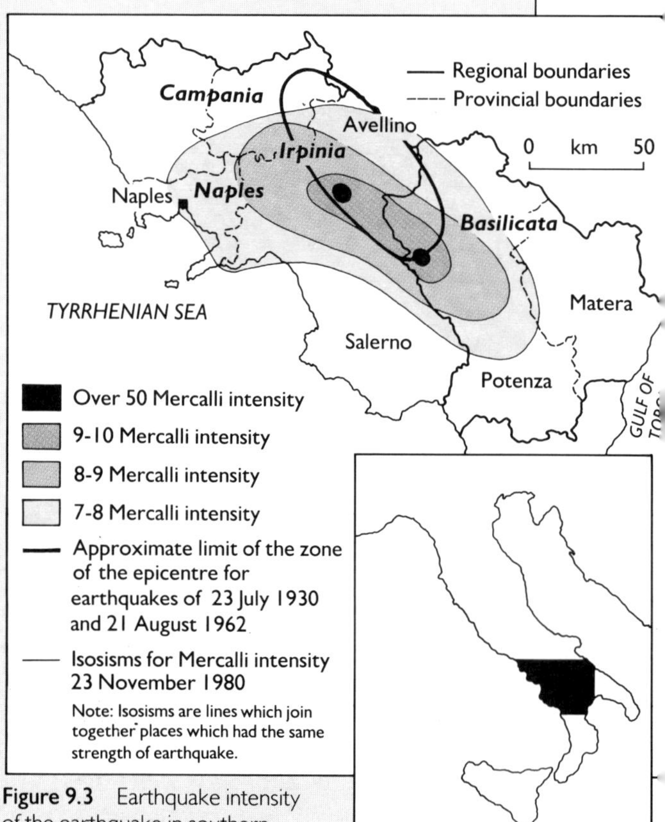

Figure 9.3 Earthquake intensity of the earthquake in southern Italy, 23 November 1980

Basic data relating to regions and provinces affected by the 1980 earthquake in Southern Italy.

	area in square kilometres	population 1976	% population change 1965-76	population density 1976 persons km²	no of comuni	total numbers of dead	total numbers of injured	total numbers of homeless	approx. no. of settlements ⩾ 50% damaged
CAMPANIA	13595	5335786	+6.5	392	544	2702	7675	453814	75
AVELLINO	2801	437911	6.3	156	120	1963	2546	118900	54
BENEVENTO	2061	292602	−6.9	142	77	7	32	143853	3
CASERTA	2639	729498	+6.2	276	101	15	135	3757	5
NAPLES	1171	2872348	+11.1	2453	89	151	1413	50446	3
SALERNO	4923	1003427	+5.0	204	157	566	3549	136853	10
BASILICATA	9988	617257	−4.2	62	129	207	522	26814	10
MATERA	3442	203118	+1.5	59	31	2	–	1130	2
POTENZA	6546	414139	−6.8	63	98	205	522	25664	8
						2909	8197	480628	85

Estimate: Dec 1, 1980

Damage to industry caused by the 1980 earthquake in Southern Italy.

	no. of factories	% factories damaged	no. of employees	% employees working in damaged factories	damage in $ million	damage in $ per employee
CAMPANIA	3062	44.7	203429	48.0	565.9	2782
AVELLINO	295	81.7	10996	78.0	50.5	4597
BENEVENTO	109	52.3	4015	23.4	11.7	2924
CASERTA	398	20.6	36317	28.2	33.3	916
NAPLES	1565	39.7	120493	49.7	347.6	2885
SALERNO	695	52.9	31608	52.0	122.8	3886
BASILICATA	160	50.0	12843	62.8	52.9	4119
MATERA	58	15.5	6734	48.8	14.9	2211
POTENZA	102	69.6	6109	78.3	38.0	6227

gure 9.4 Statistics of the effect of the 1980 Italian earthquake on people and property

Activities

▲ ■ ● **1** Study Figure 9.3 which shows the area affected by the Italian earthquake of 1980.

a Work out the approximate size of the area which had earthquake tremors of 9 and more on the Mercalli scale. Measure from north-west to south-east, and north-east to south-west.

b On an atlas map of Italy, study the area which was affected. Make a list of all the things which would have made rescue operations difficult.

▲ ■ ● **2** Study Figure 9.4 which shows the figures for the damage done in the different regions.

a Draw a series of four maps to show:
i) The number of people who died
ii) The number of people injured
iii) The number of people who were made homeless
iv) The number of settlements which had more than half their buildings damaged.

b Imagine you are responsible for co-ordinating the relief operation after the first crisis is past. Write a report based on your maps. Describe the extent of the catastrophe in the different regions. Then explain the kinds of help you think are most needed in each of the regions.

▲ ■ ● **3 a** Describe the kinds of help needed by people affected by earthquakes in the period of time immediately following the shock.

b Describe the types of help people need in the longer term after an earthquake.

c Describe the kinds of measures the Italian authorities could take to limit the loss of life, injuries and damage to property in case of another earthquake in the future.

▲ ■ ● **4 a** What problems are likely to affect people who live in an area affected by each of the following kinds of catastrophe?
i) Hurricane **iii)** Drought
ii) Flood

b For each kind of catastrophe, describe the kind of help which is likely to be needed by people who are affected. Describe the problems likely to be faced by those who try to give this help.

Using up scarce resources

Natural resources are often divided into two types. The first type includes those which are renewable, like trees. The second type includes those resources which are non-renewable, like petroleum. We described the problems which are involved in the use of fossil fuels in Chapter 6. Unfortunately, although we often describe trees, fish and wild animals as renewable resources, it is not entirely true. If any of these resources are used up more quickly than they can renew themselves, then sooner or later there will be none left.

For example, forests may take over 100 years to grow back to the state they were in before they were cut down. If timber is cut from forests more often than once in a 100 years or so, then the forests will continually become smaller until eventually they cease to exist. Another example is that of the whales. The blue whale has been hunted almost to extinction.

In Chapter 3 we described the formation of soils. Soils are not often thought of as living renewable resources. However, although soils can reform eventually, this process can take a very long time. If soil is destroyed by soil erosion or by being poisoned with pollution, it is lost for agriculture. The Great Dust Bowl of America has still not recovered fully.

There are ways of protecting ourselves and the natural environment from the effects of using up our scarce resources. These methods are usually called **conservation**.

In the case of renewable resources, conservation usually means using the resource at a rate which will allow it to recover naturally. It may mean not cutting down too many trees. It may mean not catching too many fish or not hunting too many wild animals. It may mean not growing too many crops without feeding the soil with fertilizers, and so on. Unfortunately, people or companies often find that they can make more money in the short term by not conserving a natural resource. To protect the resource for future generations it is sometimes necessary for governments to make laws to control the use of the resources.

This is particularly true in the case of fishing. Some countries, such as Iceland, have extended their control of the waters around their coasts from the original 3 mile limit to 200 miles. This can have a double effect. It can help conserve fish stocks for future generations, but it also makes sure that fishermen keep their jobs.

The problems of conserving whales is particularly difficult. This is because they are usually hunted in international waters. Agreements have to be reached between all the countries which have whaling fleets if the number of whales caught is to be reduced. It has been difficult to persuade some countries that whales need protecting if they are to survive.

In the case of non-renewable resources, conservation means slowing down the rate at which the resource is used, so that a substitute for the resource can be found. In Chapter 6 we described how renewable sources of power like alcohol made from sugar cane may eventually take the place of petroleum. Much steel is still needed in machinery and there is not yet any real alternative. In cases like this, conservation means recycling scrap metal. Most steel furnaces in the world are now fed partly with scrap metal.

Activities

▲5 ■ Look back at the section on the location of industries in Chapter 6.

- **a** If iron ore and coal are conserved by using more scrap iron in steel furnaces, describe the kinds of areas which will then become profitable locations for steel works.
- **b** Make a list of 3 areas in each continent of the world which are likely to be good sources of scrap iron.

▲6 ■ ● **a** Draw up a table like the one below to show all the products which are being recycled in your area and the non-renewable resources which are being conserved. The first one has been done for you. A clue to a second is in Figure 9.5.

Product being saved	Non-renewable resources being conserved
1 Tin cans	Tin, iron ore, coal

b **i)** Make a list of the renewable resources which could be conserved by recycling.
ii) Explain how you could save more of your waste for recycling.
iii) Explain why your list of non-renewable resources which can be recycled is longer than your list of renewable resources.

▲7 ■ Look back at the section in Chapter 3 on ecosystems (page 65). Write a paragraph to explain why animals like elephants or blue whales are more likely to become extinct than rabbits or mice.

Figure 9.5 A bottle bank

Pollution of the air, water and land

Air pollution

In Chapter 3 we described how pollution of the air, land or water is often caused by people releasing poisonous substances into an ecosystem. Some poisons are quickly dispersed until they are no longer harmful. Others become concentrated so that as time goes by they become more and more dangerous.

An example of a poison which may either become concentrated or be dispersed is carbon monoxide. Carbon monoxide is given off in the exhaust gases of car engines. In a climate where there is usually windy weather, the carbon monoxide is quickly lost into the atmosphere. It mixes with the oxygen in the air and becomes carbon dioxide which is much less dangerous. Sometimes the carbon monoxide cannot mix with the other gases in the atmosphere. It may then become changed into photochemical smog by the effects of sunlight.

Case Study

Photochemical smog in Los Angeles

Los Angeles lies between the mountains and the Pacific Ocean, on the west coast of California. Usually the winds blow over Los Angles from the mountains to the east. They are warm winds. When these winds blow, the warm air is at ground level; the temperatures drop with height. Warm air rises so long as it is warmer than the air around it. The rising air carries all the smoke and fumes up into the atmosphere and they are blown away over the Pacific. This is shown in Figure 9.6 (overleaf).

Sometimes the wind direction changes and a cooler wind blows off the sea, from the west. This cooler wind pushes underneath the warm air over the city. Instead of the temperatures reducing with height, there is warmer air on top of cooler air. This situation is called a **temperature inversion.** Figure 9.7 shows the temperature inversion over Los Angeles.

The smoke fumes can only rise until they reach the warmer air. They cannot rise any further and so they are trapped under the temperature inversion. The sunlight then acts on the fumes from the factories and cars to form photochemical smog which is very dangerous. It can be seen as a grey-green haze over the city. No one knows the full effects of photochemical smog, but people find breathing difficult and their eyes often sting and are uncomfortable. Some crops are killed by the smog.

Because of the dangers from car fumes the American Government has introduced laws to control the exhaust gases of cars. Motor manufacturers must design engines which only give off very small quantities of dangerous exhaust gases.

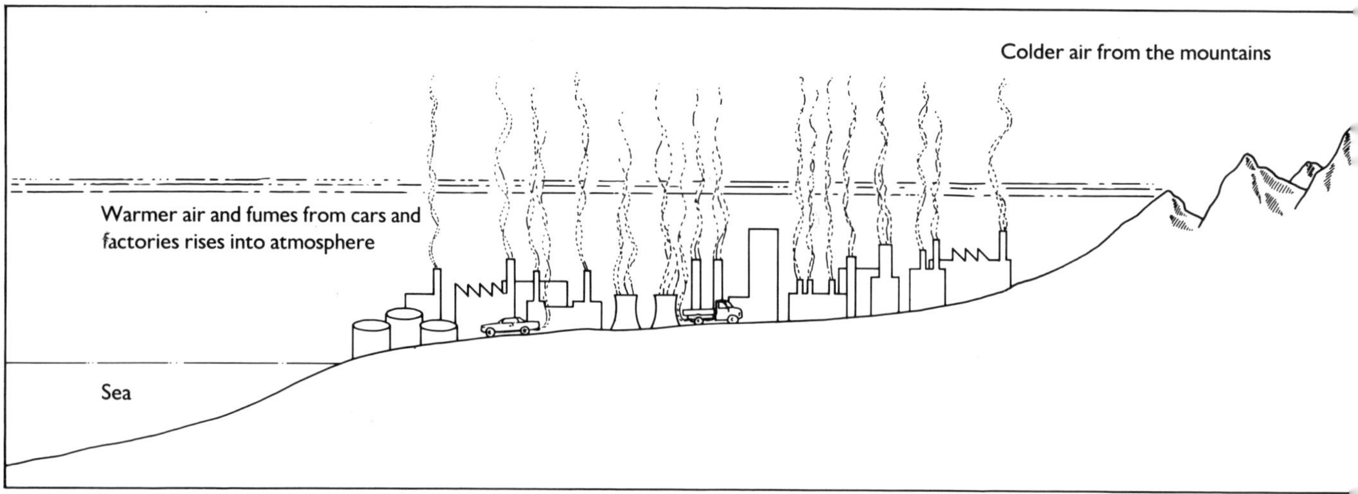

Figure 9.6 Los Angeles: normal situation with no temperature inversion

Figure 9.7 Los Angeles: with temperature inversion

It has been discovered that lead can damage the brain cells of growing children. At present most 4-star petrol is made richer by adding lead to it. This lead is given out into the atmosphere in the exhaust gases of the cars. Many governments have passed laws which force car makers to make car engines which will run on petrol which does not contain lead.

Even if gases like carbon dioxide are mixed well with the other gases in the atmosphere, they can still cause problems. The amount of carbon dioxide in the atmosphere seems to have an effect on the temperature of the air. If the amount of carbon dioxide goes up, the atmosphere could become warmer. This could result in the ice caps melting and sea level rising.

Some scientists have estimated that the amount of carbon dioxide in the atmosphere is increasing each year by 2 parts per million. Carbon dioxide makes up about 1% of the atmosphere, so this means that the amount of carbon dioxide in the atmosphere could increase significantly in 100 years.

No one is quite sure exactly what will happen, but the problems of pollution of the atmosphere are being studied carefully. The increase in sulphur dioxide in the air has caused acid rain over Sweden and other Scandinavian countries.

Water pollution

The two most important sources of water pollution are industrial wastes from factories, refineries and ships, and the untreated sewage from towns and cities.

We described the pollution problems caused by concentrations of industries in Chapter 6. Here we will briefly describe the problems faced by the Mediterranean Sea.

Case Study

The Mediterranean Sea

The Mediterranean Sea is a holiday playground for 100 million tourists each year. It is also the most polluted sea in the world. A quarter of all the oil waste dumped into the seas of the world goes into the Mediterranean. In addition, millions of tonnes of industrial waste, pesticides, chemical fertilizers, and raw sewage are poured into the Mediterranean Sea.

The biggest problem with industrial and chemical waste is that much of it is not easy to control. Mercury, for example, is extremely poisonous, even in very small quantities, but over 100 tonnes of it are dumped into the Mediterranean each year.

Many of the chemicals reach the Mediterranean by the river systems. The river Rhône in France and the river Po in Italy, flow through the centre of major industrial areas. Both these rivers are used to carry away poisonous wastes. The river Ebro in Spain, the river Nile in Egypt and the river Tiber in Italy add to the pollution.

Oil pollution reaches the Mediterranean by the rivers and also from tankers washing out their tanks while at sea. It is illegal under International Law for tankers to dump the waste oil from their tanks into the sea, but it is difficult to catch them doing it. Even if oil is dumped far away from the land, it is washed back to the shore by weak sea currents.

The countries around the Mediterranean have used the sea to get rid of their sewage for generations. The sewage would normally be broken down and 'digested' by bacteria in the water. However, the cities around the Mediterranean have been getting bigger and they all flush their household waste into the sea. The larger the city, the worse the problem. There are high population areas all the way round the coast from Barcelona in Spain, along the French coast and the west Italian coast to Naples. Along this stretch of coast, 100 tonnes of sewage are put into the sea each year for every kilometre of coastline. The sea can no longer cope with the amount of sewage being put into it. Just like the oil, the sewage is gently washed back to shore. The high concentration of sewage causes typhoid, paratyphoid, dysentry, polio, hepatitis and cholera.

This pollution has had serious effects on the safety of seafoods. Metals and other industrial wastes, as well as germs which cause the diseases mentioned above, get into the fish and then into the people who can afford to eat them. There are cases reported every year of food poisoning, which often results in death.

Figure 9.8 is a map of the Mediterranean Sea which summarizes the safe and dangerous areas.

Figure 9.8 Pollution in the Mediterranean Sea

Activity

▲8 ■ **a** Make a list of favourite holiday areas for British holiday makers. You could survey your class or school, or count the holidays offered in the travel brochures of big holiday companies.

b Mark these popular holiday areas on a copy of Figure 9.8.

c Make one list of the popular holiday areas in the 'danger zone' and another list of those in the 'safe zone'.

d Make a list of the safest areas of the Mediterranean for a 'sand and sea' holiday.

e Study Figure 9.8 and an atlas map of the Mediterranean.

i) Explain why some areas, like the eastern end of the Mediterranean, are safer than others.

ii) Give as many reasons as you can why this might change in the future. There are hints in every chapter of this book about the kinds of change which could increase the amount of pollution.

Land pollution

We have described various types of land pollution in Chapters 3 and 6. Human beings are the greatest source of all pollution because they can put large quantities of pollutants into an ecosystem. The most dangerous forms of pollution which human beings are putting into air, water and land at present all come from radioactivity. In Chapter 6 we described the leaky nuclear reprocessing plant at Windscale/Sellafield in Cumberland. The dangers can also be seen in the famous accident at the nuclear power station at 'Three Mile Island', which is near Harrisburg, in Pennsylvania in the USA. In 1979 there were a large number of breakdowns in the cooling systems in the power station and the cores of radioactive fuel were in danger of melting. Water and gas in the cooling system became radioactive and began to leak out of the station. The air and water around the power station, and down wind of it, were polluted, and radioactive particles of dust in the air polluted the ground. As a result, homes all around the station had to be evacuated. 'Three Mile Island' has never been allowed to re-open.

In 1986 there was a very serious nuclear accident at Chernobyl in the USSR. Several people died and there was widespread contamination as far afield as the UK.

No one knows the exact effects of radioactivity. What is known, is that cancers affect people who come into contact with radioactivity many years later. Large doses of radioactivity kill people and animals very quickly. No one is certain that there is a safe low dose.

The effect of radioactivity does not just come from accidents at nuclear power stations. It also comes from the waste products of nuclear fuels which are still radioactive. At present these are often thrown into the sea. The authorities hope that by throwing them into deep enough water, far enough from shore, no damage will be done. We can only hope that the containers in which the radioactive waste is dumped are strong enough to stand up to the force of the sea for the thousands of years that it will take before the waste loses its radioactivity.

The worst danger of all from radioactivity comes from nuclear war.

Activities

▲ ■ ● **9** In different parts of the world, people live on the slopes of volcanoes, in areas known to flood, in areas where tropical storms are common, and near nuclear power stations.

a Use the case studies in this book, your atlas and information you have learned from television programmes, to write lists of areas where each of these is true.

b Why do you think people chose to live in dangerous places?

▲ ■ ● **10** It has been said that 'Industrialists must bear the cost of treating their effluent (waste) so that it is no longer a danger to life in rivers'.

a Explain what this means.

b Describe the problems of this policy for:

i) Industrialists

ii) The government departments who have to police this kind of policy

iii) Customers for the goods produced.

c Who do you think should pay for treating waste materials from factories so that they can be dumped safely?

▲ ■ ● **11** Figure 9.9 shows how radioactive waste from the Sellafield/Windscale nuclear reprocessing plant can pollute several different ecosystems.

a Make up a table to show the ecosystems which are affected and how the radioactive pollution reaches them.

b Write a paragraph to explain how this pollution could be prevented. (Remember that plutonium waste will stay radioactive for almost a quarter of a million years.)

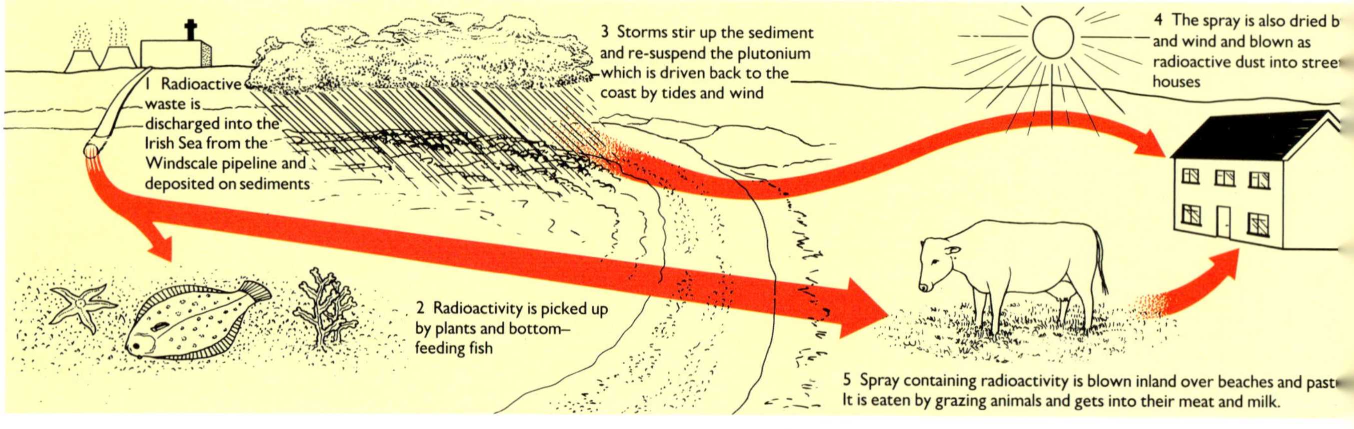

Protecting the human environment

We explained earlier in this chapter that it is difficult to define precisely the term 'the natural environment'. It is also difficult to say exactly what is meant by 'the human environment'. In Figure 9.1 the section on 'human environment problems' included all those problems which are the result of human actions and which have a direct effect on the immediate environment of human beings. For example, as we explained in Chapter 7, if cities keep on growing, then there will be problems of congestion and housing. If the result of this is that inner cities decay, then the quality of city life will also decline. Another example was given in Chapter 6. If trade between nations declines, then the total level of trade in the world will also decline. This can result in unemployment and the standard of living of some people will fall. Finally, if there are disagreements between nations of the world, there could be an increase in the barriers to movement between countries; there could even be open war. The first possibility will result in a fall in the quality of life of the people in the countries concerned. The second possibility will result in at least a fall in the standard of living. At worst it could cause the death of many people.

Problems of the built environment

Towns and cities are often called the **built environment**. This term is a reminder that towns and cities are completely made by people, and so are the problems that people find in them.

In Chapter 7 we described the problems of twilight zones and run down inner city areas (page 171). Here we will just describe two of the problems which occur in nearly all the cities of the world when they grow larger and their functions change.

Firstly, the inner city areas just outside the Central Business District (CBD) become run down and many of the houses fall into disrepair. This can be seen in the series of photographs of Singapore (Figures 9.10, 9.11 and 9.12), even though Singapore is not a very old city by European standards.

The Government of Singapore dealt with this problem in the same way as many other governments have done in Europe and Asia. They sent in bulldozers to knock down the old areas. Then they built new tower blocks of flats. Although this answer solved the first problem,

◀ **Figure 9.9** Possible effects of radioactive waste from Sellafield on the ecosystem

▲ Fig 9.10

Fig 9.11 ▶

Fig 9.12 ▼

Figure 9.10 Singapore: aerial view of the old town, 1972

Figure 9.11 Singapore: aerial view of the old town at ground level, 1972

Figure 9.12 Singapore: new developments, 1972

it added to the second problem, which is that new inner city buildings often seem to lower the quality of the environment. They do this by changing the character of the city, often just by their sheer size.

Figures 9.13 and 9.14 show Sydney, Australia. Sydney is another city which is not very old.

Figure 9.13 Sydney, Australia: tower blocks on the harbour

Figure 9.14 Sydney, Australia: central business district

Figure 9.15 Quebec city, Canada: an aerial view

Figure 9.16 Quebec city, Canada: the lower town

Figure 9.17 Quebec city, Canada: Rue de Tresor

In Figure 9.13 the view of the tower block on its own seen from across Sydney Harbour is quite attractive. Figure 9.14 shows a view of the tall buildings in the centre of Sydney's CBD from above. It seems to be very crowded and makes the people in the streets seem very unimportant little creatures.

Figures 9.15, 9.16 and 9.17 are different views of Quebec. Quebec seems to have a good balance between the older buildings which give a city its character and the new tower blocks and modern architecture which are the result of modern ideas of efficiency and design. Figure 9.15 is an aerial view over Quebec. There are a few tower blocks but they are not next to one another and do not seem to be threatening people. Figure 9.16 shows the original 18th and 19th century buildings which are left from the old town. These older buildings have been preserved and give the sense of character to Quebec. This has been encouraged even more by the older warehouses which have been preserved and converted into art galleries and museums (Figure 9.17).

Activities

▲■● **12** Study the photographs of the inner city areas of Singapore (Figures 9.10, 9.11 and 9.12).

- **a** Describe the evidence in the photographs that shows that these are inner city areas.
- **b** Explain why older buildings in inner city areas are often replaced by tower blocks.
- **c** Describe the advantages and disadvantages of living in tower blocks.
- **d** Write a paragraph to explain what other methods of redeveloping inner city areas of large cities could be used.

▲■● **13** Study the photographs of Sydney (Figures 9.13 and 9.14) and the descriptions of Sydney above. Write a paragraph to give the opposite point of view.

▲■● **14** Study the photographs of Quebec (Figures 9.15, 9.16 and 9.17).

- **a** Describe the site of Quebec from the aerial view (Figure 9.15).
- **b** Explain why there are many warehouses near the river (Figure 9.16) and why they are not used as warehouses any longer.
- **c** **i)** Describe the scene in the Rue de Tresor in Quebec city. (Figure 9.17).
  ii) Do you find the scene attractive or not?
  iii) Why do you have these feelings about the scene in the Rue de Tresor?

Case Study

The impact of development on the environment of the Languedoc area in southern France

It is usually a matter of opinion whether a new development is pleasant or unpleasant. How strongly people feel about it often depends on how much the new development actually changes the landscape. To show the impact of new developments on a landscape, we will look at what has happened in the Languedoc region of southern France. The region of Languedoc and its location in France are shown in Figure 9.18.

Up to about the mid-1960s Languedoc was an area of low Mediterranean scrub vegetation. This type of vegetation is called **garrigue** in France. The farms were old and concentrated on growing vines. The wines made from the grapes were of low quality. The scenery and one of the farms are shown in Figures 9.19 and 9.20.

There were few other jobs in Languedoc and incomes were low. Many people, particularly young people, left the area to look for better jobs in other parts of France.

The French Government decided to develop the area. They wanted to improve the farming and build new holiday resorts along the coast.

The first need for new farming methods was water. Canals were built to take water from the river Rhône. Irrigation channels then distributed the water to the farms. Because the land is so flat, new water towers and pumping stations were built. This has meant that the farming has changed from olives and vines to fruit and vegetables.

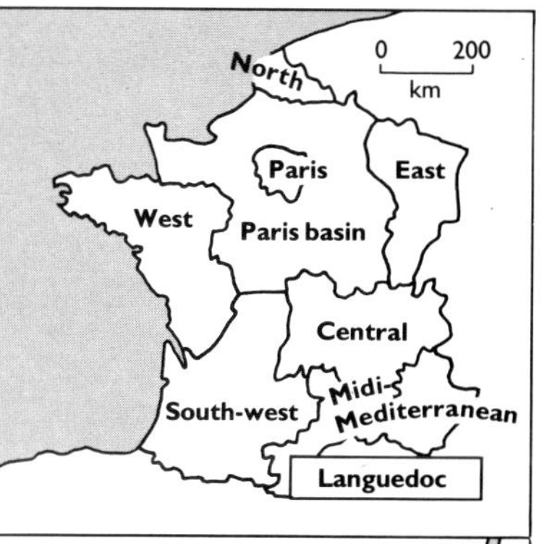

Figure 9.18 The location of Languedoc in Southern France

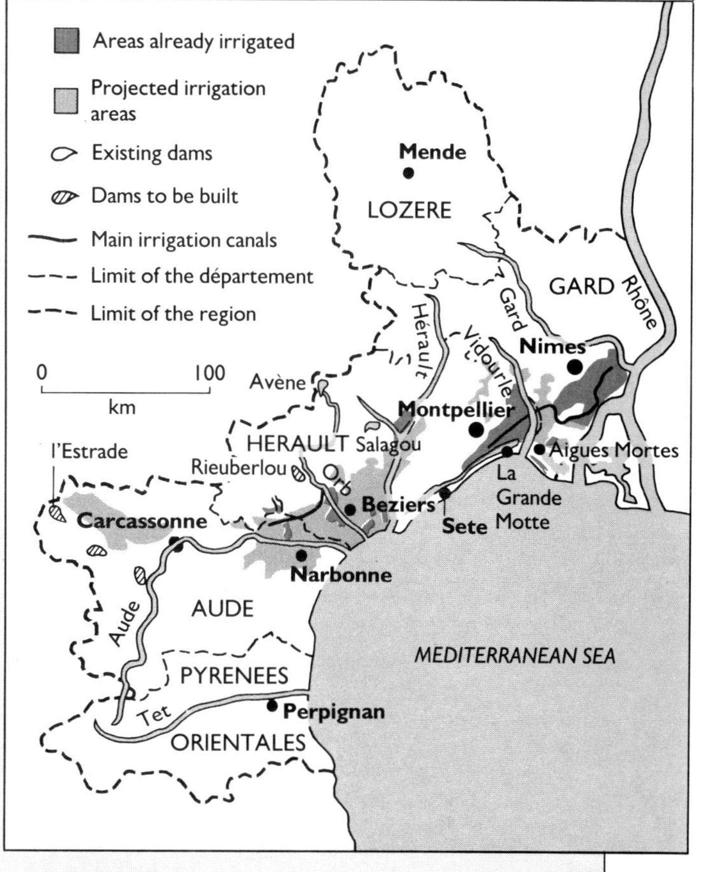

Figure 9.19 The original character of the uncultivated landscape of Languedoc

Figure 9.20 Languedoc, a typical old farmhouse with vineyard

◄ Fig 9.21

▼ Fig 9.23

Fig 9.22 ▲

Fig 9.24 ►

Figure 9.21 Languedoc, a water tower for irrigation
Figure 9.22 A new farmhouse in Languedoc
Figure 9.23 Marina La Grande Motte, Languedoc
Figure 9.24 The A9 motorway at Languedoc

A new motorway (the A9) was built to make transport easier for the farmers and to encourage visitors to the area. A whole series of summer resorts was built along the coast with marinas, beaches, camping sites and all the other facilities that people from all over Europe want for a Mediterranean holiday. Figures 9.21, 9.22, 9.23 and 9.24 show some of these new developments in Languedoc.

The problem is whether these new developments have made the landscape more interesting or less interesting. There are many questions which we can ask to help us decide the answers.

We can ask ourselves what it was about the old landscape which was worth preserving. Some landscapes are worth preserving because they are beautiful. Other landscapes may be worth preserving to remind ourselves and the people who come after us to be more careful!

We can ask ourselves if the new buildings fit in with the landscape easily or are they too 'loud' in one sense or another? This is a particular problem in the case of very old towns and buildings. Someone has to decide which buildings need to be preserved because they have special interest. This is usually done by the local authority, although often there are other groups of people with strong feelings on the subject. Some buildings need to be preserved because they are good examples of a particular style of architecture, or because they are just very old. Other buildings are preserved because the local people like them.

Once the local authority has agreed which buildings should be preserved, it then has to decide what to do with them. In the example of Quebec which we described earlier in this chapter, the warehouses have been preserved, but they are not used as warehouses any longer. In many cases, the buildings are preserved because of their outside appearance. Their inside design may be completely unsuitable for modern use. In cases like these they may be 'gutted' and refitted with a modern interior. For example, in Montpellier which is one of the oldest towns in Languedoc, most of the old buildings in the centre have been preserved but the interiors have been rebuilt to make modern shops and offices. On the other hand some buildings keep their original use for many centuries. In Nimes, for example, the Roman Arena is still used for entertainments of all kinds, including bullfighting!

Figure 9.25 shows Aigues Mortes which is a medieval walled town. You can imagine the effect that a massive rebuilding scheme would have on a town like this.

Planners have to think about the impact of their plans before change begins. The changes can go much further than just the look of the buildings. In the case of Languedoc, the changes include the effects of the large numbers of tourists who come to the area. We have already described the effects on the levels of pollution in the Mediterranean Sea. There is also likely to be pollution caused by the increase in motor cars, the new farming methods, and the factories which process the fruit and vegetables which are now being grown.

Figure 9.25 Aigues Mortes

Activities

▲■● **15** **a** Write one or two paragraphs to describe the landscape of Languedoc before the development of the area began. Mention:
i) The physical landscape
ii) The types of farming
iii) The way in which the traditional farmhouse was built – shape, building materials, types of windows, roofing materials.

b Write a brief paragraph to describe how you feel about the old Languedoc landscape. Do you find it interesting or boring? Do you find it threatening or friendly? Would you like to live in an area like this?

▲■● **16** **a** Study the new features of the Languedoc landscape which are shown in Figures 9.19 and 9.20. Write a brief description of the landscape shown in each photograph.

b Explain the effects of each of the new developments shown in Figures 9.21 to 9.24 on the landscape of Languedoc.

c Explain your own view of whether these developments have improved the landscape or spoiled it.

▲■● **17** Look back over all the photographs of the changes in Languedoc as well as the photograph of Aigues Mortes (Figure 9.25).

a Describe the changes which are likely to be needed in the towns of Languedoc as the farming and tourist industries grow.

b Describe the features of Aigues Mortes which could be in danger of being lost if these developments are not handled carefully.

c Explain how Aigues Mortes could be developed without destroying the features you have described in **b** above.

Problems of economic relations

In Chapter 4 we explained how international trade is an important part of the global system. Governments have interfered with international trading almost since such trade began. Governments interfere with trade by putting import duties on imported goods. This is a way of earning money. They also interfere with trade by putting high duties on goods to discourage people from buying imported goods. This protects home industries from foreign competition. The idea of protection may go further. Governments may limit the quantity of goods imported by imposing quotas or even an outright ban on particular types of goods. One example of this is the attempt to limit the number of Japanese cars which can be imported into the EEC.

The problem of this kind of government tactic is that other countries tend to react in the same way. The result is that trade between the countries may dwindle. This does no one any good.

Some countries have tried to come to agreements so that trade is encouraged and increased. The **European Economic Community (EEC)** is one of these groups. The idea of the EEC is to make it possible for trade between the countries to take place without any barriers. In fact this has not so far been achieved. As anyone who has travelled within Europe will know, you still need to go through customs and make a declaration of your goods. This is because countries have two types of tax. They have import duties on goods coming into their country. They also have internal taxes on goods sold in their country. In the case of wine coming into the UK, for example, the import duties have been abolished, but the excise duty on wine has been kept. From the traveller's point of view, this has the same effect.

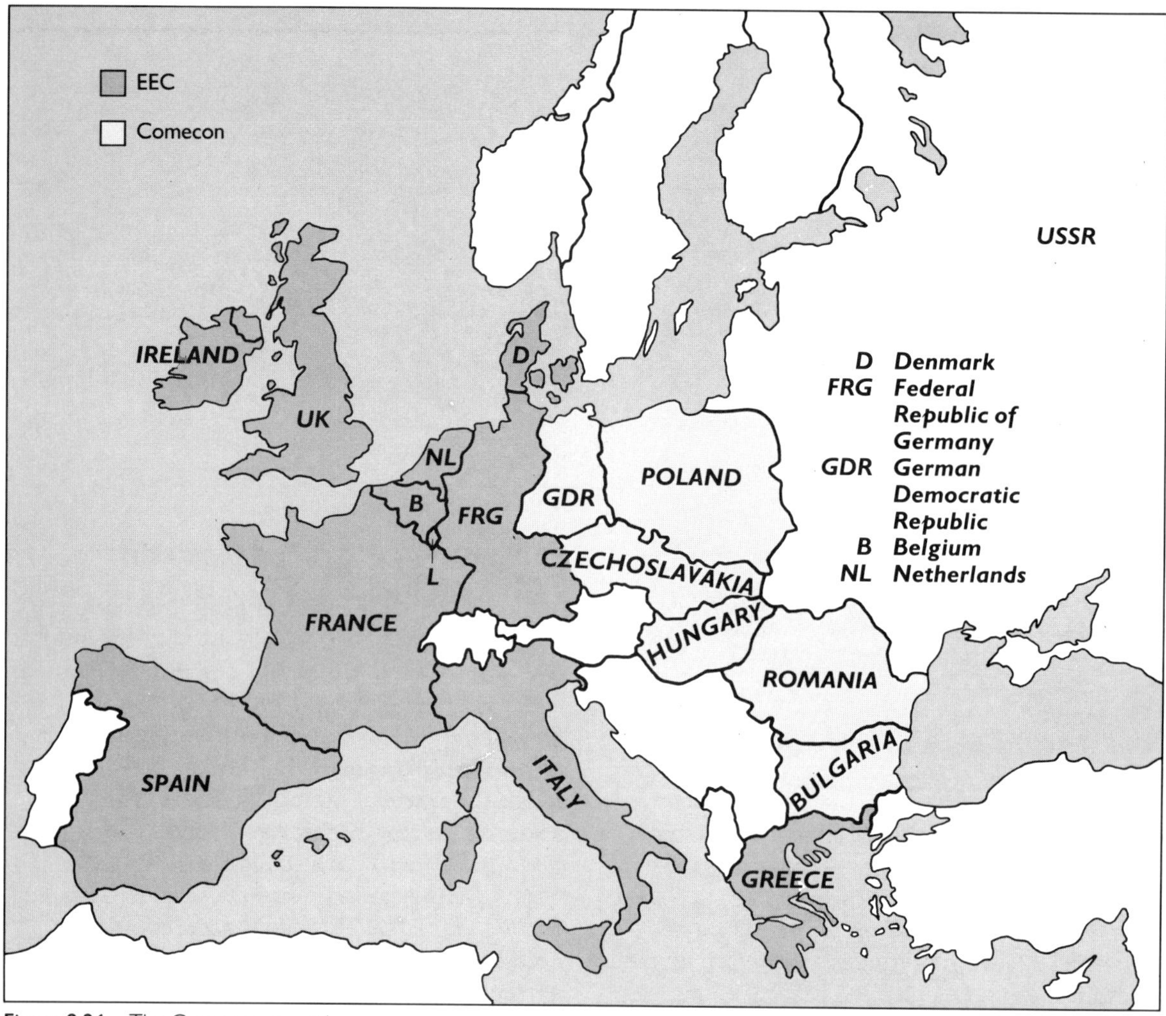

Figure 9.26 The Comecon countries

One of the main criticisms of the EEC is that customs duties are charged on goods coming in from other countries which are not members. As we explained in Chapter 4 (page 83) this can make it very difficult for developing countries to sell their goods. The EEC has been accused of being a 'rich man's club'.

Another group of countries which have come together to help their economies is called **COMECON**. This is a group of communist countries which has grouped together for economic co-operation. The proper name of this group is the **Council for Mutual Economic Assistance (CMEA)**. Figure 9.26 shows the countries of COMECON.

COMECON does not aim to make trade between different countries easier like the EEC. It is mainly concerned with planning joint projects like developing electricity grids and petroleum pipelines. Trade between COMECON countries is hampered by many regulations and controls over the exchange rates of their currencies. One of the authors recently crossed from East Germany into Poland. The paperwork at the border took over an hour! This kind of problem makes it difficult to develop trade contacts.

Problems can be caused to the environment by the internal economic relations of a single country. Industrial disputes always hurt innocent people regardless of what causes them. If railway workers go on strike, then millions of people are unable to travel. Coal and iron ore cannot reach power stations and steel works. The effects are felt in many other areas of industry. If ambulance drivers strike, then patients may find it more difficult to reach hospital.

Governments may have policies which upset the population and may cause strikes. Governments may also have policies which lead to unemployment. When millions of people who are willing and able to work cannot find jobs, then the national income may fall. If people have less money, they spend less on their own houses and gardens. Because the people pay less tax, local authorities can spend less money on improving the quality of the environment in public places.

Activities

▲ ■ ● **18** a Write one or two paragraphs to suggest how the grouping of countries in the EEC can lead to
i) Improvements and
ii) Damage to the environment.

b Write one or two paragraphs to explain how the grouping of countries in COMECON can lead to
i) Improvements and
ii) Damage to the environment.

▲ ■ ● **19** Write one or two paragraphs to describe the ways in which
a Industrial disputes and
b Unemployment
worsen the quality of our environment.

Problems of political relations between countries

War is probably the worst catastrophe which can affect the human race. Once upon a time, wars were fought between professional soldiers and the civilian population was not affected very much. Now everyone is affected in an area where there is conflict. People may be affected directly through war damage, injury or death. They may also be affected indirectly by the general lowering of the standard of living because more and more of the country's resources are given over to war purposes.

The environment also suffers both directly and indirectly. In World War II cities like Dresden, Coventry, Volgograd (Stalingrad) and Le Havre suffered immense physical damage. In the Vietnam war, towns and villages were destroyed and the leaf killing chemicals (antifoliants) which were used ruined large areas of forest and farming land. The environment also suffers indirectly because resources which would have been used in maintaining or improving the environment are used for the war.

Since war is such a pointless and wasteful activity, the problem is to try to prevent it happening. Towards the end of World War II, the Allies (UK, USSR, USA and France) set up the **United Nations** organization (**UN**). The purpose of the United Nations was to prevent future wars and to try to provide some way in which countries could settle their differences without going to war.

The United Nations machinery worked fairly

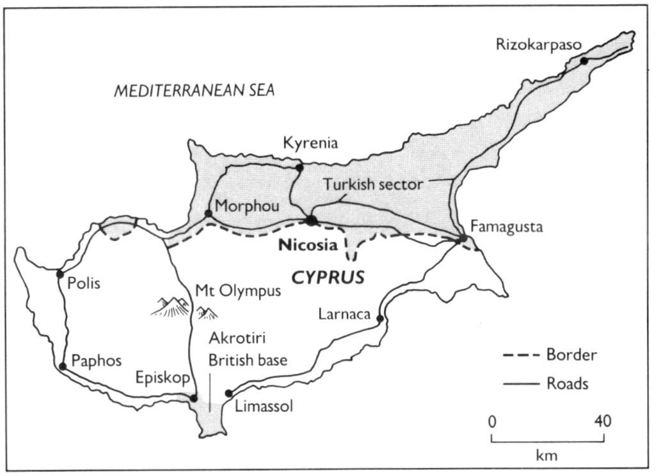

Figure 9.27 The division of Cyprus

successfully in Cyprus. In Cyprus there was friction between Turks and Greeks which eventually led to the island being divided between the two ethnic groups. United Nations observers have kept watch to keep the peace between the two communities. Figure 9.27 shows the island of Cyprus and the Turkish and Greek zones which were negotiated.

The United Nations has also been active in the Middle East. There has been conflict between Israel and Egypt over the ownership of the Sinai Peninsula for many years. The United Nations supervised the evacuation of Sinai by the Israelis. Now soldiers of many nations including the USA, Italy, Australia and New Zealand and the UK, are acting as observers in Sinai. This means that any trouble between Israel and Egypt can be dealt with before it becomes an active conflict. This should help to prevent war from breaking out between the two countries again.

If an organization like the UN is to be successful in solving problems between different nations, the governments of the world have to agree to accept recommendations about their behaviour. In other words, they have to give up the idea of absolute sovereignty.

The problems which are caused by claims of absolute sovereignty can be seen in the case of the Falkland Islands, or Las Malvinas, as they are known in the Argentine Republic. Figure 9.28 (overleaf) shows the position of the Falkland Islands in the South Atlantic Ocean.

Britain and Argentina have disagreed about who should govern the islands for 150 years. In April 1982, the Argentine Government sent troops to the islands and occupied them. The UK Government then mobilized a fleet of warships and many soldiers and sent them into

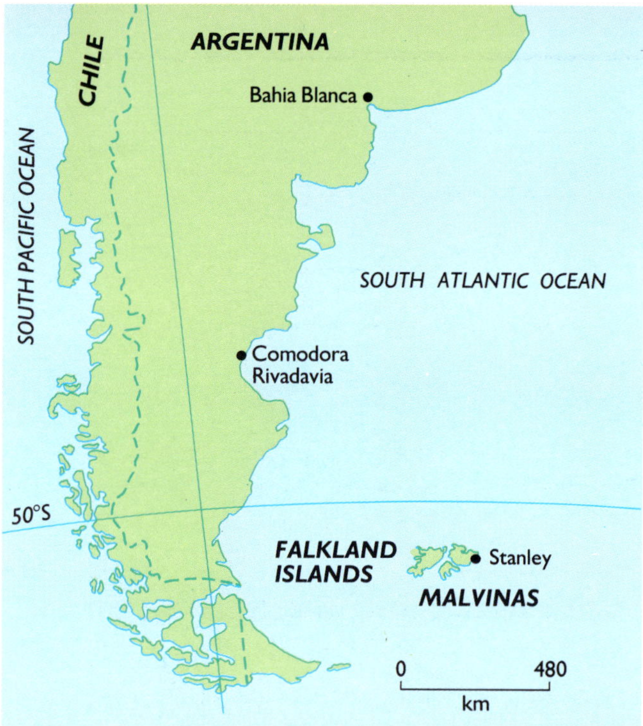

Figure 9.28 The position of the Falkland Islands

the South Atlantic. The situation quickly became open warfare between the UK and Argentina.

It is, of course, natural to feel annoyed if you are faced with something which appears to be a clear case of aggression. The UK has managed the islands for a long time and the 1800 people who live there are English speaking and of British origins. Many British people felt that Britain had a right to remain in command of the Falkland Islands, even if that meant engaging in warfare with the Argentinians.

However, there is another side to the story. Originally, the islands were claimed by both the British and the Argentinians. In 1833 a British squadron of warships effectively seized the islands and forced the Argentinian garrison which was already there to surrender. The Argentinian Government has never recognized British sovereignty over the islands. One of their reasons for this is that the islands are, after

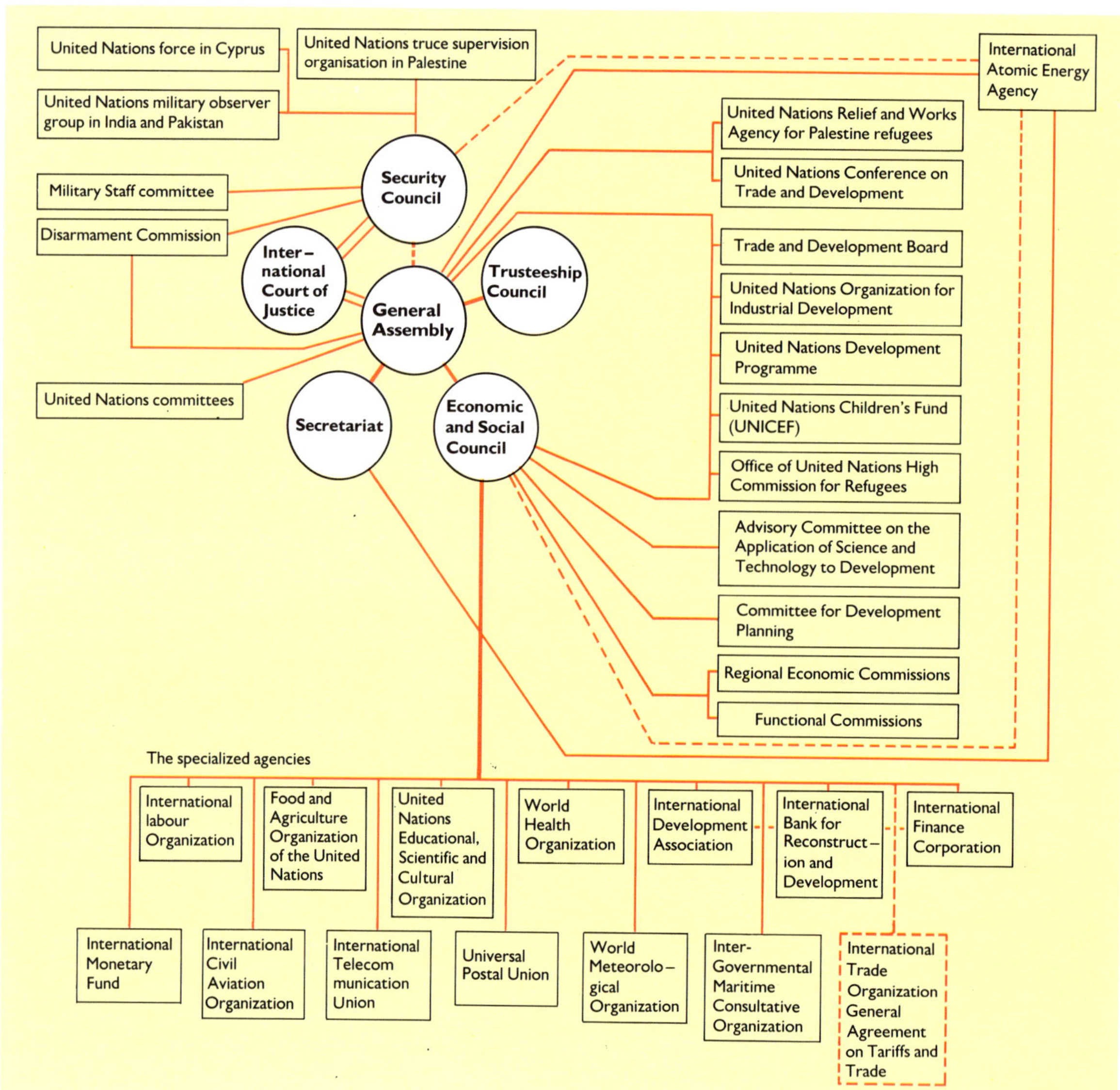

Figure 9.29 The structure of the United Nations

all, only about 500 km from the Argentinian coast, but 12 000 km from the UK.

Even though the original British seizure of the islands dates back to 1833, it is understandable that the Argentinians did not accept British sovereignty. On the other hand, it is also understandable that the 1800 people of British origin who live on the islands should look to Britain to protect them and their interests. The point is whether confrontation and war is a sensible way to decide who is right. Would a compromise be possible?

The United Nations exists to try to prevent countries settling differences like these by going to war. Figure 9.29 shows the way in which the United Nations is organized. The branch of the United Nations which is responsible for dealing with disputes between nations is called the **Security Council**. If there is a dispute between countries, the Security Council will examine both sides of the dispute and try to settle it by arranging negotiations between them. It can also arrange to police an area with neutral troops to act as a buffer between the two sides.

Activities

▲ **20** Read again the descriptions of the Cyprus
■ conflict and the Falklands dispute.
● **a** Describe how each conflict was resolved.
b Explain the advantages and disadvantages of each method of solving problems between countries.
c Write one or two paragraphs to explain how you would have solved the problems.

▲ **21** Figure 9.30 shows the claims made on the
■ continent of Antarctica by various nations.
● **a** List the countries which have made claims, in order of distance away from Antarctica. Put the closest first.
b Imagine you are a United Nations arbitrator. For each country write a paragraph explaining the reasons each could have for claiming a part of the Antarctic continent.
c Write a paragraph to explain the compromise you would want all the countries to accept.

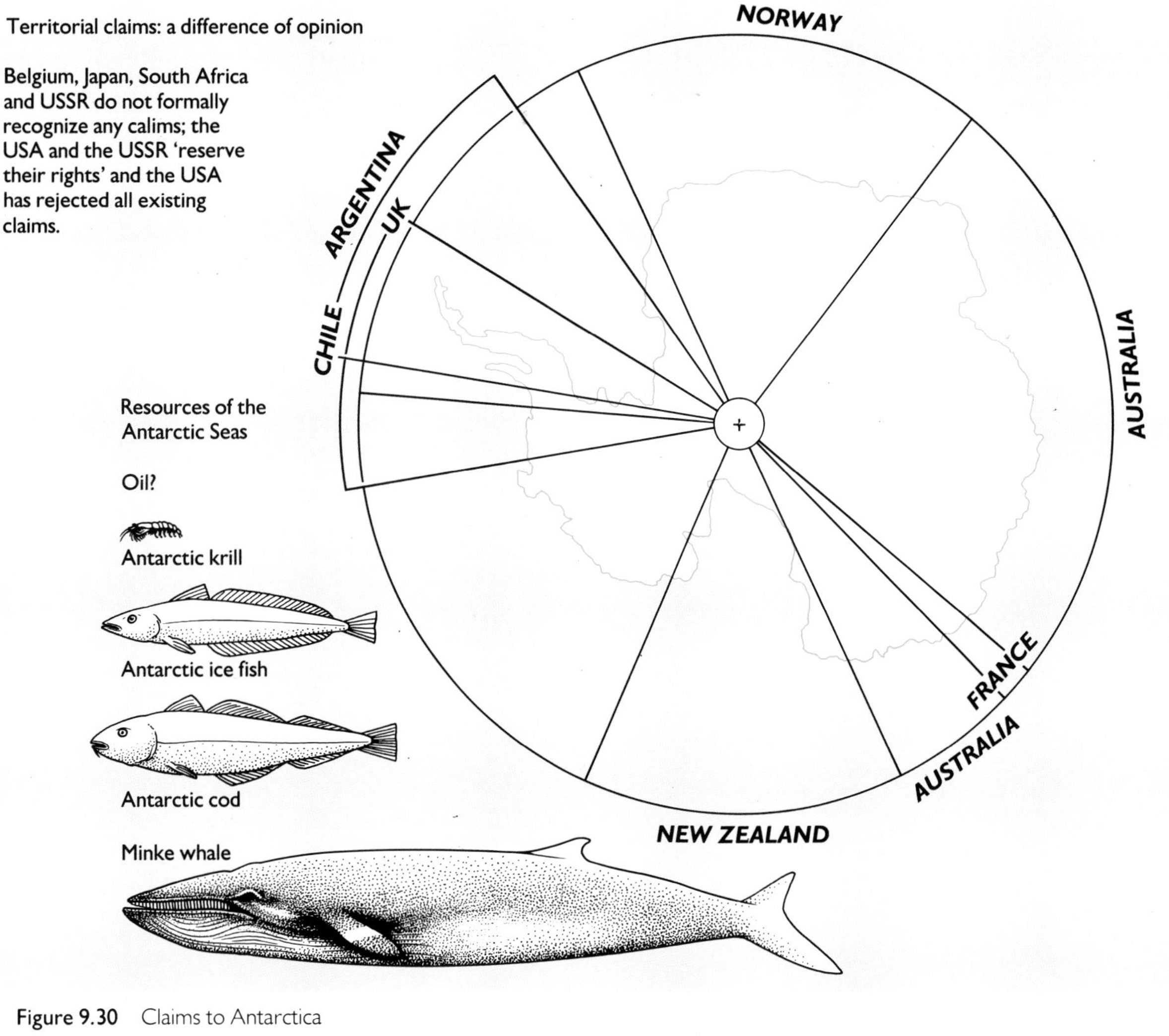

Figure 9.30 Claims to Antarctica

All peaceful solutions to disputes involve both sides giving way on some points. For example, in the Falkland Islands dispute, the basic problem was who should have sovereignty over the islands, the UK or Argentina? A compromise solution could only be one where neither Argentina nor the UK had absolute sovereignty. This would mean either both agreeing to share sovereignty or both agreeing that a third party, like the United Nations, could administer the islands until a final agreement could be reached.

Conclusion

Our planet seems very large and permanent to us. However, it is really very fragile. Figure 9.31 is a newspaper report of some research which suggests that the Earth is even more fragile than we realize. A small drop in the heat output of the Sun would cause very cold winters and immense costs for the snowed-up nations.

However, the planet is in much more danger from the unthinking actions of human beings which can upset an ecosystem which is very delicately balanced. The worst thing of all would be if the people of the world destroyed their planet by allowing a nuclear war to take place.

With all these dangers, it is very important that people learn how to deal with the problems of the planet in ways that develop harmony and not conflict. There are international organizations which have been set up to encourage co-operation between human beings. These organizations work in many of the areas which cause trouble for people and between people. Many of the organizations are parts of the United Nations. They work in education and science (UNESCO), health (WHO), food (FAO) and international relations (the Security Council and the whole UN). It is the job of all the people who live on the Earth to do their best to see that these organizations are supported and used and that our governments abide by international decisions.

Our world needs people who care – about other people and about human and physical environments. Our world needs people who understand the delicate mechanisms of systems and the possible effects of interfering with them. Are you trying to understand the world? Do you care?

Satellite records a steady fall in the sun's energy output

From Thomas O'Toole in Washington

A US satellite put into earth orbit to look at the sun has compiled data indicating an almost steady fall in the sun's output of energy – a condition that could have been a cause of this year's harsh winter.

"The duration and magnitude of the change we've seen is certainly enough to have had an effect on our climate," said Dr. Richard Wilson, of California's Jet Propulsion Laboratory where a telescope was built for the solar maximum mission satellite. "At the very least, it's a suspicious coincidence," he said.

In the 18 months starting on February 16, 1980, the telescope found an almost continuous decline in the sun's radiant energy, 99.9999 per cent of light leaving the sun from the far ultraviolet through the visible and into the far infrared regions.

On plotting the information received, Dr Wilson found that the sun's output of light in the 18 months ending in last August was one-tenth of 1 per cent less than it had been when the satellite started measuring solar luminosity.

"This is a small change in the total energy output of the sun," he said, "but it has great potential significance for the earth's fragile ecosystem."

Figure 9.31 The sun's energy output (*Observer*)

Index